N O N - P L A N   ESSAYS ON FREEDOM PARTICIPATION AND CHANGE IN MODERN ARCHITECTURE AND URBANISM

EDITED BY JONATHAN HUGHES & SIMON SADLER
NON-PLAN
ESSAYS ON FREEDOM PARTICIPATION AND CHANGE
IN MODERN ARCHITECTURE AND URBANISM

ARCHITECTURAL PRESS

OXFORD AUCKLAND BOSTON JOHANNESBURG MELBOURNE NEW DELHI

Architectural Press is an imprint of Elsevier
Linacre House, Jordan Hill, Oxford OX2 8DP, UK
30 Corporate Drive, Suite 400, Burlington, MA 01803, USA

First edition 2000
Reprinted 2002, 2007

Copyright © 2000, Johnathan Hughes and Simon Sadler. Published by Elsevier Ltd.
All rights reserved
Copyright © of individual chapters is retained by the contributors

The right of Johnathan Hughes and Simon Sadler to be identified as the authors of this
work has been asserted in accordance with the Copyright, Designs and Patents Act 1988

No part of this publication may be reproduced, stored in a retrieval system
or transmitted in any form or by any means electronic, mechanical, photocopying,
recording or otherwise without the prior written permission of the publisher

Permissions may be sought directly from Elsevier's Science & Technology Rights
Department in Oxford, UK: phone (+44) (0) 1865 843830; fax (+44) (0) 1865 853333;
email: permissions@elsevier.com. Alternatively you can submit your request online by
visiting the Elsevier web site at http://elsevier.com/locate/permissions, and selecting
Obtaining permission to use Elsevier material

Notice
No responsibility is assumed by the publisher for any injury and/or damage to persons
or property as a matter of products liability, negligence or otherwise, or from any use
or operation of any methods, products, instructions or ideas contained in the material
herein. Because of rapid advances in the medical sciences, in particular, independent
verification of diagnoses and drug dosages should be made

British Library Cataloguing in Publication Data
A catalogue record for this book is available from the British Library

Library of Congress Cataloging-in-Publication Data
A catalog record for this book is available from the Library of Congress

ISBN–13: 978-0-7506-4083-1
ISBN–10: 0-7506-4083-9

For information on all Architectural Press publications
visit our website at www.architecturalpress.com

07 08 09 10 10 9 8 7 6 5 4 3

Working together to grow
libraries in developing countries

www.elsevier.com | www.bookaid.org | www.sabre.org

ELSEVIER   BOOK AID International   Sabre Foundation

Transferred to digital printing 2008

frontispiece
ARCHIGRAM: INSTANT CITY VISITS BOURNEMOUTH, 1969

CONTENTS

PREFACE | VIII
CONTRIBUTORS | X
CREDITS | XII

#01 PAUL BARKER:
THINKING THE UNTHINKABLE | 2

#02 CEDRIC PRICE:
CEDRIC PRICE'S NON-PLAN DIARY | 22

#03 BEN FRANKS:
NEW RIGHT/NEW LEFT | 32
AN ALTERNATIVE EXPERIMENT IN FREEDOM

#04 COLIN WARD:
ANARCHY AND ARCHITECTURE | 44
A PERSONAL RECORD

#05 BARRY CURTIS:
THE HEART OF THE CITY | 52

#06 IAN HORTON:
PERVASION OF THE PICTURESQUE | 66
ENGLISH ARCHITECTURAL AESTHETICS AND LEGISLATION,
1945-1965

#07 ELEONORE KOFMAN AND ELIZABETH LEBAS:
RECOVERY AND REAPPROPRIATION IN LEFEBVRE
AND CONSTANT | 80

#08 JONATHAN HUGHES:
THE INDETERMINATE BUILDING | 90

#09 YONA FRIEDMAN:
FUNCTION FOLLOWS FORM   104

#10 JOHN BECK:
BUCKMINSTER FULLER AND THE
POLITICS OF SHELTER   116

#11 HADAS STEINER:
OFF THE MAP   126

#12 SIMON SADLER:
OPEN ENDS   138
THE SOCIAL VISIONS OF 1960S NON-PLANNING

#13 BEN HIGHMORE:
THE DEATH OF THE PLANNER?   156
PARIS CIRCA 1968

#14 JONATHAN HUGHES:
AFTER NON-PLAN   166
RETRENCHMENT AND REASSERTION

#15 CLARA GREED:
CAN MAN PLAN? CAN WOMAN PLAN BETTER?   184

#16 MALCOLM MILES:
LIVING LIGHTLY ON THE EARTH   198

#17 CHINEDU UMENYILORA:
EMPOWERING THE SELF-BUILDER   210

#18 MARTIN PAWLEY:
TOWARDS AN UNORIGINAL ARCHITECTURE   222

#19 MICHAEL RAKOWITZ:
PARASITE   232

INDEX   236

PREFACE

Should architecture obey, deny or subvert the logic of 'the plan'? This question has continued to haunt the theory, polemics and practice of architecture throughout the latter half of the twentieth century. It is a simple question, yet one which can be considered at many levels and from many points of view, challenging the established professional boundaries of the architect, problematizing the role of the official urban planner and forcing an investigation of the scope of the lay 'consumers' of architecture to seize control of the forces which manipulate the design and construction of the buildings and cities around them. At the level of the individual building one is forced to consider whether one thinks of buildings as completed artefacts or perpetual works-in-progress, as real estate or as tools. At the level of the city the power of the 'rational' modernist plan to shape the use of space, once considered the guarantor of freedom and enlightened progress, has been critiqued as a tyranny governing everything from matters of taste to the conduct of life itself.

The responses to the question can be grouped into two broad approaches: those which consider the possibility of 'non-planning' within the context of existing social and economic infrastructures and those which confront existing structures as limiting conditions which must be transgressed. The scope for differing and contradictory responses to the question is great and the resulting programmes which the post-war period has witnessed testify to the breadth of political and social perspectives which can be brought to bear on the subject. The devolution of power conjures up such notions as 'choice', 'freedom' and 'participation', words laden with the accumulated hopes and aspirations of so many partisan groupings and propagandists from across the political spectrum.

In 1997, at its annual conference, the Association of Art Historians (AAH) met to examine 'Structures and Practices', offering the ideal arena in which to explore the structures and practices of the established architectural and planning professions. The twelve papers assembled for the conference duly set about investigating the post-war strategies which have attempted to prise apart the grip of architectural determinacy: technology, prefabrication, democracy, feminism, self-help, anarchy and the free market. This book expands upon and revises the findings of that conference, presenting a collection of papers almost all of which are published here for the first time. The collection cannot pretend to be a comprehensive survey of the subject; indeed, the breadth of the subject matter has made it almost impossible to offer an exhaustive survey of an impulse which has marked both modernism and the nascent post-modernism, as well as political groupings of many hues.

PREFACE

The book borrows its title from an extraordinary article published in *New Society* magazine on 20 March 1969. On that occasion, 'non-plan' was a plea for deregulation, although elsewhere the authors of the article – Reyner Banham, Paul Barker, Peter Hall and Cedric Price – had been pursuing the problem of environmental freedom on several fronts. Likewise, this new non-plan anthology, where disparate contributions turn out, to our delight, to interlock. We have deliberately avoided ideological consistency in our selection. Indeed, one of the fascinations of 'non-plan' is surely the way in which it consistently seems to confound established political categories of left and right. The issue is, fundamentally, how people can take control of their environments, a subject on which most, if not all, political groupings proffer their views. What does unite these disparate opinions is an optimistic belief in the ability of people to gain from the devolution of power – be it through the benefits of technological progress (or its ecologically aware successors), the logic of the global consumer market (or challenges to the institutions of capitalism) and the merits of direct self-help (or the need for advocacy and professional support). The charge of naivety may easily be levelled at the project of 'non-plan', yet it is ultimately a charge which either lacks the courage to think around the existing boundaries of contemporary life or betrays an unwillingness to reconsider historical situations on their own terms.

This is not to say that all authors in the book believe that 'non-planning' is wholly desirable, let alone achievable. For several writers, past and present, there are limits to the scope for beneficial 'non-planning', limits which relate either to the impossibility of ever achieving the complete devolution of power or to the need to challenge 'planning' with an equally powerful and united counter force. In such situations the terms 'planning' and 'non-planning' become almost redundant and the task becomes one of negotiating a path between the two extremes. This book does not seek to provide easy answers, for it is in part a dispassionate critique and an historical investigation. Yet it is also a platform for proposals and solutions, usually argued with a conviction that has barely diminished over time.

We have been extremely fortunate in securing the involvement of several of the instigators and proponents of the ideas explored in this book – Paul Barker, Yona Friedman, Martin Pawley, Cedric Price and Colin Ward – and we thank them for lending their enthusiasm to the project. Likewise we acknowledge the commitment of those who participated in the original AAH conference in 1997, all of whom have contributed to the book. We are indebted to Neil Warnock-Smith, Mike Cash and Katherine MacInnes at Architectural Press for their support for the project from its earliest proposed translation into published form and to Marie Milmore and Margaret Denley for their ongoing assistance during its challenging gestation. We would also like to thank Tina Borkowski whose contribution as designer of this book stands alongside those of the other authors. Finally, we both owe a debt to all those who have lived with this project in one way or another for the last two years, including our respective families and friends. Jonathan Hughes would like to thank Kerry Bristol, Simon Dell, Margaret Garlake, Chris Green, John Higgins, Iris Hughes, Graham Larkin and Margit Thøfner.

CONTRIBUTORS

PAUL BARKER was the Editor of *New Society* from 1968 to 1986. He is a writer and broadcaster and a Senior Fellow of the Institute of Community Studies. His books include *Arts in Society* (Fontana, 1977), *The Other Britain* (Routledge, 1982), and *Living as Equals* (OUP, 1996).

JOHN BECK is Adrian Research Fellow at Darwin College, Cambridge.

BARRY CURTIS is Professor of Visual Culture and a Director of Research at Middlesex University. He has published on Archigram and urban theory as well as tourism and assimilation. He has co-edited *Mapping the Futures* (Routledge, 1992), *Travellers' Tales* (Routledge, 1994), *Future Natural* (Routledge, 1996) and *The Block Reader in Visual Culture* (Routledge, 1996).

BEN FRANKS holds a Research Studentship in the Postgraduate School of Critical Theory at Nottingham University.

YONA FRIEDMAN is an architect best known for his 'Ville Spatiale' project (1958–1962), proposing a space frame structure raised high above ground level. In the voids of the structure usable spaces were to be inserted, the layout of which would be decided by the inhabitant. His theories were implemented by other architects including Tange and Piano. He has subsequently worked for disadvantaged groups in India and elsewhere.

CLARA GREED is a Reader in the Built Environment at the University of the West of England, Bristol. Her research interests include women and planning, other minorities issues and the changing composition and culture of the construction industry. She has published widely, including *Women and Planning* (Routledge, 1994) and *Introducing Urban Design* (Longman, 1998, with Marion Roberts).

BEN HIGHMORE is a Lecturer in Cultural and Media Studies at the University of the West of England, Bristol. He is currently completing a study on cultural theory and everyday life, whilst starting a book about the imaginary geographies of 'Swinging London'. He is a founder member of the 'Everyday Life Research Group'.

IAN HORTON is an Associate Lecturer at the Open University and Sessional Lecturer at the School of Architecture at Kent Institute of Art and Design. His current research examines government legislation and its impact on architectural aesthetics.

JONATHAN HUGHES lectures and publishes on post-war British architecture. His current research focuses on the inter-relationship of artistic and architectural avant-gardes in post-war Britain.

ELEONORE KOFMAN is Professor in the Department of International Relations at Nottingham Trent University. She works on contemporary issues of urbanism in France and on gender migration in European global cities. ELIZABETH LEBAS is Senior Lecturer in the Faculty of Art, Design and Performing Arts at Middlesex University. She researches on municipal gardening and film-making between the wars. Together, the authors are the editors of *Henri Lefebvre: Writings on Cities* (Blackwell, 1996).

MALCOLM MILES teaches in the School of Art, Publishing and Music at Oxford Brookes University. He is author of *Art, Space and the City* (Routledge, 1997) and has contributed to journals including *The Journal of Art and Design Education, Parallax, Point, Urban Design International* and *Urban History*. His current research concerns the relation of art, critical theory and ecology.

MARTIN PAWLEY is a writer and critic with regular columns in the *Architect's Journal*, the Munich on-line magazine *Telepolis* and *World Architecture* (of which he was the editor until 1996). He was architecture correspondent for the *Guardian* (1984–1991) and the *Observer* (1992–1995). Recent books include *Theory and Design in the Second Machine Age* (Blackwell, 1990), *Buckminster Fuller: A Critical Biography* (Trefoil, 1990), and *Future Systems: the Story of Tomorrow* (Phaidon, 1993). His latest book, *Terminal Architecture*, is published by Reaktion Books (1998).

CEDRIC PRICE, architect, founded his practice in central London in 1960. His work in the UK and abroad is largely involved with urban issues.

MICHAEL RAKOWITZ received a Master of Science in Visual Studies from Massachusetts Institute of Technology. He is currently working as an artist in New York City and is an Adjunct Professor of Design at State University of New York Purchase College.

SIMON SADLER currently lectures in the Department of Art History at Trinity College, Dublin. He is the author of *The Situationist City* (MIT Press, 1998).

HADAS STEINER is a PhD candidate in the History, Theory and Criticism section of the Department of Architecture at the Massachusetts Institute of Technology.

CHINEDU UMENYILORA, AA Dipl, is an architect exploring the role of an 'empowerment broker'. Having worked on various small-scale projects, he is currently working with the residents of Kingsmead Estate, East London, to promote individual and community development. He is a past RIBA Medal Winner and Serjeant Award winner.

COLIN WARD worked at the drawing board between the ages of 16 and 40 years. He is author of many books of which the latest, written in collaboration with Peter Hall, is *Sociable Cities: the Legacy of Ebenezer Howard* (Wiley, 1998). He was given an honorary fellowship by Hull School of Architecture and an honorary doctorate by Middlesex University and in 1996 was a visiting professor at the London School of Economics.

CREDITS

Archigram Archives: frontispiece, 11.1–11.2, 11.4, 11.7–11.8, 12.2, 12.4–12.5
New Society: 1.1–1.10 (*New Society* pages reproduced from issue of 29 March 1969 (vol. 13, no. 338), published by New Science Publications, London)
Barnaby's Picture Library, London: 4.3 (© Hubertus Kanus)
Stewart Brand: 14.6
Buckminster Fuller Institute, Santa Barbara: 10.1–10.5 (©1960 Estate of Buckminster Fuller. Courtesy Buckminster Fuller Institute, Santa Barbara)
Cambridge University Press: 8.4, 8.6
Peter Cook: 11.3
Dennis Crompton: 11.6
Patrick Eagar: 2.3
Yona Friedman: 9.1–9.24
Richard Hamilton/DACS: 8.7 (© Richard Hamilton, all rights reserved, DACS 1999)
HMSO: 6.1–6.8
Jonathan Hughes: 8.1, 8.8, 14.2–14.5, 14.7
Charles Jencks: 12.3
Kisho Kurokawa: 12.1
Magnum Photos, London: 13.1 (© Bruno Barbey/Magnum Photos)
Kenneth Martin/Tate Gallery: 8.5
Malcolm Miles: 16.1–16.6
Constant Nieuwenhuys: 7.2
Martin Pawley: 18.1–18.12
Ann Pendleton-Jullian: 16.7
Kensington Post (Tony Ironside)/Penguin Books: 14.1
Cedric Price: 2.1–2.2, 2.4–2.8
Alison and Peter Smithson: 8.9, 11.5
John Turner: 4.1
Chinedu Umenyilora: 17.1–17.11
Nick Wates and Christian Wolmar: 3.1–3.3, 3.5
Colin Ward: 4.2, 4.4, 4.5
John Weeks: 8.3, 8.10
Front cover illustration courtesy of Comstock

#01
PAUL BARKER: THINKING THE UNTHINKABLE

In 1969, Christopher Booker published *The Neophiliacs*,[1] his attack on the passion for change which had characterized Britain from the mid-1950s. In that same year, *New Society* published a special issue under the heading, 'Non-Plan: An experiment in freedom'[2] (Figures 1.1–1.10) It came too late for inclusion in Booker's onslaught. It would, anyway, have been rather difficult to categorize. On the one hand, it was certainly imbued with the desire for change (rampant neophilia). On the other hand, it argued that what ordinary people wanted – rather than what planners, architects and other aesthetic judges said they ought to want – was the best guide (rampant conservatism or rampant anarchism, depending on your viewpoint). Its tone, however, was undoubtedly that of the period: scathing and iconoclastic. It was marked, too, by a fascination with the culture of the car which, then as now, was seen by many cultural critics as a threat to civilization as we know it.

The idea of Non-Plan, or at any rate the word, was born one day in 1967. I was then the deputy editor of *New Society*. This weekly magazine of social inquiry had been founded in 1962. It was itself a sign of the contemporary preoccupation with trying to work out what sort of place Britain really was and might become. In *Too Much: art and society in the sixties, 1960–75*, his cultural history of the 1960s, Robert Hewison said that *New Society* was launched 'as a forum for the new intelligentsia'.[3] I doubt whether, earlier, the word 'intelligentsia' could accurately have been employed in Britain.

The expansion of the universities in the 1960s gave *New Society* many of its readers and writers. But, though it was usually categorized as centre-left, it was always fiercely non-partisan. It sought to counter the usual preoccupations of magazines of opinion (party politics, foreign affairs, literature). The founder editor was a liberal Conservative and I was resolutely non-party. I saw the magazine as in the fine tradition of Dissent. I was always conscious of George Orwell's censorship troubles with doctrinaire editors and publishers. I was determined that this would not be repeated at *New Society*. The Marxist historian, E.P. Thompson, who found a friendly home in its pages, away from sectarian disputes, wrote, '*New Society*'s hospitality to a dissenting view [is] heartening evidence that the closure of our democratic traditions is not yet complete'.[4] From its launch to its demise in 1988, the magazine was obsessed with pinning down how things were, rather than how they were supposed to be. Urban change was always one of my own deepest interests.

1 Christopher Booker, *The Neophiliacs*, London: Collins, 1969 (new edition, London: Pimlico, 1992).
2 Reyner Banham, Paul Barker, Peter Hall and Cedric Price, Non-Plan: An experiment in freedom, *New Society*, 13, no. 338, 20 March 1969, pp. 435–443.
3 Robert Hewison, *Too Much: art and society in the sixties, 1960–75*, London: Methuen, 1986.
4 E.P. Thompson, *Writing by Candlelight*, London: Merlin Press, 1980.

figure 1.1
NEW SOCIETY, 20 MARCH 1969, COVER

That day in 1967 I went out for a lunchtime glass of beer and a sandwich with the urban geographer, Peter Hall, at a pub called the 'Yorkshire Grey' on Gray's Inn Road, near *New Society*'s offices. He was then best known for his book *London 2000*,[5] and he had become a regular contributor to *New Society*. We were both disheartened by what urban planning was then producing. Peter Hall, then at the London School of Economics, was always ready to think the unthinkable – which being a member of the Fabian Society executive committee did not then rule out. He was strongly influenced by his extensive knowledge of the United States of America.

Earlier in 1967, I had seized gratefully on a book by the American sociologist, Herbert Gans. *The Levittowners: ways of life and politics in a new suburban community*[6] showed how a spirit of community evolved within the most despised form of American suburban speculative housing. I ran long extracts from it in *New Society*, as a corrective to the usual we-know-best snobberies about suburbia.

Between us, Peter Hall and I floated this maverick thought: could things be any worse if there was no planning at all? They might even be somewhat better. We were especially concerned at the attempt to impose *aesthetic* choices on people who might have very different choices of their own. Why not, we wondered, suggest an experiment in getting along without planning and seeing what emerged? We called it 'Non-Plan'. The word was, I think, mine. But it evolved after the usual batting to and fro which arises on such occasions.

For other collaborators, the decision seemed obvious: Reyner Banham and Cedric Price. It would make a quartet of mavericks: paid-up members of the Awkward Squad.

In 1965, I had persuaded Reyner Banham to become *New Society*'s regular design and architecture critic. He was then at University College, London. I was enchanted by the quality of his writing and his loving observation of everyday objects. His first major essay for the magazine was a review of *The Kandy-Kolored Tangerine-Flake Streamline Baby*, by the then-unknown Tom Wolfe. With Peter Hall, he became one of *New Society*'s most characteristic voices. The Non-Plan idea was strongly influenced by Banham's essays in the magazine.[7]

It was Cedric Price, the fourth maverick in our quartet, who had first suggested to me that Reyner Banham should be writing for *New Society* (where the range of critics included John Berger, Angela Carter, Peter Fuller, Albert Hunt, John Lahr and Michael Wood). Price's designs had appeared in the pages of the magazine.[8] His proposal for

5 Peter Hall, *London 2000*, London: Faber & Faber, 1963.
6 Herbert J. Gans, *The Levittowners: ways of life and politics in a new suburban community*, London: Allen Lane The Penguin Press, 1967.
7 Reyner Banham's essays in *New Society* have appeared in three selections: Paul Barker, *Arts in Society*, London: Fontana, 1977; Penny Sparke, *Design by Choice*, London: Academy Editions, 1981; Mary Banham, *A Critic Writes*, Berkeley: University of California Press, 1997. The Tom Wolfe review was published on 19 August 1965 (*New Society*, 6, no. 151, p. 25).
8 Cedric Price, Pop-up Parliament, *New Society*, 6, no. 148, 29 July 1965, pp. 7–8; Potteries thinkbelt, *New Society*, 7, no. 192, 2 June 1966, pp. 14–7.

what he called a 'Pop-up parliament' was one of the things Booker objected to in *The Neophiliacs*. Booker missed Price's irony. The proposal to knock down, and update, the Barry-Pugin masterpiece was one way of criticizing the relationship, or non-relationship, between Parliament and people. In the mid-1960s, Cedric Price was probably best-known for his long-running battle to build a 'fun palace' in London. It was never built, but it is the acknowledged intellectual inspiration for the Piano-Rogers Pompidou Centre in Paris.

Our scheme for launching Non-Plan involved Hall, Banham and Price each taking a segment of English countryside and hypothesizing what might happen if Non-Plan were applied there. We wanted to startle people by offending against the deepest taboos. This would drive our point home. I suggested Constable Country to Banham, partly because of his East Anglian roots and partly because it represented the greatest rural taboo of all. (In the end, he shied away from this a little. We kept the title *pour épater*, but he moved the focus westwards from Constable's heartlands to Royston-Stansted, where there was no Foster airport yet.) Cedric Price chose the hinterland of the Solent. Peter Hall chose the eastern edge of the Peak District. To maintain the fancy nomenclature, we called these Montagu Country and Lawrence Country. The wider polemic would then be built around these three case studies.

During 1968 some of the material was written, but the idea marked time. I became editor of the magazine. It was a year of historic eruptions. Other issues took precedence. An anti-Communist uprising in Czechoslovakia was put down by Soviet tanks. In Paris, students rioted against President de Gaulle (the protests were strangled by a deal struck between the right-wing government and the Communist trades unions). In England and the USA there were recurrent campus and street protests against the Vietnam War.

The Non-Plan special issue was finally published on 20 March 1969. I had written an introduction, trying to capture the spirit of the enterprise. Peter Hall and I wrote the closing pages. But the issue appeared under all our names. We had all agreed the entire text and every page included thoughts from each contributor. It was illustrated mainly with specially taken night-time photographs of illuminated signs in and around London: for petrol stations, launderettes, supermarkets, burger bars. It is worth noting here that the Venturi *et al.*'s *Learning From Las Vegas*[9] was not published until 1972.

Non-Plan produced a mixture of deep outrage and stunned silence. The environmentalist and anarchist, Colin Ward, wrote later: 'If I were to choose a single article (endlessly cited by me) which most epitomised everything I believe in, in a particular field, and which was valuable to me just as a legitimation of opinions I seemed to be alone in advocating it was ... "Non-Plan: an experiment in freedom".'[10] But, at the time,

---
9 Robert Venturi, Denise Scott Brown and Steven Izenour, *Learning from Las Vegas*, Cambridge, MA: MIT Press, 1972.
10 Colin Ward, quoted in Paul Barker, Painting the portrait of 'The Other Britain': *New Society* 1962-88, *Contemporary Record*, 5, no. 1, summer 1991, pp. 45–61.

all the architects, conservationists and socialists I knew were highly offended by it. It was perhaps ten years ahead of its time. It is a key text in the intellectual counter-attack against Webbian Fabianism. Later in 1969, Non-Plan was one of the ideas put forward in a pamphlet, *Social Reform in the Centrifugal Society*,[11] on which Peter Hall and I collaborated with the sociologists, Michael Young and Peter Willmott.

Non-Plan had very practical consequences. Peter Hall, as always, carried on thinking. We had not believed that our ideas could be applied in London, but the problem of what to do with derelict docklands changed this argument. In 1977, Hall gave a paper at the annual conference of the Royal Town Planning Institute under the title 'Greenfields and grey areas'.[12] He suggested 'enterprise zones' in the run-down parts of cities, where planning restrictions would be lifted in order to spur improvement forward. In London, local authorities, including the Greater London Council, had been notably unable to come up with any useful strategies when the docks closed. Infighting and short-sightedness prevailed.

When 'Non-Plan' was first published, one of the few friendly reactions, at the time, came from an ex-Communist turned *Daily Telegraph* leader-writer, Alfred Sherman. In 1974, Sherman helped Sir Keith Joseph and Margaret Thatcher to found the Centre for Political Studies, the purpose of which was to carve out a new way for Conservatism after Edward Heath's failed corporatism. The first Thatcher government was elected in 1979 and enterprise zones were introduced as a brief legislative experiment in Non-Plan. (It was brief because the Treasury eventually decided that the associated tax breaks were costing too much.) Without enterprise zones, we would not have had the Gateshead MetroCentre, the first such shopping mall in Britain, or the London Docklands' love-it-or-hate-it trademark skyscraper at Canary Wharf. Both were built in enterprise zones.

The idea of Non-Plan never went away. It continued as a kind of underground river. Recently, it has resurfaced. Is this because we are once again surrounded by people who think that planning is the answer to everything and who believe that they alone know the way we should all live? Under guidance issued by John Gummer, as Environment Secretary, planners were once again encouraged to pay special attention to aesthetics in giving permissions. In other words: they can decide what is beautiful *for* you.

Non-Plan was essentially a very humble idea: that it is very difficult to decide what is best for *other* people.

11 The Open Group, *Social Reform in the Centrifugal Society, New Society* pamphlet, September 1969.
12 Peter Hall, Greenfields and grey areas (paper presented at Royal Town Planning Institute annual conference, Chester, 15 June 1977), reprinted in Peter Hall, *The Enterprise Zone: British origins, American adaptations*, Berkeley: Institute of Urban and Regional Development, Working Paper no. 350, 1981. Colin Ward followed up Non-Plan from a different perspective with his concept of a 'do-it-yourself new town' (which he first proposed in 1975). This linked the experience of the pre-war 'plotlands' in the English countryside with the post-war adventure of the self-built settlements that surround every city of Latin America, Africa or Asia. See Colin Ward, The unofficial countryside, in *Town and Country* (Anthony Barnett and Roger Scruton, editors), London: Jonathan Cape, 1998.

But what, exactly, did we say? What follows is the introduction to 'Non-Plan'.[13] Some of it – like the passage about petrol stations – turned out to be a very accurate forecast of what happened, though prediction was not really our purpose. The language is sometimes dated but much of the argument has an all too contemporary resonance. Our conclusions, after the three case studies, were headed 'Spontaneity and space'. We said that the British 'seem so afraid of freedom'. We argued that 'the notion that the planner has the right to say what is "right" is really an extraordinary hang-over from the days of collectivism in left-wing thought'. We concluded: 'Let's save our breath for genuine problems – like the poor who are increasingly with us.'

Today it is very striking that the 1947 nationalization of land development rights is the only nationalization left unrepealed. But the dilemmas have not gone away.

We wrote, in our conclusion, that 'as people become richer they demand more space; and because they become at the same time more mobile, they will be more able to command it. They will want this extra space in and around their houses, around their shops, around their offices and factories, and in the places where they go for recreation. To impose rigid controls, in order to frustrate people in achieving the space standards they require, represents simply the received personal or class judgements of the people who are making the decision.'

Non-Plan, however, was never against some kinds of *negative* planning (for example: this land shall not be built on); the trouble, so often, lay – and lies – with would-be *positive* planning. The British vice is bossiness. As I go around Britain in the dying days of the twentieth century,[14] I am unconvinced that our planned towns and cities have delivered the best we could hope for. Nor do I think that what now passes for wisdom will necessarily turn out to be any wiser than the misplaced confidence of previous generations.

But it is time to raise the curtain on 1969: 'Non-Plan: An experiment in freedom', by (in the alphabetical order we used then) Reyner Banham, Paul Barker, Peter Hall and Cedric Price. The subtitle said: 'Town and country planning has today become an unquestioned shibboleth. Yet very few of its procedures or value judgements have any sound basis, except delay. Why not have the courage, where practical, to let people shape their own environment?'

---

13 First reprinted in an Open University course text: Andrew Blowers, Chris Hamnett and Philip Sarre (editors), *The Future of Cities*, London: Hutchinson Educational, 1974.
14 Many of these journeys were chronicled in my weekly column in the *New Statesman*, from May 1996 to January 1999, combining social, architectural and topographical observation.

NON-PLAN

A dispute has arisen about a booklet, *Dorset Building in Rural Areas*, just issued by Dorset County Council, and aspiring to be a guide to good design for people building houses in the countryside – our Architecture Correspondent writes.[15] Most of the examples that it illustrates and recommends as models are utterly commonplace, the sort of house to be found in almost any speculative builder's suburban estate. This view is shared by the Wilts and Dorset Society of Architects, which, through its president, Mr Peter Wakefield,[16] has asked for the publication to be withdrawn.

THE TIMES, DECEMBER 1968

This news item illustrates the tangle we have got ourselves into. Somehow, everything must be watched; nothing can be allowed simply to 'happen'. No house can be allowed to be commonplace in the way that things just *are* commonplace: each project must be weighed, planned, approved and only then built, and only after that discovered to be commonplace after all. Somehow, somewhere, someone was using the wrong year's model.

Once, Rasmussen, in *London: The Unique City* (first published 1934), thought it worth printing a picture of the entirely commonplace domestic architecture built along Parkway, Camden Town, in the early nineteenth century. It was architecture that worked; it provided what the inhabitants wanted from it. Now there'd be trouble if you tried to knock it down (though the London motorway box will pass close by[17]). But at least the preservationists didn't get in at ground level, as they do today, in order to try to make sure – *before* the event – that something that is eventually worth preserving is built.

The whole concept of planning (the town-and-country kind, at least) has gone cockeyed. What we have today represents a whole cumulation of good intentions. And what those good intentions are worth, we have almost no way of knowing. To say it has been with us so long, physical planning has been remarkably unmonitored; ditto architecture itself. As Melvin Webber has pointed out: planning is the only branch of knowledge purporting to be some kind of science which regards a plan as being *fulfilled* when it is merely *completed*; there's seldom any sort of check on whether the plan actually does what it was meant to do and whether, if it does something different, this is for the better or for the worse.

The result is that planning tends to lurch from one fashion to another, with sudden revulsion setting in after equally sudden acceptance. One good recent example, of course, was the fashion for high-rise flats – which had been dying for some time before

15 This was J.M. Richards, for many years the editor of the *Architectural Review*.
16 Peter Wakefield has one credit in my editions of the *Buildings of England* volumes for Dorset and Wiltshire. A house called Low Ridge, in Crockerton, near Warminster: '1956, L-shaped, single-storeyed'.
17 Very little of this contentious Inner London motorway was ever built, but the planning blight, caused by the threat that it would run through Camden Lock, allowed hippy-ish dealers to start up in low-rent or no-rent properties. Without intending to, planners launched one of London's most vigorous, and wholly unplanned, tourist destinations.

Ronan Point gave it a tombstone. This fashion had been inaugurated with bizarre talk of creating 'vertical streets', which would somehow, it was hoped, re-create the togetherness of Bethnal Green on Saturday morning in (presumably) the lift shaft – this being the only equivalent communication channel in the structure.

Not that one can be too swiftly mocking. We may yet find that for some future twist of social or technological development, tall flats are just the thing. This happened with another fashion – that for the Garden City, as promulgated by Patrick Geddes, Ebenezer Howard and Raymond Unwin. It's worth remembering that the garden in this theory was there specifically for growing food: the acreage was carefully measured out with this fodder ratio in mind. The houses in (say) Welwyn Garden City or Hampstead Garden Suburb were also scattered thinly because of the width of space allocated (for reasons of health) to the loop and sweep of roads.

Welwyn Garden City and Hampstead Garden Suburb were therefore built – and then duly mocked for dull doctrinairism. The layout made public transport almost impossible; the tin and the frozen pack rapidly outdated the vegetable patch. But then the spread of car ownership outdated the mockery: those roads lived to find a justification; the space around the houses could absorb a garage without too much trouble; and the garden (as, even, in many inner London conversions of Georgian houses) became an unexceptional outdoor room and meeting space for children, away from the lethal pressed steel and rubber hurtling around the streets.

Now it's nice that a plan should turn out to have reasons for succeeding which the planner himself did not foresee. At every stage in the history of planning, we have cause to be grateful for the quirks of time. It's doubtful if John Nash saw how well his Regent's Park would serve as an arty but fairly democratic pause on the north edge of London – just right for football and swings and non-copulating pandas and Sunday-promenading Central Europeans; inhabited not by Regency aristos but by film people, lumps of London University and H.M. Government, the American ambassador and high-class tarts.[18] And did Scott foresee how his St Pancras hotel, superbly planned to fit in with departing trains and arriving horse-carriages would survive being a much-mocked office block[19] so successfully that it can now be argued for as a natural home for a sports centre or a transport museum or Birkbeck College?

Nor is it just the cities and towns that have benefited. How many further-education departments[20] can be duly grateful for minor Georgian country houses or their Victorian imitators – so apt for giving courses in? How many angling clubs can thank the canal builders for where they spend their peaceful Sundays? How many Highlands-

---

18 In reading this thumbnail sketch of the park, remember the date. Many refugees from Nazi Germany lived on the northern edge of the park; Bedford College, University of London, was still in buildings in the middle; and newspapers were enjoying running the story that London Zoo was having trouble persuading pandas to mate.
19 For years the hotel, which narrowly escaped demolition, housed British Rail offices. There was intermittent debate, then and long afterwards, about what to do with it.
20 As Non-Plan was published, these were being grouped into 'polytechnics'. In the 1990s they were all re-designated as universities.

addicted tourists, even, depend for the solitude they love on those harsh men who preferred the glens clear of people and who planned them out of the Highlands and into Canada and Australia?

Yet it's hard to see where, in this, the credit can go to the planner. That last example – which pushes the concept of planning altogether too far – is justified in rubbing in the coerciveness of it. Most planning is aristocratic or oligarchic in method, even today – revealing in this its historical origins. The most rigorously planned cities – like Haussmann's and Napoleon III's Paris – have nearly always been the least democratic.

The way that Haussmann rebuilt Paris gladdens the tourist; it was not such a help, though, for the poor through whose homes the demolition gangs went to create those avenues and squares. Similarly, the urban renewal programmes of the American cities gladdened the real estate men; they did not help the Negroes[21] and poor whites who were uprooted with little to compensate them. In Britain, public housing programmes gladden the housing committees and the respectable working class; they do not help the poorest, the most fissile or the most drifting families.[22]

The point is to realize how little planning and the accompanying architecture have changed. The whole ethos is doctrinaire; and if something good emerges, it remains a bit of a bonus. Not to be expected but nice if you can get it – like totalling enough Green Shield stamps[23] to get a Mini. At the moment, most planners in Britain are on a tautness jag: Camden's neatly interlocked squares, Southwark's high-density juggernauts or Cumbernauld's and the Elephant's sculptural shopping centres. Some of these look pleasant enough now – and some do not. But the fact is that, so far as one can judge, taut arrangements last much better when plenty of money can be spent on their upkeep (Oxbridge colleges, Chelsea squares) than when it can not (remember all those Improved Industrial Dwellings put up in the late nineteenth century by Mr Peabody and others?).

So it's at least plausible that some other doctrine than the current one would be right for everyday housing and building. It would be pleasant if 'doctrine' were precisely what it wasn't.

But how are we to know? Planning is being subjected to increasing scepticism. The Town and Country Planning Act, 1968, tidies up some of the abuses (especially those which caused delay in granting permissions); and the Skeffington committee is currently trying to decide how people might be given more say ('participation', in the jargon) in planning. The New City plan for Milton Keynes tries to shy away completely from planning. At universities, research is being done. The one thing that is not being

---

21 This reads oddly now; it was then standard usage. It had recently displaced 'coloured people'. At the time, 'blacks' – the usual word afterwards – was seen as offensive.
22 In the following decade this kind of criticism, commonplace then among housing experts, led to changes in official allocation policies. There is now no doubt that council estates house these once-excluded groups. The unplanned result has been to stigmatize much of what is now called 'social housing'.
23 Instead of a discount, shops gave away stamps with purchases. The stamps could then be traded in against goods from a catalogue.

done is the harshest test, the most valuable experiment, of all. What would happen if there were no plan? What would people prefer to do, if their choice were untrammelled? Would matters be any better, or any worse, or much the same? (Might planning turn out to be rather like Eysenck's view of psychoanalysis: an activity which, insofar as it gets credit, gets it for benefits that would happen anyway – minds can cure themselves; maybe people can plan themselves?) But even if matters ended up much the same, in terms of durable successes or disastrous failures, the overall pattern would be sure to be different: the *look* of the experiment would be sure to differ from what we have now.

This is what we're now proposing: a precise and carefully observed experiment in non-planning. It's hardly an experiment one could carry out over the entire country. Some knots – like London – are, by now, far too Gordian for that. Nor are we suggesting (here) that other than physical planning should be shelved.

The right approach is to take the plunge into heterogeneity: to seize on a few appropriate zones of the country, which are subject to a characteristic range of pressures, and use them as launch-pads for Non-Plan. At the least, one would find out what people want; at the most, one might discover the hidden style of mid-twentieth century Britain.

It's 'hidden' for the same reason that caused any good social democrat to shudder at the anarchic suggestion of the previous paragraph. Town planning is always in thrall to some outmoded rule-of-thumb; as a profession, in fact, planners tend to read the *Telegraph* and the *Express*, rather than the *Guardian* or the *Times*.[24] Take a specific example: the filling station.

'Watch the little filling station', Frank Lloyd Wright said. 'It is the agent of decentralization.' Like all focuses of transport, the filling station could be a notable cause of change. Self-service automats, dispensing food and other goods, could spring up around the forecourt; maybe small post offices, too; telephone kiosks; holiday gear shops; eateries (*not* restaurants): all this quite apart from the standard BP Viscostatic/ice cream/map and guidebook shop. (Thus, at Cumbernauld New Town, it's already clear that only the most repressive controls can stop the two conveniently sited filling stations from replacing the inconveniently sited town centre as a shopping focus.)

Well, you can watch as long as you like in Britain, but you will see small sign of this happening. It's hard enough to get planning permission to put up a filling station in the first place. (There's still a feeling – dating probably from the hoo-ha which broke out when the Set Britain Free Tories decided to replace pool petrol[25] in the 1950s by commercial brands – that it is very easy to have 'too many' filling stations.) To have anything else on

---

24 The *Daily Express* was still the obvious example of a popular right-wing newspaper; the *Daily Mail* was in the doldrums. The *Daily Telegraph* was much more the mouthpiece of the Conservative Party than it later became. The *Times* was still a fairly rigorous newspaper of record: conservative, but with liberal leanings.
25 'Pool petrol' was a wartime expedient, like Utility furniture. The 1945–1951 Labour government kept it. With other echoes of wartime, like food rationing, the Tories ended it.

opposite page and following pages figures 1.2-1.10
NON-PLAN: AN EXPERIMENT IN FREEDOM, *NEW SOCIETY*, NO. 338,
20 MARCH 1969, PP. 435-443

the forecourt is almost impossible. Only in the motorway service areas (themselves damply over-planned) is there anything like this; and here the unfortunately not unique combination of incompetence and non-spontaneity kills the whole thing.

And yet there's no doubt that the popular arts of our time (i.e. those on which everyone thinks he has a valid opinion) are car design and advertising; and these are doubly symbolized by such characteristic forecourt figures as the Esso tiger or the BP little man. The great recent soap-opera films have been Jacques Demy's *Les Parapluies de Cherbourg* (hero: a filling station owner) and Claude Lelouch's *Un Homme et Une Femme* (hero: a racing car driver). If you drive down the French Rhone valley motorway – not so planned as ours – one of the most memorable sights is a Total petrol station, writing the letters T-O-T-A-L huge across the valley, with a flutter of flags underneath. Stay in Moscow, and you end up yearning to see an Esso sign.

Ask yourself why it is that almost the only time you ever see flags on any *unofficial* occasion – i.e. not at an ordained festival or other jamboree and not on a public building – is on filling stations or else on the rear windows of cars.

Now the purpose of this is not to write a kind of Elegy in a Country Filling Station. The purpose is to ask: why don't we dare trust the choices that would evolve if we let them? It's permissible to ask – after the dreariness of much public re-building and after the Ronan Point disaster[26] – what exactly should we sacrifice to fashion?

Here we take a look at three zones where one might make the experiment of succumbing to the pressures and seeing where it led: the East Midlands, 'Lawrence country'; the area around Nuthampstead, 'Constable country'; and the Solent, 'Montagu country'. There are, obviously, other candidates. Anyone can fill in his own sacred cows or *bêtes noires*. (Imagine, for example, dividing the Lake District so that Coniston and Windermere could satisfy all those M6 hordes by becoming a Non-Plan zone: it might help protect the Wastwaters that are worth preserving). The main thing is that the experiment should be tried – and tried quickly. Even the first waves of information would be valuable; if the experiment ran for five years, ten years, twenty years, more and more of use would emerge. Legally, it would not be too difficult to set up. It only requires the will to do it – and the desire to *know*, instead of *impose*.

Of course, any experiment of this sort will have a tendency to endure. The megaliths are still with us; so is Paddington station; so is Harlow New Town. Non-Plan would leave an aftermath at least as interesting as these. But what counts here, for once, is now.

---

26 The new Ronan Point tower block of council flats in East London, built by industrialized methods, collapsed on 16 May 1968. It was the beginning of the end, in Britain, for tower blocks as social housing. Later, I commissioned Nicholas Taylor to write *The Village in the City* (in Paul Barker (general editor),'Towards a New Society' series, London: Temple Smith, 1973), a pioneer defence of Britain's suburban streets against planning megalomania.

NON-PLAN: AN EXPERIMENT IN FREEDOM

Town-and-country planning has today become an unquestioned shibboleth.
Yet few of its procedures or value judgments have any sound basis, except delay.
Why not have the courage, where practical, to let people shape their own environment?

**Reyner Banham
Paul Barker
Peter Hall
Cedric Price**

"A dispute has arisen about a booklet, *Dorset Building in Rural Areas*, just issued by Dorset County Council, and aspiring to be a guide to good design for people building houses in the countryside—our Architectural Correspondent writes. Most of the examples that it illustrates and recommends as models are utterly commonplace, the sort of house to be found in almost any speculative builder's suburban estate. This view is shared by the Wilts and Dorset Society of Architects, which, through its president, Mr Peter Wakefield, has asked for the publication to be withdrawn"—*The Times*, December 1968.

This news item illustrates the kind of tangle we have got ourselves into. Somehow, everything must be watched; nothing must be allowed simply to "happen." No house can be allowed to be commonplace in the way that things just *are* commonplace: each project must be weighed, and planned, and approved, and only then built, and only after that discovered to be commonplace after all. Somehow, somewhere, someone was using the wrong year's model.

Once, Rasmussen, in *London: the Unique City*, (first published 1934), thought it worth printing a picture of the entirely commonplace domestic architecture built along Parkway, Camden Town, in the early 19th century. It was architecture that worked; it provided what the inhabitants wanted from it. Now there'd be trouble if you tried to knock it down (though the London motorway box will skirt it close). But at least the preservationists didn't get in at ground level, as they do today, in order to try and make sure—*before* the event—that something that will eventually be worth preserving is built.

The whole concept of planning (the town-and-country kind at least) has gone cockeyed. What we have today represents a whole cumulation of good intentions. And what those good intentions are worth, we have almost no way of knowing. To say it has been with us for so long, physical planning has been remarkably unmonitored; ditto architecture itself. As Melvin Webber has pointed out: planning is the only branch of knowledge purporting to be some kind of science which regards a plan as being *fulfilled* when it is merely *completed*; there's seldom any sort of check on whether the plan actually does what it was meant to do, and whether, if it does something different, this is for the better or for the worse.

The result is that planning tends to lurch from one fashion to another, with sudden revulsions setting in after equally sudden acceptances. One good recent example, of course, was the fashion for high flats—which had been dying for some time before Ronan Point gave it a tombstone. This fashion had been inaugurated with bizarre talk of creating "vertical streets" which would somehow, it was implied, recreate the togetherness of Bethnal Green Road on Saturday morning in (presumably) the lift shaft—this being the only equivalent communication channel in the structure.

Not that one can be too swiftly mocking. We may yet find that for some future twist of social or technological development, tall flats are just the thing. This happened with another fashion—that for the garden city, as promulgated by Patrick Geddes, Ebenezer Howard and Raymond Unwin. It's worth remembering that the garden in this theory was there specifically to grow food in: the acreage was carefully measured out with this fodder ratio in mind. The houses in (say) Welwyn Garden City or Hampstead Garden Suburb were also scattered thinly because of the width of space allotted (for reasons of health) to the loop and sweep of roads.

Welwyn Garden City and Hampstead Garden Suburb were therefore built—and then duly mocked for dull doctrinairism. The layout made public transport almost impossible; the tin and the frozen pack rapidly outdated the vegetable patch. But then the spread of car ownership outdated the mockery: those roads lived to find a justification; the space around the house could absorb a garage without too much trouble; and the garden (as, even, in many inner-London conversions of Georgian houses) became an unexceptional outdoor room, and meeting space for children, away from the lethal pressed steel and rubber hurtling around the streets.

Now it's nice that a plan should turn out to have reasons for succeeding which the planner himself did not foresee. At every stage in the history of planning, we have cause to be grateful for these quirks of time. It's doubtful if John Nash saw how well his Regent's Park would serve as an arty but fairly democratic pause on the north edge of inner London—just right for football and swings and non-copulating pandas and Sunday-promenading Central Europeans; inhabited not by Regency aristos but by film people, lumps of London University and HM government, the American ambassador and high-class tarts. And did Scott foresee how his St Pancras Hotel, superbly planned to fit in with departing trains and arriving horse-carriages, would survive being a much-mocked office block so successfully that it can now be argued for as a natural home for a sports centre or a transport museum or Birkbeck College?

Nor is it just the cities and towns that have benefited. How many further-education departments can be duly grateful for minor Georgian country houses, or their Victorian imitators—so apt for giving courses in? How many angling clubs can thank the canal-builders for where they spend their peaceful Sundays? How many Highlands-addicted tourists, even, depend for the solitude they love on those harsh men who preferred the glens clear of people and who planned them out of the Highlands and into Canada or Australia?

Yet it's hard to see where, in this, the credit can go to the planner. That last example—which pushes the concept of planning altogether too far—is justified as rubbing in the coerciveness of it. Most planning is aristocratic or oligarchic in method even today—revealing in this its historical origins. The

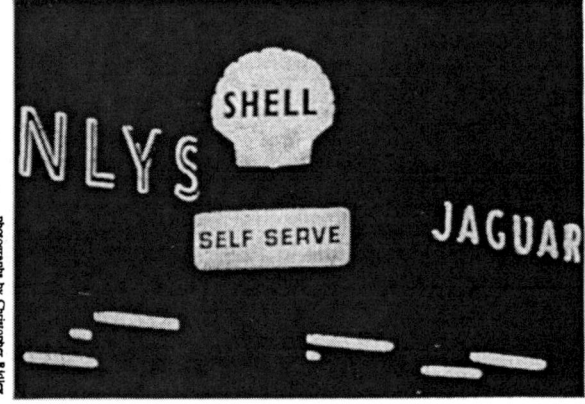

photograph by Christopher Ridley

most rigorously planned cities—like Haussman's and Napoleon III's Paris have nearly always been the least democratic.

The way that Haussman rebuilt Paris gladdens the tourist; it was not such a help, though, for the poor through whose homes the demolition gangs went to create those avenues and squares. Similarly, the urban renewal programmes of the American cities gladdened the real estate men; they did not help the Negroes and poor whites who were uprooted with little to compensate them. In Britain, public housing programmes gladden the housing committees and the respectable working class; they don't help the poorest, the most fissile or the most drifting families.

The point is to realise how little planning and the accompanying architecture have changed. The whole ethos is doctrinaire; and if something good emerges, it remains a bit of a bonus. Not to be expected but nice if you can get it—like totalling enough Green Shield stamps to get a Mini. At the moment, most planners in Britain are on a tautness jag: Camden's neatly interlocked squares, or Southwark's high-density juggernauts, or Cumbernauld's and the Elephant's sculptural shopping centres.

Some of these look pleasant enough now—and some don't. But the fact is that, so far as one can judge, taut arrangements last much better when plenty of money can be spent on their upkeep (Oxbridge colleges, Chelsea squares) than when it isn't (remember all those Improved Industrial Dwellings put up in the late 19th century by Mr Peabody and others?

So it's at least plausible that some other doctrine than the current one would be right for everyday housing and building. It would be pleasant if "doctrine" were precisely what it wasn't.

But how are we to know? Planning is being subjected to increasing scepticism. The Town and Country Planning Act, 1968, tidies up some of the abuses (especially some of those which caused delay in granting permissions); and the Skeffington committee is currently trying to decide how people might be given more say ("participation," in the jargon) in planning. The New City plan for Milton Keynes tries to shy away completely from planning. At universities, research is being done. The one thing that is not being done is the harshest test, the most valuable experiment, of all. What would happen if there were no plan? What would people prefer to do, if their choice were untrammelled? Would matters be any better, or any worse, or much the same? (Might planning turn out to be rather like Eysenck's view of psychoanalysis: an activity which, insofar as it gets credit, gets it for benefits that would happen anyway—minds can cure themselves; maybe people can plan themselves?) But even if matters ended up much the same, in terms of durable successes or disastrous failures, the overall pattern would be sure to be different: the *look* of the experiment would be sure to differ from what we have now.

This is what we're now proposing: a precise and carefully observed experiment in non-planning. It's hardly an experiment one could carry out over the entire country. Some knots—like London—are, by now, far too Gordian for that. Nor are we suggesting (here) that other than physical planning should be shelved.

The right approach is to take the plunge into heterogeneity: to seize on a few appropriate zones of the country, which are subject to a characteristic range of pressures, and use them as launchpads for Non-Plan. At the least, one would find out what people want; at the most, one might discover the hidden style of mid-20th century Britain.

It's "hidden" for the same reason that caused any good social democrat to shudder at the anarchic suggestion of the previous paragraph. Town planning is always in thrall to some outmoded rule-of-thumb; as a profession, in fact, planners tend to read the *Telegraph* and the *Express*, rather than the *Guardian* or *The Times*. Take a specific example: the filling station.

"Watch the little filling-station," Frank Lloyd Wright said. "It is the agent of decentralisation." Like all focuses of transport, the filling-station could be a notable cause of change. Self-service automats, dispensing food and other goods, could spring up around the forecourt; maybe small post offices, too; telephone kiosks; holiday-gear shops; eateries (*not* restaurants): all this quite apart from the standard BP Viscostatic/ice cream/map and guidebook shop. (Thus, at Cumbernauld New Town, it's already clear that only the most repressive controls can stop the two conveniently sited filling stations from replacing the inconveniently centred town centre as shopping focus.)

Well, you can watch as long as you like in Britain, but you will see small sign of this happening. It's hard enough to get planning permission to put up a filling station in the first place. (There's still a feeling—dating probably from the hoo-ha which broke out when the Set Britain Free Tories decided to replace pool petrol in the 1950s by commercial brands—that it's very easy to have "too many" filling stations.) To have anything else on the forecourt is almost impossible. Only in the motorway service areas (themselves damply overplanned) is there anything like this; and here the unfortunately not unique combination of incompetence and non-spontaneity kills the whole thing.

And yet there's no doubt that the popular arts of our time (ie, those that everyone thinks he has a valid opinion on) are car design and advertising; and these are doubly symbolised by such charac-

Non-Plan

teristic forecourt figures as the Esso tiger or the BP little man. The great recent soap-opera films have been Jacques Demy's *Les Parapluies de Cherbourg* (hero: a filling-station owner) and Claude Lelouch's *Un Homme et Une Femme* (hero: a racing car driver). If you drive down the French Rhone valley motorway—not so planned as ours—one of the most memorable sights is a Total petrol station, writing the letters T-O-T-A-L huge across the valley, with a flutter of flags underneath. Stay in Moscow, and you end up yearning to see a Esso sign.

Ask yourself why it is that almost the only time you ever see flags on any *unofficial* occasion—ie, not at an ordained festival or other jamboree, and not on a public building—is on filling-stations or else on the rear windows of cars.

Now the purpose of this is not to write a kind of Elegy in a Country Filling-Station. The purpose is to ask: why don't we dare trust the choices that would evolve if we let them? It's permissible to ask—after the dreariness of much public rebuilding, and after the Ronan Point disaster—what exactly should we sacrifice to fashion?

Here we take a look at three zones where one might make the experiment of succumbing to the pressures, and seeing where it led: the east midlands, "Lawrence country"; the area round Northampstead, "Constable country"; and the Solent, "Montagu country." There are, obviously, other candidates. Anyone can fill in his own sacred cows or *bêtes noires*. (Imagine, for example, dividing the Lake District so that Coniston and Windermere could satisfy all those M6-borne hordes by becoming a Non-Plan zone: it might help protect the Wastwaters that are worth preserving.) The main thing is that the experiment should be tried—and tried quickly. Even the first waves of information would be valuable; if the experiments ran for five years, ten years, twenty years, more and more of use would emerge. Legally it would not be too difficult to get up. It only requires the will to do it—and the desire to *know* instead of *impose*.

Of course, any experiment of this sort will have a tendency to endure. The megaliths are still with us; so is Versailles; so is Paddington station; so is Harlow New Town. Non-Plan would leave an aftermath at least as interesting as these. But what counts here, for once, is *now*.

LAWRENCE COUNTRY

The east midlands are perfect for Non-Plan. Stretching from Nottingham and Derby northwards through Mansfield up to Chesterfield, the Nottingham-Derby industrial zone has a population of close on 1¾ million. By the year 2000, it is expected to have 2¼ million: the same as the west midlands conurbation today. Just to the north of this zone (and, by an administrative accident, in another planning region), is Greater Sheffield with over three quarters of a million more people.

This is an anomaly in England: a big, fast-growing industrial area with a lot of people on the ground but with no Birmingham-type conurbation. The east midlands regional economic planning council, in its report back in 1966, was frightened that by the end of the century a conurbation was what they might have. It was unnecessarily afraid. The west midlands conurbation around Birmingham, which was the example that frightened them, was a product of the public transport era—first the tram, then the bus bound the towns together. The three quarters of a million extra people expected in the east midland industrial zone in the next 30 years will mostly have cars, and their tastes in housing will be quite different from those that shaped the Black Country.

As American experience shows, such people will be more mobile than previous generations. They will commute farther each day, some of them much farther. Industrial decentralisation will mean that many of them will be working outside the cities

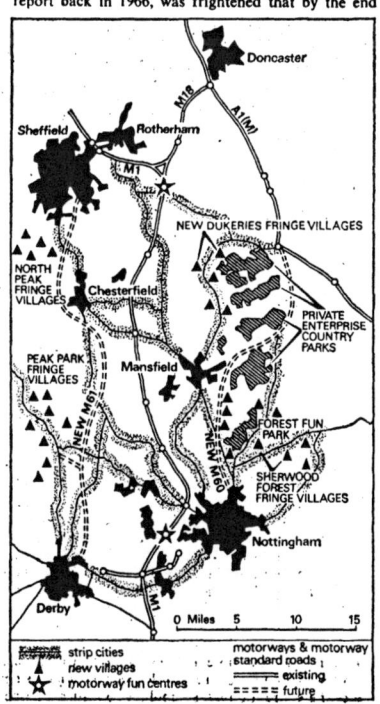

Non-Plan

too. To use the urban economists' jargon, they will "trade off" amenity against accessibility. For many the result will be life in far-flung suburbs, close to open countryside.

In the east midlands this is all the more likely, because the countryside is worth having, and because it is relatively more accessible than elsewhere. Lawrence in *Lady Chatterley's Lover* describes what industrialism had done to the countryside he knew, north west of Nottingham. But really, the impact of the towns is still remarkably small in the whole of this countryside. Everywhere, there are still patches of the old symbiosis of mining and the rural economy, which Lawrence himself describes poignantly in the opening pages of *Sons and Lovers*.

The biggest difference in fact has come in the last year or two. Now, the M1 rolls on only two miles from the village of Eastwood, where Lawrence grew up. It links northwards not only with Leeds but also with the Great North Road at Doncaster, thus forming the new main north-south route down the eastern side of the Pennines. From Nottingham to Sheffield by the motorway is now half an hour's drive. From Nottingham to Leicester, also half an hour. From Nottingham through to the outskirts of London, two hours. The transformation in space relationships is as great as anywhere in England; and, as is already occurring on the M1 between St Albans and Northampton, it will be accompanied, after a time lag, by a massive shift in commuting. In the whole 60 mile tract between Leicester and Sheffield, many people will find that they can live where they like. There will be colossal pressure for scattered, often small-scale growth in hundreds of villages and small towns. Non-Plan would permit this.

The biggest practical problem is preserving open space. There is really no difficulty about the ordinary local open spaces; they can be bought in the market, or from the land commission, in such amounts as the appropriate department thinks necessary. (But only after an examination of *actual* needs.) The problem is the large regional or national park areas. The Peak park, west of the zone, is one case; the Dukeries, forming a series of potential country parks to the east, are another.

Land for these parks would simply be bought in the market by a state Countryside Commission because the social benefits from recreation would outweigh those from development. The commission would then recoup its expenditure (like a nationalised industry) by charging for entry to the country parks, with the aim of breaking even, "taking one year with another." American experience shows this can work. It may be necessary to buy now, while the expected benefits only justify the purchase some time in the future. This may justify a state subsidy, but it does not justify an arbitrary refusal to consider the alternative uses to which this land might possibly be put.

Non-Plan, applied to this area, would keep all the options open. No land-use pattern could be regarded as sacrosanct.

What would result? Probably a pattern which intensified the present one, but without the "planning" rigmarole. The forces of dispersion, of mobility, are already strong. But there would be certain differences. Development would be more scattered and less geometrically tidy than our present planners would like. It would be low-density—the apotheosis of exurbia. There would be more out-of-town shopping centres and drive-in cinemas, and Non-Plan would let them zoom to considerable size by the end of the century. With the aesthetic brakes off, strip development would spread along the main roads on the American model. Much of this will serve the needs of a mobile society: eating places, drinking places, petrol stations, supermarkets. It would not look like a planner's dream, but it would work.

CONSTABLE COUNTRY

Nuthampstead? Only 38 miles from London—this, among the Roskill commission's four short-list sites for a third London airport, has a not-bad chance of being finally chosen. As an alternative to Stansted it would change nothing. It doesn't matter which side of Bishop's Stortford the airport is located: the ultimate disturbance to the Herts-Essex border country will be the same. The actual aircraft noise contours will be moved ten miles to the north west, but the airport project is not a cause, it is merely one symptom of what is trying to happen anyhow in this rare enclave of a dying way of life that has, so far, escaped pressures that are normal in the rest of London's exurbanite belt. Proclaiming a Non-Plan zone thereabouts would reveal what pressures are currently being held in check (but only just) by present planning routines. Even more than that, taking the planning lid off would produce a situation traumatic enough among the amenity lobbies to make their real motivations visible; to show how much is genuine concern for environmental and cultural values, how much merely class panic.

For the kind of population that rallies to its defence, this countryside and its villages have everything to recommend them, the perfect ecology for retired officers and gentlemen who are now Something In the City.

The scale of the countryside is relatively small and garden-like—the landscape does not really open out until the chalk downland rises north of the Chesterfords, where the main communication links—the railway to Cambridge, and the A11 trunk road to Newmarket—separate. Up to that point, the terrain is mostly gently folded, with shallow dips separating spot heights that rarely break the 400 foot contour. The tree cover is often thick enough to give the illusion that this might be some westward extension of that most sacred of English sacred scenery: "Constable country."

But this is largely illusory; most of the trees are in the belts of a few very handsome parks that more or less alternate with the half-timbered, or Georgian, villages along the A11, which has almost the air of a parkway in places. The rest of the area is fairly badly off for roads of this quality (with the possible exception of the east-west A120) but tends to exhibit instead the kind of intricate grid of minor roads that characterises the heartlands of Hertfordshire.

This close-grained and rather private terrain has long been immune to the development pressures that have transformed many other areas in London's exurbanite belt. If this area were freed of direct or implicit planning prohibitions, what semi-submerged tensions (which underlie the present malaise of insecurity here) could come to the surface and be studied?

By comparison with the other three suburban quadrants of London, the north-east quadrant is almost an underdeveloped country. Because of this, it was able to absorb a disproportionate amount of London's satellite New Town population—or, to express the matter another way, it had enough spare space for the working and lower middle classes to be shut away in separated ghettoes of which the Becontree Estate was the prototype, and Harlow New Town the final solution. Until recently, the north east quadrant was buffered against developmental pressures that were "normal" in the other quadrants. Urban sprawl of earlier kinds was largely blocked by the marshes of Hackney and Wanstead, and by the inviolable common lands of Epping and Hainault forests. Later developmental pressures were also abnormal, probably because these same blockages pushed the main railway lines towards the edges of the quadrant—northwards to Cambridge, eastwards to Colchester, with anything in between typically petering out at Ongar.

This has always thrown a (probably disproportionate) traffic load on the A11, which probably ought to have been let rip to develop as a thick local "midway", rather than being regarded, as at present, as an inefficient trunk route to remoter parts of East Anglia. The building of the M11 motorway (which an airport at Nuthampstead would certainly hasten) will lift the through-traffic load from the old A11 trunk, but will leave untouched the unacknowledged local pressures to which that road is increasingly subject in its role as a kind of diffuse, linear "downtown" for the whole area between Potter Street and the Chesterfords. These pressures are revealed not only by the eruption of more motels than their national average distribution would suggest (two at Epping, one at Harlow, others rumoured further north) but even more clearly by the constant widenings, re-alignments and general tinkering with the A11 to cope with the local traffic crossing or turning on and off it.

Of course, Harlow New Town is the major cause of hidden pressures on the whole area. Not in the way in which, for instance, Stevenage has become a focus for junkie activity in the northern home counties, but simply because the introduction of a large and unbalanced new population in any area brings with it many more demands and needs than can be accommodated by the building of homes, schools and community centres. Harlow has been parasitical on surrounding communities for entertainment, to take only one example, ever since it was founded—and Bishop's Stortford appeared to be profiting handsomely from the New Town's unsatisfied needs in its early days.

Pressures of this kind appear to be contained for the moment, but it will be physically impossible to contain them if Harlow grows much bigger. And, if the population target of about 100,000 is achieved, Harlow will be the largest settlement on the A11 between the Greater London boundary and Norwich, and must make dependent suburbs of all other roadside communities from Epping to the Chesterfords, including Stortford and Saffron Walden, and the Ware/Hertford bijou mini-conurbation. And then add to this the effect of an airport, with all the attraction that scheduled flights would have for factory owners—consequently for speculative house builders. (One ought to remember, too, that there's an airport at Stansted *already*—and, though small, not all that tranquil.)

The result of these pressures would not, probably, look like the prewar ribbon development (of evil fame). The lifting of planning restrictions would not simply connect all the A11 villages into a continuous

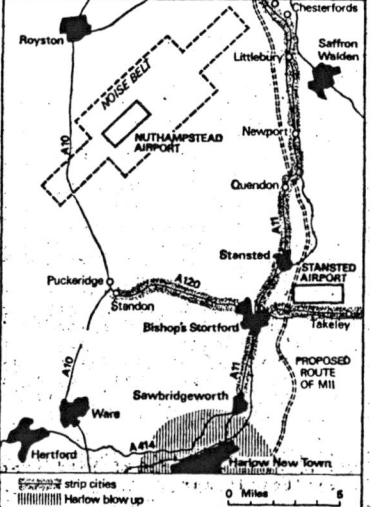

Non-Plan

ribbon running north from Sawbridgeworth. One of the national advantages of Nuthampstead is the fact that motorised traffic from the midlands and the north can (with a little ingenuity) reach it without passing through London at all, and does not need the A11.

Most conceivable airports in the other three quadrants around London would throw their main traffic load on the radial arteries leading to them from the metropolis. However, any airport near Bishop's Stortford will shed quite a bit of that load on to roads running east-west or north-westwards—in other words, moving through the area at right angles to the line of flow apparently envisaged by London-obsessed "national" thinking of the sort responsible for the M11.

A fair amount of heavy commercial traffic already moves through Stortford on this axis which, some 15 or so miles further east, connects with Braintree and the diffused zone of miscellaneous light industries in central Essex. If local (and other) authorities can respond freely to a plan-free situation, then Bishop's Stortford could shortly have an improved east-west throughway, which it probably needs even more than to be disembarrassed of the A11. This could also be a step towards the creation of a fan of better quality roads carrying an increasing amount of containerised traffic to the rest of England out of the new freight facilities at Tilbury or Felixstowe—and, again, without entanglement in the private traffic neuroses of London.

In other words, what might be in store under a planning-free dispensation might not be the simple "destruction" of the pretty coaching villages on the main road to Newmarket, but a much more evenly distributed process of infilling and backfilling of communities in an area of some five to ten miles around the Stortford airport complex with a general thickening in all parts as far as Dunmow or Royston. Nearest the airports one can expect a zone of motels, long-term parking (essential and inevitable with a largely motorised access) and secondary services, with primary and engineering services down towards Harlow because of its existing industrial zone. The motels, restaurants and so on for Stansted might well string out eastwards, however, along the A120, in a similar manner to the development of the "little Las Vegas" strip along Mannheim Road to serve Chicago's O'Hare airport.

Equally well, they might not. We don't know, because we have not seen the area around an airport develop naturally in England since Croydon in the twenties. Indeed few prospects seem less welcome to our present planning establishments, undermined culturally by Stephen Spender's identification of such situations as the landscape of hysteria and deafened by the barrage of propaganda that thunders down from the anti-noise lobby. And to have this happen in what is virtually Constable country...

Actually, the close-textured, tree-grown, Constable-type country is supposed, by bodies of opinion like the *Architectural Review*, to be able to absorb practically anything that is not taller than a grown tree, and the buildings which free enterprise would put up in this planning-free situation would not be half that height. On an open site, one and two storey buildings have overwhelming commercial attractions—it is only ultra-high urban land values or the activities of determined architect-planners like Walter Bor or Sir Hugh Casson, that make multi-storey commercial development thinkable.

So this small-scale, rather private landscape might barely reveal its new commercial buildings to the eye. But this would be very bad commercial practice, since an invisible building is no advertisement, and there would certainly have to be a compensatory efflorescence of large and conspicuous advertising signs. The overall result could thus be low commercial buildings set well back from the road behind adequate parking courts, backed by tall trees and fronted by tall signs, with a soft, rolypoly countryside appearing behind.

It might be quite graceful to the eye; certainly more so than the quasi-regimented squalor of our present suburban industrial concentration camps (or trading estates), and equally more so than the featureless boredom of the increasingly large areas of East Anglia that are being flattened out for efficient exploitation by agro-industry. I don't suppose that it will appear graceful to the eyes of the present generation of Stansted nay-sayers. But it may appear differently to their successors—as a deliverance from creeping death by economic stagnation that will await the area if it remains in its present condition of stalemate between development pressures and planning prohibitions.

MONTAGU COUNTRY

A few years ago a nuclear power station was rejected for the Isle of Wight, under the doubtful slogan of preserving the nation's heritage. In fact, this Victorian island—once one of the Old Queen's favourite roosts, and J. B. Priestley's—is losing what heritage it had. In the Solent area—Portsmouth/Southampton/New Forest/Isle of Wight—the island is one of the few parts suffering any loss of population. It might gain more from an abandonment of preservation than it has so far won from its continuance.

Altogether, the Solent is a curious hodgepodge. At Fawley, for example, it has the largest oil refinery in Europe and the most publicised productivity agreements in Britain—from which pipelines and moralisation stretch out to the rest of the country. Then there is Southampton—a major port with huge capacity for expansion—already within the orbit of Greater London. To arrive at Southampton, either by boat or by plane, is to feel yourself at the edge of an incipient megalopolis which doesn't stop till it reaches Bletchley, Ipswich and Sevenoaks. Southampton doesn't just have four tides a day (which seems like an almost sinful amount of deep water), it has a university as expansionist as the rest of them and a rapidly swelling population. Fawley and Southampton, in fact, are at present the poles of growth. They generate various secondary industries: hovercraft, synthetic rubber, electricity, technical training.

The other pole of decline apart from the Isle of Wight (with its diminishing rail network) is Portsmouth. The highly equipped naval dockyard is being run down; skilled labour is looking for work. The ditched Buchanan plan for a Solent City is intended to arc between the Southampton and Portsmouth poles like a spark looking for a gap. It will be valuable to have the check of what Professor Buchanan expected to be able to instil here.

Besides growth and decline, the Solent has a flourishing middle area which is neither growing nor declining but simply being preserved. It has historic towns, villages and monuments—like the well-known monumental village school at Winchester; the palace, abbey and lord at Beaulieu; the New Forest itself. There's the small-boats industry. The preservationist lobby is powerful: there are assorted architectural knights at Beaulieu and at Buckler's Hard, and the yachting brotherhood of Beaulieu (again the lynch pin), Hamble and Lymington; Edward Montagu and Edmund de Rothschild (the latter, at Exbury) are showmen-gentry; but they remain gentry. A consortium of landowners in the Beaulieu valley have launched a development plan.

With Non-Plan, industrial sites would be likely to spread more freely along the coast west of Southampton/Fawley. So would housing. But there would also be a spread of pleasure. It's cut out to be an zone where parking and recreation in Jermingle: the Forest, the boats, the Isle of Wight. It could mark a new kind of living for Britain. Form wall/Devon might ideally be better (for a start, they're warmer) but they're too far from the London magnet at the moment. The division between freely willed and directed (ie, between leisure and work) would erode.

Residents might become "auto-nomads" at holidays and weekends or in fine weather, and still remain within the Solent zone. The tourist pearls are remarkably evenly spread throughout the area: multi-funstops. This would not be for the big setpiece holiday—which, more and more, will be abroad (in Malta if the exchange regulations don't permit the Costa del Sol or Rimini). It will be for small, intermittent holidays. Visitors (as opposed to residents) will increasingly see it the same way—though they might stop off at the Buckler's Hard motel complex to refresh themselves en route from the continent to Stoke-on-Trent, Balham or Oxford-with-Reading. The New Forest pony sales would become a heavily plugged rodeo time.

Culturally, the prospect is bizarre. It was in Hampshire, after all, that the proposed New Town of Hook was killed: planning used in order to defeat planning. Non-Plan would upheave all that. An enclave would be irrupted into and become one of the main play-and-live edges of the London region.

Mobile homes might dot the New Forest and the Isle of Wight. Caravans to begin with; later more elaborate, or at any rate more efficient, constructions. There would be high-level, tree-top chair rides through the Forest and convoys of computer-programmed holiday houseboats (both public and private) on the Solent. Fawley refinery would have son et lumière. Floating grandstands, with public address systems and information displays, would involve visitors in the speed and performance trials of new water gear (hovercraft, speedboats, water-skis, lifesaving). Large retractable marinas would have sail-in movies and row-in bars. Beach buggies would drive through the heathland. Particular villages, especially on the Isle of Wight, would be got up as showpieces. Britain's first giant dome would rise on the Isle of Wight coast: the first all-weather, all-public Ile du

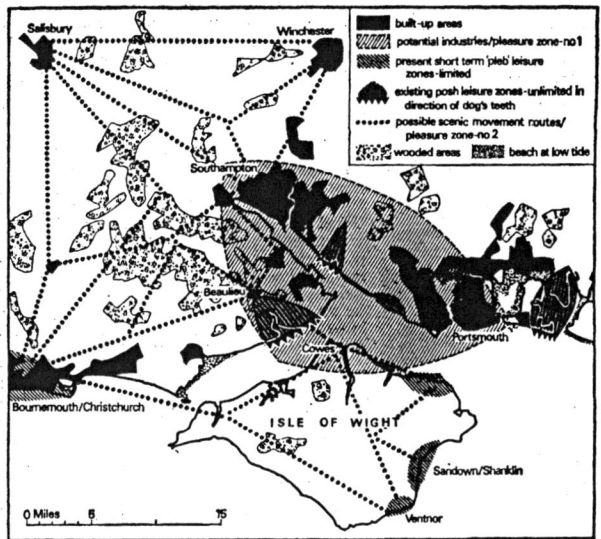

Levant nudist scene in the country—thermostatically controlled and ten bob a head.

It would be a good zone in which to tack on to the basic Non-Plan scheme a number of other possible try-outs: freedom for local authorities to raise money in ways they see fit (a sales tax, a sail tax, a poll tax, a pony tax); local commercial radio, with information for visitors and tourists; "pot" shops instead of all those declining tobacconists (and see how different the population seems, or how similar, after five or ten years); the abandonment of a few other rules, like pub hours—as at present happens, if you know where, during Cowes Week.

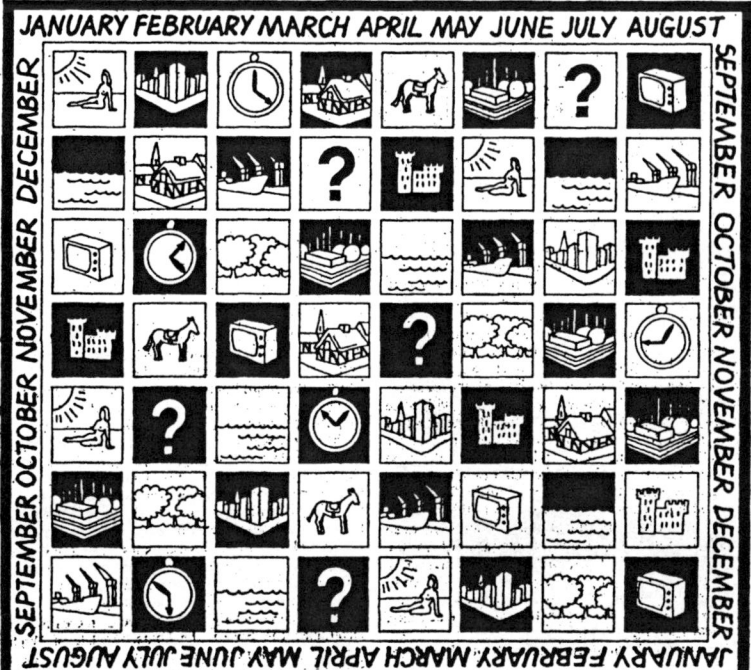

To play: Take any counter and place it on the pleasure zone board; move again before 12 hours are up; after a year or two build a new board.

SPONTANEITY AND SPACE

Any advocate of Non-Plan is sure to be misrepresented; we had better repeat what we mean. Simply to demand an end to planning, all planning, would be sentimentalism; it would deny the very basis of economic life in the second half of the 20th century.

As Galbraith has reminded us, the economies of all advanced industrial countries are planned, whether they call themselves capitalist or communist. In the United States or Japan or Germany or Britain, the need to make elaborate and long-term plans is as pressing for the individual firm, as it is for the central government. But we are arguing that the word planning itself is misused; that it has also been used for the imposition of certain physical arrangements, based on value judgments or prejudices; and that it should be scrapped.

Three developments in particular makes this argument compelling. They are developments of the last 15 years; their main force has been felt in this country in the last ten. They are: the cybernetic revolution; the mass affluence revolution; and the pop/youth culture revolution.

Cybernetics is commonly described as a technological revolution; but it is much more. It has its technological basis in the computer, as the 18th century industrial revolution had in the steam engine. But just as that revolution arose out of the intellectual ferment of the age of Newton and the Royal Society, so this has gone along with a major revolution in our ways of thought.

The essence of the new situation is that we can master vastly greater amounts of information than was hitherto thought possible—information essentially about the effect of certain defined actions upon the operation of a system. The practical implications are everywhere very large, but nowhere are they greater than in the area we loosely call planning. It is true that the science of decision-making, or management, was being developed in the United States from the 1920s, a quarter century before the cybernetic revolution; and it is almost true that it was this science of management, applied to military ends in World War Two, which made the cybernetic revolution possible.

Now, the two fields—that of scientific management, and that which embraces operations research and systems analysis—are so closely related as to be in practice inseparable. But physical planning flourished in this country when the science of management was almost unknown. Thus, simple, rule-of-thumb value judgments could be made, and were held to have perpetual validity, like tablets of the law. Since the cybernetic revolution, it has become clear that such decisions are meaningless and valueless—as, indeed, ought to have become clear before. Instead, physical planning, like anything else, should consist *at most* of setting up frameworks for decision, within which as much objective information as possible can be fitted. Non-Plan would certainly provide such information. But it might do more. Even to talk of a "general framework" is difficult. Our information about future states of the system is very poor.

If the cybernetic revolution makes our traditional planning technologically and intellectually obsolete, social change reinforces this conclusion. The revolution of rising affluence (despite the current economic problems) means that a growing proportion of personal incomes will be funnelled off into ever more diverse and unpredictable outlets. Non-Plan would let them be funnelled. Galbraith (again) has shown how the modern industrial state depends on the ability to multiply wants for goods and services; certainly a large amount of prediction is involved in this. Car manufacturers have a fair idea of how many cars will be sold in 1984. Similarly with refrigerator manufacturers, colour TV set makers and purveyors of Mediterranean or Caribbean holidays.

But in detail and in combination, the effects are not easy to relate to programmes of public investment. One change, however, Non-Plan would inevitably underline: as people become richer they demand more space; and because they become at the same time more mobile, they will be more able to command it. They will want this extra space in and around their houses, around their shops, around their offices and factories, and in the places where they go for recreation. To impose rigid controls, in order to frustrate people in achieving the space standards they require, represents simply the received personal or class judgments of the people who are making the decision.

Worst of all: they are judgments about how they think *other* people—not of their acquaintance or class—should live. A remarkable number of the architects and planners who advocate togetherness, themselves live among space and green fields.

This assertion may be most clearly demonstrated where different value judgments are involved. The most remarkable manifestation so far of mass affluence—above all in Britain—has been the revolution in pop culture. This is a product of newly emergent social groups and, above all, of age groups. Among the young, it has had a remarkable effect in breaking down class barriers, and replacing these by age barriers. Though pop culture is eminently capable of commercial exploitation, it is essentially a real culture, provided by people drawn from the same groups as the customers.

Most importantly for Non-Plan, it is frenetic and immediate culture, based on the rapid obsolescence cycle. Radio One's "revived 45" is probably three months old, and on the New York art scene fashions change almost as quickly as on the King's Road. Pop culture is anti high bourgeois culture. Though it makes many statements it does not like big statements.

All these characteristics could not be more opposed to the traditional judgments of the physical planner—which, in essence, are the values of the old bourgeois culture. Pop culture in Britain has produced the biggest visual explosion for decades—or even, in the case of fashion, for centuries. Yet its effect on the

British landscape has been nil, for the simple reason that the planners have suppressed it.

Three particularly ripe examples: one, the row over the psychedelic painting on the Beatles' former "Apple" boutique in Baker Street (objected to, and duly erased, because on a building of architectural merit—though the shop is next door but one to a fairly unreticent cinema); two, the rebuilt Jack Straw's Castle on Hampstead Heath, one of the few bits of pop fantasy to get past the taste censors, but only after a major row among the planners; three, the Prince of Wales pub in Fortune Green Road, north London, internally perhaps the most remarkable piece of pop design in Europe, externally a tedious piece of planner's Old Englishe Good Taste.

The planning system, as now constituted in Britain, is not merely negative; it has positively pernicious results. The irony is that the planners themselves constantly talk—since the appearance of Jane Jacob's *Death and Life of Great American Cities*—about the need to restore spontaneity and vitality to urban life. They never seem to draw the obvious conclusion—that the monuments of our century that have spontaneity and vitality are found not in the old cities, but in the American west.

There, in the desert and the Pacific states, creations like Fremont Street in Las Vegas or Sunset Strip in Beverly Hills represent the living architecture of our age. As Tom Wolfe points out in his brilliant essay on Las Vegas, they achieve their quality by replacing buildings by signs. In Britain you only get occasional hints of how well this could work. The prime example—Piccadilly Circus at night—is apparently so successful it needs to be *preserved*, God help us. Why preserve it? Why not simply allow other efflorescences of fluorescence in other places? Write it in neon: NON-PLAN IS 'GOOD FOR YOU; I DREAMT I FOUND FREEDOM IN MY NON-PLAN BRA.'

To say that Las Vegas is exciting and memorable and fine is also a value judgment. It cannot be supported by facts. But except for a few conservation areas which we wish to preserve as living museums, physical planners have no right to set their value judgment up against yours, or indeed anyone else's. If the Non-Plan experiment works really well, people should be allowed to build what they like. (Oh, and a word for the preservationists: much easier to relieve pressure on medieval town centres by letting the edges of the city sprawl, and give people chance to shop there in drive-in suburban superstores, than by brooding on inner-relief roads or whatever.)

At the very least, Non-Plan would provide accurate information to fit into a "community investment plan." The balance of costs and benefits to the individual is not the same as to the community. If there are social costs, the people who are responsible pay them. If low-density development is expensive to the community, the reaction should be to make it proportionately expensive to those who live in it; not to stop it. The notion that the planner has the right to say what is "right" is really an extraordinary hangover from the days of collectivism in left-wing thought, which has long ago been abandoned elsewhere.

We seem so afraid of freedom. But Britain shouldn't be a Peter Pan Edwardian nursery. Let it at least move into the play school era: why should only the under-sevens be allowed their bright materials, their gay constructions, their wind-up Daleks. In that world, Marx is best known as the maker of plastic, battery-driven dump trucks. Let's become that sort of marxist.

Let's save our breath for genuine problems—like the poor. We are increasingly with us. And let's Non-Plan at least some problems of planning into oblivion.

Reyner Banham is Reader in Architecture, Bartlett School of Architecture, University College, London; Paul Barker is Editor of NEW SOCIETY; Peter Hall is Professor of Geography, University of Reading; Cedric Price is an architect

#02
CEDRIC PRICE: CEDRIC PRICE'S NON-PLAN DIARY

A review of Cedric Price's thinking before, during and after Non-Plan, through words, images and critical reactions (Figure 2.1).

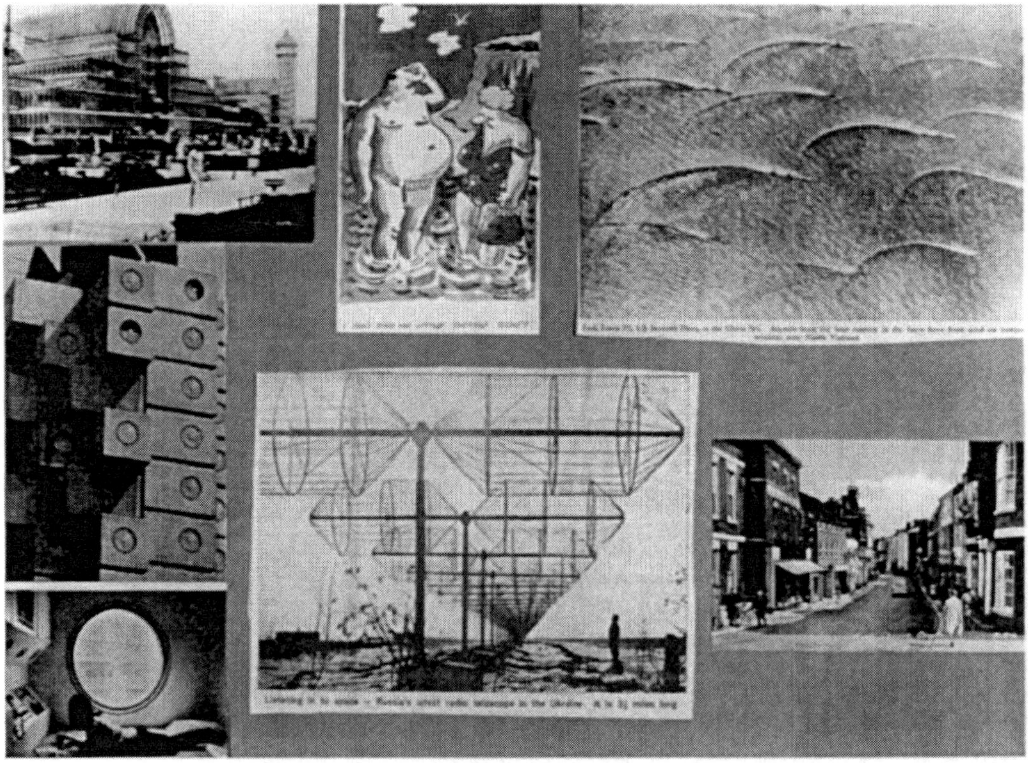

figure 2.1
CEDRIC PRICE, PAGE FROM SALMON PINK SCRAPBOOK, C.1970.
JOSEPH PAXTON, CRYSTAL PALACE, 1851: 'AN EARLY KIT OF PARTS'; KISHO KUROKAWA, NAKAGIN CAPSULE TOWER, TOKYO, 1970: 'KIT OF PARTS HOTEL'; RUSSIAN RADIO TELESCOPE, UKRAINE; HIGH STREET, STONE, STAFFORDSHIRE, UK: 'HOME TOWN'; US SEVENTH FLEET, CHINA SEA DURING VIETNAM WAR: 'MOVEMENT IN SPACE AND TIME'; CARTOON BY LARRY: 'HEALTHY VULGARITY'

figure 2.2
CEDRIC PRICE, FUN PALACE, 1961–1964

one
FUN PALACE, LONDON E15 (figure 2.2)

A large temporary (twenty years approximately) community toy and learning machine. Designed for a London East End site by Joan Littlewood and Cedric Price. 'More a launch pad than a Mecca' (1960).

ARRIVE AND LEAVE by train, bus, monorail, hovercraft, car, tube or foot at any time YOU want to – or just have a look at it as you pass. The information screens will show you what's happening. No need to look for an entrance – just walk in anywhere. No doors, foyers, queues or commissionaires: it's up to you how you use it. Look around – take a lift, a ramp, an escalator to wherever or whatever looks interesting.

CHOOSE what you want to do – or watch someone else doing it. Learn how to handle tools, paint, babies, machinery, or just listen to your favourite tune. Dance, talk, or be lifted up to where you can see how other people make things work. Sit out over space with a drink and tune in to what's happening elsewhere in the city. Try starting a riot or beginning a painting – or just lie back and stare at the sky.

WHAT TIME IS IT? Any time of day or night, winter or summer – it really doesn't matter. If it's too wet that roof will stop the rain but not the light. The artificial cloud will keep you cool or make rainbows for you. Your feet will be warm as you watch the stars – the atmosphere clear as you join in the chorus. Why not have your favourite meal high up where you can watch the thunderstorm?

WHY ALL THIS LOT? 'If any nation is to be lost or saved by the character of its great cities our own is that nation.' Robert Vaughan, 1843.
We are building a short-term plaything in which all of us can realise the possibilities and delights that a twentieth-century city environment owes us. It must last no longer than we need it.

CEDRIC PRICE AND JOAN LITTLEWOOD, PROSPECTUS FOR FUN PALACE, C. 1964

figure 2.3
CEDRIC PRICE, MECHANICAL MOBILITY: ARCHITECTURE'S GREEN LIGHT,
GRANTA, 69, NO. 1236. 14 MAY 1964

two
MECHANICAL AND SOCIAL MOBILITY (figure 2.3)

Now we are all travelling observers. The *Radio Times* or Cadbury chocolate is recognisably available throughout the land, and no-one should lament that the outskirts of Glasgow and Southampton look alike – the real cause for regret is that at present they both look bloody.

HERE THEN IS ONE OF THE POSITIVE CONTRIBUTIONS TO A VALID ARCHITECTURAL AESTHETIC MADE BY THE ADVENT OF THE AVAILABILITY OF RAPID TRANSIT TO ALL.

The way to improve Oxford Street is to make it easier and more pleasant to shop in Hendon and thus contribute to its destruction rather than add escalators and pedestrian walkways thus prolonging its lethal economic life.

Thus, roads must not be considered as objects whose social value change dependent on their position and siting in relation to existing large scale artefacts. Rather, it must be realised that the provision of sufficient space for a particular form of human movement – whether called 'road' – must be considered at the same time and be invested with the same degree of importance as the provision of fresh air.

CEDRIC PRICE, MECHANICAL MOBILITY: ARCHITECTURE'S GREEN LIGHT,
GRANTA, 69, NO. 1236, 14 MAY 1964

Cedric Price, the architect, thinks that there is too much emphasis on caravans as an answer to the housing *problem*; 'it should be the housing *potential*'.

JOHN BARR, HOMES ON WHEELS, *NEW SOCIETY*, VOL. 9, NO. 228, FEBRUARY 1967, PP. 189-191

Cedric Price has pointed to the major upheavals in social mobility which may follow the participation in higher learning of a greater and greater proportion of the population.

STANFORD ANDERSON (EDITOR), *PLANNING FOR DIVERSITY AND CHOICE: POSSIBLE FUTURES AND THEIR RELATIONS TO THE MAN-CONTROLLED ENVIRONMENT*, CAMBRIDGE MA: MIT PRESS, 1968. DOCUMENTATION OF A CONFERENCE HELD AT ENDICOTT HOUSE, DEDHAM MA, 13-16 OCTOBER 1966

figure 2.4
CEDRIC PRICE, VIEW FROM A RAILBUS, LONGTON FACULTY AREA, POTTERIES THINK BELT, 1964

three
POTTERIES THINK BELT (figure 2.4)

A twenty to twenty-five year 'university' for North Staffordshire, largely science-based, including a range of variable housing available equally to local residents and students with associated communal rail-based facilities, and links to both national and international academic grid (1964).

I doubt the relevance of the concepts of Town Centre, Town, and Balanced Community. Calculated suburban sprawl sounds good to me.

CEDRIC PRICE, POTTERIES THINK BELT, *ARCHITECTURAL DESIGN*, VOL. 36, OCTOBER 1966, PP. 483-497

The public embarrassing back-pedalling on the definition of a 'balanced community' from the New Town Mark I version, demanding juxtaposition of income (class) roots, to the Hook Plan, requiring merely an even distribution of 'age groups', has not rid us of the planners' determination to try to predetermine the 'Good Life'.

CEDRIC PRICE, LIFE CONDITIONING, *ARCHITECTURAL DESIGN*, VOL. 36, OCTOBER 1966, P. 483

four
POP-UP PARLIAMENT (figure 2.5)

A new two-chamber parliament building on the same Westminster site incorporating new electronics and including a temporary shelter to a Parliament Square 'stadium' (1965).

'If we want an efficient parliament, let's give it a whole efficient building to work ... replace the present historic monument with an up-to-date structure – flexible, accessible and dispensable.' So wrote *New Society* in 1965. A large but comparatively simple supermarket of democracy spreading its information and shelter to adjoining but less committed areas such as the vastly enlarged Parliament Square.

CEDRIC PRICE, *CEDRIC PRICE WORKS*, LONDON: ARCHITECTURAL ASSOCIATION, 1984

figure 2.5
CEDRIC PRICE, POP-UP PARLIAMENT, 1965

five
NON-PLAN (see chapter 1)

A constructed alternative to the present UK planning legislation that not only abhors change but reverses the natural social progress of land usage (1969).

General recommendations.
Restrictions to be lifted.
Controls – physical or legislative – that would need to be retained to enable normal relationships with the rest of the UK.
New controls or legislation required to enable Non-Plan to function.
Sequence of development patterning considered applicable to all selected cases.
Consideration of allowable effects of pilot areas to permanently affect areas not so designated.
Present conditions in selected areas.
'Immediate' reductions in activity and population.
'Immediate' increase in activity and production (it must not become necessary in these proposals and in fact to make estimates (either extrapolatory or by prediction) of long-term growth since this negates the self-adjusting factor implicit in Non-Plan).

CEDRIC PRICE, HEADINGS FROM 'NON-PLAN', *ARCHITECTURAL DESIGN*, VOL. 39, MAY 1969, PP. 269–273

'Non-Plan: an experiment in freedom': originally part of group project with Reyner Banham, Paul Barker and Peter Hall. Caused through growing annoyance at the positively anti-social implications of present physical planning policy and legislation in the UK.

ARCHITECTURAL DESIGN, VOL. 40, CEDRIC PRICE SUPPLEMENT, OCTOBER 1970

Fragmentation relevancy does not merely mean recognition of an increased sophistication of social-physical patterning but also a realisation of continuous unevenness in both the process and results.

Non-Plan – or as it was originally and more accurately called Null-Plan *(Architectural Design,* no. 5, 1969) detailed the advantages of such unevenness. It also proposed that by reducing the permanence of the assumed worth of past uses of space through avoiding their reinforcement, society might be given not only the opportunity to reassess such worth, but also be able to establish a new order of priorities of land, sea and air use which would be related more directly to the valid social and economic lifespan of such uses, replace utopia with Non-Plan.

CEDRIC PRICE, APPROACHING AN ARCHITECTURE OF APPROXIMATION, ARCHITECTURAL DESIGN, VOL. 42, OCTOBER 1972, PP. 645-647 ('COMPLEXITY' ISSUE, ROYSTON LANDAU (EDITOR))

Variable marina – with computer control. Holiday house boats, large environmentally controlled dome, no licensing hours, c.f. Cowes week. Short-stay holidays on the way to elsewhere.

CEDRIC PRICE, MONTAGU COUNTRY (NEW FOREST, HAMPSHIRE), THOUGHTS ON 'NON-PLAN', NEW SOCIETY, NO. 338, 20 MARCH 1969, P. 441

Sir, Congratulations on your article on non-planning. The current emphasis on physical planning at the expense of economic and social understanding has resulted in the cult of preservation as an end in itself and as one of the prime causes of our current economic malaise. We have planned ourselves into an impasse and haven't the faintest idea how to plan our way out.

It is no longer a question of substituting one set of planning ideas for another within the closed system, but the situation calls for a radical reappraisal of the whole system. Basically, our difficulty stems from a lack of clear goals – whilst those we do have are essentially paternalistic, 'the gentleman in the town hall knows best'.

We need far more discussion about goals; the plain facts are they are never publicly discussed under a cosy consensus of both political parties, planning is thought of as a mere matter of administration and left to the bureaucrats.

Determination of goals should be the politics; in fact we need to put planning back into politics; I congratulate you on firing the first shot in the battle.

NEIL WATES, NEW SOCIETY, VOL. 13, NO. 341, 10 APRIL 1969, P. 573

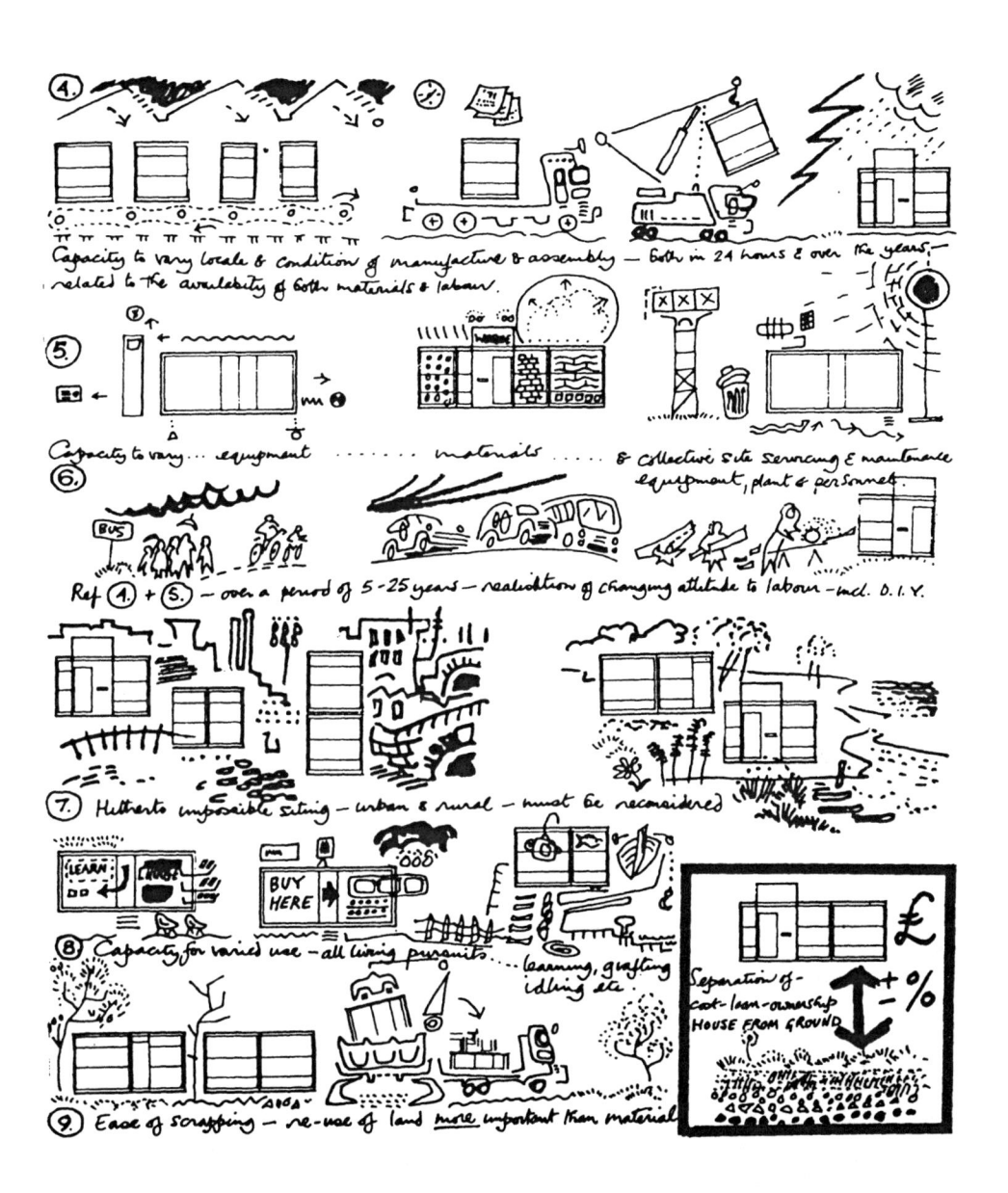

figure 2.6
CEDRIC PRICE, PRINCIPLES, *ARCHITECTURAL DESIGN*, VOL. 41, OCTOBER 1971

Sir, Peter Hall's conversion to Non-Plan seems rather sudden. Not so long ago he was writing that 'the new towns have on every criterion been a triumphant success.' *(The World Cities,* 1966.)

ALEX REID, *NEW SOCIETY,* VOL. 13, NO. 339, 3 APRIL 1969, P.535

six
INTER-ACTION CENTRE, KENTISH TOWN (figure 2.7)

A multi-purpose community resources centre providing, in its first stage, workshops, rehearsal rooms, studios, assembly hall, classrooms, eating facilities and administrative office for the Inter-Action Trust.

CEDRIC PRICE, *CEDRIC PRICE WORKS,* LONDON: ARCHITECTURAL ASSOCIATION, 1984

Yet there is one building I know which is designed to celebrate its unfettered use for changing function, to encourage do-it-yourself modification, used communally and personally, and it is a clear demonstration of a new attitude to architecture – Cedric Price's Inter-Action Centre in Kentish Town ... It is a large house with all the characteristics of informal, busy and friendly occupation.

JOHN WEEKS, DESIGNING AND LIVING IN A HOSPITAL, *JOURNAL OF THE ROYAL SOCIETY OF ARTS,* 127, NO. 5276, JULY 1979, PP. 464-480

figure 2.7
CEDRIC PRICE, INTER-ACTION CENTRE, LONDON, 1971

figure 2.8
CEDRIC PRICE, MAGNET, 1996

seven
MAGNET (figure 2.8)

Magnets are installed on existing metropolitan sites which are underused or misused. The structures are transplants providing socially beneficial movement routes. Their planning encourages adjacent future growth while the fixed-life structures enable variation and reassembly to be undertaken with speed and minimal disruption (1996).

'There are many situations in which to be systematically late, is to be systematically wrong.' (Sir Geoffrey Vickers, VC, *Value Systems and Social Progress,* 1968.) To establish a valid equation between contemporary social aspirations and architecture it is essential to add to the latter doubt, delight and change as design criteria.

ARCHITECTS' JOURNAL, ANTICIPATING THE UNEXPECTED: CEDRIC PRICE SPECIAL ISSUE, SEPTEMBER 1996

#03
BEN FRANKS: NEW RIGHT/NEW LEFT
AN ALTERNATIVE EXPERIMENT IN FREEDOM

one
INTRODUCTION

The 20 March 1969 edition of *New Society* featured an article by Reyner Banham, Paul Barker, Peter Hall and Cedric Price called 'Non-Plan: an experiment in freedom'[1] (Figure 1.1). The year of publication was one of considerable radical activity and this was reflected in this issue of the magazine which featured, amongst others, supportive articles on labour disputes, university strikes, schemes to extend the radio waves to youth and book reviews on student power and the British revolutionary movement. Amongst these items, in the main body of the magazine, was 'Non-Plan', written by intellectuals of a noted socialist background.

Reyner Banham, then an academic at the Bartlett School of Architecture, had described himself a few years earlier in the Terry Hamilton Memorial Lecture as part of the 'protest culture'.[2] Cedric Price was a 'socialist' architect[3] who, alongside his call for the demolition of York Minster, was also famous for a project, with the communist impresario Joan Littlewood, to design an interactive Fun Palace and – with Alexander Trocchi – a situationist university. These proposals, sadly, never came to fruition. Paul Barker, the youngest of the four authors, was the editor of the leftist *New Society*. So it was of no surprise that 'Non-Plan', appearing in this radical epoch and emanating from such noted egalitarian intellectuals in a left-wing publication, should be considered part of the New Left. In his book *Cities of Tomorrow*, even Peter Hall, the fourth of the article's authors, placed Non-Plan in the chapter dealing with participatory architecture, rather than in the chapter concerning free-market planning deregulation.[4]

However, Non-Plan has much more in common with the New Right than the New Left, and shares many key characteristics with Friedrich Hayek, a writer who is not only unequivocally of the New Right, but is regarded by both the New Right and their opponents as exemplifying their creed.

two
'NON-PLAN', A HAYEKIAN OUTLINE

'Non-Plan' argued that the grand architectural schemes associated with Modernism, and which were designed to resolve social problems, actually exacerbated them. These grand

---

1 Reyner Banham, Paul Barker, Peter Hall and Cedric Price, Non-Plan: an experiment in freedom, *New Society*, no. 338, 20 March 1969, pp. 435–443.
2 Reyner Banham, The atavism of the short-distance minicyclist, *Living Arts*, no. 3, 1964, pp. 91–97.
3 Cedric Price, *Cedric Price: Architectural Association works II*, London: Architectural Association, 1984, p. 7.
4 Peter Hall, *Cities of Tomorrow*, Oxford: Blackwell, 1988. Colin Ward also considered Non-Plan compatible with egalitarian projects to democratize architecture (Colin Ward, *Talking to Architects*, London: Freedom Press, 1996, p. 86; also, Colin Ward, *Anarchism in Action*, London: Freedom Press, 1983, pp. 61–62).

programmes were often married to wider socio-economic regulations. It was not simply that these grandiose blueprints, when put into practice, failed to meet the needs of inhabitants – whether manufacturer, retailer or consumer – nor that they also restricted architectural imagination. It was that planning necessarily inferred failure. Hayek argued similarly.

Social planning for given outcomes, for Hayek, was insufficiently flexible to deal with the myriad needs and desires of a large population. An imposed order, the creation of just a few minds (indeed maybe as few as one) was termed by Hayek *Taxis*. This Hayek identified with socialism, a planned ordering of society. *Taxis* was contrasted with *Kosmos*, the spontaneous order created by individuals obeying certain economic rules, specifically those of the market economy, modifying their behaviour as that of their neighbours and competitors altered. The board game was a good analogy (Figure 1.8, p. 19). The rules were set but the outcome was undecided.

Like Hayek, the Non-Planners preferred the spontaneous order of *Kosmos* to *Taxis*. Where planning had worked, it had been serendipitous. The Non-Planners cited the heavily planned Welwyn Garden City and Hampstead Garden Suburb. The latter had been the subject of numerous criticisms because its road layout was difficult for public transport to negotiate and the back-garden cabbage patches were redundant in an age of supermarket frozen and tinned vegetables. However, with the increased penetration of the motor car, the road layout was no longer a problem and the back gardens became a safe haven for children away from the 'lethal pressed steel and rubber hurling around the streets'.[5] The plan succeeded, but not for the reasons envisaged by the planners.

As the Non-Planners pointed out, social planning could not cope with the myriad desires of a large group of individuals whose choices grow ever more complex and divergent, as incomes rise.[6] Attempts to overcome social disutilities by planning merely exacerbated the social problems that planning was meant to solve. Hayek provided an example of how benign social engineering cannot improve on spontaneous order, no matter how well intentioned. Socially planned slum clearance, he argued, distorted the housing market and encouraged greater depopulation of rural areas, thereby leading to greater concentration of people in the cities and consequently more slums. The Non-Planners, too, rejected the zoning of building land to create pleasant rural areas, as this merely increased the building concentration of the cities. The rural areas became increasingly featureless as the land could only be used for farming, such as the huge monotonous fields of Banham's native East Anglia.[7] Cedric Price, in his singular version of 'Non-Plan' published in *Architectural Design* two months later, gave a detailed account of which legislation should be withdrawn – a list which included housing subsidies and land use control.[8]

5 Banham, Barker, Hall and Price, *op. cit.*, note 1, p. 435.
6 *Ibid.*, p. 442.
7 *Ibid.*, p. 440.
8 Cedric Price, Non-Plan, *Architectural Design*, 39, no. 5, May 1969, p. 269.

The Non-Planners, like Hayek, criticized the regulation of buildings and the zoning of space, as these were viewed as reflecting the values of a small, paternalistic élite. The planners were from a different class and had no idea nor appreciation of the interests of the majority. The bureaucrats had outmoded views indicated, according to the Non-Planners, by their choice of newspapers: the *Daily Telegraph* and *Daily Express*. The planners who had disparaged consumers' desires were dismissed by Barker, Banham, Hall and Price with the most pejorative epithet of the New Left lexicon, they were condemned as 'bourgeois'.

Like Hayek, the Non-Planners distinguished between two types of planning: the unacceptable static-state and that which was broadly desirable. This second type of planning came in two forms. The first was from commercial concerns which needed to plan; this planning was considered legitimate as it was receptive to individual choice. The other type was State intervention, which sought to encourage further commercial activity, opening up markets and disbanding planning laws. The 'Non-Plan' solution was in this vein – setting up three Non-Plan areas where regulations based on the zoning of land, preservation orders and paternalistic social welfare legislation would be reduced or eliminated.

These experimental districts were to provide a template for Britain as a whole.[9] The trial areas were: Lawrence country, stretching from the East Midlands of Derby and Nottingham to the south of Yorkshire of Sheffield and Doncaster (Figure 1.4); Constable country, ranging northwards from Harlow New Town, bounded by Royston in the west and Saffron Walden in the east (Figure 1.6); and Montagu country, located south of Hampshire, taking in Southampton, Portsmouth, slices of the Isle of Wight and bits of Bournemouth (Figure 1.8). Price's own version had an additional Non-Plan region based in the Lake District.

The ideal for both Hayek and the Non-Planners was free-market capitalism, which for both was synonymous with freedom itself. They shared not only the analysis of the cause of social problems and the type of solution, but also the source of that solution: North America. Hayek was lavish in his praise for the US for its economic-individualist society. He dedicated his 1960 book, *The Constitution of Liberty*, to 'the unknown civilization that is growing in America'.[10] The Non-Planners, too, saw the excitement and lack of coercion of the marketplace, as embodied by North America, as the perfect model for 'restoring vitality and spontaneity to city life'.[11] They pointed to the Pacific states, creations like Fremont Street in Las Vegas or Sunset Street in Beverley Hills as 'represent[ing] the living architecture of our age'.[12] The photographs that illustrated the article were either of imported neon signs for 'Motel'[13] and 'Coca-Cola' (Figure 1.10, p. 21)[14] or of

9 *Ibid.*, p. 443.
10 Friedrich Hayek, *The Constitution of Liberty*, London: Routledge and Kegan Paul, 1960. See also Friedrich Hayek, *Law, Legislation and Liberty*, London: Routledge and Kegan Paul, 1973.
11 Banham, Barker, Hall and Price, *op. cit.*, note 1, p. 443.
12 *Ibid.*, p. 443.
13 *Ibid.*, p. 442.
14 *Ibid.*, p. 443.

quintessential British institutions Americanized in the same illuminated medium. To illustrate how Britain could become as vital and energized as the US 'Tesco', 'Petrol Open', 'Shell' and 'Fish Bar' were emblazoned in bright light (Figure 1.3, p. 14).

The reason for this adoration of the USA might be guessed at by the choice of another sign: one for the British footwear company 'Truman's' (Figure 1.9, p. 20). This was redolent of Harry S. Truman, the US president who had governed during the Marshall Plan redevelopment of Europe, an exercise which demonstrated US bounty in contrast to the drab, ration-inflicted Britain under Attlee's governorship. This was at a time when all the Non-Planners except the youngest (Barker) were in their economically liberated twenties.

American and British cultural signifiers were hybridized in the illustration, signed by Graham Percy, which accompanied 'Non-Plan' (Figure 1.6, p. 17). British High Street names 'Safeway', 'BP' and 'ICI' were featured on American highway boards in a scene which resembled an Iowan small town. It is hard to figure out whether the cars are obeying American or British road protocol, as the vehicles are on both sides of the street and seem to be travelling off into the horizon.

Even the three experimental Non-Plan regions were described in terms of a travelogue for visiting American tourists: Lawrence country, Constable country and Montagu country currently sound perfectly normal in heritage-dominated Britain. However, in the 1960s, the reduction of the heavy industrial and mining districts of Nottingham and Sheffield to an author notorious for a prosecution about a smutty book (and who had little love for Nottingham itself) was redolent of the marketing concepts of Madison Avenue.

In terms of identifying the problem, the key enemies, the solution and the source of the solution, the Non-Planners were in step with Hayek and the New Right. The problems appeared to be twofold: the inability of the paternalistic Welfare State to meet the needs of its population and economic stagnation. The enemies were identified as the officials in the planning offices, and bureaucrats of local councils and the liberal-democratic State. The solution, indicated by America, was the reinvigoration of the entrepreneurial spirit. Big business – in the form of petro-chemical multinationals – should be given the freedom to build their gas-stations in the locations they desired. This would promote architectural diversity and bold colourful experiment, combined with the excitement of a play-school.[15]

There are a number of reasons why a New Right proposal coming from this particular part of the New Left milieu should not appear particularly surprising. First and foremost the division between New Left and New Right, in 1969, hardly existed. A movement identifiable as the New Right had yet to fully coalesce. Although a body of

15 *Ibid.*, p. 443.

theory did exist, with substantial outpourings from Ayn Rand, Ludwig von Mises and other hyper-capitalists alongside Hayek, it had not been associated with any actually operating social policy, nor aligned with a major political movement (although Hayek had allied himself with the anti-trade union Institute of Economic Affairs). In Britain coalescence did not occur for another six years until the election in 1975 of Margaret Thatcher as the Conservative Party leader under the tutelage of Keith Joseph.[16]

Similarly the New Left was hardly an unproblematic category. It was open to differing interpretation. Its interests and its personnel were diverse, although some had considered it synonymous with just one part: the white, predominantly middle-class student revolts (1964–1969) of which the Non-Planners were clearly not a part.[17] The New Left pre-dated the campus rebellions; the unifying feature was the development of an egalitarian social theory in opposition to the repressive orthodoxy of Marxist-Leninism. Yet even here there were problems as New Leftist ideas began to percolate into the Old Left; indeed, the British Communist Party's own youth section criticized the Soviet invasion of Czechoslovakia in 1968, albeit hesitantly.

Similarly, many participants who would naturally be associated with anti-Stalinist radicalism did not wish to associate themselves with the label New Left as they distrusted those who had loyally trusted Stalin until the tanks rolled into Budapest, having previously excused or ignored other Soviet atrocities. Alternatively, they disliked the types and backgrounds of the personnel associated with the movement and so refused to identify themselves with it, although sharing many key ideas.[18]

The antagonism that the New Left felt toward the orthodox Communists and their paternalistic forms of socialism was one of the reasons why a piece of New Right thinking could be generated under the guise of the New Left. The writers of the New Left and the New Right had the same enemies: the planned economies of the Soviet Union and the paternalistic liberalism of the Western Welfare States. For the New Left, the socialism of Stalinism lacked democracy and freedom, while the liberal establishment had involved the West in the genocide in Indochina. The New Left despised the Welfare State because it failed to meet the needs of the poor, but also restrained proletarian revolutionary instincts. Similarly the New Right opposed the same figures, albeit for different economic reasons. The Stalinist left was unpatriotic and a restraint on trade. The neo-imperialism of the Vietnam conflict made Western citizens poorer, not wealthier, and the Welfare State involved taxation and expropriation preventing a fully free market. 'Non-Plan' attacked the same targets as the New Left – the petty bureaucrat and restrictive laws – but did so from a New Right perspective.

16 Sir Keith Joseph, on becoming a minister in Margaret Thatcher's cabinet, handed out copies of Hayek's *Roads to Freedom* to his civil servants.
17 W. Breines, *Community and Organisation in the New Left, 1962–1968: the great refusal*, London: Rutgers University Press, 1989, p. 8.
18 A. Meltzer, *The Anarchists in London 1935–1955*, Sanday, Orkney Islands: Cienfuegos Press, 1976, p. 35. Also, S. Christie, *The Christie File*, Sanday, Orkney Islands: Cienfuegos Press, 1980, p. 31.

These similarities led to concurrence in the choice of terminology. Both the New Left and New Right talked of 'freedom' and 'choice' and of opposing 'paternalism' and 'bureaucracy'. They shared the same nomenclature, but interpreted the terms in incompatible ways. As a result of these apparent similarities a proposal for one programme could be mistaken for the other.

The schema of criticism was the same for the Non-Planners and Hayek. There were only two choices: paternalistic *Taxis* or free-market *Kosmos*. The contemporary critics of 'Non-Plan' also shared this view, although they did not share the Non-Planners' preference. 'Non-Plan' generated eleven letters, more than any other article that spring (although Hall believed 'Non-Plan' was ignored). Some made incidental criticisms: I. Martin took offence at the suggestion that planners read the *Telegraph* and *Express*, and sent a detailed break-down of the reading habits of his planning office.[19]

Remaining criticisms fell into two categories. The majority admitted that planning was not perfect, but that planning was superior to the laissez-faire of 'Non-Plan' as this would restrict the freedom of the poor even further. The minority, led by the ex-communist Alfred Sherman (a soon-to-be confidant to Margaret Thatcher), supported Non-Plan as he found it hard to see how imposing planners' choices would increase the opportunities of those at the lower end of the income scale.[20]

These two groups of critics, like Hayek and the Non-Planners, shared the view that the choice was between State or quasi-State planning on the one hand or laissez-faire on the other. It was a debate which prefigured the political battles of the 1980s, in which State intervention was contrasted solely with the free-market, and these two options were presented as if they were the only possibilities.

However, these two positions were not exhaustive. For there are other forms of social organization, one of which shows far greater critical insight and experimental and liberating features than 'Non-Plan', and which also developed out of the New Left. Its first major eruption occurred in Redbridge on the Essex/East London boundary, about 15 miles from the edge of 'Constable country', a few months before the publication of 'Non-Plan'.

three
ADVENTURES IN REDBRIDGE

In November 1968 the London Squatters Campaign was formed, its membership coming predominantly from New Left backgrounds – that is members or supporters of anarchist, libertarian socialist and other anti-Stalinist left-wing groupings. The spur to the squatting movement was the failure of the Welfare State to deal adequately with the

---

19 *New Society*, vol. 13, no. 341, 10 April 1969, p. 573.
20 *New Society*, vol. 13, no. 342, 17 April 1969, p. 610.

problem of homelessness and poor housing. Their inspiration were the Vigilantes and other squatters who had taken over military land for homes in the aftermath of the Second World War, a movement Cedric Price had himself witnessed and supported.[21]

The shortcomings of family hostels in the public and private sectors had been the impetus for campaigns since the mid-1960s. With the showing in 1966 and the later repeat of the BBC drama *Cathy Come Home* (and the subsequent formation of the organization Shelter), homelessness and the shortcomings in housing provision had become an issue of public concern. The edition of *New Society* in which 'Non-Plan' appeared contained pleas for more social housing and a rent subsidy to prevent further homelessness.

It was against this background that the London Squatters held their first protest, the symbolic occupation of The Hollies, a luxury private housing development in Essex which had stood empty for a number of years following the collapse of the higher echelons of the housing market. This gained some local publicity for the squatting group and led them from symbolic to practical direct action. Over a period of three months in spring–summer 1969 they moved approximately a dozen homeless families into empty council properties in Redbridge. These had been bought by the council for a large redevelopment programme and were expected to remain vacant for as long as seven years.

The squatters successfully fought off legal and extra-legal attempts by the council to evict them, including unlawful physical violence by the bailiffs. This gained the squatters significant support locally from residents' groups, so much so that the mayor's 200-signature petition against the squatters was trumped by one of 2000 in support. They also received favourable publicity, both locally and nationally, and spurred a wider squatting campaign.

The squatting movement was not homogeneous. On one side were the reformers such as Ron Bailey, a housing activist, who regarded squatting as part of a campaign for more efficient use of council residential stock. Bailey was happy to deal with the local State and admired other reformers from other political groupings. He held particular affection for the Conservative mayor of Lewisham at the time of the campaign. On the other side were those Bailey labels 'a small group of the worst type of "anarchist" – they had established the free society at "their" house. The interests of the squatting families became subordinate to the "revolution".'[22] Amongst this 'revolutionary' group were activists like Chris Broad, also involved in the Redbridge campaign, who in a 1978 edition of *Anarchy* magazine described the events as part of a programme for more radical social change.[23]

21 Interview with Cedric Price, 25 March 1997.
22 Ron Bailey, *The Squatters*, Harmondsworth: Penguin, 1973, p. 102. See also: Ron Bailey, *Homelessness What Can Be Done: an immediate programme of self-help and mutual aid*, Oxford: Jon Carpenter, 1994.
23 Chris Broad, Anarchy and the art of motor-cycle maintenance, *Anarchy*, no. 26, 1978.

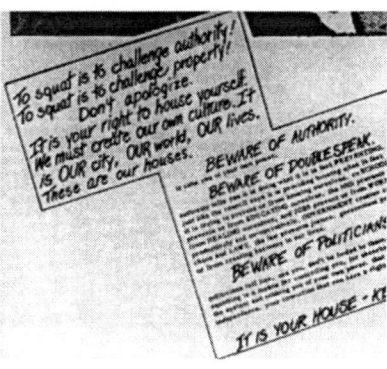

figure 3.1
FRONT PAGE OF *THE SQUATTER*

Robert Goodman made a similar distinction between those squatters who did not threaten the given framework of administration, and guerrilla architecture which helps 'promote political consciousness of the people ... expose[s] the repression of the established order ... [and] address[es] itself to the people's real needs ... [whose] successes and even failures lead to further political acts and the creation of a larger movement ...'.[24] It was this guerrilla section which became more prominent in the early 1970s, as squatting campaigns took off throughout London and spread and developed in other parts of Britain (Nottingham, Birmingham and Glasgow amongst others).

The squatters shared with the Non-Planners and Hayek the belief that the Welfare State was failing to meet people's needs and desires. Current planning was adding to their problems not resolving them. However, the practices of the squatters demonstrated the conservativeness of Non-Plan, and its valuative similarities with Hayek. The five main beliefs differentiating the squatters from the Non-Planners were that, first, capitalism was not value-neutral, but a system of class domination; second, that dominant architectural presuppositions and practices were repressive; third, that the current social divisions were due to hierarchies which could be directly confronted; fourth, that this confrontation itself provided opportunities for the realization of libertarian ways of living; and, lastly, that squatting itself was part of a wider social and political struggle against capitalism.

THE FREE-MARKET IS VALUE-SPECIFIC

Unlike the Non-Planners, the guerrilla architects saw private enterprise as value-specific (Figure 3.1) and believed that its imposition was incapable of resolving the problems of

[24] Robert Goodman, *After the Planners*, Harmondsworth: Penguin Books, 1972, p. 228.

39

left figure 3.2
PHOTOGRAPH OF PREBBLE AND CO. BEING
PROTECTED BY THE POLICE, 1974

right figure 3.3
PICTURE OF ANTI-YUPPIE RIOT FROM *CLASS WAR*,
NO. 30, C.1988, (N.D.), PP. 4-5

the poor. Symbols of the failure of capitalism to fulfil its consumer promises were particular targets. The office block Centrepoint was squatted for accommodation in 1974 after standing vacant for several years, as was the one-time target of the Angry Brigade, the Biba boutique in Kensington, in 1977.

Private property for the guerrilla squatters was not immutable and sovereign as it was for Hayek and the Non-Planners. The squatters viewed ownership in terms akin to the anarchist-communism of Peter Kropotkin and Alexander Berkman, where ownership was determined by use rather than title. Squatters did not enter homes in which people were living but only entered those buildings which were unoccupied.

The squatters' rejection of the primacy of private ownership went further than the direct action of taking over buildings. They also rejected capitalism's distribution of housing space on the basis of wealth. Campaigns were waged against speculators, such as the harassment of Islington estate agents Prebble and Co. (Figure 3.2) – an ultimately unsuccessful attempt to prevent the gentrification of the area. Squatters' groups led other similar campaigns in Sweden, Germany, the Netherlands and Denmark (Figure 3.3).

Of course, not all squatters were guerrillas. There were those who tried, through squatting, to build a lifestyle which was within capitalism, using the low-rent costs of squatting to create or win new markets for themselves. Wholefood stores, ethnic jewellery shops, vegan cafés and 'alternative' music outlets represent particular interests and predominantly middle class desires.[25] These commercial concerns have helped in the 'yuppiefication' of working class districts,[26] where non-guerrilla squatters have been the first wave, followed by the artists and then the liberal professionals, as the takeover of London's Camden, Islington, Notting Hill, Stepney and Hoxton areas bear witness.

25 N. Wates and C. Wolmar (editors), *Squatting: the real story*, London: Blackrose Press, 1980, pp. 42–43.
26 S. Reilly, The middle class, *The Heavy Stuff*, no. 3, n.d., pp. 2–9.

40

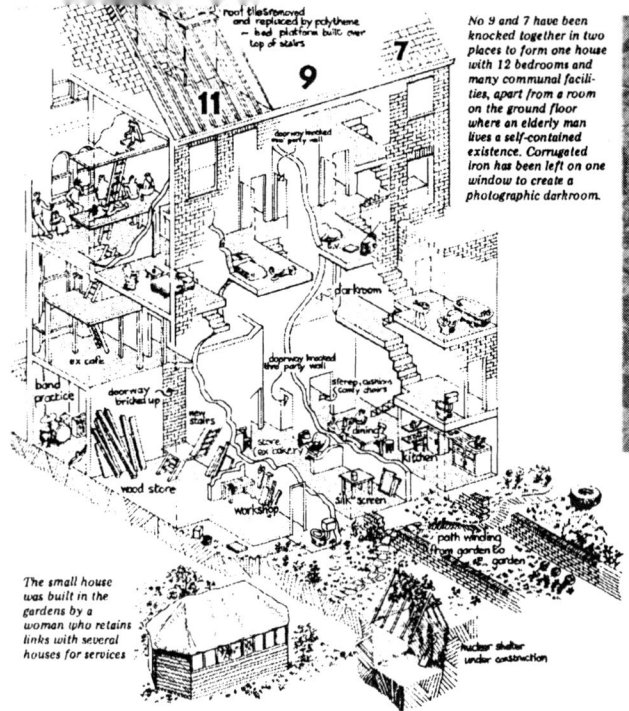

left figure 3.4
SQUATTING STRUCTURE

right figure 3.5
TREE-HOUSE IN SQUATTED TREE
AT POLLOCK (1995-1996)

AGAINST THE ESTABLISHED ORDER

Neither Hayek nor the Non-Planners viewed architecture outside of traditional terms of built spaces designed for predetermined ends. Squatters' practices, on the other hand, were drawn from wider afield, particularly from the artistic *avant-gardes* of Dada, Surrealism and Situationism. They incorporated aspects of the ready-made, of appropriation and *détournement*. Office buildings, such as Centrepoint, were turned into delimited zones. The separation of the work-place from the residential which came with the industrial revolution and the factory system were questioned by the squatters (Figure 3.4). Buildings had multiple uses: cafés, print-shops and dark-rooms were placed alongside bedrooms and dormitories.[27]

PARTICIPATORY AGENTS, NOT CONSUMERS

Social divisions and hierarchies were rejected by the squatters but not by the planners (who wanted to save their professional role) or the Non-Planners (who wanted to keep the division between those who build and the consumers who will use the building). The division of labour and the primacy of the individual as consumer was also maintained by Hayek. This division between architects and planners on one side, and the building's users on the other, was questioned through the radical squatters' self-build projects and participatory democratic decision-making. This egalitarian method stripped the experts of their claims to uniqueness in creativity. Hence the phrase on the poster at the 121 Bookshop (Railton Road, Brixton): 'Everything is architecture and we are all architects' – a phrase which has its roots in the Fluxus movement.

27 Wates and Wolmar, *op. cit.*, note 25, *passim*.

PREFIGURATIVE EXPERIMENTS

The way in which squatters confronted social problems provided examples of possible liberated forms of living, and allowed for experiments in communal ways of living, even if they seemed to be at the expense of personal dignity. The decision to sacrifice privacy was at least up to the individual. As Colin Ward, one of the architectural theorists who supported the squatting movements, wrote: 'It is not up to the planners to decide if we should be communal or isolated'.[28]

The squatters' attempts at more egalitarian social relations has subsequently been criticized by feminist activists. The sexist attitudes of male cohabitants and the division of labour and space often replicated those of the non-squatting world.[29] Anti-social behaviour, such as hard drug-taking and excessive noise, have also been associated with the squatting movement, but there is not necessarily a connection between such activities and squatting. The practice provides a possibility, even if only occasionally successful, for more egalitarian social relations.

REVOLUTIONARY PERSPECTIVES

The radical squatters also had overtly political or social revolutionary objectives. They attempted to strengthen working class communities through the provision of arenas for gigs and local events, rather than through the creation of an exclusive squatters' ghetto, which saw their neighbours as hostile. The squatted zone has often provided a centre for political activity, most recently organizing against the Criminal Justice Act, workfare or environmental campaigns.[30] Squatting has provided the tactic for the anti-roads protests, such as the tree-houses at Newbury (1994) or Pollock (1995–1996)[31] (Figure 3.5), or at Claremont Road against the M11 link, less than a mile from the original Redbridge squats.

While not all those partaking in the environmental squatting movements would consider themselves revolutionary, in a world of capitalist ascendancy, control and repression, squatting can provide a glimpse of a different, more spontaneous, communal and exciting future. It can provide a Temporary Autonomous Zone (TAZ, to borrow a term from the American 'ontological anarchist' Hakim Bey). Bey's thesis is that by taking on heteronomous power, forces of resistance frequently replicate the power structures they seek to overthrow. For instance, the way a centralized party takes on and over the power of the centralized State. Consequently, revolutions, even when successful, do not liberate but merely reproduce heteronomous power. Even the most libertarian insurrections, while in the short term providing intense excitement and the opening up of possibilities 'peak experience' – in becoming permanent, drift into the everyday.

28 Colin Ward, *Housing: an anarchist approach*, London: Freedom Press, 1976, p. 39.
29 F. Jackson, *Squatting in West Berlin*, London: Hooligan Press, 1987, p. 17.
30 See for instance the Autonomous Centre of Edinburgh or the 1 in 12 Centre, Bradford.
31 See: Grrrt (fish) and S. Wakefield, *Not for Rent: conversations with creative activists in the U.K.*, Amsterdam, Netherlands: Evil Twin Publications, 1996, p. 69.

The TAZ, by avoiding permanence, seeks to recreate these intense peak experiences by opposing the State, in its creation of liberated spaces, but not by confronting it. Once the State intervenes, the zone dissolves to reappear elsewhere. It is, for Bey, a microcosm of an anarchist society, but with no aim at permanence. A small TAZ may avoid the interest of the State for a long time, or TAZs may become so frequent that they form wider liberated zones. The TAZ is a 'guerrilla operation which liberates an area ... and then dissolves itself to re-form elsewhere'.[32]

four
CONCLUSION

Despite the egalitarian impulses of the authors of 'Non-Plan' and their desire to overcome the stultifying paternalistic State, their response, in 1969, would have been to strengthen the power of multinationals and to impose business priorities on the public. Yet commercial predilections do not lead to ludic spontaneity, but to heteronomous control to check efficiency and the maximization of profit. The response of the guerrilla squatters, by contrast, was to encourage playfulness and autonomy rather than the garish matronly games in the privately funded 'play-school' of 'Non-Plan'.

five
ACKNOWLEDGEMENTS

The author wishes to acknowledge the assistance of Millie Wild (Advisory Service for Squatters, 2 St Paul's Road, Islington, London, N1. Tel.: 0171 359 8814) and Class War (PO Box 467, London).

---

32 Hakim Bey, *T.A.Z.: the temporary autonomous zone, ontological anarchy, poetic terrorism*, Brooklyn, NY: Autonomedia, 1991, p. 101.

#04

COLIN WARD: ANARCHY AND ARCHITECTURE
A PERSONAL RECORD

My architectural life began in 1941 and my anarchist life in 1943. So my sole qualification for the exploration of implied contradictions between anarchy and architecture, between plan and non-plan is that I have been attempting to make the links longer than most explorers. When I was fifteen my second job was in the office of the Borough Engineer of Ilford, Essex, where I lived, and one of my tasks was sorting out the dockets about repairs and maintenance to that council's housing estates. Some tenants we favoured and they got repairs, but others were put on a second pile. This depended on the power and influence of their councillors. I had stumbled, without realizing its implications, on one of the unmentioned facts of public housing management. The whole sad story has been carefully chronicled by Anne Power.[1] In support of her interpretation of the history of public housing in Britain, I must cite the opinion of a lifelong socialist, Tony Judge. Writing of his experience of the Greater London Council's Housing Management Committee, he declared that 'the impression, often confirmed as accurate on deeper examination, is of a vast bureaucracy concerned more with self-perpetuation than with either efficiency or humanity'.[2]

When I was sixteen, my third job was for an elderly architect, S.B. Caulfield, whose work was then confined to war-damage repairs, but whose own working life had begun in the 1890s, drawing full-size details on brown paper on a barn floor in Devon for Truro Cathedral in Cornwall, whose architect was the gothic revivalist John Loughborough Pearson. Caulfield urged me to go and gaze, while I had the chance, at the remains of the newly bombed St John's, Red Lion Square, one of Pearson's London churches, ('big-boned' as Pevsner was to describe them), for the rare opportunity of seeing a life-size cross-section of a Gothic church. He left me with a lifetime interest in lettering and typography and in the people he had met at the Central School of Arts and Crafts, like Edward Johnson and Eric Gill, and especially in that school's principal, the architectural philosopher W. R. Lethaby, one of the figures celebrated in my book about *Influences: voices of creative dissent*.[3]

As soon as I was 18 years old I was conscripted into the army and in 1943 found myself working on the drawing-board for a military unit in Glasgow. There I fell under the influence of the busy anarchist propagandists in that city, who urged me to contribute

---

1 Anne Power, *Property Before People: the management of twentieth-century council housing*, London: Allen and Unwin, 1987.
2 Tony Judge, The political and administrative setting, in Nabeel Hambdi and Bob Greenstreet (editors), *Participation in Housing*, Oxford: Oxford Polytechnic, 1981.
3 Colin Ward, *Influences: voices of creative dissent*, Bideford: Green Books, 1992.

to the journals published by Freedom Press in London. This I have done, from December 1943 to the present day, and my first contribution on housing was in 1945.[4]

By 1946, I had been posted south after several years in Orkney and Shetland. I was in southern England at the time when squatting families were occupying empty army and air force camps, and was able to report these events in *Freedom*.[5] In 1947, belatedly released from the army, I returned to the drawing-board for a series of architectural firms. They included the Architects' Co-Partnership and then, for 10 years, Bridgwater, Shepheard and Epstein, and finally Chamberlin, Powell and Bon, which I left as director of research in 1964.

Readers familiar with the professional world will recognize that my employers in those years had completely different design ideologies but had several common characteristics. They were small (or smallish) private firms engaged in large public jobs. Their work in the 1950s and 1960s was mostly housing, schools and health buildings for public authorities. It often reflected the architects' own situation in the family life-cycle: they were involved with nursery and primary schools when their own children were of that age, and grew up with their children's contemporaries into the building of secondary schools and universities.

That generation of architects was nurtured by, and employed by, the Welfare State. They shared its social ideology but also, of course, its paternalistic assumptions.

In discussing the buildings that resulted, one question seldom raised is that of the freedom of action of architects in the fields of both housing and schools, both of which were subject to a long series of design requirements from the clients in local government and the paymasters in central government. Several of the architects I worked for had confrontations over school design.

The Architects and Buildings Branch of the then Ministry of Education was quite often in advance of current practice in relating school design to teaching methods, but I well remember how that department had a map on its wall showing which of the various consortia for system-built schools the various local authorities had joined at the Ministry's recommendation. On this map there was a reproachful white space in the middle of southern England. This was Buckinghamshire, where the county architect, Fred Pooley (who was the original instigator of what became the New Town of Milton Keynes) had argued that you would get more school for your money, and a more adaptable building, if you built with brick walls and pitched, tiled roof. School buildings in that county proved to be cheap, simple and durable and provided about 15 per cent more school for the capital invested just through not following the bureaucratization of design.[6]

4 Colin Ward, Direct action for houses, *War Commentary – For Anarchism*, 28 July 1945.
5 Colin Ward, The people act, *Freedom*, 27 July, 10 August, 24 August, 7 September, 21 September, 5 October and 19 October 1946. Reprinted in Colin Ward, *Housing: an anarchist approach*, London: Freedom Press, 1976.
6 Colin Ward, The future of the design professions, in Colin Ward, *Talking to Architects: ten lectures*, London: Freedom Press, 1983.

Something very similar is true of housing. In those post-war decades the word was synonymous with local authority housing and, although experience had shown that traditional building methods cost less in first costs and in maintenance, a series of (usually Conservative) Ministers cajoled local authorities to adopt building systems. Not only this, but almost all significant decisions were made not by architects but by their employers. Peter Malpass in Newcastle examined the extent to which decisions were made by either architects or building users and found that:

> Instead of meeting his clients face to face, getting to understand their clients, needs and preferences ... these are mediated by other departments and by the central government, all of whom are equally innocent of any systematic contact with tenants.[7]

Several decades later those architects of the post-war years are long retired and I have a friend, a community activist in East London, Ken Weller, who posts me their obituaries, highlighting political commitments, in order to stress the links, as he puts it, 'between authoritarian State socialism and the appalling disaster of municipal housing in the post-war decades'. As I knew plenty of these people I have to say, 'Yes, but ...' and to explain lamely that there were no voices calling for dweller control as the first principle of both housing and planning. Instead, the debate was concentrated in matters of design, which are totally subject to changes in fashion and to individual whim and self-advertisement.

There were very few links between the anarchists and the architects. One was the architect Giancarlo De Carlo, nurtured during the years of war and resistance by the Italian anarchist propagandists and by the stream of ideas they channelled from earlier generations. Thus, as Colin St John Wilson explained when De Carlo was awarded the RIBA Gold Medal in 1993:

> As the most lucid of his generation of architect-philosophers-in-action his point of departure lay in the work of Kropotkin and Patrick Geddes and above all perhaps in William Morris. In 1947 he wrote a book on William Morris, and I believe that the ethical drive of his work, undeflected during the ensuing 40 years of practice, lies in that famous question of William Morris, 'What business have we with art at all unless all can share it?'.[8]

In 1948 De Carlo wrote in the anarchist journal *Volontà* on the housing problem and I translated his article, inaccurately, for *Freedom*.[9] One of our readers was John Turner, then a student at the Architectural Association School, having been seduced from military service by that journal (Figure 4.1). As a schoolboy he had been given the task of summarizing a chapter from Lewis Mumford's *The Culture of Cities,* and this led him to the work of Mumford's mentor, Patrick Geddes (Figure 4.2). Turner was to con-

---
7 Peter Malpass, Professionalism in architecture and the design of local authority housing, Newcastle University Thesis, 1973.
8 Colin St John Wilson, Master of the resistance, *Architectural Review,* July 1993.
9 Giancarlo De Carlo, Il problema della casa, *Volontà,* 2, no. 10/11, 15 April 1949. Reprinted as The housing problem in Italy, *Freedom,* 12 June, 19 June 1949.

top figure 4.2
PATRICK GEDDES IN INDIA 1919 (FROM COLIN WARD, *INFLUENCES: VOICES OF CREATIVE DISSENT,* GREEN BOOKS, 1992)

right figure 4.1
JOHN TURNER. THE ARCHITECT WHO DID MOST TO CHANGE THE OFFICIAL MIND ON UNOFFICIAL SETTLEMENTS

tribute to the 1949 reprint of *Cities in Evolution*,[10] and was deeply influenced by the 1947 volume *Patrick Geddes in India,* where Geddes (reporting on the towns in the Madras presidency in 1915) remarked that,

> Town-planning is not mere place-making, nor even work-planning. If it is to be successful it must be folk-planning. This means that its task is to find the right places for each sort of people; places where they will really flourish. To give people, in fact, the care that we give when transplanting flowers, instead of harsh evictions and arbitrary instructions to 'move on', delivered in the manner of officious amateur policemen.[11]

In 1952 Turner, Patrick Crooke, De Carlo and I met in Venice, and Turner also met the architect Eduardo Neira who invited him a few years later to work in Peru, learning through mistakes in assisting self-build housing projects (Figure 4.3).[12] John Turner absorbed in Latin America the important lesson of illegal squatter settlements: that far from being threatening symptoms of social malaise, they were a triumph of popular self-help which, overcoming the culture of poverty, evolved over time into fully serviced suburbs, giving their occupants a foothold in the urban economy. More, perhaps than anyone else, Turner changed the way in which we perceive such settlements anywhere. It was his paper at the 1966 United Nations seminar on Uncontrolled Urban Settlements that was most influential in setting in motion 'site-and-services' housing programmes – policies about which Turner himself had and has reservations.

10 Patrick Geddes, *Cities in Evolution,* second edn, Edinburgh: Outlook Tower Association and London: Association for Planning and Regional Reconstruction (Jacqueline Tyrwhitt, editor), Williams and Norgate, 1949.
11 Patrick Geddes, *Patrick Geddes in India* (Jacqueline Tyrwhitt, editor), London: Lund Humphries, 1947.
12 John F.C. Turner, The re-education of a professional, in Turner, J.F.C. and Fichter, R. (editors), *Freedom to Build,* New York: Collier Macmillan, 1972.

figure 4.3
DWELLER-BUILT SETTLEMENT AT LIMA, PERU.
© HUBERTUS KANUS

When he moved from South to North America, Turner found that the ideas he formulated in Peru were also true of the richest nation in the world and, when he returned to Britain after seventeen years abroad, he found that the housing situation in Britain too fitted his formulation.[13] Yet in Britain, architects and planners, both employed by local authorities and both involved in vast programmes of comprehensive redevelopment, were failing to notice the gulf between their pre-occupations and the concerns of the citizens who saw themselves as victims.

John R. Gold begins his account of *The Experience of Modernism* with a preface describing his own childhood recollections from Ilford, Essex (now the heart of the London Borough of Redbridge) a quarter of a century after I was a child in the same town. His family lived in one of those late-Victorian terraces near the High Road, with 'narrow but substantial gardens where a child could get on with things unobserved by interfering adults'. The 1962 plan for a new town centre of gleaming concrete and glass was to provoke outraged opposition when those houses were described as slums, for which demolition was 'in the best interests of the town'. They were boarded up and vandalized by the council (to keep out the squatters) and cleared piecemeal to become temporary car parks. Residents 'quickly cut their losses, accepting a selling price based on "site-value only" and moved out. Those who could not afford alternative housing, like my parents,' explains John Gold, 'eventually accepted rehousing in a block of high-rise council flats some miles distant'. Comprehensive redevelopment never happened and the area today is a windswept mess justifiably regarded as 'much worse than existed previously'.[14]

It was in those streets of fit but condemned housing near Ilford town centre that the squatters' movement was reborn in 1968, thanks to two activists, Ron Bailey and Jim Radford. Councils sent in wrecking crews and bailiffs to intimidate squatters (Figure 4.4), but several councillors, embarrassed by their grotesque neglect of empty houses they had bought, eventually entered into agreements for short-life housing co-operatives, some of which, because of the changed climate of policy, have had a very long life. In London, some of the housing co-operatives have grown out of squatting groups.[15]

13 John F.C. Turner, *Housing by People: towards autonomy in building environments*, London: Marion Boyars, 1976.
14 John R. Gold, *The Experience of Modernism: modern architects and the future city, 1928–1953*, London: E. and F.N. Spon, 1997.
15 Ron Bailey, *Homelessness: what can be done: an immediate programme of self-help and mutual aid*, Oxford: Jon Carpenter Publishing, 1994.

figure 4.4

THE ASSAULT ON THE SQUATTERS, ILFORD 1969, *DAILY MIRROR*, 26 JUNE 1969 (FROM COLIN WARD, *VIOLENCE*, PENGUIN CONNEXIONS SERIES, 1970)

In the 1960s, experience was demonstrating that the shortcomings of accepted ideologies of housing and planning and, at last, at quite different levels and with different audiences, there were journals propagating alternatives. In the architectural world the magazine *Architectural Design,* by then under the editorship of Monica Pidgeon, featured not only the fantasies of Archigram, but the self-build in Britain, including the plotlands of the first 40 years of the century (Figure 4.5), the lessons of the squatters' campaign and the global message of the *bricoleur*. In the world of the dissident Left, there was the monthly *Anarchy* relating these alternatives to anarchist traditions and, in the world of weekly journalism, there was *New Society* whose special enquiry, as Paul Barker, its former editor claimed, was that 'it tried to see the world as it was rather than as it ought to be'. In his recollection the 'Non-Plan' article was the result of the question that he and Peter Hall asked themselves, which was, 'Could things be any worse if there were no planners at all?'.[16]

The fact that the Non-Plan article suggested not abandonment of the planning legislation, but simply a series of 'plan-free zones' in various parts of the country, was useful

16 Paul Barker, Non-Plan revisited: or the real way cities grow, lecture at the Victoria and Albert Museum, 13 March 1998.

figure 4.5
PLOTLANDS, LAINDON, ESSEX, IN THE 1930S
(FROM DENNIS HARDY AND COLIN WARD,
*ARCADIA FOR ALL: THE LEGACY OF A MAKESHIFT
LANDSCAPE,* LONDON: MANSELL, 1984)

for propagandists since it implied a controlled experiment rather than a wholesale rejection of the planning system. The interesting thing is that we have not yet won that small concession. I was asked to lecture on this topic in 1975, urging an experimental 'Do-It-Yourself New Town'.[17] Like the Non-Plan paper itself, my lecture had its ripples of influence. I, meanwhile, was exploring with Dennis Hardy the unrecorded history of the plotlands of southeast England, those places where agricultural depression had enabled low-income city dwellers to build their own shack, chalet, chicken-farm, holiday home or retirement idyll.[18]

By the 1980s there were several attempts to develop alternative do-it-yourself settlements on land acquired by the New Town Development Corporations. The Greentown proposals at Milton Keynes failed, and the Lightmoor project at Telford had fourteen houses, not 400. The difficulty that killed these efforts after endless labour was the absence of a resolve to adopt a non-plan policy. As Don Ritson of Milton Keynes Development Corporation explained to me in 1978, 'We can't get planning permission, even in outline, without a clear statement of what is going to happen on the site, but if we specify what is to happen we are limiting in advance the aspirations of the people who we expect to settle there. And the whole idea is to give *them* freedom of choice'.[19]

Today the Non-Plan concept is further from acceptance than ever. In the climate of the turn of the century, the massed ranks of 'nimbyism' would march on London to object if the idea were to gain a hearing. But a more recent propagandist is conscious of the injustice done to the poor and to those who choose alternative lifestyles by the assumptions of the planning system and by its effect on land prices. Simon Fairlie seeks slight changes to the planning machinery that exists to enable, or oblige, local planning authorities to foster experiments in what he calls low-impact development. He claims, persuasively, that,

17 Colin Ward, The do-it-yourself new town, lecture at the Garden Cities/New Towns Forum, 22 October 1975, reprinted in Colin Ward, *Talking Houses: ten lectures,* London: Freedom Press, 1990.
18 Dennis Hardy and Colin Ward, *Arcadia for All: the legacy of a makeshift landscape,* London: Mansell, 1984.
19 Colin Ward, *New Town, Home Town: the lessons of experience,* London: Gulbenkian Foundation, 1993.

If permission to build or live in the countryside were to be allocated, not just to those who can afford artificially inflated land prices, but to anyone who could demonstrate a willingness and an ability to contribute to a thriving local economy, then a very different kind of rural society would emerge. Low impact development is a social contract whereby people are given the opportunity to live in the country in return for providing environmental benefits. Planners will recognize this as a form of what they call 'planning gain'. The mechanisms to strike such a bargain are for the most part already written into the English planning system ...'[20]

For me, and for people who want to make room for freedom of experiment in architecture and planning, the importance of flying the Non-Plan kite was the attempt to make room for do-it-yourself alternatives to the rival orthodoxies of the bureaucracy and of the speculative development industry. The attempt was not successful, but the fact that we discuss it 30 years later indicates what a rare challenge it was.

---

20 Simon Fairlie, *Low Impact Development: planning and people in sustainable countryside*, Charlbury: Jon Carpenter Publishing.

#05
BARRY CURTIS: THE HEART OF THE CITY

This chapter addresses the last relatively untroubled conference of the International Congress of Modern Architecture (CIAM), referred to throughout this chapter as CIAM 8, and considered here as the moment when the difficulties of implementing architectural and planning theories conceived in the interwar years began to become apparent. More generally, the record of the proceedings, published in 1952 as *The Heart of the City: towards the humanisation of urban life*[1] (Figure 5.1) can itself be presented as a manifestation of the discourse of humanism and the 'organic', put under severe pressure by post-war and Cold War circumstances and the emerging priorities of a new generation of architects.

The 'humanism' referred to throughout this chapter is intended to describe a pervasive mood within which cultural production was assessed. It was deeply imbued with notions of continuity and tradition, and marked by the terms 'Man' or 'Modern Man'. Younger artists and designers of the 1950s sought alternatives to this formulation in their admiration of a culture of consumption which recognized the fragmentation of the market and the indifference of the dominant humanist way of thinking. Humanism was an organizing principle in architectural thinking in the post-war period, both in terms of reconfiguring traditions and seeking lost or exotic alternatives. But humanism also implied a new mode of sensitivity to values which responded to recent experiences of totalitarianism and scientifically planned mass destruction. The architect in post-war Britain was required to address a wider range of human aspirations and needs in the context of social democracy.

This is not to suggest that there was any widespread agreement on the specific terms of a humanist approach. In the architectural discourse of the time the need to humanize could range from an essentialist desire to establish the invariable nature of 'Man' to more complexly informed attempts to deploy sociological and conjunctural understandings.

The notion of the 'organic' was related to this new mood and stood as a concept which had evolved within Modernism to describe an essential relationship integrating form and function, part and whole, appearance and value. It implied a holistic quality in which there were no superfluities of ornament or association; it was frequently used in relation to a 'return' to lost unity and integrity which enabled architectural ensembles to meet basic needs and, in terms of structures and spaces, to conform to 'natural laws'. One of the defences of Modernism was that its solutions were natural and innate: as

---

1 J. Tyrwhitt, J. Sert and E.N. Rogers, *The Heart of the City: towards the humanisation of urban life*, London: Lund Humphries, 1951.

figure 5.1
CIAM 8, THE HEART OF THE CITY, 1952

Giedion suggested in the introduction to *Space, Time and Architecture: the growth of a new tradition*, not only that 'architecture' was an 'organism' but also that Modernism sought to promote 'an approach to the life that slumbers unconsciously within us all'.[2]

'Organic' is a confusing term since it can be deployed to describe very different appearances: rectilinear as well as biomorphic architecture has been described in this way. It must be accepted that although organicism implies an essential relationship between structure and appearance, it primarily addresses the functional empathy of parts to the whole. As with the term 'plastic' there is an implication of perception in depth, an awareness that is related to the experiential and haptic, rather than the merely optical.

Notions of the 'human' and 'organic' and their ubiquity in the architectural writing and thinking in the early post-war world indicate a characteristic desire to address fundamental needs and to provide models which incorporate a complexly articulated concern for detail, connectivity and spatiality. They signal a concern for ordering and relationship which had a particular significance at a time when architects were expected to 'lay the foundations' of a widely accepted future. One of the recurring injunctions at CIAM 8 was to respect and remedy the causes of totalitarianism and authoritarian thinking. The paradox was whether this was best done by contriving a plan which excluded those possibilities or by abandoning the concept of planning altogether.

CIAM 8 took place in Britain in 1951, just before the incoming Conservative government ignited its 'bonfire of controls'[3] which marked the relaxation of much of the 1946 Labour government's interventionist planning and development legislation. The sense of empowerment which was evident at the conference was soon to be destabilised. Indeed, Le Corbusier, still a looming presence and the virtual host of the next meeting at Aix-en-Provence, seems to have conceded the shortcomings of his own generation of

2 Siegfried Giedion, *Space, Time and Architecture: the growth of a new tradition*, Cambridge, MA: Harvard University Press, 6th edition, 1946, p. 20.
3 Lionel Escher, *A Broken Wave: the rebuilding of England 1940–1980*, Harmondsworth: Penguin, 1983, p. 51.

architects and planners in a letter to CIAM 10 at Dubrovnik, when he admitted that they were no longer 'subject to the direct impact of the situation'.[4] This should not support a case for an earlier 'great divide' between the discourses of modernism and post-modernism, although most of the issues relevant to that debate are present at CIAM 8 in explicit or symptomatic forms.

The proceedings of CIAM 8 present the reader with the fascination of familiar and yet vague and imprecise terminology. The values which the conference enshrined belong to the same formation as the ones encountered in literary criticism in the mid-1960s – a seemingly arbitrary articulation of metaphysics and empiricism, the centrality of anecdote, the persistent reference to depth and duration, the assumption of shared responses – a systematic yet inconclusive discourse which at CIAM 8 oscillated between the stark simplifications of the 'Four Functions' and moments of Kiplingesque portentousness, like Maxwell Fry's exhortation: 'let us try to perfect the idea in our search for the truth of men and things'.[5]

In contrast to this, the young architects referred to by Le Corbusier as being 'in the heart of the present period' demonstrated a structuralist sensibility. Their desire to make lateral and extensive links provided the basis for communication between disciplines and institutions and the breaking up of assumed hierarchies of value in ways which conclusively rendered the humanist-visionary mode obsolete. Certainly the reaction against 'value', which is so evident in the ideas of the Independent Group and the Brutalists in Britain, can be seen as a corrective to this discourse if not a direct response to structuralist theories.

It is difficult to assess the extent to which the proceedings of a conference held in 1951 were influenced by the recent experience of wartime, or the extent to which that experience would have differential impacts on the older and younger generations of delegates. The opportunities to participate in reconstruction and the utopian potential for beginning anew have to be weighed against the impact of the erasure of place by blitz and atomic weapons and the ultimate challenge to humanist-based theories posed by the creation of non-places like Auschwitz. Yet one justification offered for the use of tower blocks and surrounding parkland was that they were less susceptible to aerial bombardment, and the spectre of future conflicts is present in many of the contributions to conference proceedings.

CIAM 8 was held in a lonely Victorian mansion at Hoddesdon to coincide with the Festival of Britain. There was no direct rail link to London at the time and, as in 1947 when the venue was Bridgwater in Somerset, there seems to have been an intention to keep delegates from the distractions of city life. This was particularly ironic in 1951, as the theme of the conference was 'The heart of the city', subtitled 'towards the humanization of urban life'.

---

4 Le Corbusier, in a letter to the Dubrovnik Conference, quoted in Kenneth Frampton, *Modern Architecture: a critical history*, London: Thames and Hudson, 1980, pp. 271–272.
5 Maxwell Fry, The idea and its realisation, in J. Tyrwhitt, J. Sert and E.N. Rogers, *op. cit.*, note 1, p. 89.

figure 5.2
FRONTISPIECE TO PART ONE:
THE PIAZETTA, VENICE, FROM CIAM 8,
THE HEART OF THE CITY, 1952

A polemical context for this theme had been set by debates on monumentality initiated during the war by J.L. Sert, Siegfried Giedion and Fernand Léger and continued at a symposium reported in the *Architectural Review* in 1948.[6] It was clear from this debate how carefully Modernist proposals needed to be weighted to avoid accusations of undemocratic functionalist solutions and it is worth bearing in mind other work, notably by Colin Rowe and Rudolph Wittkower, which served to 'humanize' modern building, as well as the numerous initiatives which looked for continuities with the Georgian and Picturesque traditions in Modernism.

The two previous post-war conferences had been held in Bridgwater in 1947 and at Bergamo in 1949. Aldo van Eyck, who was to play a key role in revising the modernist trajectory of CIAM, noted of the first post-war conference that 'the tyranny of common sense had reached its final stage' and that 'the imagination and the natural flow of existence' were beginning to emerge.[7] Certainly there was a widespread awareness that what Giedion referred to as 'the spring cleaning'[8] phase of modernism was over, and at Bergamo the agenda was focused on the historic centres of cities, although a great deal

6 Gregor Paulsson, Henry-Russell Hitchcock, William Holford, Siegfried Giedion, Walter Gropius, Lucio Costa, Alfred Roth, In search of a new monumentality, *Architectural Review*, 104, no. 621, September 1948.
7 Aldo van Eyck, quoted in Oscar Newman, *CIAM '59 in Otterlo*, London: Alec Tiranti, 1961, pp. 26–27.
8 Siegfried Giedion, The heart of the city: a summing up, in J. Tyrwhitt, J. Sert and E.N. Rogers, *op. cit.*, note 1, p. 163.

figure 5.3
HYDE PARK ORATORS, LONDON.
'FREE THINKING DID NOT FIND ITS SHAPE IN RURAL REGIONS, NEITHER IS IT A PRODUCT OF PRESS, RADIO OR TELEVISION, IT OWES MORE TO THE CAFE TABLE THAN TO THE SCHOOL, AND THOUGH OTHER MEANS HAVE HELPED, IT WAS MAINLY SPREAD BY THE SPOKEN WORD AND BORN IN THE MEETING PLACES OF THE PEOPLE' J.L. SERT, P. 8

of attention was given to 'The Grid' drawn up by the French 'Ascoral' group under the supervision of Le Corbusier. This 'thinking tool' was to be used in conjunction with the key principles of town planning established at CIAM 4 in 1933 – the functional zoning of city plans and high-rise, widely spaced apartment blocks.

In 1951, J.M. Richards recalled, 'the world of the architect had suddenly expanded to embrace that of the town planner and even the sociologist'.[9] The enhanced scope of practice which had been anticipated by CIAM and was an assumption of much avant-garde practice before the war was a major preoccupation of CIAM 8. The opening addresses by Sert and Giedion commented on the new internationalism of the conference, which now extended beyond European and American domination, albeit patronizingly presented by Giedion as 'the emerging consciousness of remote people'.[10] Although examples of the work of CIAM members were drawn from Morocco, Peru, India and Colombia, the main exemplars of the hearts of cities were Mediterranean and overwhelmingly taken from Italian sources. (Tellingly, when the young Lawrence Alloway was accused by the critic Basil Taylor of defecting to America in the 1960s, he accused the previous generation of cultural critics of 'defecting to the Mediterranean'.) Of the examples, the most conspicuous was Venice's Piazza San Marco – a pedestrian precinct par excellence – which figured as endplate and frontispiece (Figure 5.2). The almost universally perceived priorities for humanizing the city core were the careful control of commercialism and the banishment of traffic.

Considerations of the politics of urban space expounded in the conference were focussed on the promotion of democratic participation and the construction of contexts which would stimulate citizens to activity. The anxiety this was intended to remedy was the fear of mass communications and the passive states of acquiescence they were assumed to produce. Sert suggested that 'lack of civic centres leads to the rule of the few'.[11] Many of the images which accompanied the texts offered long shots of informal

9 J.M. Richards, *Memoirs of an Unjust Fella*, London: Weidenfeld and Nicholson, 1980, p.192.
10 Siegfried Giedion, The heart of the city: a summing up, in J. Tyrwhitt, J. Sert and E.N. Rogers, *op. cit.*, note 1, p. 162.
11 J.L. Sert, Centres of community life, in *ibid.*, p. 11.

figure 5.4
FROM J.L. SERT'S INTRODUCTORY ESSAY: 'CENTRES OF COMMUNITY LIFE',
ILLUSTRATING THE PRINCIPLE OF FREE ASSOCIATION AND SPONTANEITY FOR
'PLANNED AND UNPLANNED MEETINGS'

groups forming and dissolving. Understandably after the experience of dictatorships and war, the classification of crowds was an inevitable preoccupation, and a premium was placed on casual encounter and free speech (Figures 5.3 and 5.4). The images of meeting places simultaneously captured the hoped-for freedoms which the planners were seeking an architectural language to endorse, and which David Mellor has identified as a major thematic of the 1950s: the phenomenology of the body unsettled in space.[12]

The spatial criteria of the conference resemble the priorities established by critics for quality cinema in the immediate post-war period.[13] The new cinematic realism was conceived in terms of the establishment of shots from the point of vantage (which ensured an objective documentary account), individualized and representative images of 'ordi-

12 See David Mellor, Existentialism and post war British art, in Frances Morris, editor, *Paris Post War: art and existentialism*, London: Tate Gallery, 1993.
13 See John Ellis, Art, quality, culture: terms for a cinema in the forties and seventies, *Screen*, 19, no. 3, Autumn 1978, pp. 9–50.

57

nary people' and a narrative and deeply focused *mise en scène*. For CIAM 8 the essential humanity of 'the heart of the city' could only be secured by separating it from the architecture of work and residence. Inevitably, however, the suspicion of commercialised leisure was moderated by its place in a new definition of everyday life in the 'Free World'. One delegate mentioned the positive psychological impact of the turning on of the lights on V.E. day.[14] Sert's introduction suggested that commercial techniques could be brought into play by public art to establish new symphonic integrations for the enjoyment and education of people (Figure 5.5).[15]

figure 5.5
TIMES SQUARE, NEW YORK, 'THE NOISY HUB OF A GREAT METROPOLIS IS CLEARLY AN ORGANIC PART OF THE BIG CITY', FROM CIAM 8, *THE HEART OF THE CITY*, 1952

One contribution by Ian McCallum, titled 'Spontaneity at the Core', celebrated the 'casual commerce' which was described as a picturesque tableaux of soapbox orators, flower girls and fishmongers' blackboards.[16] These were likened, rather ambivalently, to flowers and weeds pushing their way between even the best laid paving stones.

Some of the presentations indicated that the problematic of containing space was being conceived in terms which increasingly questioned the compositional verities of Modernism. The assumption that residential problems were best solved by a combination of two- to three-storey walkups and slab blocks was presented in terms of a vague explanation that they separated families from single people and that the slabs functioned as expressions of the use of the elevator or as symbols of community. Le Corbusier had announced the death of the street[17] in 1933 and Giedion had claimed that the *rue cor-*

14 J. Tyrwhitt, J. Sert and E.N. Rogers, *op. cit.*, note 1, p. 103.
15 *Ibid.*, pp. 3–16.
16 *Ibid.*, pp. 64–66.
17 See Romy Golan, *Modernity and Nostalgia: art and politics in France between the wars*, New Haven and London: Yale University Press, 1995, in which the complex meanings of Le Corbusier's antagonism to 'the street' is explored p. 77 *passim*.

figure 5.6
AIR VIEW OF THE BOMB-DAMAGED AREAS OF THE CITY OF LONDON – NEARLY
A THIRD OF THE CITY'S ACCOMMODATION, DEMONSTRATING THE OPPORTUNITY
AVAILABLE IN 1951 FOR REBUILDING THE CORE OF LONDON

ridor belonged to the optical vision of another day;[18] and significantly, the dysfunctional street of 1951 was illustrated by the Hausmann-esque Champs Elysées. But other contributors to the conference questioned in general terms whether the life of the city was not to be found in those very streets. Some, like Jacob Bakema and Paul Wiener who gave a discordant paper on technology called 'New trends will affect the core', stressed as a characteristic of the new era a science concerned with relational and contextual issues.

Wiener's contribution introduced some of the predictive assumptions which were to be taken as axiomatic by the avant-garde of the next generation: the onset of an era of magical abundance, the 'problem' of leisure, the overthrow of the concept of property, a society where remuneration was no longer linked to effort and the new paradigm of a flow-continuous confluence of atoms, molecules and energy no longer linked to locations.[19] Ernesto Rogers cited Alexander Calder's mobiles as conceptual models of the mobile and relative which he took to be a characteristic of urban life.[20] In his summing up Giedion implicitly dismissed these indications of an emerging tolerance of relativity by suggesting that they needed to be taken under control in the interests of a need for wholeness, integration and universality.

There are indications throughout the published version of the proceedings that the problems which were being confronted exceeded the solutions that were being offered. Giedion quoted Jean-Paul Sartre to support his primitivist concept of 'bare and naked man' seeking a direct means of expression through signs and symbols, but there is no indication that Existentialism's stress on personal authority, choice and situation played any part in his thinking. The ways in which the 'needs of the people' were to be expressed provide little evidence of the dialectic demanded by Henri Lefebvre of the trivial and exceptional in daily life. Nor is there any psychogeographical sensitivity capable of conveying the 'unity of atmosphere' of various segments of the city.

18 Siegfried Giedion, *Space, Time and Architecture: the growth of a new tradition*, op. cit., note 2, pp. 465–501.
19 P.L. Wiener, New trends will affect the core, in J. Tyrwhitt, J. Sert and E.N. Rogers, *op. cit.*, note 1, pp. 81–86.
20 E.N. Rogers, in *ibid.*, pp. 72–73.

Giedion's suggestion that life fills out the plan in the way that a river occupies and shapes its bed sits uneasily with the demands of the grid and the need to 'avoid mutual interferences in the various functions of a section'. Perhaps the clearest indication of a sense of potentially disruptive opposition is Le Corbusier's 'A word to critics of the grid' in which he exhorts those critics to 'improve the grid by all means, but do not smash it'.[21]

Throughout the record of the proceedings, 'Humanity' and 'Mankind' were the categories which were persistently addressed. The citizen was ideally a man and reference was sometimes made to the single man as the unit of identity. The family appeared only as an entity which needed low-rise accommodation, or as an aggregate of mankind. The 1955 international photographic exhibition, 'The Family of Man', which belonged to the same ideological climate, was criticized in these terms by Roland Barthes. He saw the deployment of the term 'family' as a device for magically propagating a myth of diversity in order, through the suppression of history, to produce a spurious unity and referred to it as 'the ambiguous myth of the human community which serves as an alibi to a large part of our humanism'.[22]

Women played little part at 'the heart of the city' or at the conference itself – Jacqueline Tyrwhitt, the secretary, seems to have been the only female member of the council. Indeed one contribution suggested that a measure of the quality of humanized space is that it provided the opportunity for men to pay women compliments. Perhaps a guide to the mood of the time is supplied by Thomas Sharp who, in his 1936 survey of British planning (reprinted in 1950), consigned women to the suburbs: 'woman is by nature far more individualistic than man ... in aesthetic matters she has few of the makings of a citizen. All these qualities are reflected in a thousand Motorvilles'.[23]

The discourse of Modern Man has been extensively explored by Michael Leja, although most of his examples are taken from American middle-brow literature.[24] Leja has demonstrated the impact of a *film noir* existential mood on existing assumptions about the 'primitive' in 'man' after 1945. He has particularly stressed the alienation and fallibility which are assumed to be fundamental to membership of the 'Free World'. Some of this unease is evident in the proceedings of CIAM 8, sitting ambivalently in relation to the mood of reconstruction. Giedion noted that 'our period has lost so many of the formally accepted codes of human behaviour and human relations that a new interest has arisen in the continuity of human experience'.[25]

Certainly, a retreat from functionalist and mechanistic visions of heroic modernism had started well before the outbreak of war and the imbrications of the modern and the ver-

21 Le Corbusier, Description of the CIAM grid, Bergamo 1949, in *ibid.*, p. 175.
22 Roland Barthes, *Mythologies*, London: Paladin, 1973, p. 100
23 Thomas Sharp, *English Panorama*, London: J.M. Dent & Sons, 1936; revised edition London: Architectural Press, 1950, p. 91.
24 See Michael Leja, *Reframing Abstract Expressionism: subjectivity and painting in the 1940s*, New Haven and London: Yale University Press, 1993, Chapter 4.
25 Siegfried Giedion, Historical background to the core, in J. Tyrwhitt, J. Sert and E.N. Rogers, *op. cit.*, note 1, p. 17.

nacular are still being explored in the 1990s. The drive to discover the fundamentals of architecture and human nature was heavily invested in the post-war period of reconstruction. In the process, an attempt to install Nature at the root of History was a fundamental strategy. For CIAM 8 the 'agora', introduced by way of a quote from the work of Ortega y Gasset, was a compelling site of origin and the sense of a progressive European tradition was still strong. Giedion's category of 'bare and naked man' was consistent with a consensual strategy to conceive 'the heart of the city' as a space defined against Nature but united with it.

In 1951 Jacquetta Hawkes, advisor to the 'People of Britain' pavilion at the Festival, published *The Land* – a metaphorical expression of the need to reintegrate – in which she challenged architectural rationalism, writing:

> But with classical building Man was giving expression to that upper part of his consciousness which would cut itself more and more from its background to live in the Ionic temple of the intellect. Yet in spite of the Ionic temple, in spite even of the greater perils of the concrete office block, the most sensitive and the simplest men have never forgotten their origins, their relationship with the land.[26]

The Humanism which was at the heart of CIAM discourse was not the 'progressive Humanism' which Barthes saw as a commitment to scouring the laws and limits of Nature. It was, however, a humanism against which the various angry, existential, anthropological, new, *autre* and brutalist sensibilities of the 1950s defined themselves. The new generation of architects represented by Team X, who had not yet found their voices in Hoddesdon, attacked the mandarins of CIAM both for losing the visionary plot and for failing to understand the relationship between form and the full complexity of human need and response. Far from seeking to sustain the organism of the 'heart of the city', they interested themselves in a logic of the supplement of the things that by-passed the heart. They were interested in identity, association and solutions from below. In their reaction to the CIAM 7 report they suggested 'the short narrow street of the slum succeeds where spacious redevelopment frequently fails'.[27]

Humanism in architecture is closely associated with anthropomorphy and empathy. It assumes a unified subject and a fundamental need for compositional integrity. As it engaged with the humanistic culture of post-war Europe, it focused on a future which would see the fulfilment of human potential, a future predicated on a past of essential humanity which had to be retrieved from the superficial accumulations of everyday life. New Humanisms were being formulated after 1945. Existentialism defined itself for experience and against essence. Henri Lefebvre reacted to the structuralism of Lévi-Strauss as an episode in the history of capitalism: 'an infusion of

26 Jacquetta Hawkes, *The Land*, London: The Cresset Press, 1951.
27 Quoted in Kenneth Frampton, *op. cit.*, note 4, p. 271.

technocratic thought into the intellectual field',[28] and proposed instead a more adequate version, 'a genuine humanism ... a humanism which believes in the human because it knows it'.[29]

The 'Universal Man' for whom CIAM were planning was conjunctural in other ways. In 1950 (and again in 1951) UNESCO published statements on race and difference. 'Man' was incorporated into the discourse of science as an affirmation of the mental equality of all races and evidence of a species trait which favoured educability and co-operation. As Donna Harraway has demonstrated, at the outset of the Cold War UNESCO's social democratic 'Man' was in competition with the more aggressive and exploratory version of 'Man the Hunter' who sustained the military industrial effort. Harraway's summing up of the challenges mounted to this myth by the 1970s indicates some of the difficulties involved in sustaining a humanist analysis of urbanism. She writes:

> 'Early Man in Africa' in his 1950s and 1960s incarnations had to contend with the pretenders to humanity cast onto the surface of the earth by post colonialism, feminism and late capitalism. In his humanist guises he was assailed by post modernism in the critical disciplines that used to speak for man.[30]

Although difficulties with difference dogged CIAM 8, its internationalist perspective coincided with a continentalization of British culture of which the Festival was a foretaste. It also hinted at the encounters with the non-modern which were to become such a feature of the architectural discourse of the 1950s. The quest for a *tabula rasa* has been well documented in Parisian and New York artistic avant gardes of the post-war years.

Kristin Ross, in her analysis of French culture of that time, identifies what she describes as a Blochian theme of non-synchronicity in novels of the 1950s and 1960s.[31] In these romances of middle class life, encounters with peasants who inhabit an older economic consciousness play a significant role. Ross sees these encounters as formative of what she calls 'neo-bourgeois space'. Similar strategies are evident in seeking a heart for the city which evades contemporaneity. In Sert's introduction to the CIAM 8 proceedings he affirms that the new cores will be 'the opposite of what Main Street is today'.[32]

The fundamental assumptions of CIAM 8 with regard to planning held that the relationship between parts was crucial, that it should be formal and coherent, yet adaptable and, importantly, that it should be 'organic'. Sert suggested that this was only achievable by rigorous separation: 'when a city is replanned it is divided into zones of different land uses ... the resulting pattern should then become organic'.[33] Throughout the pro-

28 Kristin Ross, *Fast Cars, Clean Bodies: decolonisation and the re-ordering of French culture*, Cambridge, MA and London: MIT Press, 1995.
29 Henri Lefebvre, *Critique of Everyday Life*, 1945, trans. London: Verso, 1991, p. 252.
30 Donna Harraway, *Primate Visions*, London: Routledge, 1989, p. 187.
31 See Kristin Ross, *op. cit.*, note 28.
32 J.L. Sert, in J. Tyrwhitt, J. Sert and E.N. Rogers, *op. cit.*, note 1, p. 6.
33 *Ibid.*, p. 11.

ceedings of the conference there is a tension between, on the one hand, a sense of cities as embodying the human, and on the other, a sense of their inherent inhumanity – an inhumanity explored in terms of Georg Simmel's assumptions that they lead to langour and indifference.[34] Ordering seems to have been the remedy.

Exploring the notion of the 'organic' is essential to an understanding of humanism in architectural thinking. For CIAM 8, the organic implied a relation to human needs and scale, and also a corrective to the programmatic phase of modernism deemed no longer suitable for democracies. As such, it differed from the sense in which F.R. Leavis used the term from the 1930s onwards to describe a culture destroyed by the 'organized' State. Bruno Zevi, in 1950, sought to analyse the term and proposed it as corrective to the fundamental contradiction in early modernism between the rational utilitarian and the philosophy of purism.[35] He also posed the organic against the two-fold corruptions of Fascism – monumentalism and provincialism. In the light of his analysis England fared best. England not only resisted Fascism but was resistant to 'genius', preferring instead to concentrate on a decent way of life and a constantly improving sequence of buildings. Whereas for Giedion the organic was opposed to the rational and geometric, for Zevi it was a sign of resistance to any aesthetic dogmatism. Organic architecture could therefore describe both processes of ordering and of *laissez-faire*.

The predicament for CIAM 8 lay partly in its lofty conceptualization of the role of the architect/planner. Jos Boys has recently suggested the continuing dangers of their disinterested high-mindedness: 'the architectural establishment in seeking to stand above the cash nexus, the market and "fashion" had developed a body of knowledge which centred on offering representational solutions to economic, social and political inequalities'.[36] The centrality of 'Man', both metaphorically and actually, was subsequently countered by a shift in attention to family and kinship and to exemplars drawn from architecture without architects, nomads, space travel and even Las Vegas.

In 1959 at the Otterlo CIAM conference, organised by the younger generation of architects, Team X, Giancarlo de Carlo recalled CIAM 8 as 'such a huge amount of inaccurate statements and idle nonsense that on re-reading the report today we wonder how it is possible for so many serious minded persons ... to put up with them'.[37] By the late 1950s matters arising from the *dérive*, the 'long front of culture', the 'as found' aesthetic and the 'urban fix' had consigned the ordering of functions for the human spirit to history. The narrow line 'between chaos and the slave state'[38] which the post-war architects had regarded themselves as treading had broadened out into a pluralist practice.

34 George Simmel, The metropolis and mental life, in Albert N. Cousins and Hans Nagpaul, *Urban Man and Society: a reader in urban sociology*, New York: Alfred A. Knopf, 1970, pp. 136–144.
35 Bruno Zevi, *Towards an Organic Architecture*, London: Faber, 1950.
36 Jos Boys, Neutral gazes and knowable objects, in Katerina Ruedi, Sarah Wigglesworth and Duncan McCorquodale, *Desiring Practices*, London: Black Dog, 1996, p. 41.
37 Oscar Newman, *op. cit.*, note 7, p. 86.
38 L.T.C. Rolt, *High Horse Riderless*, London: George Allen & Unwin, 1947, p. 84.

CIAM 8, trapped in an attempt to compromise the everyday practices of city dwellers with universal solutions, found it difficult to account for what was political and spontaneous in urban culture, or to take into account what Jane Jacobs at the end of the decade was referring to as 'the unaverage',[39] or to appreciate the overlay of function in a single territory which Richard Sennett defined as the essential characteristic of a city.[40]

Shortly after Hoddesdon and before the next and divisive CIAM conference at Aix-en-Provence, the role of the planner in Britain (which had been likened by one of the delegates to that of a dietitian)[41] changed again as the likelihood of achieving a de-commercialized centre became more remote. In 1953 the *Parallel of Life and Art* exhibition at the Institute of Contemporary Arts – incongruously opened by Herbert Read, who embodied for the young artists of the Independent Group the humanist values which they were attempting to supplant – provided a preview of interdisciplinary, de-hierarchicalized units of information purposefully contrived to have no organic rationale.

It is tempting to see the fate of CIAM 8 as evidence of a grand narrative succumbing to complexity and contradiction. Similar faultlines were appearing at the same time in British drama, film, literature and scientific discourse. The loss of values or a questioning of the concept of value were hotly contested issues in the cultural politics of the period. It is interesting to note the role played by 'the street' in architectural polemics since then. The street had fulfilled most of the requirements sought from the 'heart'. It has figured as an arena for subcultures and a sign of credibility, particularly in association with an emphasis on marginality and nomadic and heterotopian moods. In Paolo Portoghesi's introductory essay to the first Venice Architectural Biennale in 1980,[42] the street famously figured as the instrument for the reintegration of the urban organism.

Perhaps the most constructive way of rethinking the troubled discourse of CIAM 8 is as part of a dialectic between the claims of a return to stable or absolute verities and an opposing desire to recognize a field of competing values. If we can assume that there is not a procession of more and more adequate theories each replacing the other, it is interesting to contemplate what might have been lost in the rejection of humanism. It is clear that the dominance of structuralist and post-structuralist theory has, to some extent, repressed 'value' at a time when it has become a key issue in everyday politics. Clearly there is no way back to the essence and indifference of the early 1950s, but the question of whether Main Street is nearly right is still an open one.

---

39 Jane Jacobs, The kind of problem a city is, in Albert N. Cousins and Hans Nagpaul, *op. cit.*, note 34, p. 436.
40 Richard Sennett, *The Fall of Public Man*, Cambridge: Cambridge University Press, 1976, p. 297
41 G. Scott Williamson, The individual and the community, in J. Tyrwhitt, J. Sert and E.N. Rogers, *op. cit.*, note 1, pp. 30–35.
42 Paolo Portoghesi, The end of prohibitionism, in Gabriella Borsano, *The Presence of the Past*, Venice: La Biennale di Venezia, 1980, pp. 9–13.

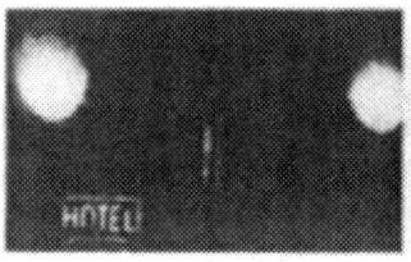
HOTEL

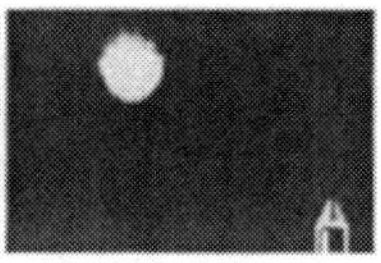

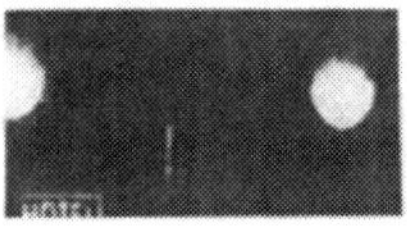

#06
IAN HORTON: PERVASION OF THE PICTURESQUE
ENGLISH ARCHITECTURAL AESTHETICS AND LEGISLATION, 1945-1965

Non-Plan solutions of the 1960s have generally been acknowledged as a rejection of the rigid compartmentalization and prescriptiveness of planning strategies promoted by the State. However, if the debate concerning Non-Plan is contextualized it is evident that such alternative proposals were not as oppositional, in terms of broad aesthetic considerations, as their promoters believed. To explore this issue it is essential to examine government policy in the post-war period as most accounts which focus on planning legislation fail to account for the ramifications in terms of architectural aesthetics.[1]

To rectify this situation it is necessary to look at the important role played by the Royal Institute of British Architects (RIBA) in assisting the government to frame both planning controls and prescriptive advice on architectural matters. An analysis of this material, unexpectedly, shows that the dominant aesthetic promoted by both the government and the RIBA was a variant on the English Picturesque tradition.

This is surprising as concurrent debate in the architectural press promoting the Picturesque aesthetic has usually been regarded as an oppositional force challenging government legislation and the dominant planning ideology. Clearly such accounts simplify this debate and fail to accommodate the notion that Picturesque aesthetics pervaded most aspects of post-war architecture. To investigate the complexity of these issues it is necessary to examine Picturesque theory and practice in both its simple and complex forms: as an evocation of pastoral and rural associations, and as an elaborate aesthetic employing mixture, variety and connection. Through this analysis it can then be shown that this aesthetic has implications for the 'radical' solutions outlined by advocates of Non-Plan, many of which employed the Picturesque aesthetic in a complex form.

Given the importance of the RIBA in advising the government on architectural matters it must be acknowledged that the Institute needed to assert control over planning issues because of a perceived threat to the profession's autonomy – a factor which led it to take the protectionist measure of supporting the statutory regulation of architects in the 1930s.[2] The danger faced was seen to come from two directions. Firstly, it came from a growth in the technological solutions to architectural problems which could be handled by structural engineers – a situation which became particularly evident in the 1940s and

---

1 J. Punter, A history of aesthetic control: part 2, 1953–85, *Town Planning Review*, 58, no. 5, pp. 29–62. This is the only study that specifically focuses on this issue but it does not give either a detailed outline of the actual legislation or its ramifications.
2 B. Kaye, *The Development of the Architectural Profession in Britain*, London: Allen and Unwin, 1960, pp. 147–153. This provides a clear and concise account of these events as does H. Barnes, The RIBA and statutory regulation of architects, in J.A. Gotch (editor), *A History of the RIBA 1835–1935*, London: RIBA Publications, 1936, pp. 68–84.

1950s as industrialized building methods were promoted as the solution to building shortages.³ Secondly, the threat came from the growth of town planning as an independent profession, drawing on a wide range of expertise from outside traditional architectural discourse. This was made apparent in 1932 when, for the first time, the Town Planning Institute was empowered to examine candidates without them first having passed examinations set by architectural institutions.⁴ As a result of these pressures the RIBA increasingly felt that architectural aesthetics was the only field in which it could be considered the dominant force.

Since 1914 the RIBA has been consulted by successive governments of all political allegiances in matters of architectural legislation and its involvement can be traced by examining such legislation (Table 6.1).⁵ The important factor to be noted from this list is the concentration of activity in the period 1942 to 1947. Post-war planning was actually formulated during the second half of the war, which is not surprising considering that many buildings had been damaged, destroyed or fallen into disrepair owing to the ongoing hostilities and that reconstruction was an important national issue. In this period of coalition government and focus on the war effort the detail of planning legislation was formulated by civil servants. Instead of facing opposition from political parties, the fledgling Ministry of Town and Country Planning faced only the constraining force of the treasury and other government departments. These factors explain why legislative changes were so sweeping and passed into law with little dilution of power or intent.⁶

The main thrust of these measures was the use of zoning to control all future planning schemes. This was outlined very clearly in a government White Paper, *The Control of Land Use*, published in 1944:

> Provision for the right use of land ... is an essential requirement of the government's programme of post-war reconstruction. New houses ...; the new layout of areas devastated by enemy action or blighted by reason of age or bad living conditions; the new schools which will be required ...; the balanced distribution of industry ...; the requirements of sound nutrition and of a healthy and well-balanced agriculture ...; a new and safer highway system ... all these related parts of a single reconstruction programme involve the use of land, and it is essential that their various claims on land should be harmonized so as to ensure, for the people of this country, the greatest possible measure of individual well being and national prosperity.⁷

The White Paper summarized the Town and Country Planning Acts of 1943 and 1944, with suggestions for improvement and implementation. These Acts, the 1944 White Paper and the Uthwatt Report of 1942, influenced the framing of the complex Town and

---

3 J.M. Richards, *An Introduction to Modern Architecture*, Harmondsworth: Pelican, 1940. This was the first populist account to promote industrialized building techniques in England.
4 G. Cherry, *Cities and Plans: the shaping of urban Britain in the nineteenth and twentieth centuries*, London: Edward Arnold, 1988.
5 The increasing importance of the RIBA as an advisory body is outlined in A. Mace, *The RIBA: a guide to its archive and history*, London: RIBA Publications, 1986, pp. 211–212. For a listing of Acts of Parliament relating to architectural matters see A. Ravetz, *The Government of Space: town planning in modern society*, London: Faber and Faber, 1986, pp. 149–150.
6 G. Cherry, *op. cit.*, note 4, p. 149.
7 *The Control of Land Use*, Cmd 6537, London, HMSO, 1944.

Country Planning Act of 1947. Under this Act every potential development had to secure planning permission. If granted, the landowners had to pay a development charge rated and collected by a Central Land Board. If permission was refused then landowners were not entitled to the development compensation they received under the previous system. The result of these changes was that any future development was to be governed by plans produced by local authorities that had to be passed by central government.

These factors limited private enterprise in building and promoted State control of architectural matters. Planning was controlled by partitioning land into differentiated activity zones such as residential, commercial, industrial, agricultural and recreational spaces. This zoning affected aesthetics by denying an admixture of different building types; however, the 1947 Act was more remarkable for its depth of financial consideration and lack of advice concerning the appearance of new developments. Only 6 of the 120 sections of the Act related to the external appearance of buildings. Two sections were concerned with the preservation of buildings of special historic or architectural interest. This was related to wider planning concerns in that all new developments should take account of such existing buildings and permission be denied when the existing character of sites would be damaged. Two other sections of the Act concerning external appearance were limiting controls in regard to advertisements on buildings. As was the case with advice regarding buildings of special interest, the Act was vague and open to interpretation. The final two sections related to external appearance had nothing to do with buildings themselves but were advisory measures concerning the preservation of existing trees in new development areas.[8]

The 1947 Act contained nothing that related directly to architectural aesthetics, so in order to explore the issue of aesthetics it is necessary to look at the activities of the RIBA as an advisory body (Table 6.2). The planning committees of the RIBA were effectively the same body throughout the period and changes in name reflected changes in external circumstances. The inclusion of slum clearance in the committee's title in 1936 was a consequence of the Housing Act of 1936 which gave local authorities more powers in this area. During the war it was renamed the Reconstruction Committee and was assisted by the Central Advisory Committee on National Planning. Together these committees reflected the concerns of the White Paper of 1944 and so their decisions were in accord with government policy.

The Town and Country Planning and Housing Committee that sat between 1944 and 1959 also supported government legislation. Subjects covered in its meetings included: control of land use, distribution of industry and development areas, road design and layout and, of course, town and country planning legislation. In addition to the subjects already noted it discussed matters directly related to architectural aesthetics including the control of elevations, design of buildings, control of advertisements and design of electrical signs. In these instances the committee agreed with government

---

8 *Town and Country Planning Act 1947*, 10 and 11 GEO. 6 CH. 51, London: HMSO, 1947.

policy and did not wish to see rigid legislation. It supported the notion of considering each case on its own merits in the context of the local environment and believed that control was possible through advisory bodies attached to local planning authorities.[9]

As early as 1929 the RIBA, in conjunction with the Council for the Preservation of Rural England, had formed the Control of Elevations Joint Committee to deal with such matters (Table 6.3). Its concerns were to secure means for ensuring that the elevations and siting of new buildings were in accord with their surroundings and that alterations to existing buildings of interest were controlled by an independent body. It was replaced in 1933 by the Central Committee for the Architectural Advisory Panels. These panels were set up as a consequence of the 1932 Town and Country Planning Act which gave central government the powers to insist that local planning authorities appointed panels with architect members to advise on the aesthetic merits of submitted designs. This committee was originally formed by members of the RIBA and the Council for the Preservation of Rural England but, when it disbanded in 1978, it included representatives from fifteen other bodies including the Town Planning Institute and the Institute of Building. During the period in question the committee's membership included the leading pre-war planning theorists Stanley Adshead and Patrick Abercrombie. The latter also had a major influence on post-war planning, as his 1944 Greater London Plan was adopted as a model by many local authorities for their own development plans.[10]

The Central Committee for the Architectural Advisory Panels also advised government on the 1947 Town and Country Planning Act, the 1950 Schuster Report on the qualification of planners and the General Development Order, also of 1950. Although this committee commented on the use of suitable building materials, standards of house design and the layout of open spaces, it did not promote a particular aesthetic solution to these design problems. The position of the RIBA on this matter was outlined in 1949 when a statement of policy was released:

> ... the Institute is not in favour of the principle of the control of the external appearance of buildings and will endeavour to secure removal of all such control as soon as the employment of an architect in all building projects has become the established practice.[11]

From the legislation examined there is no indication that the government or the RIBA were interested in specific aesthetic solutions. However, it is possible to draw out such elements embedded in the legislation by examining prescriptive advice on architectural matters published by government agencies and written in conjunction with architects drawn from the local government advisory panels. In the immediate post-war period priority was given to house building with the government pledging to build 240 000 new dwellings a year.[12] Given that building activity was focused on housing, the most useful

9 A. Mace, *op. cit.*, note 5, pp. 215–225. This gives an outline of the minutes of meeetings and papers circulated by RIBA committees concerned with planning issues. These minutes and papers are held in the RIBA archive.
10 See minutes and papers of the Central Committee for the Architectural Advisory Panels held in the RIBA archive.
11 Minutes of meeting of the Central Committee for the Architectural Advisory Panels held on 27 October 1949, RIBA archive.
12 G. Cherry, *op. cit.*, note 4, pp. 151–154.

source materials for investigating prescriptive advice are the *Housing Manual* of 1944 and its companion volume and supplements published by the government between 1949 and 1953.[13] These were intended as exemplars of good practice for both local authority architects and private developers. Each manual covered three main areas. The first was general advice on the type of accommodation to be provided, economic use of sites and materials and recommended layouts for estates. A second area was technical advice refining economic use of materials with reference to British Standards and building regulations. A third section consisted of photographs of recent houses and flats, the majority built by local authorities, which were considered to be examples of good practice.

The manuals were consistent in that all recommended the employment of architects on housing projects. The 1944 manual stated that:

> Successive Ministers of Health have drawn attention to the importance of employing qualified architects on housing work ... It is essential that the housing schemes promoted by local authorities should set a good standard for the country, as many have already done, and that this standard should apply, not only to accommodation and construction which can largely be prescribed, but also to questions of arrangement, taste and harmony with the surroundings, which depend largely on professional knowledge and its right application. The services of a qualified architect should therefore be secured by local authorities for their housing schemes.[14]

The manuals also stressed the importance of accommodating existing trees within new designs, drawing attention to the provisions of the Town and Country Planning Act of 1947. The 1944 manual included a photograph of Welwyn Garden City titled 'Division of a building line to preserve an existing tree' (Figure 6.1).[15] The 1949 manual was more evocative and the titles of supporting illustrations included, 'Forest trees of the old hedgerow retained' and 'Terraces with parkland character retained', both titles highlighting the importance of Romantic rural associations.[16] From the first the Picturesque aesthetic had utilized associational values to evoke a rural heritage under threat. The retention of trees had been advised by Uvedale Price in 1798 when commenting on the Picturesque aesthetic. In his opinion this prevented ribbon development and the employment of symmetry, therefore making it possible to retain some of the original character of the site.[17]

The government's housing manuals were also consistent regarding the type of accommodation to be provided. The 1944 manual stated that:

13 Ministry of Health, *Housing Manual*, London, HMSO, 1944. Ministry of Health and Works, *Housing Manual*, London, HMSO, 1949. Ministry of Local Government and Planning, *Housing Manual Supplement*, London, HMSO, 1951. Ministry of Local Government and Planning, *Housing Manual Supplement*, London, HMSO, 1953.
14 *Housing Manual*, 1944, ibid., pp. 9–10.
15 Ibid., p. 55.
16 *Housing Manual*, 1949, op. cit., note 13, pp. 124–125.
17 U. Price, *An Essay on the Picturesque as Compared with the Sublime and the Beautiful, and on the Use of Studying Pictures for the Purpose of Improving Real Landscape*, Hereford, 1798. For an examination of these issues see C. Hussey, *The Picturesque: studies in a point of view*, London: G.P. Putnam, 1927, pp. 204–206.

The great majority of the new houses built by local authorities will be of two storeys. Hitherto the semi-detached pair has been the type most usually adopted. This type has been, and will probably continue to be, generally preferred. The great difficulty in developing an estate of semi-detached houses is to avoid the monotonous repetition of identical units and the consequent lack of repose and interest, which is specially marked where hipped roofs are much used. These defects may largely be avoided by skilful grouping and by linking blocks by use of outbuildings and occasional curtain walls. The use of longer blocks and terraces, besides being more economical in construction as well as road and service works, gives much greater scope for an orderly architectural treatment, and enables a wider variety to be obtained between street and street.[18]

This statement, and the recommendations to retain existing landscape elements reflected, unconsciously, the Picturesque aesthetic as developed in the eighteenth century in the writings of both Uvedale Price and Richard Payne Knight with their focus on mixture, variety and connection.[19] Uvedale Price's interest in these issues has been examined in detail by Sidney Robinson:

The balance between parts and whole is largely achieved by means of 'small connecting ties and bonds.' If the parts of a composition are to retain their identities, then the connections with other parts must be achieved by means of elements that function specifically as linkages. However trifling these bonds may appear in scenery, 'they are those by which the more considerable objects in all their different arrangements are combined, and on which their balance, their contrast, and diversity, as well as union depends.'[20]

This passage parallels the recommendations contained in the housing manuals and this Picturesque aesthetic was also evident in the layouts and buildings used in the manuals as examples. In 1944 the layouts were rigid grids derived from pre-war examples where the uniformity was only broken by the retention of existing trees (Figure 6.2). In contrast, the 1949 manual included a development plan for a new estate where informality replaced such rigidity (Figure 6.3). This layout conformed to the Picturesque aesthetic by containing a variety of different housing types mixed across the site linked by a combination of curved and straight roads and paths. Three major roads led to the heart of the development with one curving across the slight gradient of the site. This arrangement was irregular but the whole was dominated by an encircling ring road which set its boundary and highlighted the zoning of the site. These points are reinforced if the plan is examined in relation to photographs included to illustrate a model made of the estate (Figure 6.4). The caption to the first photograph suggested that the curve of the road was determined initially by the retention of a line of trees. The caption to the second photograph referred to an informal arrangement of terraces. Both statements stress the Picturesque notions behind such arrangements.

18 *Housing Manual,* 1944, *op. cit.,* note 13, p. 15.
19 See U. Price, *op. cit.,* note 17, and R.P. Knight, *An Analytical Inquiry Into the Principles of Taste,* London: T. Payne, 1808. For an analysis of connection and mixture as essential characteristics of the Picturesque see S.K. Robinson, *Inquiry into The Picturesque,* Chicago: University of Chicago Press, 1991.
20 S.K. Robinson, *op. cit.,* note 19, p. 123.

figure 6.1
PHOTOGRAPH OF AN ESTATE AT WELWYN GARDEN CITY FROM THE
HOUSING MANUAL, 1944, TITLED 'DIVISION OF A BUILDING LINE TO
PRESERVE AN EXISTING TREE'

These themes were also present in a second series of photographs illustrating the model (Figure 6.5). The captions to the first two photographs focused on the central area as the symbolic heart of the estate, conjuring images of an idyllic rural past in imitation of the village green, an image reinforced by the inclusion of allotments and the adjoining market gardens. As well as containing a church, schools, public house and park, this central area contained a community centre adapted from an existing building. The retention of existing buildings such as the church and community centre was in accordance with government legislation. It is worth noting that Price had also recommended the retention of old buildings, for their associational value, when examining Picturesque qualities in landscape design.[21] The apparent licence of these recommendations actually contained its own restrictions. For example, by including the community centre and nursery it is possible that the housing manuals were attempting to reconcile the traditional values of village life with the creation of a Welfare State. This sense of restriction is emphasized by the caption to the final photograph which referred to the retention of trees as a barrier to traffic and industry. However, it can also be considered as a form of containment emphasizing the enforced zoning of the site.

This informal approach to planning was retained in the 1953 supplement to the manuals. The conventional layout of an estate contained the same curved road system and was built on a slight gradient (Figure 6.6). The symbolic heart was removed to the outskirts in this proposal but still contained the same ingredients with the community centre replaced by the more traditional church hall. This layout was followed by other potential arrangements with different means of access. One utilized increased footpath

21 C. Hussey, *op. cit.*, note 17, p. 204.

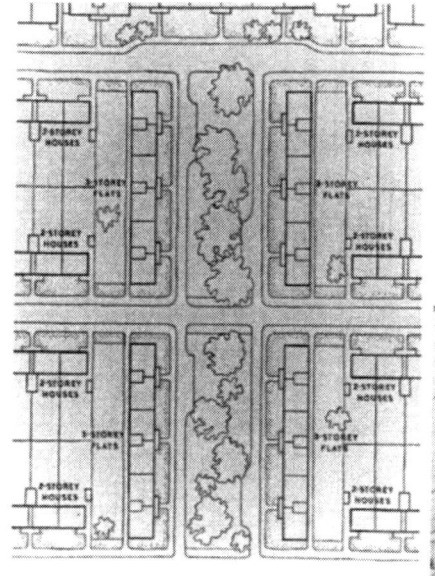

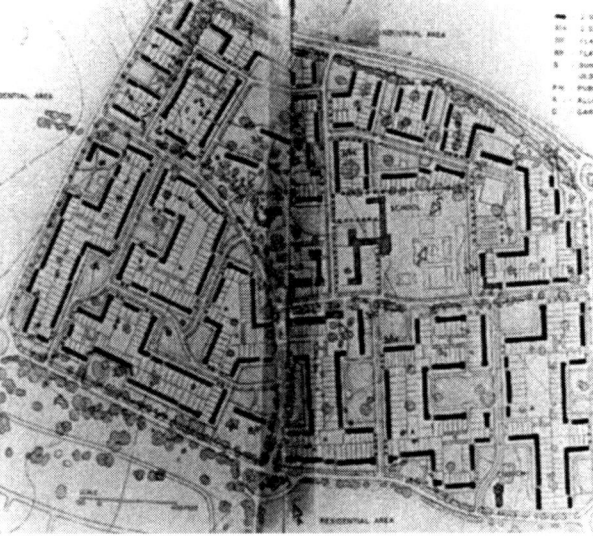

top figure 6.2
'HOUSES AND FLATS' LAYOUT FROM THE *HOUSING MANUAL*, 1944

right figure 6.3
'LAYOUT FOR A NEW RESIDENTIAL AREA' FROM THE *HOUSING MANUAL*, 1949

access to houses, a device that gave a higher population density but meant space reductions in the accommodation and gardens (Figure 6.7). In all these alternatives the basic principles remained the same: life centred around a symbolic communal area, allotments were included at the fringes and existing trees defined the main roads and boundaries of the site.

These higher density levels were also reflected in the photographic examples of the 1953 manual; pre-war Neo-Georgian and Arts and Crafts now being replaced by more multi-storey flats and maisonettes with sparse detailing. One example showed flats at Elstree captioned as belonging to a new tradition (Figure 6.8). This new tradition appeared to utilize non-traditional building materials but this was in fact a rendered brick construction. The design retained an existing tree by the setback of one of the blocks, a bland solution when compared with the example from 1944 where the existing tree was incorporated by the informal device of breaking the building line.

All these manuals referred to flat living and high-rise solutions but the latter were seen, at least initially, as a minor consideration. The 1944 manual stated that,

> While the great majority of people prefer to live in houses with gardens there is likely to be in any large community a minority who prefer to live in flats, e.g. single persons and some childless couples or families without young children.[22]

The 1949 manual echoed this sentiment but was more pragmatic about the situation and its comments appear to be almost an admission of failure:

22 *Housing Manual*, 1944, *op. cit.*, note 13, p. 15.

A STUDY FOR THE LAY-OUT OF A NEW RESIDENTIAL AREA
FIGS. 5 to 9 illustrate views from the model of the lay-out shown in Fig. 4.

FIG. 5. From point 'A' on plan—The entrance to the residential area showing an eight-storey block of flats grouped with two-storey terrace houses and bungalows. A belt of existing trees is preserved.

FIG. 6. From point 'B' on plan—An informal arrangement of interrelated squares in which long terraces are used.

FIG. 7. From point 'C' on plan—View of the local centre in which public buildings and shops are grouped with three-storey houses and blocks of flats.

FIG. 8. From point 'D' on plan—View of the local park and centre. Parkland encloses an existing building retained as a community centre and two new three-storey blocks of flats.

FIG. 9. From point 'E' on plan—Light traffic lanes giving access from within the estate to houses adjoining a principal traffic road. The estate is shielded from traffic noise and the industrial area by an existing belt of trees serving also as a windbreak.

left figure 6.4 and right figure 6.5
PHOTOGRAPHS OF A MODEL CREATED TO ILLUSTRATE THE 'LAYOUT OF A NEW RESIDENTIAL AREA' FROM THE *HOUSING MANUAL*, 1949

There is no really satisfactory substitute for a house with a garden for families with young children, but in most high-density areas the provision of a house for all such families will be impracticable. To enable as large a number of two- or three-storey houses as possible to be built in such areas, the blocks of flats in them should be high. Where families with children cannot be provided with houses, they should be offered accommodation on the lower floors of blocks of flats or maisonettes.[23]

Given that the manuals were promoting a Picturesque aesthetic with rural associations it is not surprising that the prescribed layouts included few blocks of flats, a situation that was mirrored in the photographic examples included in the manuals. Of forty-eight examples in the 1944 manual only six were for blocks of flats, three of three storeys and three of five storeys. In the 1949 manual of eighty-six examples only sixteen were for blocks of flats or maisonettes. The majority of these were of three or four storeys with one seven-storey block, two eight-storey blocks and only one of ten storeys. None of these flats or maisonettes utilized an industrialized building system and the manuals on the whole ignored non-traditional building methods. There was no mention of the subject in the 1944 manual and in the 1949 manual there was only one page on the subject in the main text with seven examples for houses included in the illustrated examples. The text did, however, encourage the use of prefabrication for internal fittings and finishing, if not for the main fabric of the building.

23 *Housing Manual*, 1949, *op. cit.*, note 13, p. 82.

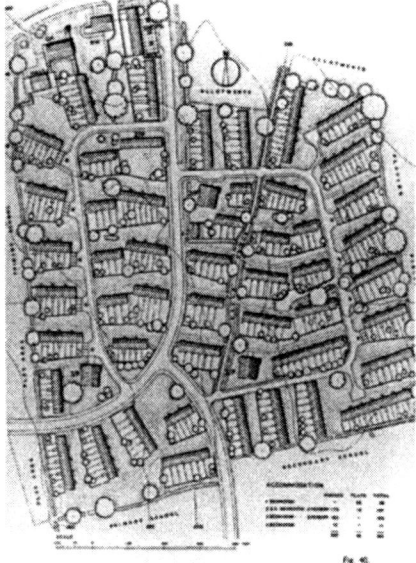

figure 6.6
'CONVENTIONAL LAYOUT FOR A NEW ESTATE'
FROM THE *HOUSING MANUAL SUPPLEMENT,* 1953

figure 6.7
'LAYOUT FOR A NEW ESTATE WITH DOUBLE ACCESS FOOTPATHS' FROM THE *HOUSING MANUAL SUPPLEMENT,* 1953

Apart from being the implicit aesthetic promoted by government and the RIBA the Picturesque informed concurrent debate in the architectural press. The *Architectural Review* provided a forum for this debate from the 1930s onwards while also promoting International Modernism. This debate started under the assistant editorship of John Betjeman between 1930 and 1935, when he gave equal coverage to both Modernist and traditional architecture in the selection of essays and juxtaposition of photographs.[24] The journal continued to promote Picturesque values in the early 1940s and as early as 1944 one member of its editorial board, H. de Cronin Hastings, was promoting Sharawaggi, a transliteration of the Chinese term for irregular gardening, as a new theory for urban design.[25] This approach was also promoted by Pevsner, co-editor with Hastings, in a number of articles on the English Picturesque landscape tradition which were additionally critical of government planning policy. Pevsner believed the existing legislation was restrictive and unwieldy but he failed to recognize the Picturesque principles underlying the prescriptive advice provided by the government and the RIBA.[26] Using the Picturesque to criticize government policy soon became a central issue for the journal and in 1946 the ardent Modernist

24 K. Hiscock, Modernism and 'English' tradition: Betjeman at the *Architectural Review.* Paper delivered at the Association of Art Historians annual conference April 1998. Betjeman continued to promote such values after 1935 as editor of the Shell Guide series.
25 H. de Cronin Hastings, Exterior furnishing or Sharawaggi: the art of making urban landscape, *Architectural Review,* 95, 1944, p. 5.
26 For a listing of Pevsner's articles and his involvement in the debate concerning the Picturesque and Modernist architecture in the 1940s and 1950s, see R. Banham, Revenge of the Picturesque: English architectural polemics, 1945–1965, in J. Summerson (editor), *Concerning Architecture,* London: Allen Lane, 1968.

figure 6.8
PHOTOGRAPH OF AN ESTATE AT ELSTREE FROM THE *HOUSING MANUAL SUPPLEMENT*, 1953, TITLED 'A NEW TRADITION SCHEME OF THREE-STOREY FLATS AT ELSTREE'

J.M. Richards, another co-editor along with Pevsner and Hastings, published *The Castles on the Ground*, a study of the English suburb focused on the Romantic rural associations of informal gardens.[27]

In 1949 Hastings dealt with contradictions in the journal's editorial policy by reconciling Picturesque aesthetics with International Modernism in an article titled 'Townscape'.[28] The opening passages of this article noted the relationship between English Picturesque traditions and political freedom, in contrast with continental examples. This section concluded with the observation that the Picturesque was the only original contribution made to aesthetic theory by England and was indeed a national characteristic. These comments on national character were followed by an analysis of the development of Picturesque theory by Price and Knight, noting their opposition to any absolute aesthetic standards and the overall belief that the Picturesque was established in relations of differences. In this phrase he attempted to distance the Picturesque from its Romantic rural associations and noted the importance of the more abstract notions of mixture and connection, which had informed this aesthetic from the outset. Hastings linked this theoretical position to concurrent needs concerning the overt stylization of International Modernism, which had split into two factions: the rational or Classic as exemplified by Le Corbusier, and the organic or Romantic as exemplified by Frank Lloyd Wright. Hastings then proposed an investigation of the English architectural tradition which could inform planning solutions while still utilizing industrialized building methods. To this end the article concluded with photographic examples of the Picturesque drawn from English cities, towns and villages.

Townscape became an important issue for the journal and many articles on the subject followed.[29] Pevsner was a leading advocate of this planning philosophy and in 1956 published *The Englishness of English Art*, which was dedicated to Hastings and concluded with a chapter on the Picturesque.[30] In this he praised the Alton Estate at Roehampton as an example of Picturesque principles reconciled with the industrialized building

27 J.M. Richards, *The Castles on the Ground*, London: Architectural Press, 1946.
28 I. de Wolfe [H. de Cronin Hastings], Townscape, *Architectural Review*, 106, 1949, pp. 355–363. This article was published under the pseudonym I. de Wolfe but it was revealed by Betjeman that this was in fact Hastings in an interview broadcast on Independent Television on 29 July 1967. See R. Banham, *op. cit.*, note 26, p. 267.
29 For a detailed analysis of this approach to planning and a listing of related *Architectural Review* articles see W.M. Whistler and D. Reed, *Townscape as a Philosophy of Urban Design*, Monticello: Council of Planning Librarians, 1983 and R. Maxwell, An eye for an I, *Architectural Design*, 46, 1976, pp. 534–536.
30 N. Pevsner, *The Englishness of English Art*, London: The Architectural Press, 1956.

systems of Modernism. In contrast, when the government finally supported non-traditional building methods in the 1950s, they did so without raising aesthetic questions, as they saw political and economic advantages that could be accommodated within the framework they had prescribed in the previous decade. As Banham noted, in his 1968 article 'Revenge of the Picturesque: English architectural polemics, 1945–1965', Townscape principles were initially opposed by a younger generation of architects still enamoured with the functional and modular aesthetic of International Modernism. This opposition was, however, short lived and by the early 1950s these architects – the Smithsons, Stirling and Gowan, Llewelyn-Davies and Weeks – were producing designs displaying Picturesque characteristics.[31]

This is not to suggest that government legislation met with universal approval even though it promoted the Picturesque aesthetic. In 1955 the *Architectural Review* published a special issue, *Outrage*, which focused on planning issues. Under the influence of Townscape principles its main areas of criticism were: the fragmentation of planning control, the inflexibility of zoning and bye-law regulations, and the failure of advertisement control.[32] This was followed by another special issue, *Counter Attack Against Subtopia*, in 1957, which focused on the retention of aesthetic controls and the removal of exemptions from development controls. In addition, it criticized the planning standards for density, daylighting and road widths as wasteful of space and administratively unwieldy.[33]

This advice went unheeded, and it was against this legislative background that the 'radical' opposition of the 1960s articulated the argument for Non-Plan. It was suggested at the outset of this study that the Picturesque aesthetic was embedded in some of these alternative planning solutions and it can be argued that they share many common qualities. The basic characteristics of the Picturesque are mixture, variety and connection, factors that Robinson considered as centring on the relation of parts:

> In the clearest possible terms, [Uvedale] Price positions his work to refer to the relationship between parts, rather than the parts for themselves. It may come as a surprise to realize that the Picturesque is not about the inherent virtues of roughness, irregularity, and abrupt variation, but about their contribution to a larger composition. Its motivation is to keep things alive by mixing in the marginal qualities, to maintain vividness, to resist the tendency for systematic application of any form of selection to become despotic.[34]

These are qualities that were manifest in Archigram projects such as Peter Cook's Plug-In City of 1964 with its underlying notions of infinite flexibility and social exchange (Figure 11.3). With its focus on compositional vividness and resistance to system, Robinson's statement could almost be perceived as a manifesto of Archigram's interests. Additionally, Archigram promoted the belief that technological solutions for architec-

31 R. Banham, *op. cit.*, note 26.
32 Ian Nairn, *Outrage*, London: The Architectural Press, 1955.
33 Ian Nairn, *Counter Attack Against Subtopia*, London: The Architectural Press, 1957.
34 Sidney Robinson, *op. cit.*, note 19, p. 27.

tural problems must account for individual freedom and provide a liberating, supportive and enabling environment. As such, they were highlighting the failure of Modernism which had become a philosophy of constraint and containment, ideas which can be linked to Robinson's comments concerning system and the despotic.[35] During the nineteenth century the Picturesque had been used as a metaphor for liberty in political debate, a factor which links this aesthetic to the ethical dimension of Archigram's theoretical stance. The relationship between liberty and the Picturesque went beyond mere rhetoric and liberty actively stood as a mediating force between licence and tyranny, much as the Picturesque itself stood between the extremes of the beautiful and the sublime. In these respects Archigram's projects were clearly utilizing, albeit unwittingly, the Picturesque aesthetic which had dominated architectural polemics over the previous twenty years.

TABLE 6.1

ACTS OF PARLIAMENT AND GOVERNMENT REPORTS RELATING TO ARCHITECTURE
1930 TO 1957

YEAR	LEGISLATION OR REPORT
1930	Housing (and Slum Clearance Act), *Greenwood Act*
1932	Town and Country Planning Act
1936	Housing Act
1938	Green Belt (London and Home Counties) Act
1942	Report of the Committee on Land Utilization in Rural Areas, *Scott Report*
1942	Report of the Expert Committee on Compensation and Betterment, *Uthwatt Report*
1943	Town and Country Planning (Interim Development) Act
1944	Town and Country Planning Act
1944	Design of Dwellings, *Dudley Report*
1945	Distribution of Industry Act
1946	New Towns Act
1947	Town and Country Planning Act
1949	Housing Act
1950	General Development Order
1950	Report of the Committee on the Qualification of Planners, *Schuster Report*
1952	Town Development Act
1957	Rent Act
1957	Housing Act

---

35 For an account of liberty and its relationship to the picturesque see *ibid*, pp. 73–89.

TABLE 6.2

RIBA COMMITTEES CONCERNED WITH GENERAL PLANNING ISSUES 1930 TO 1957

YEARS ACTIVE	COMMITTEE TITLE
1921–1936	Town Planning and Housing Committee
1936–1939	Town Planning and Housing and Slum Clearance Committee
1941–1943	Reconstruction Committee
1943-1945, 1948	Central Advisory Committee on National Planning
1944–1959	Town and Country Planning and Housing Committee

TABLE 6.3

RIBA COMMITTEES CONCERNED WITH SPECIFIC PLANNING ISSUES 1929 TO 1957

YEARS ACTIVE	COMMITTEE TITLE
1929–1933	Control of Elevations Joint Committee
1933–1978	Central Committee for the Architectural Advisory Panels
1942–1944	Architectural Use of Building Materials Committee
1956–1958	Architectural Control under the Town and Country Planning Act 1947 Special Committee

#07
ELEONORE KOFMAN AND ELIZABETH LEBAS:
RECOVERY AND REAPPROPRIATION
IN LEFEBVRE AND CONSTANT

Pour une architecture de situation (1953) by Constant is one of the handful of books which have illuminated these pages

HENRI LEFEBVRE, 1986[1]

Henri Lefebvre held Constant Nieuwenhuys in high esteem, considering him to be the leading figure behind what has been labelled situationist architecture.[2] Lefebvre explained at some length in *Le Temps des Méprises*[3] what he particularly liked about Constant's anti-functionalist architecture. It was an architecture which aimed to generate a direct response from its users, as well as a variety of sensations and passions. As such, it paralleled – and was surely indebted to – Lefebvre's concept of moments, a highly influential notion in early situationist thinking. Constant's multifaceted production also sought to elaborate a new unity operating on the nexus between the micro-urbanistic and the macro-architectural in the production of a concrete or practical utopia. These were the principles Lefebvre also aimed to elicit in his engagement with practising architects such as Ricardo Bofill and Mario Gaviria.

Equally, Constant's work can be used to explore the ideas of urbanism and planning in Lefebvre's thought, and their location in the social and cultural history of experimental urban design and utopian thinking in the post-war period. For Lefebvre, planning as an arrangement for living did not belong to the technocrat. Only the poet could really know the city; therefore, planning as *poesis* belonged to the artist, for only the artist could transform everyday life into a practical utopia. As we shall see, Lefebvre's ideas on planning evolved over a period of almost twenty-five years, during which society became increasingly dominated by technological rationality. In response, Lefebvre developed principles for a project of recovery which included as much the physical and emotional whole of the individual as it aimed to reconnect the social, cultural and economic dimensions of society to rhythms of space and time redefined again by use over commodity. In turn, Constant provided him with elements for a practical utopia. However, to understand how Constant's urban writings and later models, paintings and drawings, inspired Lefebvre to consider another possible way of planning in the future, we must first turn to the diverse strands of Situationist thinking on the urban with particular attention to Constant's contribution.

1 We cannot find any reference to this text by Constant Nieuwenhuys cited by Henri Lefebvre in three texts (*Introduction à la Modernité*, 1962; *Le Temps des Méprises*, 1975 and *Le Retour de la Dialectique*, 1986) and in an interview with Kristin Ross (Lefebvre on the Situationists: an interview, *October*, no. 97, 1997, pp. 69–83). The most likely reason is that Lefebvre may have been referring to a piece Constant had written with Aldo van Eyck in 1953 entitled 'Towards a Spatial Colourism'. We would like to thank Marcus Risdell for letting us have access to his unpublished work, including interviews with Constant.
2 Simon Sadler, *The Situationist City*, Cambridge, MA: MIT Press, 1998.
3 Henri Lefebvre, *Le Temps des Méprises*, Paris: Stock, 1975.

one
LEFEBVRE AND THE SITUATIONISTS

Lefebvre's contact with and influence on the International Situationists, and particularly with Guy Debord, are acknowledged. His significant contribution to their urban and socio-political thinking is subsumed in his key work on the critique of everyday life and in the concept of 'moments'.[4] The latter, though considered by the Situationists as too abstract and unsituated, provided the pivotal concept for the construction of situations. Lefebvre himself singles out *Le romanticisme révolutionnaire* – a tract he wrote in 1957 following his break with the French Communist Party – as the text which instigated the collaboration with the newly formed Situationist International movement in 1957.[5] Both Lefebvre and Debord depicted the relationship as a turbulent and intense collaboration for a short period of time until its dissolution in 1960, when they parted company over ideological differences and accusations of plagiarism.

In our introduction to *Henri Lefebvre: Writings on Cities*, we suggested that the relationship between Lefebvre and the Situationists was worth investigating. The publication since then of an interview conducted by Kristin Ross with Lefebvre over a decade ago has confirmed the significance to Lefebvre of Constant's proposals for an utopian architecture whose seeds had been planted earlier in the Cobra group.[6]

Both the immediate post-war period of reconstruction prompted by the disintegration of the existing fabrics of ancient cores in Amsterdam, London and Paris, and also the building of new towns in response to an expanding post-war economy, had alarmed Constant and Lefebvre. Constant was particularly struck by the rebuilding of London after the Blitz, which he witnessed in the early 1950s, and also by the expansion of 'green cities' – new towns – around Amsterdam. For Lefebvre, the turning point was the sudden appearance during the mid-1950s in deepest rural France of the new town of Mourenx – not far from his ancient and beloved birthplace, Navarrenx – on the site of a newly discovered natural gas field. The contrast between Navarrenx, whose every stone Lefebvre knew 'as the rings of a tree', and the 'inexorable boredom of Mourenx' could not have been greater (Figure 7.1).[7] It was this kind of loss which for Constant made 'urbanism into one of today's key cultural problems'.[8]

Concern about the transformation of everyday life and the nature of urban forms were prominent in pre- and early Situationist thinking.[9] Constant's specific interest in spatial

---
4 A moment refers to discontinuous *durées* which define and are defined by forms. The everyday is composed of a multiplicity of moments such as play, love, struggle. Each moment has its specific rules, affirmed as each is repeated. For example, play follows specific categories of rules, partners, stakes, etc. (Henri Lefebvre, *La Somme et le Reste*, 3rd edition, Paris: Méridiens-Klincksieck, 1989, p. 648).
5 Ross, *op. cit.*, note 1.
6 Eleonore Kofman and Elizabeth Lebas (editors), *Henri Lefebvre: writings on cities*, Oxford: Blackwell, 1996. Kristin Ross, *op. cit.*, note 1.
7 Henri Lefebvre, *Introduction à la Modernité*, Paris: Editions de Minuit, 1962, pp. 121–124.
8 Constant Nieuwenhuys, Another city for another life, *Internationale Situationniste*, no. 2, 1959, pp 37–40. Other writings on urbanism by Constant include: By our means and our perspectives, *Internationale Situationniste*, no. 2, 1959; Description of the yellow zone, *Internationale Situationniste*, no. 4, 1960; New Babylon? An urbanism of the future, *Architectural Design*, June 1964, pp. 304–305; New Babylon, *Informatief*, no. 4., 1966, p. 1.
9 Sadler, *op. cit.*, note 2.

figure 7.1
MOURENX, FROM *INTERNATIONALE SITUATIONNISTE*, NO. 6, AUGUST 1961

issues had already been sparked by his collaboration in the early 1950s with the architect Aldo van Eyck, who had proclaimed an architecture of the imagination rather than of the intellect. Having received training as an architect, Constant for a while earned a living from architectural practice (like Van Eyck, he designed playgrounds and public sculptures), but in the late 1960s returned to painting full-time.[10]

Constant's association with the Situationist International (SI) was short-lived: from 1958 to 1960. He had met Debord in 1956, but did not attend the SI's founding meeting in Alba in 1957. Moreover, much of the literature on the group has tended to blur differences within, as well as stages in the evolution of, the SI, focusing instead on later political writings and reducing the influence of its northern European members.[11] With the recent publication of original texts focusing on art, politics and urbanism[12] and a more historical and critical contextualization of situationism,[13] it is becoming possible to identify more clearly the preoccupations, contributions and membership in various periods.

Before Constant's expulsion from the SI in 1960 for colluding with an urbanistic ideology and daring to visualize and give material substance to a future city, ideas of unitary urbanism were at the forefront of Situationist thinking.[14] Discussions of *dérive* and psychogeography were more associated with the group which had come from the Lettrist International (i.e. Debord and Bernstein), and regularly appeared in the pages of *Potlach* and *Internationale Situationniste* until the early 1960s. After Kotányi and Vaneigem took over the *Bureau d'Urbanisme Unitaire* in 1960, urbanism was irrevocably dismissed as nothing but a packaged ideology. This was roughly the time when Constant and Lefebvre began to develop their own urban thinking into more mature pieces and writings. Indeed, by 1968 Constant had completed his project for New Babylon (Figure 7.2) and Lefebvre had published *Le Droit à la Ville*,[15] and there soon followed afterwards an explosion of State-led critical urban research.[16]

10 Marcus Risdell, From Old Amsterdam to New Babylon, unpublished M.A. Report, Courtauld Institute of Art, 1995.
11 Sadie Plant, *The Most Radical Gesture: the Situationist International in a postmodern age*, London: Routledge, 1992. Peter Wollen, Bitter victory – the Situationist International, in Iwona Blazwick (editor), *An Endless Adventure ... An Endless Passion ... An Endless Banquet: a Situationist scrapbook*, London: ICA/Verso, 1989.
12 Libero Andreotti and Xavier Costa (editors), *Situationists: art, politics, urbanism*, Barcelona: Museu d'Art Contemporani de Barcelona, 1996; also, Sadler, *op. cit.*, note 2.
13 Thomas McDonough, Rereading Debord, rereading the Situationists, *October*, no. 79, 1996, pp. 3–14.
14 Constant Nieuwenhuys, Another city for another life, *Internationale Situationniste*, no. 2, 1959, pp. 37–40; also, Constant Nieuwenhuys, The great game to come, *Potlach*, no. 30, 15 July 1959.
15 Henri Lefebvre, *Le Droit à la Ville*, Paris: Anthropos, 1968.
16 A history needs to be written on different modes of knowing the city: one which acknowledges dependence on the State for this knowledge, and whose critical (and often structuralist approaches) were in turn promoted by institutional research (M. Amiot, *Contre l'Etat, les Sociologues*, Paris: Maison des Sciences de l'Homme, 1986).

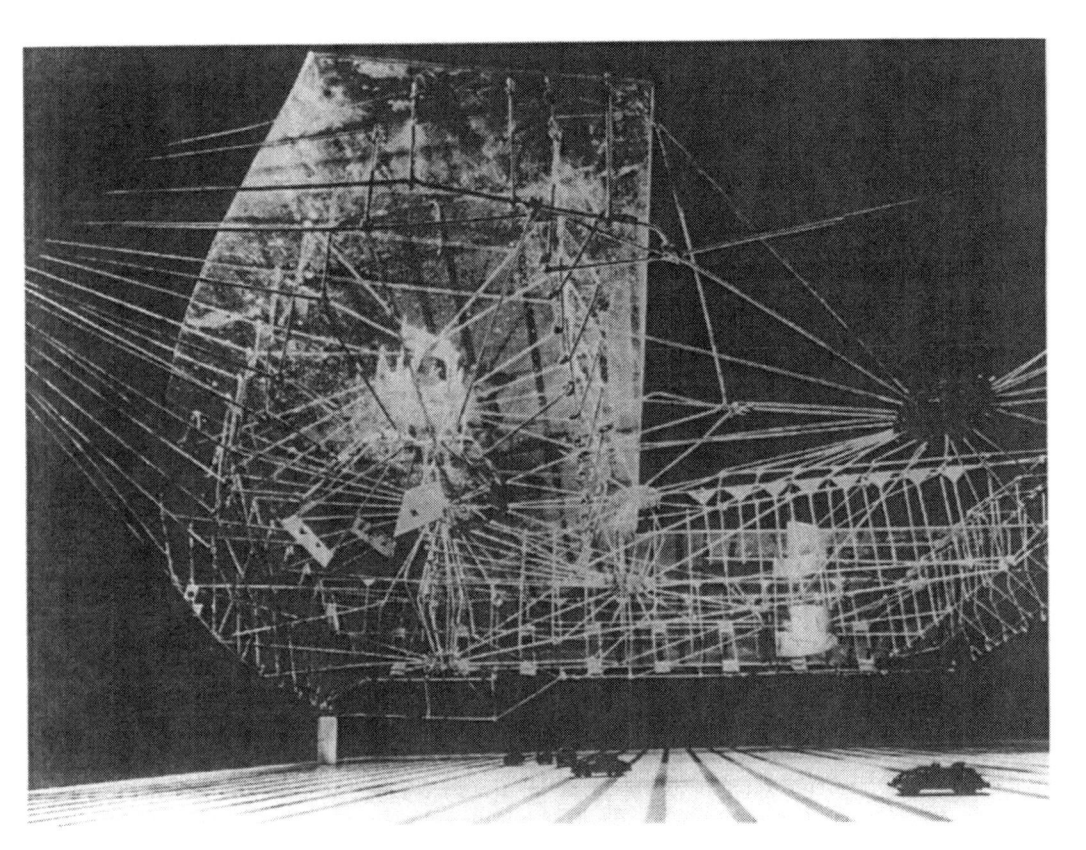

figure 7.2
CONSTANT NIEUWENHUYS, NEW BABYLON, YELLOW SECTOR, 1958

The idea of the *dérive*, attributed to Debord, arises from the attraction and repulsion we feel for different areas of a city. It was elaborated in the context of existing cities such as Paris and Amsterdam, and expressed reactions to the systematic destruction of its fabric. Issues of *Potlach* (for example, August 1954) reported the incursion of developers into areas such as the *rue Sauvage*.[17] Clearly, the notion of the *dérive* as urban wandering and meditative observation associated with the transformation of the city by capitalist economic forces has a long history going back to Restif de la Bretonne, Charles Baudelaire and the Surrealists. The repertoire of the *dérive* was therefore readily available; its originality lay in new kinds of interventions into the urban fabric and new ways of representing them as the city was being ravaged for a renewed cycle of accumulation. For the Situationists the *dérive* became a political and psychological strategy in itself, meant as both objective study of the conditions propitious for the construction of an attractive urban environment, as well as a game of communication. For example, while Jorn and Debord created sensual maps of inner urban areas as part of their 'psychogeographical' project, Constant and others equipped with walkie-talkies would set out – as Constant did in Amsterdam in 1960 – on a *dérive* lasting several days.[18] The *dérive* was therefore a mapping technique, the production of a new aesthetic, a means of locating

17 Andreotti and Costa, *op. cit.*, note 12.
18 Risdell, *op. cit.*, note 10.

opportunities for the creation of situations, a subversion of conventions – and altogether enormous fun. And it was these ludic and creative dimensions which, for the Situationists, ultimately made it political.

An outcome of Constant and Debord's meeting in Alba in 1956 was further thinking on the principles of unitary urbanism first espoused by Gilles Ivain (also known as Ivan Chtcheglov) in the early 1950s.[19] Unitary urbanism was proposed as an antidote to the absences of contemporary town planning. It was to be a new way of living, a totality embracing space and time, and a bringing together of the different activities of inhabitants, most notably the activity of play. Unitary urbanism would promote a participatory urban environment that would dislodge the passivity of the capitalist economic spectacle through a permanent transformation of urban locales.

Constant attempted to give material substance to ideas of unitary urbanism through his project for a New Babylon. It began in 1956, quite independently from Debord, with a model for a gypsy camp in Alba and evolved into a full-time preoccupation from 1959 until 1969, during which time Constant produced some sixty texts, drawings and models expressing aspects of urbanism as seemingly disparate as theoretical speculations on the nature of a cybernetic urbanism, technical aspects of load-bearing structures, experiments in multimedia aesthetics, love and play.

Debord soon came to oppose what he considered to be Constant's materialization of the ideas of unitary urbanism whilst the existing capitalist system remained intact. How could urbanism be anything else than an ideology comparable with that advertising Coca Cola?[20] In contrast, for Constant, unitary urbanism and the New Babylon project were intended for the 'man of tomorrow': New Babylonians did not yet exist but in the meantime it was necessary to visualize and concretize these principles.

Clearly, unitary urbanism was the aspect of situationist architecture which most influenced the development of Lefebvre's conceptualization of a progressive urban project – one which attempted to promote the conditions of possibility of what Marx called the society of associated producers: a society beyond advanced capitalism, one based on the remaking of everyday life and the satisfaction of radical needs. The 1950s had been a period of optimism in the possibilities of a positive, State-sponsored urbanism, and it was only following the implementation of the *Code du Plan* in 1961 and of the Ministry of Culture's imposition under André Malraux in 1962 of the *secteur sauvegardé* (protected sectors), that the rigid codification of new developments, accompanied by the museumification of ancient urban cores such as the Marais in Paris, began to take place. At this point, in his second volume of *Critique de la Vie Quotidienne: fondements d'une sociologie de la quotidiennete* (Paris: L'Auche, 1958), Lefebvre argued that everyday life was being

---

19 Gilles Ivain, Formulary for a new urbanism, *Internationale Situationniste*, no. 1, 1953, reprinted in Ken Knabb (editor), *Situationist International Anthology*, Berkeley, CA: Bureau of Public Secrets, 1981, pp. 1–4.
20 Attila Kotányi and Raoul Vaneigem, Programme élémentaire du bureau d'urbanisme unitaire, *Internationale Situationniste*, no. 6, 1961, reprinted in Knabb, *op. cit.*, note 19, pp. 65–67.

increasingly colonized by capitalist imperatives, and that exchange values were rapidly displacing use values. This analysis, which he had begun to expound in the first volume *Critique de la Vie Quotidienne: introduction* (Paris: Guasset, 1947) had been highly influential in early Situationist thinking about the nature of space, time and urbanism.

Very often, unitary urbanism is simply treated as the translation of *dérive* and psychogeography[21] and of interest only for architects and planners. Yet it represented much more. Constant himself, as we have noted, envisaged it as a model for a way of living and for cities of the future.[22] More than any of the Situationists, Constant saw the necessity of embracing technology for the purpose of cultural production. He criticized Asger Jorn, one of his fellow members in the earlier Cobra movement (1948–1950) and founder of the Imaginary Bauhaus Movement in 1953, for his continuing support of an artisanally produced aesthetic (although Constant's own sculptural models for the New Babylon Project, derived from Constructivist aesthetics, were largely hand-made from found industrial objects). In a debate begun by Constant in the *Internationale Situationniste* in December 1958, he wrote:

> Industrial and machine culture is an indisputable fact and artisanal techniques ... are finished ... Those who scorn the machine and those who glorify it display the same inability to utilize it. Machine work and mass production offer unheard-of possibilities for creation ... without this, the integration of art in the construction of the human habitat remains as chimerical as the proposals of Gilles Ivain.[23]

Constant envisaged a state of complete mechanization which would free people from the necessity of work. New forms of technology, no more than a means to an end, would enable him to create lightness, playfulness and flexibility for this ideal city. The abolition of work was a compelling slogan in Situationist circles, with antecedents in the anarchist movement of the nineteenth century and in Paul Lafargue's *Droit à la Paresse* (Paris: Moulins, 1883). In his interview with Ross, Lefebvre also noted that there was much discussion (probably in the 1950s) of the science fiction novel *City* by Clifford Simak, in which work is performed by robots.[24] It was also in the 1950s that the idea of cybernetics, defined by Norbert Wiener in 1947 as the comparative study of control and communication in the animal and the machine, gained growing currency in certain artistic and intellectual circles. Cybernetics represented a particular kind of intimacy between humans and machines, and would have been central to the ever-changing and artificial micro-environments proposed in Constant's New Babylon. Certainly Constant and Lefebvre noted its ramifications. Initially, science fiction and high technology scenarios were seen in Situationist thinking as a means of undermining mainstream modernist principles.[25] Yet by the 1960s Lefebvre was launching trenchant attacks on what he called the *cybernanthropes*, or the technocrats of an informational rationality,

21 T. Levin, Geopolitics of hibernation: the drift of situationist urbanism, in L. Andreotti and X. Costa, *op. cit.*, note 12, pp. 111–146.
22 Risdell, *op. cit.*, note 10.
23 Constant, Sur nos moyens et nos perspectives, *Internationale Situationniste*, no. 2, December 1958.
24 Ross, *op. cit.*, note 1.
25 Sadler, *op. cit.*, note 2, p. 148.

who wielded power over a new planning system and an informational society.[26] For Lefebvre, hierarchical apparatuses were taking command of the management, planning and control of all social activities: this was the *société de consommation dirigée* – the society of programmed consumption.

two
THE CRITIQUE OF PLANNING IN A CAPITALIST SOCIETY: REAPPROPRIATION AND RECOVERY

Envisaging Lefebvre's writings on urbanism as a binary opposition between the planned and the non-planned only invites closure. From his first specific writing on urbanism,[27] continuing in such texts as *Introduction à la Modernité* (1962), *Le Droit à la Ville* (1968), *Du Rural à l'urbain* (1970), and culminating in what we could call an analytical apotheosis in *La Production de l'éspace* (1974), Lefebvre unfolds an increasingly precise and critical analysis of capitalist planning as an historically specific form of production of space integral to the society of programmed consumption. This critique cannot be juxtaposed to 'non-planning' in the sense of anarchy or disorder, as any programmation under capitalism cannot be the opposite of these. Indeed, capitalist planning – as Lefebvre is at pains to demonstrate from *Le Droit à la Ville* onwards – is not a practice of 'order' or ordering, but a strategic and punctual practice of power promoted and executed by the State, with its objective being the extraction of profit from every possible aspect of everyday life. In this practice, planning promotes a virtual *disembodiment* – fragmenting the body's activities, disorienting the senses, and giving sight empire over the other senses.

This is not to say that 'planning' – understood as social and meaningful arrangements for everyday life – has not existed, or does not exist within nodes of everyday life less dominated by the division of labour and commodity consumption, nor that it cannot be re-appropriated. All great cities of the past have been 'planned' and indeed 'ordered', but for Lefebvre their planning had another ontological genesis generated by the tragedy of the ineluctability of death, and the vitality of the ludic, the sacred and sexuality – all sustained by a collective engagement. These were values opposite to those generated by neo-capitalism whereby death is denied and, as a corollary, the celebration of life is repudiated. In such a system play is replaced by leisure, the sacred mysticism of religion is replaced by material commodities, and sexuality, now castrated, becomes mere genitality. In the urban realm, capitalism cannot but also pervert authenticity, to be replaced by planning.

Under a capitalist system planning inevitably hierarchizes and fragments functions, whilst homogenizing space within these zones, producing spaces abstracted for their very commodification and the programmation of everyday life for planned commodity consumption.[28] This production of abstract space is planned on a planetary scale

26 Henri Lefebvre, *Position. Contre les technocrates*, Paris: Gonthier, 1967.
27 Henri Lefebvre, Utopie expérimentale: pour un nouvel urbanisme, *Revue Française de Sociologie*, 11, no. 3, 1961, pp. 191–198.
28 Henri Lefebvre, *The Production of Space*, Oxford: Blackwell, 1991 (1974 French original).

according to a binary correspondence in which needs, functions, places and social objects appear to be placed in a neutral, innocuous and seemingly innocently objective space. Capitalist planning becomes the production of prohibition, a constitutive repression symbolized by the object offered to the gaze – yet banned from any possible fulfilling use. In short, planning is a negative appropriation of space under the reign of private property.[29]

However, in his attacks on neo-capitalist planning and its ideological code, Lefebvre does not dispute the necessity for a set of prescriptions and arrangements for urban living. Where he parts company with the *cybernanthropes* is how planning under capitalism separates different spheres of living from each other and focuses primarily and ultimately on promoting exchange values which entirely disregard the city as an arena for tragedy and play. For the *cybernanthropes*, capitalist planning is not an emancipatory praxis – as it is for both Constant and Lefebvre. All it does is to seek to control the unregulated expansion of cities and, in turn, produces savage and empty spaces for inhabitants who lead conformist lives in pursuit of 'métro, boulot, dodo' (commuting, work and sleep). In short, under capitalism, modern urbanism has emerged as an array of techniques of separation, circulation and communication to control and manage both the explosion of time and space, and the incoherence between different spheres of everyday life.

Lefebvre pushed Marxist thinking on the city well beyond the confines of the relations and spaces of work which in the post-war period were the sites of struggle, class consciousness and political activity.[30] The city not only encompassed everyday life, it also connected work and non-work, the humdrum and the sublime and, increasingly more so than work, was becoming the site of social and political struggle and transformation. Furthermore, it also stood for the mediation between the local and the global.

What Constant and Lefebvre both desired was for planning to repair fractured existences and restore the artistic and poetic qualities of people's lives. Emancipatory planning, therefore, constituted a dual project of recovery and re-appropriation. It resisted separation between activities, people and *ambiences* – the core idea of unitary urbanism – and created places for meeting and sociability. Constant emphasized nomadism, flexibility and the choice of environments; in turn, Lefebvre oscillated between movement and a more rooted existence. Venice and the old Paris were his ideal cities.

29 *Ibid.*, p. 319.
30 By the end of the 1960s the new generation of urban critics were professional urban sociologists (rather than artists and writers) who shifted the analysis of urban change towards a notion of collective consumption which bore a direct connection to the PCF's *(Parti Communiste Français)* thesis of State Monopoly Capitalism (M. Castells, *The Urban Question: a Marxist approach*, London: Edward Arnold, 1976). This contended that State planning had to sustain effectively what was a deep restructuring of the economy by means of a planned and subsidized consumption. Although this took the emphasis away from production and its particular spatial relations, the analysis nevertheless remained fairly mechanistic in the relationship posited between service provision and politics. The study of everyday life as the art of doing was taken up later in the late 1970s by non-Marxists such as Michel de Certeau (Michel de Certeau, *L'Invention du Quotidien*, 2nd edition, Paris: Gallimard, 1994). An examination of the 'everyday' reveals the subterranean forms of dispersed creativity and tactics of *bricolage* adopted in the face of networks of surveillance. This is a similar position to that of Lefebvre's, except that for him, everyday life was not only the place of resistance but also the place of radical change.

Both Constant and Lefebvre re-appropriate planning as part of a creative act: *poesis* (to employ Lefebvre's, rather than Constant's term). While for Constant, the maker, the architectural, artefactual dimensions of this ideal of planning are far less important than creating ambiences which stimulate creativity in New Babylonians, for Lefebvre, the thinker, *poesis* is what generates the *oeuvre:* an unproductive, sumptuous and not necessarily democratic expenditure of collective resources for the creation of a thing of beauty, of which the city as *oeuvre,* as a work of art representing the sum, is the expression most appropriate to the human being.[31] However, in Lefebvre's view, the city as a work of art is the opposite of a simple architectural or aesthetic product. The work of art is valued foremost for the collective relations embedded in it. In opposition, planning by the *cybernanthropes* precisely converts what were the integrating, regenerating and fecund spaces of what Lefebvre terms absolute and social spaces into commodifiable ones (as in the process of museumification). If for Constant New Babylon floats above existing cities and the only trained professionals allowed will be Situationists (a photomontage shows a drawing of the project superimposed over an aerial view of Rotterdam[32]), for Lefebvre the possibilities of re-appropriation can be found by wanderers, idlers, artists and poets within the fractured spaces of the city itself. Capitalism, he reminds us, can no more commodify all spaces than it can all human relations and it is within this process of commodification that its contradiction can be found – and ultimately as can be emancipation from it.

For Lefebvre, the Cobra movement and later the Situationists (until their split) shared similar views on a project of recovery based on the unity of the lived and the conceived in everyday life. Afterwards, Lefebvre was to comment that the Situationists had forgotten the State and the political in their thinking. Yet both parties agreed that revolution could not be the promotion of economic growth or the replacement of political personnel; it must have as its goal nothing but the transformation of everyday life. It must also reject the fetishism of competence and performance under an ideology proclaiming the 'end of ideology' sanctioned by authority and knowledge,[33] ideas that were also propounded by Cobra and the Situationists. Therefore, the increasing complexity of everyday life implies another way of living and the right to create another experience of the social, another social time, another way of existing: another way of 'planning'. The impossible is attained through the possible, through practical utopias.

Utopianism is often associated with a radical break with the existing society and an opening out to a less programmed system. However, for Lefebvre, concrete utopias do not entail a historical break but are part of a conscious process of re-appropriation of fundamental rights – to the city, the body, work and play – and as such gives it sense and purpose. He distinguishes between the *utopian* (concrete ideas) and the *utopist* (abstract dreamer). Constant is the prototype and leading exponent of a modern utopian who works in a concrete utopian schema but claims to be an abstract dreamer.

31 See Lefebvre, *Le Droit a la Ville,* 1968; *Du Rural à l'urbain,* 1970; *The Production of Space,* 1974.
32 Constant Nieuwenhuys, New Babylon, *Informatief,* no. 4, 1966, in Risdell, *op. cit.,* note 10.
33 Henri Lefebvre, *Critique de la Vie Quotidienne,* vol. III, Paris: L'Auche, 1981, pp. 28–29.

For Lefebvre, then, the project of change and planning would seek to transform abstract spaces in cities into differential ones which could counter homogenization and restore the functions, elements and moments of social practice and put an end to the shattering of the human body. In Lefebvre's view, if planning is conceived as social arrangements for everyday life in differential spaces, it begins by reflexive thought, by real knowledge which includes the understanding of how societies generate their social space and time, the rational spaces conceived by technocrats and bureaucrats, and the spaces of everyday life. Lefebvre[34] could outline a project of recovery with the following principles:

1. *difference against homogeneity*, not as a justification of social inequality but as right to equality in difference;
2. *unity against fragmentation*, as a concrete principle and not as abstraction;
3. *centrality implying simultaneity*, in space and time (offering a multiplicity of centre mobility and dynamism);
4. *subjectivity of reconstructed individuals*, substituting 'egos', and reconnecting the ludic and the tragic to everyday life, subjectivity and identity;
5. *sociality*, not in opposition to the individual but to the State, the economy etc., as abstractions.

There is no 'equivalence' between Constant and Lefebvre, yet their works are held by a whole – a project of re-appropriation and recovery, of reconciliation of needs and desire, a belief in the possibility of the impossible, a philosophy of pleasure, a subversion of power (including those of technology and urban planning), a critical analysis which is not perceived as immutable but as product of historical moments and an over-arching generosity. For Lefebvre, the project for a New Babylon represented – as an *oeuvre* in its own right and a concrete not a futurist utopia – his principles of recovery and the possibility of another way of planning, another way of being. It would seem that once Lefebvre had moved from the moment of regret for the passing of ancient towns to that of anger at the prohibitions and castration of the planned New Town, Constant's proposals and aesthetics represented a critical re-appropriation of what were the best ideals of modernism as technological liberation.

---

34 *Ibid.*, p. 165.

#08
JONATHAN HUGHES:
THE INDETERMINATE BUILDING

one
INTRODUCTION

The goal of flexibility within modern architecture is far from new, nor are the problems it has generated for designers seeking to cater for technological and functional change. If it is accepted that large, highly serviced buildings require professional design input at least to ensure they are safe, how then does the designer step back from dictating the form of the building over time? An attempt to resolve this dilemma was undertaken during the 1960s under the banner of 'indeterminacy', a strategy which found built expression at Northwick Park Hospital (1961–1974, Figures 8.1, 8.2 and 8.3). Notably, its designer, John Weeks of architects Llewelyn-Davies and Weeks, had been involved with both the abstract 'Constructionist' and 'Independent Group' sections of London's artistic avant-garde during the 1950s, and the strategy of indeterminacy might be seen to exhibit characteristics indicative of both groups' concerns – be it analogies with biological growth patterns, or 'pop' notions of transience and expendability.[1]

Constructionist notions of organic abstract design analogous to biological patterns of growth may appear to sit uneasily with the perceptions of transience and expendability of mid-century consumer society embraced by the Independent Group. Yet they may ultimately be related through parallel discourses of optimization – the attainment of an equilibrating, efficient, outcome – be it via a neo-Darwinian emphasis on the intrinsic 'necessity' of form, or an implicit approval of the market's ability to adapt continually to satisfy consumer demands. The architectural outcome is a notion of functionalism justifiable on both para-biological and para-economic grounds, at its most efficient when allowed to operate freely, unfettered by distorting constraints, ceaselessly adjusting to changing circumstances. Yet within the constraints of a mixed economy such architectures are utterly contingent on the economic and political frameworks within which they are located, and by which they are constantly compromised; indeed, such tensions are inscribed in the very architecture and programme of Northwick Park.

two
PROPORTION, PROCESS AND POP

The analogy of architecture with models of natural growth and evolution has persistently underwritten modern architecture – the forms and processes of organic development being variously considered to offer exemplars of efficient structural organ-

---

[1] The two groupings should not be viewed as mutually exclusive, 'members' of each camp knew each other and often exhibited at each other's shows. See Alistair Grieve, Towards an art of environment: exhibitions and publications by a group of avant-garde abstract artists in London 1951–55, *Burlington Magazine*, November 1990, pp. 773–781.

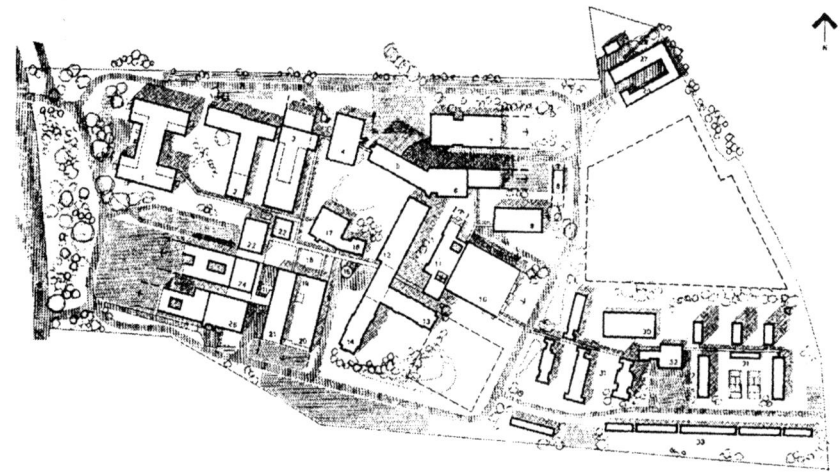

top figure 8.1
NORTHWICK PARK
HOSPITAL, VIEW

middle figure 8.2
NORTHWICK PARK
HOSPITAL, PLAN

bottom figure 8.3
NORTHWICK PARK
HOSPITAL,
CONCEPT SKETCH,
1962

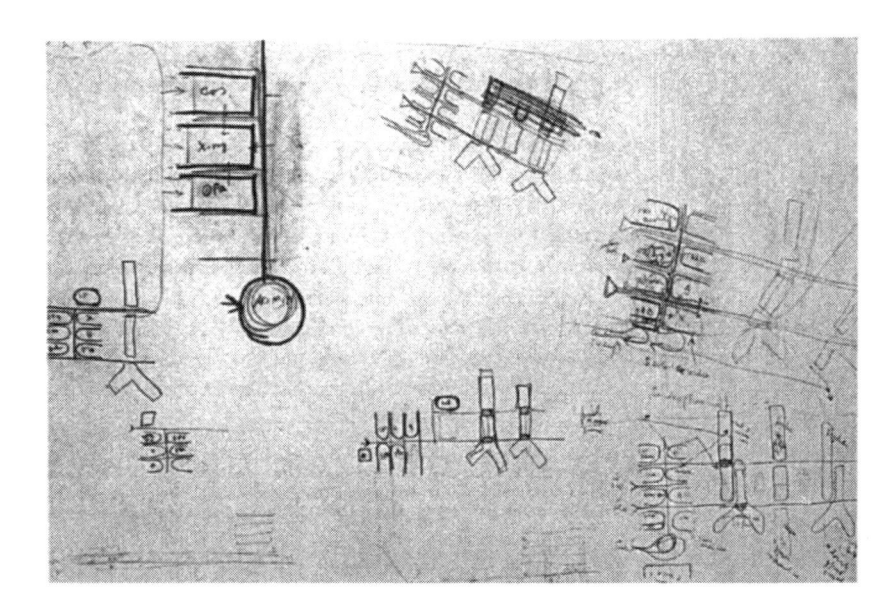

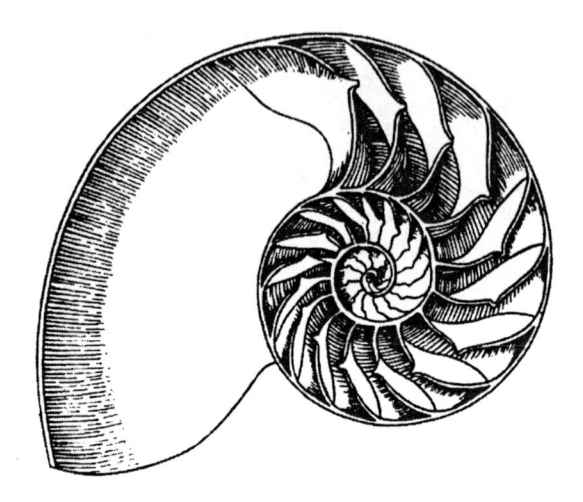

left figure 8.4
SHELL OF THE NAUTILIUS POMPILIUS, FROM D'ARCY
WENTWORTH THOMPSON, *ON GROWTH AND FORM*

right figure 8.5
KENNETH MARTIN, *COMPOSITION 1949*,
TATE GALLERY (LONDON)

ization. At its simplest, the architect could find precedents for constructional forms in living matter, most notably plants: Joseph Paxton celebratedly claimed to have based the structural principles of his 1851 Crystal Palace on the Victoria Regia lily. Alternatively, the *growth* patterns of organisms might be mimicked in the design of architectural form – typically via some mathematical or proportional rule witnessed in the natural world. Finally, the development of architectural form over time might be compared with processes of evolution, dictated by transcendent rules of necessity. These modes of analogy are clearly not mutually exclusive, and have been variously combined to provide both *intra-* and *inter-*generational explanations of form.

During the nineteenth century science had demonstrated a growing interest in the architectonic qualities of natural form resulting, most famously, in D'Arcy Wentworth Thompson's 1917 magisterial work *On Growth and Form*[2] in which he outlined the mathematical rules which appeared to underwrite the growth of natural organisms. Subsequently, in the 1920s, Raoul Francé popularized this meld of natural technology and biology under the label 'biotechnics'. Although Francé's books rarely focused solely on architecture, his sentiments were clear: 'I had pursued my search from the builder's art to the loveliest products of nature, and had found nothing new'.[3] Clear parallels with modernist thinking surface in Francé's law of 'the least expenditure of energy':

---

[2] D'Arcy Wentworth Thompson, *On Growth and Form* (2nd edition), Cambridge: Cambridge University Press, 1942.
[3] Raoul Francé, *Plants as Inventors*, London: Simpkin, Marshall and Co., 1926, p. 18 (first published in Germany, 1923). A wide-ranging account of the employment of organic analogies in architecture and design is provided in Philip Steadman, *The Evolution of Designs: biological analogy in architecture*, Cambridge: Cambridge University Press, 1979.

'Necessity prescribes certain forms for certain qualities. Therefore it is always possible ... to infer the activity from the shape, the purpose from the form. In nature all forms are ... a creation of necessity'.' For Francé, the law of necessity was akin to Adam Smith's 'invisible hand', guiding the development of form in nature, dictating that form and function be profoundly related. Indeed, the natural world appeared to have evolved forms which, as well as being admirably suited to their function, were governed by mathematical-mechanical laws open to appropriation by designers for their own use.'

Natural processes of growth could also be reconciled with notions of proportionality via the Fibonacci series – a mathematical series of numbers; namely 1, 2, 3, 5, 8, 13 ..., where each successive number is the sum of the previous two. The applicability of the series to the positioning of leaves around plant stems (amongst numerous phenomena) had been discovered during the nineteenth century, although for many writers its significance ultimately lay in a property of the number series itself – namely that the ratio of successive numbers converged on the Golden Section ($\phi = 0.618...$). Thompson's *On Growth and Form* made much of such relationships, noting that 'the harmony of the world is made manifest in Form and Number'.[6] Indeed, Thompson found the ratio in all manner of natural forms, including sunflower heads, pine cones, cacti and shells (Figure 8.4).

Such biological analogies were employed by post-war architectural avant-gardes in Britain, and rapidly gained in complexity and radical intent. The brief round of neo-Palladianism occasioned in part by Rudolph Wittkower's 1949 study of Renaissance architecture, *Architectural Principles in the Age of Humanism*, had heralded the employment of simple mathematical proportional systems by such modernists as Alison and Peter Smithson and Ernö Goldfinger.[7] For a short period, avant-garde modernists in Britain deemed it acceptable to formulate designs variously rooted in formal notions of axiality, symmetry and the Golden Section. However, the 1950s soon saw the increasing conflation of notions of static proportionality with concepts of dynamic biological process and system. Thompson's *On Growth and Form* found a new audience amongst the London-based abstract Constructionist artists of the 1950s (including Adrian Heath, Anthony Hill, Kenneth and Mary Martin and Victor Pasmore) who found in Thompson's text mechanisms for the creation of 'concrete', self-referential art works with their own organic genesis. The mathematical systems described by Thompson could be employed by the artist to create objects whose beauty and validity arose from the inherent logic of the dynamic system itself. As Kenneth Martin (Figure 8.5) put it in 1952:

4 Raoul Francé, *op. cit.*, note 3, p. 15.
5 Francé's ideas were critically considered in the 1937 constructivist manifesto *Circle* (see Karel Honzik, A note on biotechnics, in J.L. Martin, Ben Nicholson and Naum Gabo (editors), *Circle*, London: Faber and Faber, 1937, pp. 256–262). Whilst not dismissing the applicability of natural forms, Honzik considered Francé to have over-stated the case for their structural efficiency.
6 D'Arcy Wentworth Thompson, *op. cit.*, note 2, pp. 1096–1097. Thompson continued: 'So the living and the dead, things animate and the inanimate, we dwellers in the world and this world wherein we dwell are bound alike by physical and mathematical law'.
7 Goldfinger's 1955 Albermarle Street office block shows his application of the Golden Section to the design of the façade (RIBA drawings collection). The Smithsons' 1950–1951 proposals for the new Coventry Cathedral are also cited as examples of neo-Palladian planning.

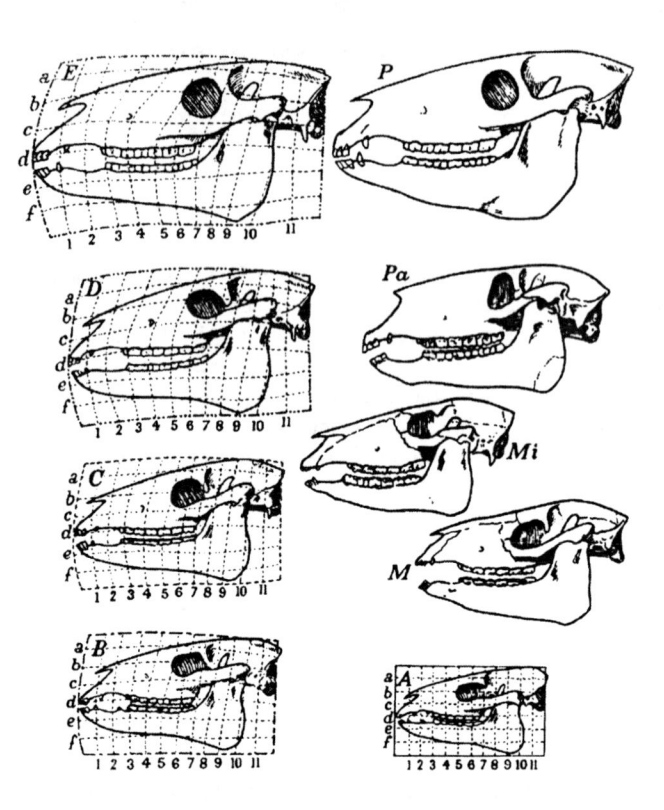

figure 8.6
CO-ORDINATE TRANSFORMATION OF HORSE SKULL (BOTTOM RIGHT),
AND COMPARISON WITH OTHER SKULLS, FROM D'ARCY WENTWORTH THOMPSON,
ON GROWTH AND FORM

Such works can grow outwards by proportion, like a tree repeating its form ... it follows that old systems of proportion cannot be used in the old way, so that proportion becomes functional again and becomes a vital developable thing ...[8]

For other sections of the avant-garde questions of change, flexibility, disorder and flux also came to occupy centre stage, and interest in simple proportional rules transformed into the consideration of organic growth and change. At London's Institute for Contemporary Arts (ICA), these ideas were also being considered by a loose affiliation of artists, architects and critics labelled the Independent Group (including Richard Hamilton, Eduardo Paolozzi, Nigel Henderson, Alison and Peter Smithson and Reyner Banham). The Independent Group's ICA exhibitions *Growth and Form* (1951) and *Parallel of Life and Art* (1953) were exemplary. Plundering Thompson's work and manifesting an anti-hierarchical inclusiveness, the shows suggested the Independent Group's catholic diet of communications theory and science-fiction, philosophy and comics. Their adoption of a non-Euclidean, non-Aristotelian approach to aesthetics blurred the distinctions between 'high' and 'low' art and embraced the relativity of individual value judgements – all of which seemed more relevant to the complexities of the mid-twentieth-century world, one apparently no longer ruled by classical certainties but by the speculative probabilities of

8 Kenneth Martin, An art of environment, *Broadsheet*, no. 2, June 1952, mimeo.

figure 8.7
RICHARD HAMILTON, *JUST WHAT IS IT THAT MAKES TODAY'S HOMES SO DIFFERENT, SO APPEALING?* 1956, © DACS, 1999

Werner Heisenberg's 'uncertainty principle', and the ideological pluralism of Karl Popper's *Open Society*.[9] Books on composition and proportion rooted in biological process alerted students to the possibilities of dynamic, organic systems and to the microscopic world. At the 1951 ICA exhibition *Growth and Form* (self-consciously drawing on Thompson's work for its title and content) the *Architectural Review* noted 'the "new landscape" which modern science has opened up for the artist'.[10] Furthermore, introducing the 1953 show *Parallel of Life and Art* at the ICA, Peter Smithson now could declare that 'We are not going to talk about proportion and symmetry'[11]: rather it was the understanding of actual organic process than the application of static proportional models which offered a more pragmatic, realistic guide to the generation of form. Thompson had himself investigated such morphological transformations within biological form (Figure 8.6) – a theme subsequently paralleled by Banham's discussion of the mathematics of topology in relation to the 'New Brutalism'.[12] The implications of all this for young architects were reported in 1957 by Independent Group architect James Stirling:

> The application of orthogonal proportion and the obvious use of basic geometrical elements appears to be diminishing, and instead something of the variability found in nature is attempted. 'Dynamic cellularism' is an architecture comprising several elements, repetitive or varied. The assemblage of units is more in terms of growth and change than of mere addition, more akin to patterns of crystal formations or biological divisions than to the static rigidity of the structural grid.[13]

Stirling's work of the period duly evinced such concerns: a project for an expandable house undertaken with James Gowan in 1957 proposed accommodation spiralling around a service core, varying in size with need.[14] Indeed, a preoccupation with vitality

---

9 Karl Popper, *The Open Society and its Enemies*, London: G. Routledge and Sons, 1945, etc. Popper's attack on determinism paralleled Friedrich Hayek's aversion towards planned societies and constituted a virulent defence of western democracy in the early years of the Cold War. In *The Open Society and its Enemies* Popper employs Hayek's 1952 work, *The Sensory Order*, in support of his attack on determinism.
10 *Architectural Review*, October 1951.
11 Quoted in Reyner Banham, The new Brutalism, *Architectural Review*, vol. 118, no. 708, December 1955, pp. 355–361.
12 Reyner Banham, *ibid.*, p. 361.
13 James Stirling, Regionalism and modern architecture, *Architects' Year Book*, no. 8, 1957, pp. 62–68.
14 Reproduced in Peter Arnell and Ted Bickford (editors), *James Stirling: buildings and projects*, London: Architectural Press, 1984, pp. 59–60.

in various guises informed the interests of many of the members of the Independent Group – be it the perceptions of the cathartic *élan* of Pollock's painting, or the vitality of ever-changing consumer culture; indeed, the market itself could be deemed to have a life of its own. In 1957 Richard Hamilton (Figure 8.7) proposed a definition of mass-market products in a letter to the Smithsons; they were 'Pop': 'Popular, Transient, Expendable, Low cost, Mass produced, Young, Witty, Sexy, Gimmicky, Glamorous and Big Business'.[15] A positively Baudelairean discovery of value in the contingent and fleeting products of consumer society, Hamilton's stance – common to many in the Independent Group – carried an endorsement of the workings of the mass market, especially in its promotion of technological advance but equally in its displays of excess, built-in obsolescence and waste. For here was the market apparently responding to demand *(popular* demand), satiating the requirements of new and unfulfilled markets and supposedly fostering a valid popular culture. The mass market's validity was vouchsafed by its apparent authenticity and vitality, its democratizing responsiveness to the demands of the public.[16] This too, then, was a living system, cybernetically reacting to consumer desire and organically developing in a manner akin to Adam Smith's ideal free-market economy, albeit one in which obsolescence and excess could now be understood as logical market strategies.[17]

three
THE INDETERMINATE BUILDING

Weeks crystallized the notion of indeterminacy in a series of talks and unpublished papers between 1962 and 1964, although the concept should be traced back to Weeks' involvement with the Constructionist and Independent Group avant-gardes in the 1950s. The theory itself was to underwrite Weeks' design for the new Northwick Park Hospital, in northwest London (1961–1974). Whilst the Constructionist, systems-derived façades of the building were analogous to necessity-driven intra-generational processes of growth, the emphasis on the inter-generational growth and change of individual buildings and the whole hospital was indicative of a model of evolution or ecological adaptation concerned more with the impact of changing external forces and cybernetic feedback and, in this respect, equally paralleled the Independent Group's interest in the complexities and responsiveness of consumer culture.

Weeks' firm, Llewelyn-Davies and Weeks, had received the commission for Northwick in 1961, with a complicated brief for over 800 beds, laboratories and research facilities. In response, Weeks developed the strategy of 'indeterminacy' in order to cope with the increasingly rapid growth, change and obsolescence of hospital departments. The approach was inflected by the 'uncertainty principle' formulated

---

15 Quoted in Richard Hamilton, *Collected Words 1953–82*, London: Thames and Hudson, 1982, p. 28.
16 The opposite of Theodor Adorno and Max Horkheimer's 1940s attack on *The Culture Industry: enlightenment as mass deception*, in which the market is condemned as homogenizing and pernicious.
17 See, for example, Reyner Banham, Design by choice, *Architectural Review*, vol. 130, no. 773, July 1961, pp. 43–48. Banham notes of pop: 'its visual characteristics, as in advertising or Detroit car-styling, were often endowed with a vitality (not always bogus) that seemed absent from the fine arts and "good" design'.

figure 8.8
NORTHWICK PARK HOSPITAL, EXTENDABLE END

by quantum-mechanics physicist Werner Heisenberg in 1927, which had stated the impossibility of determining simultaneously both the position *and* the velocity of atomic particles. The degree of uncertainty was, in everyday experience, thought to be negligible; nonetheless at sub-atomic level the principle opened up the possibility of systemic ambiguity, of a world based on probability rather than certainty. In a similar manner, and contrary to accepted thinking, Weeks' indeterminacy openly acknowledged that the size of a hospital was not fixed, and that the growth of different departments would typically be unequal and hard to predict.[18] As a result, Weeks proposed that hospital design should acknowledge change and obsolescence rather than devise some ideal but static solution which would quickly prove inflexible. Prompted by Heisenberg's thinking, Weeks proposed a series of departmental hospital buildings whose width alone, and not length, was determined – length being free to change with need. The buildings were to be conceptually endless – reflecting an ongoing concern of Weeks' since a 1951 article 'Endless architecture' in which Mies van der Rohe and Mondrian were cited as designers preoccupied with conceptual notions of endlessness.[19]

For precedents for the design of the individual hospital buildings Weeks considered two Victorian projects. Firstly, Paxton's 1851 Crystal Palace was marshalled as a structure built rapidly from standardized components, as free as possible from internal walls and thereby permitting flexible sub-division.[20] Secondly, Brunel's Renkioi Hospital built in 1855 during the Crimean War demonstrated the possibilities of modular design by linking together pre-fabricated ward units to form a corridor building whose length was indeterminate.[21] Weeks combined these notions of loose-fitting and extendable building envelopes to devise a modular system of load-bearing external mullions supporting reinforced concrete beams, permitting flexible internal subdivision largely unrelated to

---

18 Weeks' exposition was originally published in: Indeterminate architecture, *Transactions of the Bartlett Society*, no. 2, 1963–1964, pp. 83–106.
19 Richard Llewelyn-Davies, Endless architecture, *Architectural Association Journal*, July 1951, pp. 106–112. Weeks has stated to the author that the article was written by himself. The theme was also pursued by Weeks in a number of unpublished papers in the early 1960s on 'caterpillar buildings' – the length of a caterpillar only being ascertainable when dead.
20 Paxton's account appeared in the *Illustrated London News*, 6 July 1850, p. 13.
21 For a recent account see David Toppin, The British hospital at Renkioi, 1855, *Arup Journal*, 16, no. 2, July 1981, pp. 3–18.

the elevations of the buildings. The ends of these buildings were capped with removable corrugated steel panels and a temporary fire stair (Figure 8.8). These 'extendable ends' could be removed and the building lengthened as required.

Weeks subsequently inferred support for this approach from a joint performance of John Cage's music and Merce Cunningham's dance at the Phoenix Theatre in 1964, where dance and music were incidental – just like independence of the plans and elevations at Northwick Park. Notably, Cage had referred to his own music as indeterminate in 1958,[22] and the development of atonal music by Schoenberg and his pupil Anton Webern provided Weeks with another analogy for the design of the elevations and a substitute for classical proportion. In Webern's music, a set cluster of, say, twelve notes (a 'tone row') occurred melodically and harmonically in every one or two bars, whilst their rhythm varied. Of interest to Weeks was the notion of form being generated through the action of local constraints (like rhythm) on a given system (the fixed cluster of notes). A parallel approach generated the elevational treatment of Northwick Park's indeterminate buildings,[23] with the accommodation requirements of individual buildings modulating a standardized structural system. The system acted as a 'form-giving and unifying criterion',[24] reconciling the capacity for growth and change with a desire for architectural coherence across the scheme. Not only did the system manifest Weeks' interest in series (an interest he associated with Pop artist Andy Warhol's work), Weeks also sought to invest Northwick with structural integrity by making its vertical mullions load-bearing and by locating them in accordance with structural necessity. With the loads carried by the lower floors greater than those above, more mullions would be required at the bottom than the top. Hence Northwick Park's pyramidal elevational patterns were effectively system-generated in response to local loadings.

The sketches for Northwick Park were displayed at the 1968 ICA exhibition, Cybernetic Serendipity, organized by Jasia Reichardt. Devoted to the interaction of computer technology and 'art', the show featured computer-generated paintings and music, robots and machines. Cybernetics had been a key concept amongst the avant-garde (including the Independent Group) since Norbert Weiner's *The Human Use of Human Beings* (1947) had outlined how the feedback of information was central to the creation of machines capable of responding to their environment. Weeks' sketches were granted their place since, as the catalogue stated, 'The visible structure has its appearance determined wholly as a result of a computer-orientated programme ... the designers of the building did not intervene'.[25] The interior decoration was also system-generated – via the application of Webern's 'tone row' to the allocation of colour – and

---

22 For a discussion of Cage, Boulez, Stockhausen and Xenakis's experiments in the assimilation of chance into musical production see: Ivanka Stoianova, Oeuvre Ouverte, Oeuvre Indéterminée, in Paris: Musée National de l'Art Moderne, *Les Années 50*, Paris: Editions du Centre Pompidou, 1988, pp. 370–381.
23 In conversation with the author, December 1992. Weeks has recalled the impact of Moldenhauer's *The Death of Anton Webern* (London: Vision Press, 1962), which included a discussion of Webern's 'tone row' and serial music. Some of Webern's pieces have been characterized as 'a straightforward bit of numerology' and that Webern was a 'fanatical lover of plants and everything that grows' (Robert Craft, Anton Webern, *The Score: A Musical Magazine*, September 1955, pp. 9–22).
24 John Weeks, *op. cit.*, note 18.
25 Indeterminate dimensions in architecture, in *Cybernetic Serendipity* (exhibition catalogue), London: Institute of Contemporary Arts, August 1968, p. 69.

was undertaken by Weeks with Phoebe de Syllas. Internal walls were generally white, except at junctions where each wall in turn took a different colour selected sequentially from an unco-ordinated palette. Once selected, the palette was to be used systematically, working through its range until exhausted and then starting again. Such ideas were indicative of Weeks' Constructionist allegiances – these artists' ideas providing support for Weeks' belief that design should be rooted in dynamic processes and systems, not static proportional rules. Weeks' involvement with the Constructionist artists included his involvement in the design of the group's celebrated Fitzroy Street studio exhibitions in the early 1950s,[26] as well as a collaboration with Adrian Heath at the 1956 'This is Tomorrow' exhibition, creating a wall of bricks (dubbed 'Adrian's Wall') in which the position and colour of individual elements resulted from a notional system.

However, whilst indeterminacy proposed that individual hospital departments be housed in independently flexible buildings, this alone did not suggest how to group the various elements. The conceptual solution was outlined in Weeks' 1962 sketch of his indeterminate hospital which simply depicted an entrance area with an extendable corridor leading from it and extensible departments plugged into this 'street' (Figure 8.3). By creating a communications system independent of the plug-in departments, growth and change in the overall hospital could occur without detriment to the comprehensibility of the street.

A precursor for the notion of plug-in had already surfaced in Alison and Peter Smithson's 1953 Sheffield University competition entry. The Smithsons' work of the 1950s evinced an eclectic referencing of sources, reinforced by the inclusivist agenda of the Independent Group. Their interest in Dubuffet, Paolozzi and Pollock's art was indicative of their interest in anti-Classical form-making – its complexity underwriting their Cluster City projects, part of their assault on the zoning and rectilinear geometry of orthodox Modernist urbanism, stressing change, linkage, mobility and complexity (not simply pointless complication). In a similar manner, their Sheffield University scheme deployed pedestrian walkways and a free-form plan, envisaging a horseshoe of buildings skewered on a central circulation spine (Figure 8.8). The design opted for 'an architecture of involvement' in which

> Any new building must establish a 'flow' relationship with its sources of supply, for faculty buildings are 'open' rather than 'closed' ... [reflecting an] aesthetic of change ... Their shape must not only be able to 'take' change but should imply change ... The rooms can be changed in height and length to meet changing faculty requirements, the façades being built up from screens ... whose function and scale change to reflect any change within.[27]

The consideration of the impermanence and flexibility of buildings along a core circulation route was explicit, and whilst not explicitly a 'plug-in' design, the importance of the Smithsons' 'transient aesthetic' – comparable with Hamilton's def-

26 Alistair Grieve, *op. cit.*, note 1.
27 Alison and Peter Smithson, The aesthetics of change, *Architects' Year Book*, no. 8, 1957, pp. 14–22.

figure 8.9
ALISON AND PETER SMITHSON, SHEFFIELD UNIVERSITY PROJECT, 1953

inition of 'pop' – was one appreciated by Weeks. In a similar way, Northwick Park Hospital was transformed into a collection of buildings along a circulation spine, each suited to its particular use, and capable of independent evolution (Figures 8.2 and 8.3). Constructional components were standardized and pre-fabricated and, when coupled with the systematized generation of structure subject to local departmental constraints, produced unique yet generically related buildings. As such the theory marked a radical development of the Corbusian wine-rack analogy deployed at the Marseilles Unité d'Habitation where functionally different but identically shaped units of accommodation were inserted into a fixed structure as required, like bottles of wine in a rack. Northwick Park imposed far fewer constraints (on both the size and arrangement of elements over time) and formed a parallel to fellow Independent Group artist John McHale's Construction Kit sculptures (c.1954) where a kit of parts could be adjusted subject to desire, thereby producing an indeterminate sculpture.[28] McHale's own description of his pieces could equally be applied to Northwick: 'The work is in a state of "becoming" rather than simply "being", and though static in actual space, it is kinetic in a space/time sense'.[29] Yet these were not the only concerns apparent to Weeks, and it is telling that not only were the ward blocks arranged to form the shape of a chromosome, the collection of forms at the top of the ambulance ramp to the casualty department was modelled as 'a Cubist collage' by the architect.[30]

Whilst the building's shape sought to challenge what Weeks saw as the inhibiting pretensions of the Classical architectural language, the blunt treatment of the hospital's detailing hinted at the building's engagement with Brutalist ethics, privileging the usage of materials – not just concrete – supposedly 'as found' in an attempt to connote honest rigour and candid unsentimentality. Window frames were of untreated aluminium, concrete was left as moulded, and mechanical services were exposed in public areas. Similarly, the roof-top plant-rooms were encased in clear, patent glass. Just like the patients beneath, boiler plant and air-conditioning ducts were exposed to scrutiny, examination and repair. Whether the hospital's brutal image was appropriate was not

28 The sculptures are reproduced in John McHale. Magda Cordell, *Uppercase*, no. 1, c. 1958, n.p.
29 John McHale, notes on 'Spectator relationship', c.1952–1955, mimeo. I am indebted to Magda Cordell-McHale for sight of these notes. McHale also suggested, in relation to architecture that 'the person, in constant interaction with this created structure and by experiencing it, collaborates with its creator' and attributed similar qualities to his constructions.
30 In conversation with the author, March 1993.

an issue: as the architect put it, 'That was never a concern, it was extraordinary really. It just seemed to me to be so sensible really, and so beautiful probably. There was no question that the public would love it, obviously'.[31]

Northwick Park, then, engaged with both intra- and inter-generational analogies of growth and form. Its individual buildings were generated by systems deemed analogous to processes of growth, whilst the overall form was amenable to homoeostatic and evolutionary adaptation over time in line with operational necessity. Just like a tree, as Weeks put it, new branches could grow as required, whilst others could wither away.

four
THE LEGACY OF INDETERMINACY

The application of indeterminacy to building was not confined to Northwick Park Hospital. The project was widely publicized throughout its construction and spawned a brief flurry of indeterminate schemes on student drawing boards. Its influence may be noted in the new buildings for the Polytechnic of Central London, Marylebone Road (Greater London Council, 1964–1971) where capped-off extendable ends were provided for the future expansion of the building.[32] Furthermore, subsequent hospitals by Llewelyn-Davies and Weeks developed the strategy into three dimensions, envisaging a lattice of communications routes into which indeterminate structures could be inserted. Whereas Northwick had offered a communications spine which offered only the possibility of branches off the main route, the demands for greater degrees of indeterminacy and flexibility were to be met by increasingly elaborate two- and three-dimensional networks of streets. Such a development was paralleled by Christopher Alexander's influential 1965 article, 'The city is not a tree',[33] in which Alexander criticized the sterility of modern planning and blamed the reductiveness of simple hierarchical organizational structures – as had been employed at Northwick.

Simultaneously, Weeks' business partner, Richard Llewelyn-Davies, was applying similar ideas to the planning of the new town of Milton Keynes (Figure 8.10). Rather than propose the standard post-war solutions of ring and radial road systems, Milton Keynes was to offer a neutral net of communication routes, establishing a grid of 1 km^2 plots within which any activity could be located.[34] Such a strategy reflected American planner Melvin Webber's notion of a motorized urban environment which no longer required the provision of traditional, centralized, urban focal points.[35] Equally, the design paid homage to the model of Los Angeles' urbanism, a form which had been captivating

31 In conversation with the author, December 1992.
32 *Architect's Journal*, 2 June 1971, pp. 1245–1264.
33 Christopher Alexander, A city is not a tree, *Architectural Forum*, vol. 122, no.1, April 1965; published in Britain in *Design*, no. 206, February 1966, pp. 46–55.
34 Llewelyn-Davies, Weeks, Forestier-Walker and Bor, *The Plan for Milton Keynes*, Milton Keynes: Milton Keynes Development Corporation, March 1970.
35 See Melvin Webber, The urban place and the non-place urban realm, in Melvin Webber (editor), *Explorations into Urban Structure*, Philadelphia, PA: University of Pennsylvania Press, 1964. For a recent discussion see *Le Visiteur*, no. 3, Autumn 1997, pp. 103–180.

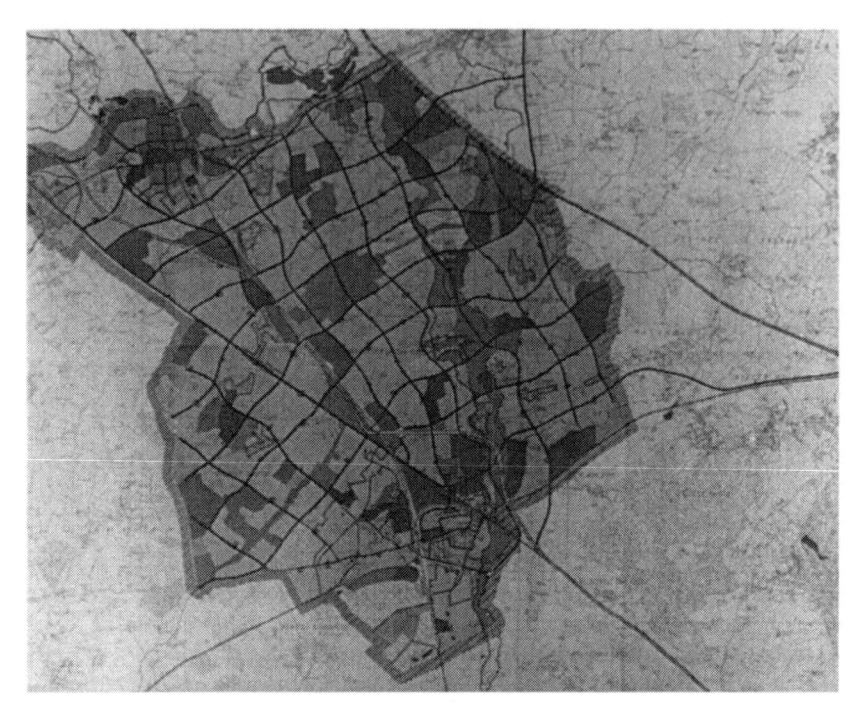

figure 8.10
LLEWELYN-DAVIES, WEEKS, FORESTIER-WALKER AND BOR,
MILTON KEYNES NEW TOWN, PLAN, 1970

British critics with a mixture of wonder and horror for the best part of the post-war period.[36] Notably, the plan for the new city made it clear that industrial and residential areas should be freely dispersed about the city, and that the functional designation of individual grid-squares be made as required in response to need rather than some predetermined zoning strategy. Yet whilst the Milton Keynes plan proclaimed indeterminacy of use, it retained a resolutely planned infrastructure, locating roads according to the planners' wishes and designating such areas as the central business district.

five
INDETERMINACY AND NON-PLAN

The problem encountered at Northwick Park and Milton Keynes was one of reconciling responsiveness and flexibility with the inertness of architectural and urban infrastructure: how to reconcile the ideal of freedom with practical constraints. The authors of 'Non-Plan' put it differently: 'I dreamt I found freedom in my non-plan bra'.[37] For the Non-Planners, building development was to be permitted wherever wanted, granting freedom from the impositional value-judgements of planning committees. Nonetheless, 'Non-Plan' dared not transgress the political–economic boundaries of the capitalist framework within which it was located. With no consider-

36 For criticism see the *Architectural Review*, December 1950; for a positive discussion see the *Economist's* California edition, 9 July 1960.
37 Banham, Barker, Hall and Price, Non-Plan: an experiment in freedom, *New Society*, 20 March 1969, pp. 435–444.

ation of the productive and distributive constraints imposed by the economy, Non-Plan's liberalism would now be constrained not by ideologically reinforcing planning regulations but by individual command over resources, and hence by the economic (in)efficiencies and social (in)justices of the free market.

A fundamental disjunction clearly exists between the ideal of freedom implicit in such projects as Northwick Park, Milton Keynes and 'Non-Plan' and the architectural constraints and institutional frameworks within which they were located. Whilst the rhetoric of flexibility and adaptive efficiency could draw credibility from neo-Darwinian models of evolution (themselves analogous to Smithian free-market economic optimization), the programme of these buildings was circumscribed by the *dirigiste*, interventionist framework of Britain's Welfare State. Clearly, free-market efficiency was not considered irreconcilable with socially redistributive justice, although economic theory suggests that both are not in practice likely to be coincidental.[38] The result, then, was likely to be a compromise: part freedom, part control.

This tension between freedom and control, indicative of a Welfare State operating in a mixed economy, is paralleled by the architecture of Northwick Park itself, where the freedoms of the indeterminate buildings are generated out of pre-determined systems of control. The aim, of course, had been simple: to ensure the transparency of architecture in the provision of flexible health-care buildings. Yet Northwick Park was situated within a capitalist economy with a high degree of State intervention, its architecture poised between states of political and economic freedom and control. This was neatly paralleled by Weeks' retention of architectural control by designing not only the system out of which most of the hospital's buildings were then 'objectively' generated, but also the standardized kit of parts out of which they were then constructed. Architectural coherence, if still deemed to be a relevant goal for the indeterminate building (and clearly at Northwick Park it was), could lie only at the extremes of the architectural gesture – in the totality of the system, or the minutiæ of the details – and Weeks had retained control of both.

[38] We cannot *a priori* rule out the possibility that the economically most efficient distribution of resources might be the most socially just. However, we can note that the establishment of the redistributive mechanisms of the Welfare State were largely based on the perceived failure of the market to achieve a socially just distribution of wealth.

#09
YONA FRIEDMAN: FUNCTION FOLLOWS FORM

'Form follows function' was the battle-cry of twentieth-century architecture.

one
WHAT IS FUNCTION?

figure 9.1
FUNCTION OF EACH ARCHITECTURAL SPACE IS DETERMINED
BY THE EQUIPMENT SPECIFIC FOR THAT SPACE

Function, for architects, is a mechanistic concept: how should a building be used? The function of each architectural space is determined, first of all by the equipment specific for that space: furniture and fixtures (Figure 9.1).

figure 9.2
LINKAGE SCHEME

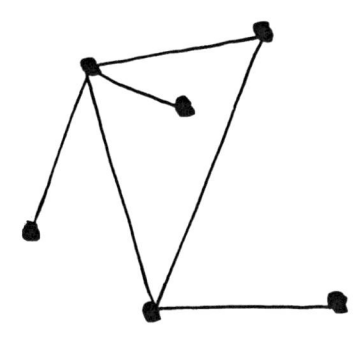

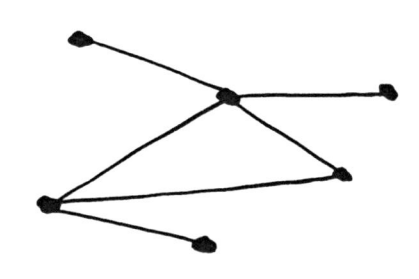

figure 9.3
TOPOLOGIC TRANSFORMATION OF A
LINKAGE SCHEME

Functional spaces, for architects, are points in a linkage scheme. To map a linkage scheme graphs are used: their nodes represent specialized equipment, their lines are the paths linking these specialized spaces (Figure 9.2).

A graph is a topological figure (made, for example, with buttons and thread). A graph has no definite form: it can be deformed, laid in any desired pattern (Figure 9.3).

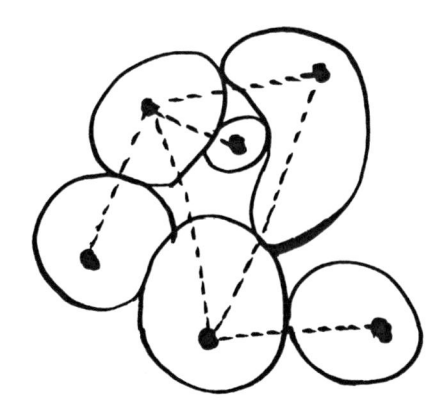

figure 9.4
THE DUAL OF THE LINKAGE SCHEME

Graphs, representing linkage schemes for architects, besides being topological are also metric: equipment and people who use it have sizes, and paths have length. These metric factors cannot be optimized: they are prefabricated, partly emotionally defined.

Function, mapped by a graph, can follow any form (Figure 9.4).

two
WHAT IS FORM?

"MONOMORPH" "POLYMORPH"

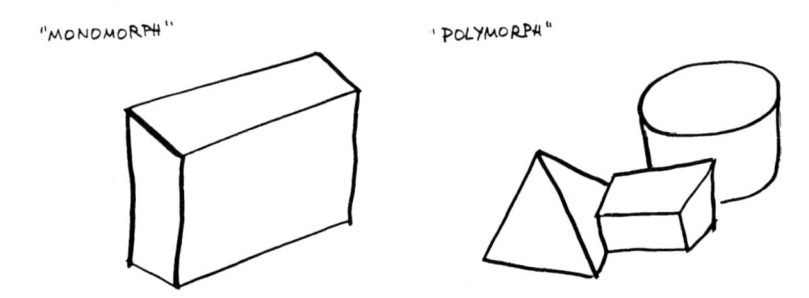

figure 9.5
(A) MONOMORPH; (B) POLYMORPH

Architecture's products, buildings, have plastic forms. Seen from the outside, they are like sculptures. This outside form can be a 'monomorph', a body without any articulation. It can also be a 'polymorph', a composite made of a number of elementary forms (Figure 9.5).

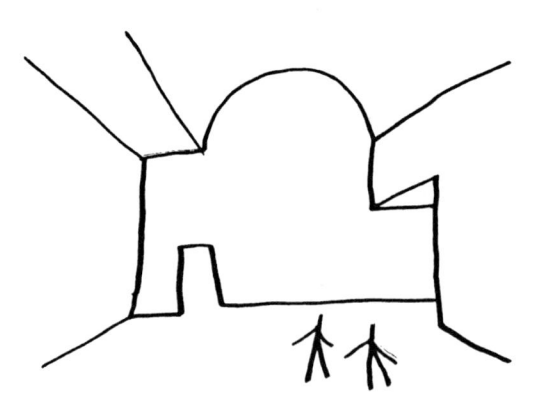

figure 9.6
THE 'HOLLOW'

This is true for all artefacts, not only for those conceived by architects. An artefact of architecture also has, beside its outside form, an inside, of a size that people can enter (Figure 9.6).

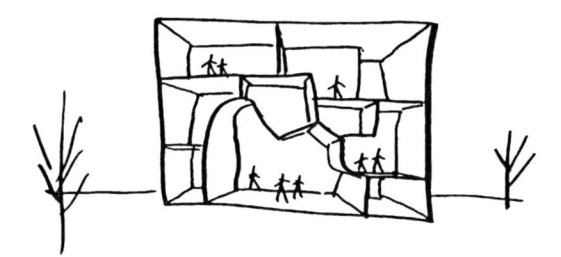

EXTERNAL FORM DOES NOT DEPEND
ON INTERNAL FORMS

OUTSIDE AND INSIDE ARE INDEPENDENT

figure 9.7
(A) EXTERNAL FORM DOES NOT DEPEND ON INTERNAL FORMS; (B) OUTSIDE AND INSIDE ARE INDEPENDENT

But, it is not a logical necessity that the inside of a building should be the negative of the outside. A building's inside can be fundamentally different from its outside form (Figure 9.7).

Both the outside form and the inside form are determined largely by emotional factors. Thus, an architectural artefact is a body with a hollow, eventually of a volume different from its external shape. Within and around that body a graph mapping functions can be fitted. This is the first step towards function following form.

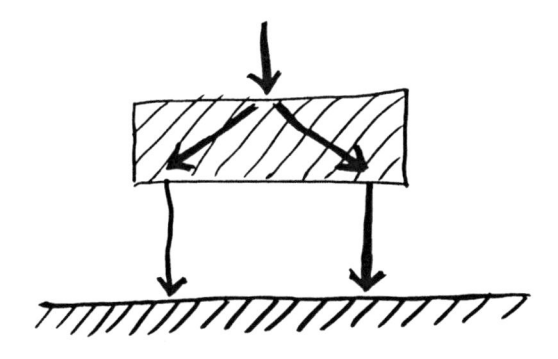

figure 9.8
STRUCTURE: A DEVICE CHANNELLING GRAVITY

The next step starts with structure. We call structure the device which channels gravity around the hollow inside and which keeps the building's external shape upright (Figure 9.8).

figure 9.9
THE PRINCIPAL ACTOR: THE USER

At this stage it is necessary to examine what I call decision.

Decision in architecture is complex: first (but not necessarily in this order) it means the graph mapping functions. The function of the map concerns the inhabitant, the user of the building (Figure 9.9).

figure 9.10
THE INHABITANT AND THE PASSER-BY

There is no optimal function map: the choice of the function map, to be made by the user, is an emotional choice.

The envelope of the function map, the body of the building, might be as good as the first choice. This choice is also an emotional one. But the inhabitant is not the only user. The external form of the building also concerns the public, the passer-by. Both the inhabitant and the passer-by evaluate the external form following emotional criteria (Figure 9.10).

figure 9.11
EMOTIONAL CHOICE

As for the negative form, the hollow, this concerns first of all the inhabitant. This choice is an emotional choice too (Figure 9.11).

The metric component of the function map, thus the enveloping form, positive and negative, is not completely free for choice. People and equipment have pre-existing sizes. If the choice of the function map and its envelope made by its user are largely emotional (consciously or not), the process is a dynamic one. Emotions change with time, so do preferences. Users change too.

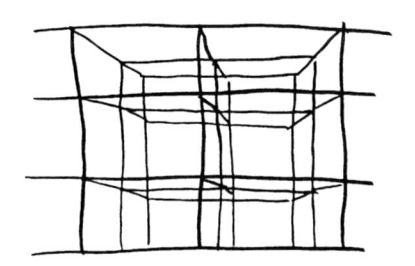

figure 9.12
STRUCTURE IS RIGID

figure 9.13
ENVELOPES WITHIN THE STRUCTURE ARE MOBILE

Now, to return to structure: structure (the device against gravity) has to be rigid (Figure 9.12).

The envelope is not necessarily synonymous with structure. Envelopes protect against climate, against intrusions. Envelopes are not necessarily rigid (Figure 9.13).

Structure can be evaluated emotionally; envelopes will surely also be. Structure and envelope can be separated from each other. It was noted before that users' emotions might change. However, structure can only be changed with great difficulty. Envelopes can be changed relatively easily. What can be changed most easily is the function map. Functions can follow form.

The dynamic process of architecture can be summed up as follows:

– function maps (topological graphs) can be changed most easily;
– envelopes (which determine the external shape and the hollows) can be changed relatively easily;
– the supporting structure (the skeleton) is the most unchangeable component of the architectural artefact.

figure 9.14
RATIONALISM IS ALSO A KIND OF EMOTION

These are the material components. But there are also the immaterial ones, the most important of which are the users' preferences. Users' preferences are necessarily emotional. Rationalism is a kind of emotion too (Figure 9.14).

figure 9.15
THE PLAN TRIGGERS AN ERRATIC PROCESS

Users' preferences manifest themselves as use patterns. Use patterns are always personal. Users' preferences manifest themselves as taste, as unstated aesthetic criteria, which are always personal. Finally, users' preferences are concerned with status symbols: illusions made for other people. Users' preferences are kept within limits by economic factors: how much effort will the final output cost?

Function can adapt to all desiderata: function follows form, but also pre-conceived personal ideas, and one's pocketbook.

Architecture was never simply functionalist. Architecture follows ever-changing day-to-day life.

The style of a building consists in its users. An unused building is nothing else than a ruin.

An architectural plan is only the triggering of a long-wearing erratic dynamic process (Figure 9.15).

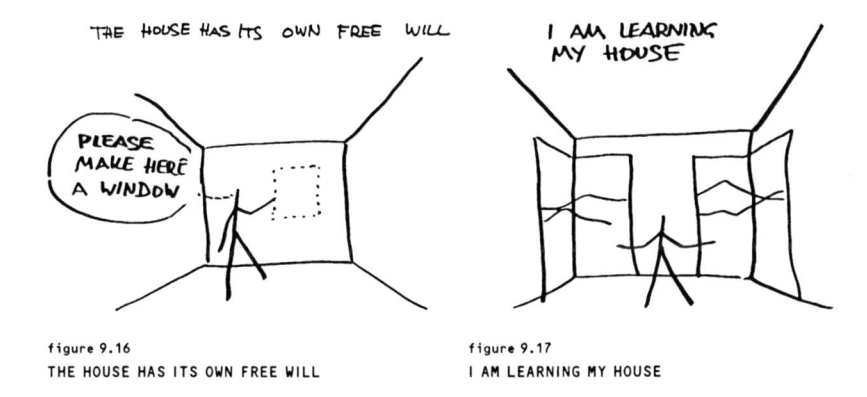

figure 9.16
THE HOUSE HAS ITS OWN FREE WILL

figure 9.17
I AM LEARNING MY HOUSE

The process cannot be mastered by the architect, nor by the user. Architectural artefacts seem to possess their own 'free will' (not conscious but effective) (Figure 9.16).

Both the technician (master of the structure) and the 'artist' (the user, in a way) who decide about form and function, cannot know the outcome in advance.

Many years ago I promoted self-planning (user-design) and mobile architecture (techniques of making the alteration of form and function easy, within a rigid, pre-existing 'infrastructure'). But later I came to believe that the complex system making a building decides everything for itself. Users, once the building exists, learn to play the game (Figure 9.17).

three
FINAL NOTE

It is interesting to remark that this analysis cannot be translated into urban design without some reservations.

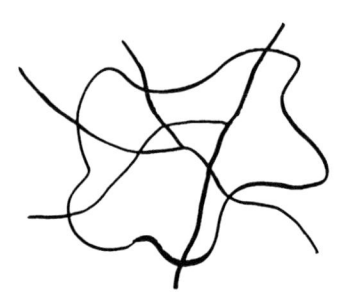

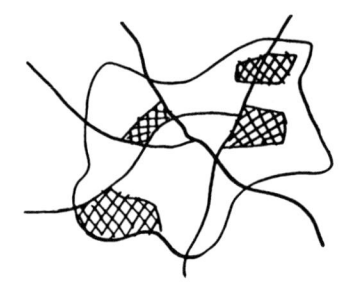

figure 9.18
CITIES ARE FORMLESS

figure 9.19
CITIES ARE MULTIFUNCTIONAL

First of all, opposite to buildings which can have a 'form', cities are formless (Figure 9.18).

Secondly, as for 'function', cities have no precise function: they are 'multi-functional' (i.e. they contain all social functions) (Figure 9.19).

figure 9.20
CITIES ARE SHAPED THROUGH THE
INHABITANTS' BEHAVIOUR

'Multi-functionality can go hand in hand with formlessness' would be the urban analogue to 'function follows form'. The role of users, as for urban reality, is all-important and totally unconscious (Figure 9.20).

figure 9.21
THE HARDWARE FOR MOBILE TOWN PLANNING + THE INHABITANTS'
INITIATIVES = *'VILLE SPATIALE'*

Mobile town planning is the urban equivalent to mobile architecture. Contrarily to classic town planning, where urban space is restricted to the void between buildings, mobile town planning is not reduced to traffic space alone.

Urban hardware for mobile town planning consists of simple 'impact points' at ground level (staircase pillars) laid out on a large-scale pattern and supporting an overhead small-module structure. Effective space would be the voids enveloping the privately used and ever-changing 'enclosures' from all sides (Figure 9.21).

Cities do not follow plans, even less than buildings do. People reorganize them daily through their behaviour. Townscape and behaviour mutually adapt themselves.

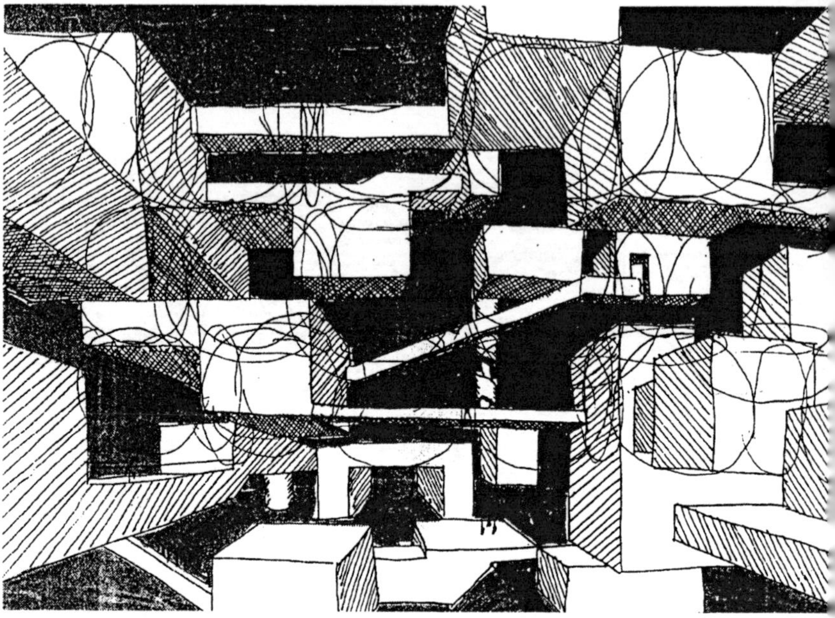

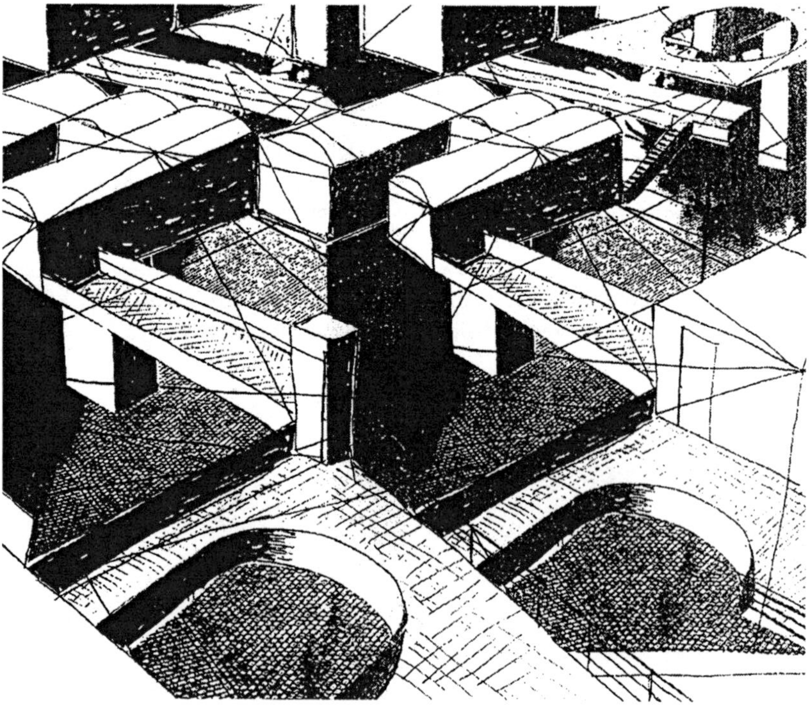

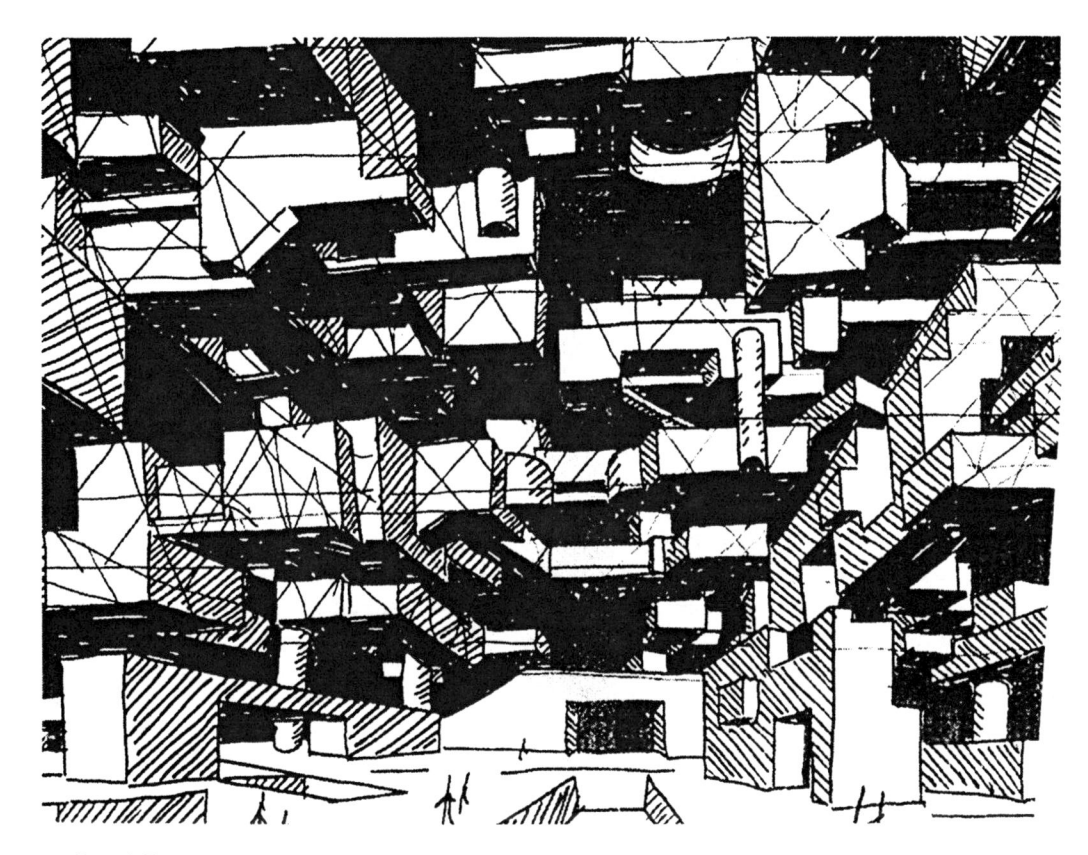

top figure 9.24
YONA FRIEDMAN, PROJECTION OF
LA VILLE SPATIALE, 1958

opposite page top figure 9.22
YONA FRIEDMAN, PROJECTION OF
LA VILLE SPATIALE, 1958

opposite page bottom figure 9.23
YONA FRIEDMAN, PROJECTION OF
LA VILLE SPATIALE, 1958

#10

JOHN BECK: BUCKMINSTER FULLER AND THE POLITICS OF SHELTER

In Nathaniel Hawthorne's *The House of the Seven Gables* (1851),[1] Holgrave, the freethinking daguerreotypist lodging with Hepzibah Pyncheon, the reclusive owner of the seventeenth-century house of the title, is pontificating to Phoebe, Hepzibah's young country cousin. 'Shall we never get rid of this past!' he complains, 'It lies upon the Present like a giant's dead body!' The burden of the past is everywhere a tyranny of habit and repetition, housing the present in its dilapidated forms. After a gloomy litany of restrictions imposed by the 'Dead Man's icy hand', however, Holgrave soars in rebellion as he envisions the day 'when no man shall build his house for posterity':

> If each generation were allowed and expected to build its own houses, that single change, comparatively unimportant in itself, would imply almost every reform which society is now suffering for. I doubt whether even our public edifices – our capitols, state-houses, court-house, city-halls, and churches – ought to be built of such permanent materials as stone or brick. It were better that they should crumble to ruin, once in twenty years, or thereabouts, as a hint to the people to examine into and reform the institutions which they symbolize.[2]

Buckminster Fuller (1895–1983) is an inheritor of a powerful tradition of New England nonconformism, characterized most memorably by the Transcendentalists of the midnineteenth century, which included Fuller's great aunt Margaret Fuller, and of which Hawthorne was a sceptical satellite. A hybrid of German idealism, Jeffersonian republicanism and Yankee self-help, Transcendentalism was didactic, utopian, organicist, supremely individualistic. The children of revolutionaries, its adherents saw the USA as a democracy and as a nation, as a source of moral and social salvation, philosophical argument bleeding effortlessly, if not always intentionally, into a discourse of expansionist imperialism. Reading the USA's founding principles as natural serves to universalize the US model and de-natures all other ways of life. While this is a familiar argument, the conjunction of the revolutionary democratic impulse and the celebration of a manifest destiny inheres in Fuller's vision of an emancipatory 'comprehensive design science', and might explain why he was courted by both the hippies and the Marines.

'I was born cross-eyed', Fuller writes. It was four years before his acute long-sightedness was corrected with glasses. 'Until four I could see only large patterns, houses, trees, outlines of people with blurred colouring […]. I did not see a human eye or a

---

1 Nathaniel Hawthorne, *The House of the Seven Gables*, New York: Norton, 1967 (originally published 1851).
2 *Ibid.*, pp. 182–184.

teardrop or a human hair until I was four.'³ We may deduce two things from this. Firstly, the useful intervention of technology to adjust natural dysfunction, as in Herman Melville's *The Confidence Man* (1857): 'Nature made me blind and would have kept me so. My oculist counterplotted her'. Secondly, that despite Fuller's 'new ability to apprehend details, my childhood's spontaneous dependence only upon big pattern clues has persisted'.⁴

This mix of romantic enchantment counterplotted with technological realignment embeds Fuller's industrial innovations within an organic universe where human ingenuity confirms a sense of belonging and sovereignty in the face of an indifferent environment. It is quite an ingenious manoeuvre which enables industrial manufacture on the largest scale to be presented as coterminous with natural process. Fuller's structures, in following the most basic mathematical models – triangle, tetrahedron, icosahedron – are thereby confirming their similitude to molecular forms – the 'big pattern clues' are also the details.

Fuller served in the Navy between 1917 and 1922, then went into the construction business with his father-in-law until the company's failure five years later. 1927, the year Lindbergh flew the Atlantic, was Fuller's much vaunted 'year of silence', when, so he claimed, he spoke to no one, not even his wife. The mass of drawings, designs and writing produced during this year – much of which was privately printed in an edition of 200 and distributed to friends and possible sponsors in 1928 as *4D* – reveal Fuller's main ideas to be in place. By 1938, with the publication of Fuller's first real book, *Nine Chains to the Moon*,⁵ the vision has taken the form of a dwelling-led, full-on critique of corporate capitalism. During this eleven years the USA had enjoyed unprecedented prosperity and endured unparalleled economic hardship. Fuller's designs are a consequence of both. The Depression confirmed for Fuller what his own lack of commercial success had revealed: capitalism worked inefficiently, self-interest and short-term gain inhibiting experimentation and truly beneficial technological change. Housing suffered under the tyranny of the architect, planner, manager, local politician and government bureaucrat. Fuller believed that efficiency of design would reveal these hindrances for what they really were: obstacles placed by backward looking, power hungry beneficiaries of a corrupt system.

Fuller's vision was of a technological utopia based on mass-produced, prefabricated shelter, airlifted to site in canisters and retailing at around the same price as a top of the range family automobile. This idea is first formulated with the 4D towers (4D for 4-

3 Richard Buckminster Fuller, *Utopia or Oblivion: the prospects for humanity,* London: Allen Lane, 1970, p. 11. For other studies of Fuller's work see: J. Baldwin, *BuckyWorks: Buckminster Fuller's ideas for today,* New York: Wiley, 1996; M. Ben-Eli (editor), R. Buckminster Fuller retrospective, special issue of *Architectural Design,* 42, no. 12, 1972; Richard Buckminster Fuller and R. Marks, *The Dymaxion World of Buckminster Fuller,* New York: Anchor, 1960, 1973; H. Kenner, *Bucky: a guided tour of Buckminster Fuller,* New York: Morrow, 1973; Lloyd Steven Sieden, *Buckminster Fuller's Universe: an appreciation,* New York: Plenum, 1989. For more information about the work of Buckminster Fuller contact: The Buckminster Fuller Institute, 2040 Alameda Padre Serra, Suite 224, Santa Barbara, CA 93103, USA (tel. (805) 962-0022).
4 Richard Buckminster Fuller, *Utopia or Oblivion: the prospects for humanity, op. cit.,* note 3, p. 11. Herman Melville, *The Confidence Man: his masquerade,* New York: The Library of America, 1984, p. 956 (originally published 1857).
5 Richard Buckminster Fuller, *Nine Chains to the Moon,* London: Cape, 1973 (originally published 1938).

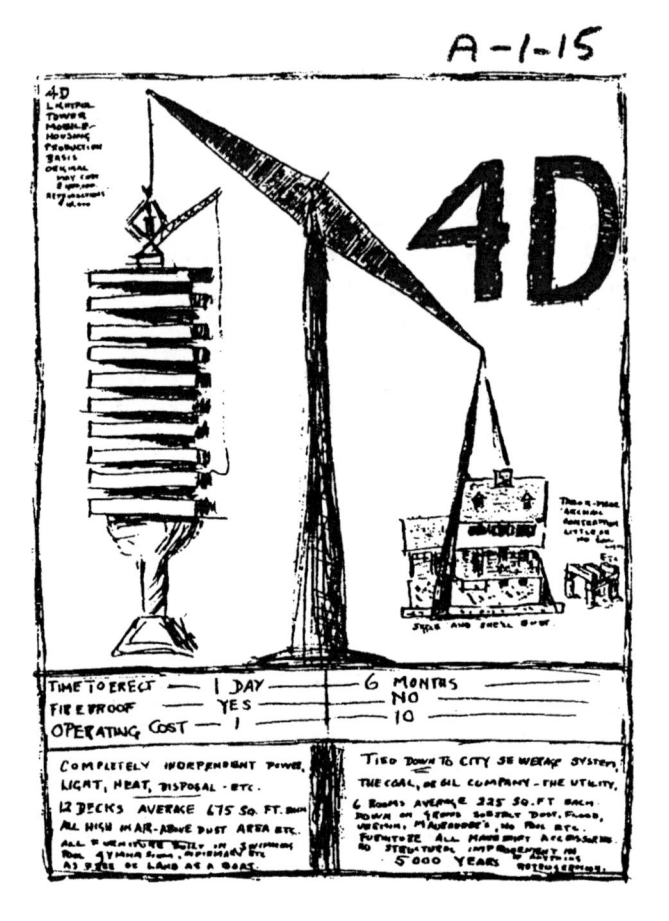

figure 10.1
SKETCH BY FULLER FROM 1927 COMPARING A CONVENTIONAL HOUSE TO HIS
TWELVE-DECK TOWER. ©1960, ESTATE OF BUCKMINSTER FULLER

dimensional thinking – an Einsteinian space–time influence) and the Dymaxion House (Dynamic + Maximum + ion) of 1927. A model of this house, mast-supported, and made of high-stretch alloys and plastics developed for the aircraft industry, was first exhibited in a Chicago department store in 1929, and its design published in *Architectural Forum* and *Shelter* in 1932 (Figure 10.1). Within twenty-four hours (the time taken for delivery, Fuller promised), the new occupant could expect the elimination of 'drudgery, selfishness, exploitation, politics and centralized control'.[6]

The scales in Fuller's primitive drawing tell the oppressive truth about conventional housing: heavy, expensive, time-consuming, dirty and vulnerable. By contrast, Fuller's twelve storey tower is 'completely independent', self-regulating, raised above the squalor of ground level, 'as free of land as a boat' (Figure 10.2). Weight is the enemy of freedom because it is resistant to movement, and the immovable demands maintenance and preservation. For Fuller, such dwellings irrationally resist the energies of space and time

6 Martin Pawley, *Buckminster Fuller*, London: Trefoil, 1990, p. 56.

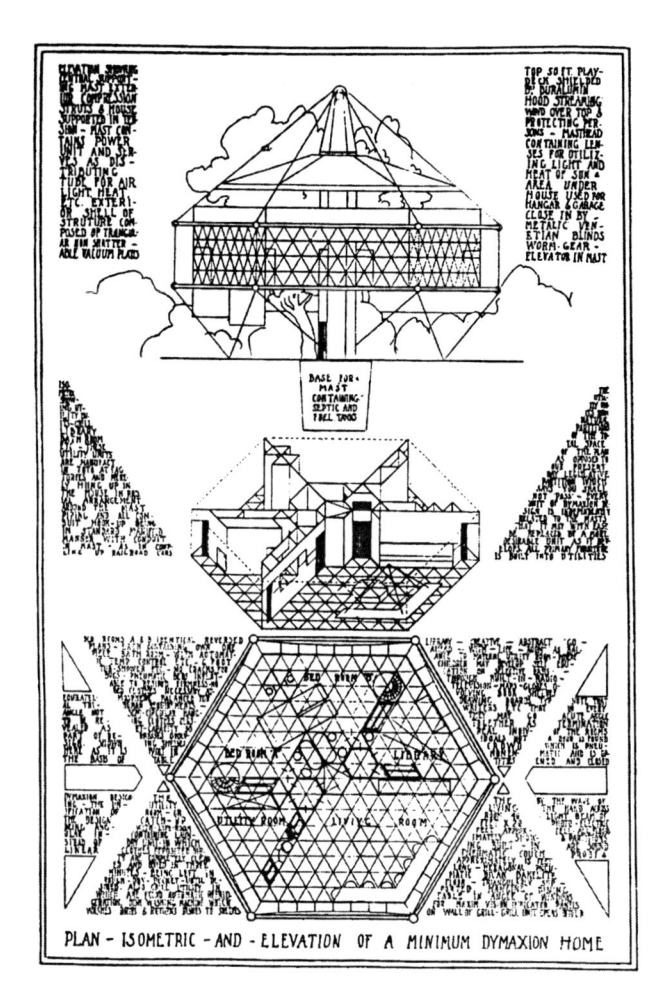

figure 10.2
PLAN, ISOMETRIC, AND ELEVATION OF THE 1927 DYMAXION HOUSE.
© 1960, ESTATE OF BUCKMINSTER FULLER

and are no more than monuments to an arrogant and untenable belief in fixity. Fuller is not interested in the least in architecture as a profession or as an art form, he is interested in social action: 'In architecture "form" is a noun; in industry, "form" is a verb. Industry is concerned with DOING, whereas architecture has been engrossed with making replicas of end results of what people have industrially demonstrated in the past'.[7] The modern movement, for Fuller, went no further than to update the shell of an obsolete artefact – the permanent dwelling. As such, he would agree with Roger Scruton's point that the functionalist theories of modern architecture 'have been used not to condemn but to articulate aesthetic values'.[8]

Given the remarkable impact on daily life and social organization effected by the motor car as a result of Henry Ford's production methods, Fuller's hopes for his house are

7 Richard Buckminster Fuller, *op. cit.*, note 5, p. 41.
8 Roger Scruton, *The Aesthetics of Architecture*, London: Methuen, 1979, p. 38.

perhaps not unreasonable. And his admission that it would cost $100 million to produce a prototype is less extravagant considering it cost Ford $43 million to develop the Model-A.[9] Fuller had more than an eye on the car industry when designing his own future for the USA. Nothing confirmed the practical wisdom of the inventor/pioneer like Ford's production line, introduced in 1913. As a consequence, by 1924 six cars could be built for what it cost to make one in 1904. Fuller was not alone in seeing possibilities for dwelling machines. Walter Gropius compared figures in 1938: between 1913 and 1926 the average cost of building a house rose by 200 per cent, the cost of living by 178 per cent. The cost of cars had fallen in the same period by 22 per cent, the cost of Ford cars by 50 per cent.[10] The lesson is clear.

The car always meant more than transportation in the USA. It embodied foundational American values: individual freedom, perpetual movement, self-transformation through geographical displacement. When Emerson said that 'everything good is on the highway', he was declaring an expansive faith that Ford merely made manifest. The liberty suggested by such rootlessness is at the heart of Fuller's houses. His rejection of weight and mass in architecture in favour of tensional structure is a rejection of monumentality and permanence in preference for the contingent and ephemeral. This is a state of mind as well as a design strategy, signalling an American suspicion of fixed and immutable form which can be traced back at least as far as Jefferson.

Fuller's mobile housing is a proposal for social revolution which relies for its validity upon peculiarly American readings of open space as somehow free for occupation, of land as horizonless, of the innate benefits of mobility as an agent of individual and civic well-being. One of the greatest fears harboured by Americans since the time of the Revolution was that the republic would stagnate, become fixed and immobile, degenerating into nothing but another version of European rigidity and corruption. My opening passage from Hawthorne's novel is an articulation of Jefferson's suggestion that a revolution was needed every twenty years in order to keep the country fresh and young, a project of perpetual reinvention. Fuller's frequent and sustained attack on the meaninglessness of modern life, its routine, its creative barrenness, the alienation generated by its cramped and filthy cities, is a Jeffersonian attack. Cantilevered onto Jefferson's pastoralism is a utopian vision of manufactured reconstruction, a form of industrial production that will bring about the end of capitalism through the elimination of the false needs that an economy of consumption endlessly generates. A contempt for place is relieved by a libertarian notion of space. The globe becomes an open prairie and air travel gives access to all areas. The Dymaxion house is a cross between the covered wagon and the tepee, shelter for a wandering people. The nineteenth-century notion of the frontier as a safety valve against urban disaffection and individual suffocation is renovated through modern technology and the American self is enabled to return to his or her proper state – that of the nomad.

9 Martin Pawley, *op. cit.*, note 6, p. 56.
10 Martin Pawley, *Architecture versus Housing*, London: Studio Vista, 1971, p. 50.

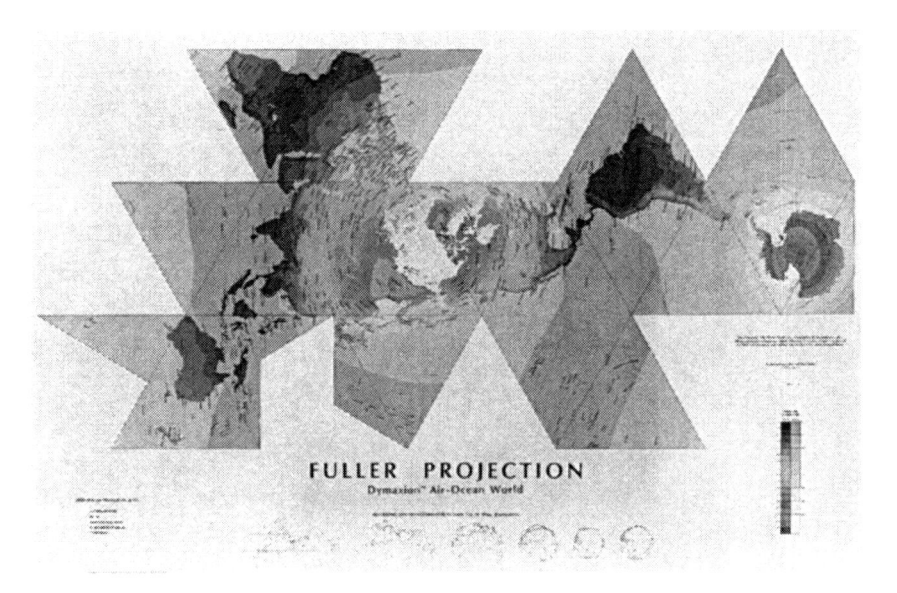

figure 10.3
WORLD MAP ON DYMAXION PROJECTION.
©1960, ESTATE OF BUCKMINSTER FULLER

A nomadic people is free-ranging, unsettled, and therefore open to adaptation as conditions change. Unchained from fixed horizons and habits of thought, physical and intellectual structures are dismantled in favour of exploration and experimentation. A nomadic community, organized around the principles of mobility and necessity, must be flexible and therefore non-hierarchical. Bonds formed through mutual interest can be more easily broken than when society is confined by economic, racial or class imperatives.

Perhaps Fuller's most vivid display of a nomad sensibility is his world map (Figure 10.3). A rejection of Eurocentric deformations of global representation, Fuller's map manages to chart the Earth's surface with minimum distortion. Keeping the shape constant, the continents can be shifted around to reveal different global patterns and networks. In the Air-Ocean version, the land masses of the planet seem peculiarly clustered together. The shortest route between places is across the Arctic. This is the world of air transport, a smooth space of undirected movement. The first map was published around 1940, although preliminary sketches go back at least to 1936. The houses are wedded to a cartography of delimited nomadic space.

While the USA has made a virtue of rootlessness and celebrated geographical wandering as a metonym for national liberty, the American nomad is fraught with contradictions. It is, in fact, the indigenous population of much of the USA which should most properly be considered nomadic, with its attendant fluid and communal notion of land rights. It is this very vagrancy of the Indians which enabled settlers to legally claim land to be free, that is, unsettled and available. Equating settlement with ownership leaves Indian conceptions of habitation literally ungrounded. The white nomad – the pioneer – is, for Americans, the necessary but temporary phase which precedes the staking out of property boundaries. The American nomad is, then, the carrier of the very system of restriction he or she symbolically stands against. As Paul Virilio has remarked, 'revolution is movement, but movement is not revolution'.[11]

In rejecting settlement in terms of property ownership, Fuller is rejecting the bourgeois revolution of 1776 and reinstating a prior notion of land as smooth space. On the other hand, this shaking off of boundaries serves to open up all space for colonization and domination. The movements of multinational corporations have confirmed this in their unhindered vagrancy around the planet, opportunistically alighting on favourable sites where labour, land and materials are cheapest. In terms of labour, the idea of mobility is promoted by business but is largely impossible in practice, enabling a loosening of responsibility on the part of companies no longer rooted in local communities. Workers, of course, are not able to follow jobs as easily as the ideology of the free market suggests.

Fuller's reasoning, then, assumes an ideal liberal democracy which his plans in themselves cannot create. The construction of the mobile dwelling industry might, indeed, engender such a society, but how is business to be persuaded that it should invest in an industry which will bring about the end of its hegemony? With Fuller, as with so many liberal progressive theories of social change through planning and technique, there is no adequate vocabulary with which to deal with the issue of power and, in this silence, power moves in and takes over nomadic thinking as its own domain.

Fuller liked to claim that he learned everything he needed to know about design and engineering in the Navy. Those brief years of military service also signal the beginning of a sporadic but lifelong collaboration with the US armed forces. During the Second World War Fuller converted steel grain bins into mobile military dwellings, which he called the Dymaxion Deployment Unit (DDU) (Figure 10.4). Hundreds were used in the Pacific and the Persian Gulf. After the war he turned to a new domestic dwelling design, the Dymaxion Dwelling Machine, or Wichita House as it became known

---

11 Paul Virilio, *Speed and Politics: an essay on dromology* (trans. Mark Polizzotti), New York: Semiotext(e), 1986, p. 18.

top figure 10.5
THE DYMAXION DWELLING MACHINE, OR WICHITA HOUSE, OF 1947,
SHOWING THE CYLINDER WHICH CONTAINED ALL THE COMPONENT PARTS.
©1960, ESTATE OF BUCKMINSTER FULLER

left figure 10.4
THE DYMAXION DEPLOYMENT UNIT (DDU), MANUFACTURED BY BUTLER FOR THE
US MILITARY, 1940-1941. ©1960, ESTATE OF BUCKMINSTER FULLER

(Figure 10.5). War-driven developments in materials and production methods made the project more feasible than the 1927 model, and a demobilized bomber factory in Wichita, Kansas, was authorized to produce prototypes for the Air Force. Despite media and customer interest, however, as with the earlier house, a combination of problems shut down the project. Union difficulties, lack of trained installation crews and a viable distribution infrastructure, Fuller's own reluctance to market what he saw only as a prototype and, most fundamental of all, absence of funds for tooling costs, revealed that the strength of design did not guarantee commercial success. A market-driven social revolution looked unlikely.

After the collapse of the Wichita House Fuller moved away from commercial projects into research and education, working as a visiting professor at colleges throughout the USA. Much of his research, in fact, was made possible through the exploitation of facilities and student labour that teaching made available. It is this campus-based work which led to the development of Fuller's most famous innovation, the geodesic dome, a potentially infinitely extendible tensile frame of equilateral triangles. The spherical shape distributes load in all directions throughout the structure and the dome increases in strength the larger it gets.

As an educationalist Fuller found an ideal site for pure research and for spreading the word about an efficient, sustainable, dwelling-led revolution. Certainly, the students were enthusiastic. The communal environment fostered by Fuller's university research projects, so inspirational to the countercultural generation of the 1960s, has, however, overshadowed the fact that Fuller always claimed ownership of work done by his students and that, more seriously, many of the experiments and prototypes were directly utilized by the military. Indeed, as Alex Soojung-Kim Pang has shown, the rise of the geodesic dome, and of Fuller, are largely due to their extensive role in Cold War security and propaganda programmes.

The prospect of nuclear war seemed to threaten Fuller's chances of leading a consumer-sponsored overthrow of the status quo through housing design, since the arms race and permanent preparedness swallowed up the resources and manpower he had counted on convincing American government and business was needed to help power the non-plan nation. Ironically, however, military strategies being developed to disperse population and industry as preventative and post-apocalyptic measures share much with Fuller's view of unrestricted spatial movement.[12] Supporters of 'dispersal' in government and among architects and town planners also saw the strategy as a way of eliminating poverty, crime and overcrowding in cities and as a means of reinforcing the values of American small-town life. Fuller had imagined for twenty years that his Dymaxion projects would fulfil these very aims. As Kim Pang persuasively suggests, Fuller's popularity rises so radically after two decades of indifference precisely because his ideas are in line with Cold War strategists.[13]

The military had shown interest in the dome as early as 1949 and, by 1953, Fuller was working directly with the Marine Corps and the Air Force. He drew upon student experiments at North Carolina State, Tulane in New Orleans, MIT and the University of Michigan, using materials often donated by industry to produce various hangar and barrack domes. By 1957 the Marines were using some 300 geodesic domes world-wide, including the 55-foot diameter fibreglass radomes stretched along the Distant Early Warning (DEW) line along the northern rim of Canada.

As propaganda, the domes became an essential element of the USA's ideological war during the 1950s, used to house government-sponsored International Trade Fairs in the Third World and behind the Iron Curtain. Consisting of ostentatious displays of American technological prowess and material abundance, the Fuller domes in many places became the central attraction. The success of the large (>100 foot in diameter) trade domes enormously boosted Fuller's reputation at home, where he and his designs were touted in the media as the acme of American individualism and ingenuity.

The adoption of Fuller, or Bucky, as he became known, by an anti-institutional counterculture is thus made possible through the visibility his ideas enjoyed as part of the American military-industrial complex's aggressive cultural imperialism during the early years of the Cold War. Although it is possible and perhaps necessary for insurgent forces to refigure the materials and symbols of the status quo, implicit in Fuller's ideas is a form of social engineering which outstrips the smaller freedoms his work more obviously offers. The mobile dwelling machines from the beginning were designed for factory production – Ford was always a hero to Fuller, and Ford's authoritarianism is legend. Only under factory conditions could the necessary precision be guaranteed, as many commune dwellers discovered as they sat beneath leaky handmade versions. The open, undifferentiated, notionally vacant space of the Air-Ocean world might liberate human beings from the stasis of the quotidian, but it also shirks off the bonds of community, of a grounded, accumulated experience of everyday life. When being *here*

---

12 A.S. Kim Pang, Dome days: Buckminster Fuller in the Cold War, in Francis Spufford and Jenny Uglow (editors), *Cultural Babbage: technology, time and invention*, London: Faber, 1996, pp. 167–192, 172.
13 *Ibid.*, p. 177.

converts into anywhere, identity might fold into itself, having no place, and give itself over to a manufactured vagrant force driven, still, by the unplanned but all-pervasive machinery of capitalism.

Fuller's holistic understanding of global networks of trade and communications, and of the ecological problems written into them, is still pertinent, and still seemingly irresolvable. His response to need assumes an elimination of status and power by a kind of value-free technology before the project can begin. We still live in dead men's houses, if we can find shelter at all. Fuller was right to focus on property as the seat of power, but design science cannot in itself disperse that power, it can merely streamline our confinement.

The House of the Seven Gables concludes with Holgrave's inheritance of a not inconsiderable fortune. Moving to the late Judge Pyncheon's 'elegant country-seat', Holgrave wonders why the judge 'should not have felt the propriety of embodying so excellent a piece of domestic architecture in stone, rather than wood', so that each generation could alter the interior to suit their needs while the exterior 'through the lapse of years, might have been adding venerableness to its original beauty, and thus giving that impression of permanence, which I consider essential to the happiness of any one moment'. Phoebe is amazed at this about-face. With a 'half-melancholy laugh' Holgrave admits: 'You find me a conservative already! Little did I think ever to become one'.[14]

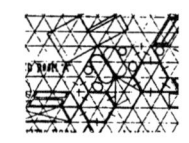

14 Nathaniel Hawthorne, *op. cit.*, note 1, p. 315.

#11
HADAS STEINER: OFF THE MAP[1]

Disenchantment with the modernist plan by the young avant-garde during the 1960s led to a fixation on the spaces outside of the disciplinary conventions of architectural graphics: limitless fields of outer space, undersea pastures and cybernetic meadows. With an intricacy foreign to architectural drawing, the structural potential of this terrain was explored in what the critic Reyner Banham (1922–1988) called the 'underground architectural protest magazines'.[2] A slump in impromptu publications had followed the Second World War in Britain because of legal restrictions on paper;[3] the proliferation of small magazines in the late 1950s and 1960s filled this gap with a vengeance.[4] Indeed, Banham went so far as to consider the little magazine phenomenon an architectural movement.[5] The consensus in these dissident publications, *Archigram* (1961), *Megascope* (1964) and *Clip-Kit* (1966) being the most popular, was of a profession in crisis (Figure 11.1).[6] 'Thinking architects', they agreed, had no choice but to diverge sharply from the security that had been offered by the Modern Movement and to question the 'constraint of the single layer, two dimensional urban plan'.[7] The shift from industrial to complex technology rendered the standard zones of work, leisure, transport and home, never truly adequate, thoroughly insufficient.

Thus the search for precepts for the second half of the twentieth century was on: 'We are in pursuit of an idea, a new vernacular, something to stand alongside the space capsules,

---

1 I am grateful to Dennis Crompton, David Greene, Paul Davies, Simon Sadler, Gordon Sainsbury and Mark Steiner for their generous and constant contributions to my scholarly obsessions.
2 Reyner Banham, Zoom wave hits architecture, *New Society*, vol. 7, no. 179, p.21, 3 March 1966. *Architectural Design* was the rare exception amongst established periodicals, dedicating issues to these extremes.
3 'The most serious consequence of the crisis in publishing was the widespread destruction of little magazines. This was to have long-term effects, for the little magazines are the seed-bed of literature. Their existence is always precarious and never financially profitable, but they provide the freedom to experiment with new ideas and develop fresh lines of criticism. In 1940 it actually became illegal to start a new magazine' (Robert Hewison, *In Anger: British culture in the Cold War 1945–60*, New York: Oxford University Press, 1981).
4 For an analysis of the 'underground protest magazines', see Denise Scott Brown, Little magazines in architecture and urbanism, *Journal of the American Institute of Planners*, XXXIV, no. 4, July 1968, pp. 223–232: 'Little magazines are usually one-track – led by a guiding spirit, trying to make one point, the vehicle of a single school of thought, and usually representing that school at its most iconoclastic. Little magazines are often scurrilous, irreverent, mis-spelled, improvisatory, anti-smooth, funny-format, cliquey, art-oriented but stoned out of their minds with science fiction images of an alternative architecture that would be perfectly possible tomorrow if only the Universe (and especially the Law of Gravity) were differently organized' *(ibid.)*.
5 *Ibid.*
6 The *Archigram* newsletter led the consensus building. The other magazines excitedly reported on the group's activities, reproducing *Archigram* images to promote their cause.
7 Paraphrased from the 'Statement of intention and aim' for the *International Dialogue in Experimental Architecture* (IDEA) conference, Folkestone, 1966. Included in *Clip-Kit*, 1966.

126

figure 11.1
COVER OF *ARCHIGRAM*, NO. 4, 1964

computers and throw-away packages of an atomic/electronic age' declared Warren Chalk, one of the core members of the Archigram group.[8] Hoping to move beyond the constraints of the plan, 'thinking architects' sought inspiration outside of the architectural, even the urban, tradition.[9] 'We want to drag into building some of the poetry of the countdown', was scrawled across the first *Archigram* broadsheet.[10] In the première issue of *Megascope*, the students of Bristol wrote, 'We must rocket ourselves so high that even when the paralysing missiles of regulation are shot at us our satellite is still orbiting, transmitting data of potential workable solutions ... countdown for Utopia'.[11] Their aerodynamical rhetoric expressed the urge to displace the technological symbolism which continued to haunt the construction industry; to pull technology out of its cosmetic rut, as a disguise for a post and lintel system, albeit one of graceful steel members.

Under the sea and outside the Earth's atmosphere, 'pure' expressions of technology were to be found. Untouched by architects and planners, the spaces were being negotiated via the techniques of advanced engineering. Cape Canaveral, the Apollo space crafts, the underwater villages of Cousteau, the Aluminaut submarine, the US Navy's Sea Lab, the Alvin ocean explorer, Buckminster Fuller's Undersea Island – images of these, and more, appeared in the magazines (Figure 11.2). Extreme conditions demanded the innovative structural solutions represented by these engineered examples; in turn, avant-garde architects eagerly seized them. The space-race furthered the development of lightweight synthetics, and pneumatics rapidly became the mark of the radical architectural practice.[12] The autonomous, self-sustaining capsule, essential for outer space

---

8 Written for the 'Living City' exhibition (1963), this statement was reprinted in *Archigram*, no. 4, 1964, p. 6.
9 Including the pre-existing fascination with industrial buildings, silos, bridges, cars, etc.
10 Excerpt from 'The love is gone', a poem by David Greene which kaleidoscoped across the cover sheet of the two-paged *Archigram*, no. 1, 1961; the first two issues of *Archigram* were edited by Peter Cook and Greene, only two of the six who were to form the group's core in 1963.
11 Ellipsis in the original, 1964 (quoted in Scott Brown, *op. cit.*, note 4, p. 225).
12 Materials were developed for spacesuits and lightweight structures easily assembled in space. See R. Sziland, Structures for the Moon, *Civil Engineering*, October 1959, or Frei Otto, *Tensile Structures, vol. I*, Cambridge, MA: MIT Press, 1967, pp. 26–29.

figure 11.2
UNDERWATER HARDWARE, *ARCHIGRAM*, NO. 5, 1964

and underwater explorations, became standard in architectural dreamworlds. The invisible impulses of the cybernetic system were programmed to manifest physical changes in the architectural environment. Photographs taken from space throughout the 1960s were particularly powerful in suggesting the previous limits of human imagination.[13]

By exploring the limits of technological invention, these architects were struggling to convey a structural model which violated the principle of *firmitas*. They wanted mobility to be functionally intrinsic to shelter as it was in the spaceship, the submarine, or even the trailer home. Two significant models for an architecture without fixed co-ordinates had been inherited from the previous generation: Buckminster Fuller's pipeless Dymaxions and Yona Friedman's extendible, multi-layered spaceframes. Fuller wanted his buildings to be movable, unbound by any predetermined infrastructure such as that of the sewage system. Friedman's vision was not so much about being literally on the move as about the flexibility of parts within the infrastructure since he believed the rigidity of the built environment to be the greatest hindrance to a fully contemporary,

13 The more famous Earthrise series was taken by Apollo 10 (18 May 1969) but the first view of Earth from the Moon came from the Orbiter spacecraft: 'At 16:35 GMT on August 23, 1966, the versatile manmade lunar Orbiter spacecraft responded to a series of commands sent to it from Earth, across a quarter-million miles of space, and made this over-the-shoulder view of its home planet from a vantage point 730 miles above the far side of the Moon. At that moment the Sun was setting along an arc extending from England to Antarctica. Above that line, the world with the east coast of the United States at the top, was still bathed in afternoon sunlight. Below, the major portion of the African Continent and the Indian Ocean were shrouded in the darkness of evening. By this reversal of viewpoint, we here on the Earth have been provided a sobering glimpse of the spectacle of our own planet ... We have achieved the ability to contemplate ourselves from afar and thus, in a measure accomplish the wish expressed by Robert Burns: "To see ourselves as others see us!".' (*Exploring Space with a Camera*, Washington DC: NASA, 1968, pp. 84–85).

mobile society.[14] Both of these men were touted as role models in the little publications. But Friedman stuck with the schematic diagram and Fuller with the technical drawing, neither of which captured a spirit of dynamism. The young architects of the 1960s were searching for ways both to convey useful information *and* capture the vitality of something that did not retain a shape long enough to be drawn.

Though he adamantly rejected Utopian solutions, Cedric Price was among the few practitioners who used state-of-the-art technology to animate his proposals.[15] The producers of the little magazines admired Price's plans for flexible buildings and, as a result, his visual and verbal constructions were a ubiquitous feature of their publications. In an essay for the seventh *Archigram*, Price wryly assessed the 'puerile pattern-making' of mathematical modernism:

> For centuries now it has been both convenient and at times practical to represent existing or proposed urban settlements (cities, towns, camps) in two-dimensional, diagrammatic form. Where for instance, defence was of prime importance, such diagrams could, with little alteration, serve as a scaled blue print for the real thing. While Ebenezer Howard was still prepared to put a physical scale to his theoretical Garden City, succeeding though less successful folk-utopians have produced diagrams (plans) purporting a two-dimensional validity while avoiding both measurable physical commitment and in doing so avoiding a degree of integrity in their chosen genre.

Price then went on to note the limitations that the existing graphic techniques posed in the search for a 'new vernacular':

> There is no particular objection to suggesting an operational design shorthand but the distinction must be drawn between one which merely clarifies or reinforces one's thought processes in relation to the necessary interaction, and one which is literally taken too far and starts to become an over-simplified indicator of desirable physical planning or form – the major fault in current thinking and the resultant proposals for future physical urban concentration is the inability to let go of the concept of the City and Town and their fast multiplying incumbents – City Regions, linked Town etc.[16]

The difficulty, then, was that the conventions of architectural notation – the very language of architectural discourse – threatened to reiterate received wisdom about the urban environment, and to justify Henri Lefebvre's severe critique that planners can see only what can be translated by the nib of a pen.[17] It was crucial, therefore, to develop a

---

14 Friedman's 'general theory' of a mobile society extended beyond the limits of architectural practice. Institutions, for example, would be subject to periodic renewal: marriage every five years, property rights every ten (see Joan Ockman and Edward Eigen (editors), *Architecture Culture 1943–1968*, New York: Rizzoli, 1993, pp. 273–275).
15 'To write about Utopia shows symptoms of mental exhaustion: to design it is criminal.' (Cedric Price, in *Archigram*, no. 7, December 1966, unpaginated).
16 *Ibid.*
17 'What interferes with the general tendencies of those involved with planning is understanding only what they can translate in terms of graphic operations: seeing, feeling at the end of a pencil, drawing.' (Industrialization and urbanization, *Writings on Cities*, trans. Eleonore Kofman and Elizabeth Lebas, Oxford: Blackwell, 1996, p. 83).

mode of representation that enabled interrogation of the standing model for the city.[18] This quest lent significance to an otherwise puzzling over-emphasis on the part of Banham, the group's most vocal proponent, that Archigram was in the 'image business'. The group's power was in its graphics, Banham repeatedly reminded his audience, combining between them the most drawing talent 'since Wren was in charge of the Royal Works'.[19] His statement, 'Archigram is short on theory, long on draftsmanship' became a motto even of some of the members themselves,[20] their shared agenda with art school students stressed to explain their atypical experiments with colour, drawing strategies and newly available tools while still attending the architecture schools.[21]

Indeed, some of the make-over sustained by architectural graphics at this time in the small magazines and elsewhere occurred as new equipment became available, from popular utensils, such as Zip-a-Tone, to the more obscure 'Banjo' stencil.[22] Felt pens, also recently added to the tool box, made it possible to emulate the vivid colours of advertisements, further broadening the visual context in which the drawings were seen. More fundamentally, however, the orthogonals of the modernist plan, section and elevation became insufficient; the axonometric which combined all three in one volumetric drawing was increasingly employed. Like a perspective illustration, the point of the view from which an axonometric drawing is derived can be chosen strategically; when the view is taken from above, Charles Jencks argued, the axonometric can 'analyse and dissect the whole project showing its underlying anatomy'.[23] Moholy-Nagy had already associated the elevated vantage point with technological development and flux in the manual for his American Bauhaus: 'In our age of airplanes, architecture is viewed not only frontally and from the sides, but also from above – vision in motion'.[24] In contrast to the perspective, Jencks and Moholy-Nagy agreed, the bird's eye axonometric could be used as a design method by these architects for it allowed them 'to work out the space, structure, geometry, function and detail altogether without distortion'.[25] Whether the axonometric lent itself to such clarity, however, was in itself a matter of perspective.[26]

18 'The problem facing our cities is not just that of their regeneration, but of their right to existence.' (Peter Cook, Living city, *Living Arts Magazine*, no. 2, 1963, p. 70).
19 This comparison is made in a film by Dennis Postle about the design of the Pompidou Centre, Paris (*Four Films*, Tatooist International Production, Arts Council Film, 1980), in which the Archigram group travel to Paris to see a building often referred to as the logical outcome of their provocations.
20 Quoted by Sutherland Lyall in a review of the Pompidou exhibition (Bubble writing on the wall, *Building Design*, 8 July 1994) it has also been repeated by group members in lectures accompanying recent retrospectives.
21 Conversation with Gordon Sainsbury (27 April 1998), an architecture student who went, as did Peter Cook, from studying with Ron Simms at Bournemouth to the Architectural Association, London. He collaborated with Cook on a project for Picadilly Circus featured in *Archigram*, no. 1.
22 Banjo stencils were initially available only in France and acquired a cult status.
23 Charles Jencks, *Modern Movements in Architecture*, London: Penguin, 1985, p. 263.
24 Laszlo Moholy-Nagy, *Vision In Motion*, Chicago: Paul Theobald and Co., 1947, p. 244.
25 Jencks, *op. cit.*, note 23. Moholy-Nagy described the overhead view as the 'next step in the development of cubism giving a more inclusive vista. To see an object frontally means to see it in elevation. From above not only the elevation can be seen, but also the plan and some of the sides. Also from above, the original shapes are seen with greater clarity than in the central-perspective-vistas and vanishing point renderings which distort the real proportions. One sees "truer". Instead of an egg shape one sees the undistorted sphere; instead of an oval, the circle.' (*Ibid.*, p. 117).
26 Banham called the 'Plug-In City' axonometric 'the vision that made Archigram famous ... this enormous and much wrought axonometric drawing assembles the whole "kit of parts"'. He quoted Cook's own commentary: 'The axonometric is usually assumed to be the definitive image ... It is "heroic", apparently an alternative to known city form, containing "futurist" but recognizable hierarchies and elements. Craggy but directional. Mechanistic but scaleable whatever else it was to be, it was not going to be a deadly piece of built mathematics.' (Reyner Banham, *Megastructures*, London: Thames and Hudson, 1976, p. 94).

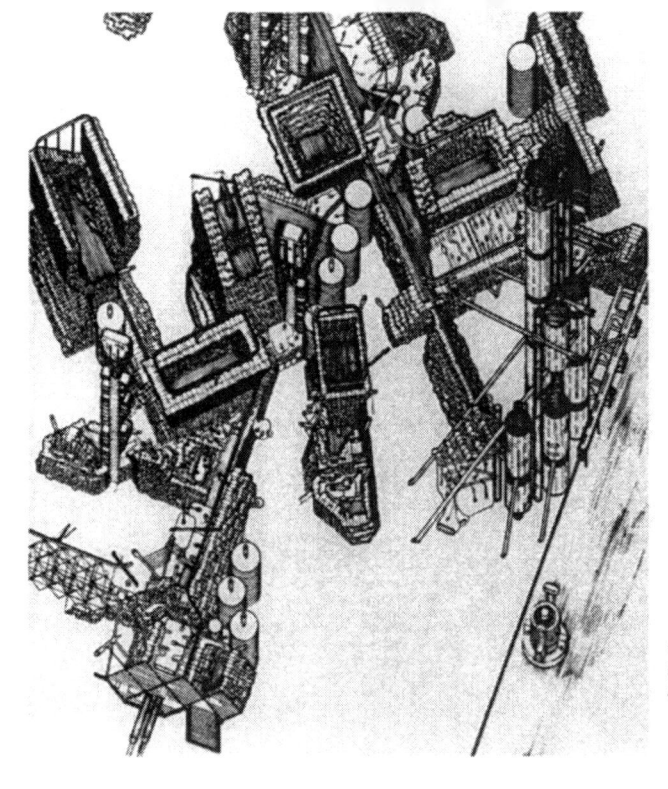

figure 11.3
PETER COOK, PLUG-IN CITY,
AXONOMETRIC, 1964

While the plan-generated abstraction of the machine had resulted in a transparent and hygienic vision of the city, the axonometric often sprawled out in three dimensions, resulting in a series of complex, even chaotic, outlines and shapes taken from angles which did as much to obscure as to clarify (Figure 11.3).

A logical companion to the elaborate contours of the aggregate line drawing was the composite image, already a staple of the avant-garde repertoire. Cubism, Dada, Futurism, Situationism, Surrealism: all these precedents used collage and photomontage to capture a multiplicity of perspectives in a single image. As Marshall McLuhan observed, an accumulation of disjunctions such as those on the cover of the newspaper charted a legible map: 'To achieve coverage from China to Peru, and also simultaneity of focus,' McLuhan asked, 'can you imagine anything more effective than this front page cubism?'.[27] In the case of the small magazines, cut-outs from glossy journals placed ads and comics, what McLuhan called 'extensions of situations elsewhere',[28] side by side with text and architectural patois. The 'found' imagery self-consciously harkened back to Duchamp's ready-mades, co-opting the impersonality of serial repetition to launch an idiosyncratic attack on the boundaries of architectural production (Figure 11.4). Though the layering of advertising imagery was already familiar from the collages of the Independent Group, images of consumer culture were still a rare sight within the realm of architectural drawings, not least because an affiliation with American culture might render one's social leanings suspect in the eyes of the architectural bureaucracy. Even Peter and Alison Smithson, architects with Independent Group credentials, had been sensitive to this sort of criticism.

27 Marshall McLuhan, *The Mechanical Bride*, New York: Vanguard Press, 1951, p. 3. Moholy-Nagy had also pointed out that the 'modern newspaper tries to organize the many events of the day similarly as the futurists: the reader should read all the news almost at once.' (*op. cit.*, note 24, p. 307, note to Figure 398).
28 Marshall McLuhan, Comics, *Understanding Media*, New York: McGraw-Hill, 1964, p. 169.

131

figure 11.4
RON HERRON, *URBAN ACTION: TUNE UP,* 1969

Their inclusion of Marilyn Monroe and Joe DiMaggio, veritable icons of the USA, in the perspective illustration for their Golden Lane project was a strategic exception within their oeuvre. With the new generation, all restraint was abandoned by the new generation and the collage was promoted to the level of a presentation drawing. Visual pilfering from the American adventure comic, a world in which everyone was Superman, was particularly prevalent, for the aim was to imbue structure with the spirit of the blast-off. *Archigram* 4, the space comic issue, was the most blatant example of how borrowed comic imagery of futuristic cities was transported into the present-continuous of the architectural proposal. The reproduction of that *Archigram*'s images in journals world-wide attested to the interest provoked by the visual hybrid of architecture and fantasy. The architecture of 'change', inspired by science fiction, proffered an antidote to 'one of the greatest weaknesses of our immediate urban architecture ... the inability to contain the fast-moving object'.[29]

Radicalization of the professional journal was an important aspect of the small magazine project. Shunning the glossy slickness of the professional journals, the small magazines made their content evident, not only by leaning heavily on visual trends that suited their message but by reflecting that message in the overall form of the journal itself. Each edition of *Clip-Kit* was to be added to a single pink plastic binder, the toggles of which actually interfered with the binding. No two issues of *Archigram* were of the same shape or size; some were unpaginated and unbound, one was posted in a plastic bag.[30] These variations

---

29 Peter Cook, Zoom and real architecture, *Archigram*, no. 4, 1964, p. 18. He continued, 'comic imagery has always been strongest here', reiterating the truism that science fiction is the literature of 'change'.
30 Scott Brown pointed out that for these and other reasons the publications honoured the 'little magazine tradition of making the medium echo the message.' (*op. cit.,* note 4, p. 228).

kept alive that which would have been absorbed by a standardized format: the task of questioning graphic strategy and means of communication. The professional publication as informational leaflet, or *samizdat,* reflected a larger cultural shift in focus – from production to communication. This shift was pivotal in a field primarily about raw materials, the very stuff of building. Structure was being reformulated as infrastructure; in an architecture of flux, information about architecture merged, self-referentially, with an architecture of information. In the search for adequate expression, the architects looked to media which by definition thematized flow – of information, of consumption, of electronics.

Clearly this was not the first time that new concerns produced changes in drawing conventions. The shift in the role of the architect from the creator of monuments piecemeal to the co-ordinator of the urban plan was another example of a significant disciplinary paradigm shift which resulted in a new graphics. When the *Congrès Internationaux d'Architecture Moderne* (CIAM), the institutional mouthpiece of a Modern Architecture gone mainstream, directed an official lens towards economic and sociological factors at the urban scale, the members agreed that they lacked a symbolic language through which to represent their revised responsibilities. Though the organization recessed from 1930 to 1933 as Cor van Eesteren's Dutch contingent devised a preliminary system, it was not until after the Second World War that Le Corbusier, driven to distraction by the clutter of both rubble and paper, pronounced 'I am going to talk to you about a sort of poetry – the poetry of classification'.[31] The resulting verse of the *Grille* format was the culmination of CIAM's obsession with order, systems and strategy. The grid simplified the presentation of complex problems and forced the chaotic strains of the city into the tidy categories of the CIAM work-leisure-transportation-home model, ridding the planner of 'extraneous' diversions.

By 1963, the carefully constrained urban map did more than uninspire: it sparked architectural resistance movements. Architects had found that solutions which had snugly fitted into the grid were, alas, lamentable when built. Members of CIAM scrutinized Britain's suburban Garden Cities and lacklustre New Towns during the Hoddesdon conference (1951); those urban developments brought out the weaknesses of the Athens charter better than any theoretical debate. The Smithsons, doggedly loyal to the Modern back home, subverted the standard *Grille* when presenting their Golden Lane project – the same project in which Monroe and DiMaggio had made their London debut – to the conference at Aix-en-Provence (1953). To contrast the fluid nature of the urban fabric with the diagrammatic purity of the grid's divisions, they included Nigel Henderson's 'nitty-gritty' photographs of children playing in the streets of Bethnal Green in their presentation (Figure 11.5).[32] Though the use of photographs in CIAM presentation boards was not unusual, the harsh 'as found' aesthetic of these slum images certainly was.[33]

---

31 Le Corbusier's Description of the C.I.A.M. Grid, Bergamo 1949 appeared as an appendix to *The Heart of the City: towards the humanization of urban life,* J. Tyrwhitt, J.L. Sert, E.N. Rogers, editors, London: Lund Humphries, 1952, pp. 171–175. 'Improve the grid,' he implored, 'but do not smash it'.
32 Bethnal Green would have been familiar to the CIAM members from J.L. Sert's study of the urban slum in *Can Our Cities Survive?,* Cambridge, MA: Harvard University Press, 1941.
33 The 'as found' is explained in: The 'as found' and the 'found', in David Robbins (editor), *The Independent Group: postwar Britain and the aesthetics of plenty,* Cambridge, MA: MIT Press, 1990, pp. 201–202.

Furtively, the Smithsons innovated within the representational standard of the grid, replacing Le Corbusier's four urban zones with their own 'patterns of association'.³⁴ It was this sort of internal manipulation of the preordained graphic framework for cultural control that the young architects of the 1960s found problematic. 'To hell with

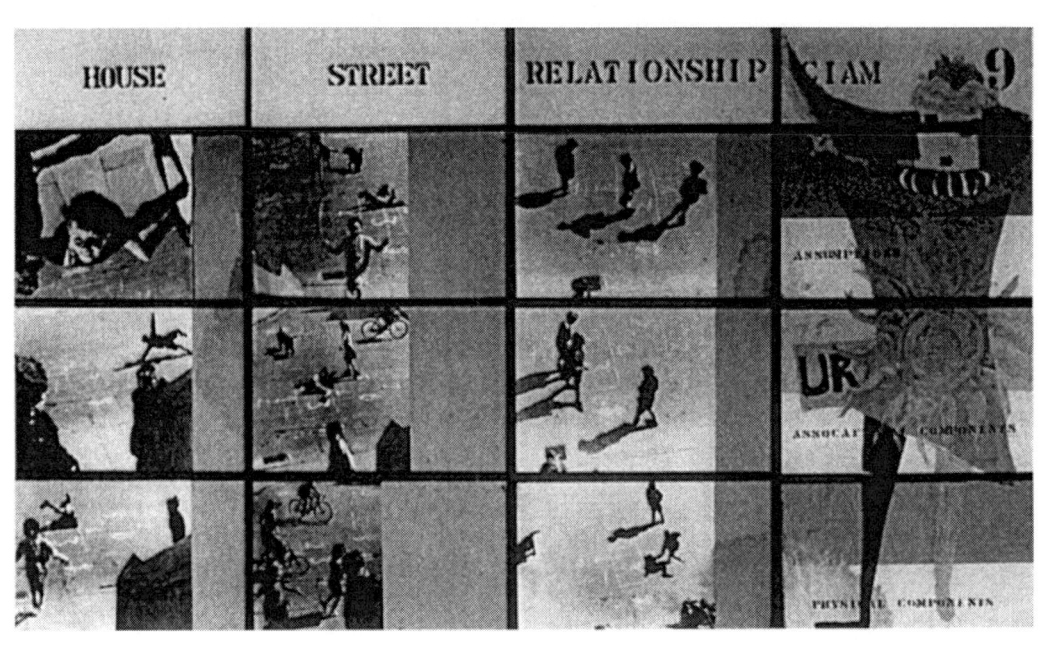

figure 11.5
ALISON AND PETER SMITHSON, *CIAM GRILLE,* 1953

all that', wrote Price of collective constraint, including its revisionist critique. 'Social corsetry is not the architect's job.'³⁵ The rejection of the dominant view of the architect as a devisor of ethical community blueprints resulted in a pervasive critique of technologically based design for freedom of individual choice as immoral and apolitical, as if the pose of politically disengaged, flux-oriented technocentricity was not ideological in itself.

Architecture, the young avant-garde believed, had to reflect the reality – made visible by the technologically enabled, refugee-making destruction of the Second World War – that a building might not, or even should not, outlast its occupants. In place of the anxiety provoked in some quarters by transience, a condition commonly seen as antithetical to

34 For the Smithsons' theories of Urban Re-Identification, including the four levels of human association, see *Ordinariness and Light*, Cambridge, MA: MIT Press, 1970.
35 *Op. cit.*, note 15.

civilization,[36] the collages of disposables and superheros brimmed with futuristic promise for a logic of shelter that could accommodate the instability of place. More than an antidote to the predicament of instant mass homelessness, the images of a new architecture expressed a passion for the liberating potential of structural mobility in a way obstructed

by the empirical formulae used by the modernists. The celebration of mobile forms clashed with the view of a building as an artefact, a sentiment that the building-as-machine motif of modernism had done much to reinforce. A series of projects which appeared in the *Archigram* publications of 1964 made this particularly clear. In 'Walking City', 'Plug-In City' and 'Computer City', the role of architecture shifted from its traditional task as hardware (walls, floors, masonry) to that of designing 'software' that would enable diverse social situations in a given space (Figure 11.6). The articulation of buildings as transmitters for intangible entities as transient as energy transfers and information relays raised fundamental questions for the nature of architecture. By challenging the machine-based model of technology that had defined modernist architectural theory and

---

36 In *The Open Society and Its Enemies* (London: Routledge, 1945), Karl Popper traced the idea of a universe in flux from its inception, attributed to Heraclitus, through to a world full of objects deteriorating away from their ideal forms; Aristotle's reversal of that principle lead, in turn, to the Hegelian nation struggling to reveal its essence. Popper reminded his battle-weary public that philosophical systems which embraced instability also promoted war as a legitimate method of social transformation.

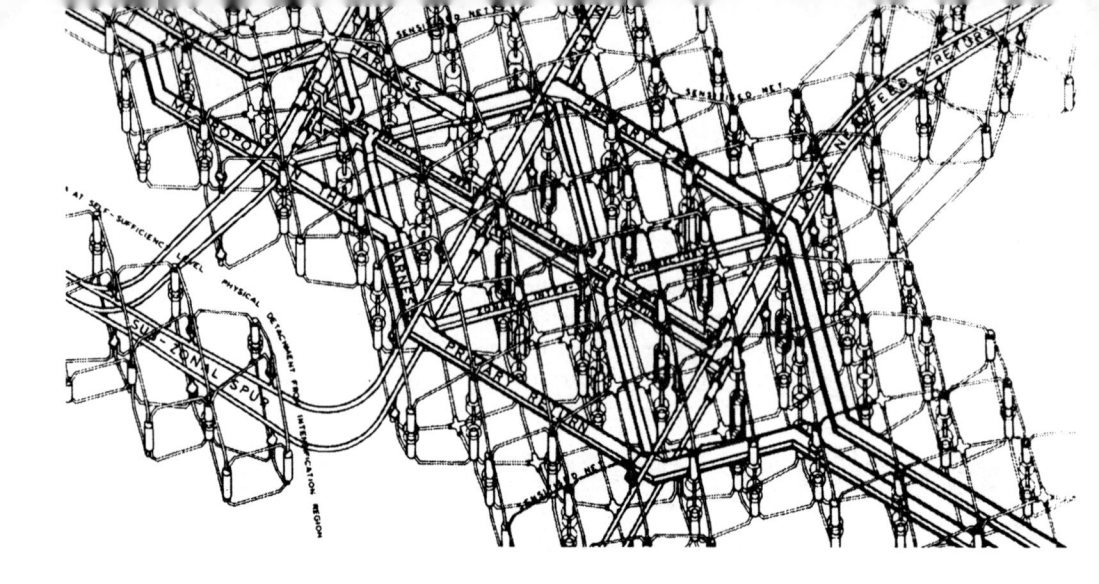

production, the *Archigram* began to represent that which the mind resisted: the dissolution of the artefact – the very concept of an object – into a landscape of complex and indeterminate systems. As Banham rhetorically asked: 'When your house contains such a complex of piping, flues, ducts, wires, lights, inlets, outlets, ovens, sinks, refuse disposers, hi-fi reverberators, antennae, conduits, freezers, heaters – when it contains so many services that the hardware could stand up on its own, why have a house to hold it up?'.[37]

The vanguard attempt in the little magazines to conceive a fundamentally material object, such as a city or a house, in a world viewed as a series of impulses was among the first to explore the dilemmas presented to architecture by electronic culture. In radically adapting buildings to sensory input, the very concept of a building evaporated. But while the concept of the building was disappearing, the drawing of an architecture as a network of information was becoming increasingly overwrought, burdened by an opaque syntax and obfuscating viewpoints. Moreover, the connectivity of proliferating systems was rendered exceedingly complicated, as in the elaborate comic devices of mad inventors designed to perform elementary mechanical tasks. Computer scientists, in turn, applied their efforts to simplifying the sketching of increasingly complicated building systems. Way before the prevalence of the personal computer it was clear to Price that computers were merely replicating what modernist graphics had already instituted. He wrote:

> It is disturbing, that a large proportion of work being undertaken on computer and other models still uses elements of the city as the 'base-line'. Thus much of this work may well result in little more than accurately tabulating the weakness of existing cities, and thereby increasing the attractiveness of propositions for the urban band-aid. The immense value to planners of computer simulation is likely to be under-exploited for as long as the demands made are based on forms and functions of existing cities and metropolises.[38]

The inability to overcome the groove of the pen was perpetuated by computer-aided graphics which merely substituted the mouse for the hand.[39] Architects extended this

---
37 Reyner Banham, A home is not a house (1965), in Penny Sparke (editor), *Design By Choice*, New York: Rizzoli, 1981, p. 56.
38 *Op. cit.*, note 15.
39 See Robert Bruegmann, The pencil and the electronic sketchboard: architectural representation and the computer, in E. Blau and E. Kaufman (editors) *Architecture and its Image*, Cambridge, MA: MIT Press, 1989.

left figure 11.6
DENNIS CROMPTON, COMPUTER CITY, 1964

top figure 11.7
RON HERRON, WALKING CITY, 1964

further by using the computer as a time saving – not form breaking – device. Ironically, the computer, the emblem of complex technology, was reinforcing the simplification inherent in the reductive, hand-drawn diagram.

In the end, then, practices which had purported to break the standard mould of urban form ended up strengthening it. 'The straight line of modern architecture was in for some twisting', the editorial of *Archigram* 2 declared (1962), but the line of modernism it nonetheless remained. Some of the twists even elicited the visual nostalgia of previous centuries. The fold-outs and cut-outs of *Archigram's* high-tech ramblings for planned 'random' interactions, for example, resembled the 'before and after' pages of eighteenth-century landscape books.[40] The translation of the lumbering structures of Cape Canaveral into Walking City evoked the prehistoric aura of the dinosaur (Figure 11.7).[41] Representation's inevitable contradictions and baggage made the Archigram group member David Greene, influenced by Joseph Kosuth's 'Art after philosophy', conclude that drawing should be abandoned.[42] The dematerialization of the object inherent in the tenets of conceptual art, he concluded with Kosuth, implied that architects need not be 'directly concerned with the physical properties of things'.[43] If, Greene wondered, architecture was, as Archigram insisted, 'no more important than the rain',[44] why carry on drawing the buildings?

40 This whiff of the Picturesque, an aesthetic theory itself formed by the intersection of representation and the motion of bodies through space, contributed to the contemporary controversy *Archigram* caused. While Nikolaus Pevsner busily argued the case of what he thought was a peculiarly English invention sharing fundamentals with Modernism in his Reith Lectures of 1955, the Picturesque was achieving an increasingly bad reputation amongst the younger architects for whom it came to signify suburban banality and the 'most debased English habits of compromise and sentimentality'. For a discussion of the politics of the Picturesque, see Reyner Banham, Revenge of the Picturesque: English architectural polemics, 1945–1965, in John Summerson (editor), *Concerning Architecture*, London: Allen Lane, The Penguin Press, 1968.
41 Anthony Vidler pointed out this visual association in 'Planets, comets and dinosaurs: mutant bodies/virtual spaces', lecture at MIT, 7 April 1998.
42 Conversation with Greene (1 June 1998).
43 Joseph Kosuth, Art after philosophy, in Charles Harrison and Paul Wood (editors), *Art In Theory 1900–1990, An Anthology of Changing Ideas*, Oxford: Blackwell, 1992, p. 864. Or as number ten of Sol LeWitt's Sentences on conceptual art claimed: 'Ideas alone can be works of art; they are in a chain of development that may eventually find some form. All ideas need not be made physical' (*ibid.*, pp. 837–839.)
44 'When it is raining in Oxford Street the architecture is no more important than the rain; in fact the weather has probably more to do with the pulsation of the living city at that given moment.' (Living city, *op. cit.*, note 18, pp. 70–71).

#12
SIMON SADLER: OPEN ENDS
THE SOCIAL VISIONS OF 1960S NON-PLANNING

one
FROM MEGASTRUCTURE TO MONAD

The impact of 'non-planning' upon mainstream construction in the 1960s, an era of high-rises and city-centre reconstruction, was marginal at best. But in experimental work, non-planning was played out upon the printed page and in the studio with a fervency unmatched before or since, spurred on by the social and cultural debates about the nature of freedom that characterized the period.

Non-planning represented a subtle shift in modernist paradigm. However much the cutting-edge 1960s architectural group Archigram revered the work of the pioneer modernists, it could not accept the wisdom bestowed upon it by one of its mentors, the pioneer modernist Arthur Korn, that a building should be 'conclusive'.[1] The imperative for Archigram's generation was instead to create 'open ends'[2] (as an editorial in Archigram's eponymous magazine put it), an architecture that would express its inhabitants' supposed desire for continuous change. The certainty with which Korn's generation felt able to identify the social 'programme' lying behind the design process, let alone cleanly 'resolve' it into 'a visually comprehensible whole',[3] was becoming alien to Archigram's generation, and pricked the consciences of some of the pioneers too. 'You know, it is always life that is right and the architect who is wrong', Le Corbusier generously conceded to the extraordinary modifications made by residents of his early model housing at Pessac.[4]

Sensibilities had been steadily shifting since the 1950s, when (through the work of Team 10 in particular) an earlier phase of modernism had been largely terminated by the consideration of how human communities actually function, rather than how they *should* function.[5] Part-and-parcel of such an approach was the recognition that if society grows

---

1 Korn discussed his beliefs with Peter Cook, his one-time pupil at the AA in London. Korn himself ultimately derived the notion from Marcel Breuer. See James Gowan, Arthur Korn interview (24 February 1972), pp. 101–113, in James Gowan (editor), *A Continuing Experiment: learning and teaching at the Architectural Association*, London: The Architectural Press, 1975, p. 105.
2 See Archigram, Open ends, editorial from *Archigram* no. 8, n.p., reprinted in *A Guide to Archigram 1961–74*, London: Academy Editions, 1994, pp. 216–222.
3 Sir John Summerson, The case for a theory of modern architecture, address to the RIBA on receipt of the Gold Medal, 1957, published in *RIBA Journal*, June 1957, pp. 307–310; reprinted in Joan Ockman and Edward Eigen (editors), *Architecture Culture 1943–1968: a documentary anthology*, New York: Rizzoli, 1993, pp. 226–236 (p. 233). Summerson's paper can be fairly considered to summarize the thinking of an entire generation or more of modernists.
4 Quoted in Philippe Boudon, *Lived-in Architecture: Le Corbusier's Pessac revisited*, trans. Gerald Onn, London: Lund Humphries and Cambridge, MA: MIT Press, 1972 (first published 1969), p. 2.
5 See, for instance, the summary by Team 10 member John Voelcker: 'To oversimplify, the idea of "social responsibility" (Gropius) was directive, an imposition. Whilst the idea of "Moral Function" (Bakema) is libertarian in that the onus placed on the architect is to seek out the existing structure of the community and to allow this structure to develop in positive directions. Induction instead of deduction'. Draft Framework 5, of CIAM X, *Arena*, June 1965, p.13, quoted in Charles Jencks, *Modern Movements in Architecture*, Harmondsworth: Penguin, 1973, p. 306. Jencks' book provides an excellent summary of many of the phenomena revisited in the present essay.

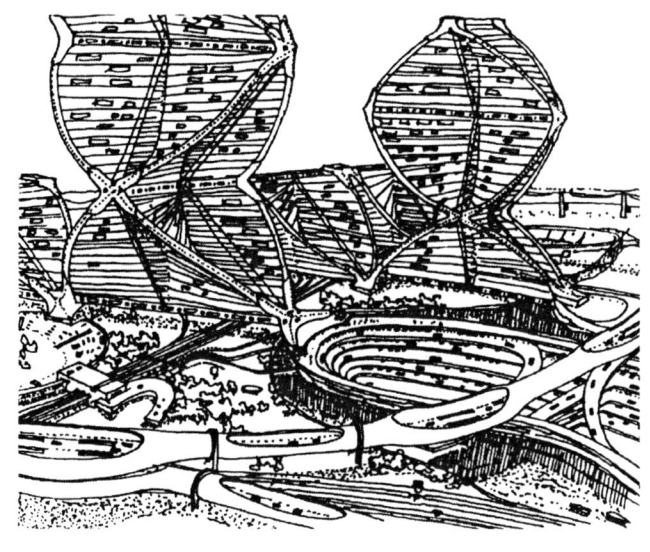

figure 12.1
KISHO KUROKAWA,
HELICOIDS PROJECT, 1961

and changes, then so should its architectural container. Two key models, the frame and the stem, were in theory infinitely extendible, and boasted a certain capacity for remodelling after construction. Gaining 'clip-on' units much as a tree gains fruit, in the 1960s the stem found its most extreme advocates amongst the Japanese Metabolists (Figure 12.1), and its most popular image in Peter Cook's Plug-in City project (1964) (Figure 11.3), exemplifying the drive to purify architecture into a sophisticated, dedicated servicing and circulation that could support its clients' needs with equanimity. In Cedric Price's Fun Palace project (1961) (Figure 2.2) and Ezra Ehrenkrantz's SCSD school (1960), the frame became a 'well-serviced shed' that nurtured an infinitesimal number of permutations of modular architectural elements slotted inside. Yona Friedman took the giant frame into the air, finding there fewer limitations to architectural growth and change than those besetting landlocked non-plans (Figures 9.22–9.24).

There was an important note of urban permissiveness in Friedman's 'Spatial City' (1958–1961). He recognized that despite the apparent 'open-endedness' of the stem plans of the previous decade, like Alison and Peter Smithsons' Golden Lane drawings (Figure 11.5), they were actually rather limiting, since they implied that extension was the same thing as flexibility, the plan expanding 'naturally' as if unimpeded by the prospect of changes in people's *desires* and *lifestyles*. There was, indeed, the implication of an omnipresent, deep-seated cultural order and social stability. Friedman believed, however, that society would find its *own* form in his Spatial City, its citizens specifying their private abodes by using 'Flatwriters', machines that would compute the best fit between the resources available, private desire and impact upon the public realm.[6] As modular architectural elements spread in three dimensions, society could expect a wide range of organizational patterns: continuous or discontinuous; centralized or decentralized; based either upon family or upon 'interest groups' (the latter a phenomenon of urban social organization identified in the mid-1960s by sociologist Melvin Webber).

6 See Yona Friedman, *Vers une Architecture Scientifique*, Paris: Editions Pierre Belfond, trans. *Toward a Scientific Architecture*, Cambridge, MA: MIT Press, 1975.

The incipient non-plan crisis was, however, still disguised by its containment within the frame, within a system as a whole. The 'programme' may no longer have been authoritatively defined in a way recognizable to earlier generations of modernists, but at least it looked more or less resolved, contained within the frame, supervised by a stem, or managed within a plan that was 'topologically' connected: in essence, solutions traceable all the way back to Le Corbusier's Algiers project of 1931. Whatever permutations and choices were contained therein, the image was of mass social unity and, to draw upon an observation made by Reyner Banham in 1963, in this things had perhaps barely progressed beyond 'the apparently permissive aesthetics of the Tecton schemes for Finsbury [London, 1950], where you had a big façade full of little windows' which 'kept such firm quotation marks round the inhabitants that they were not deciding the aesthetic of their own dwelling or anything of the sort'.[7]

Metabolist architects, meanwhile, had been demanding a still more seamless, accelerated socio-architectural organicism – 'we are trying to encourage the active metabolic development of our society through our proposals'.[8] Yet Peter Smithson himself seemed to recognize that experimental architecture was itching to break out of the great singular solution and unity, a fact recognized in his critique of Metabolism in 1964: 'One should be free to opt out, or to work in ways that might in the long run redirect the economy. That would be a real open society. The centralized nation-city seems to be the opposite of this'.[9] Smithson's Team 10 colleague, Aldo van Eyck, also worried that the attempt to take an architectural cue from culture 'as found' was increasingly difficult in an era of social dispersal: 'If society has no form,' he asked in 1966, 'how can architects build its counterform?'.[10]

two
THE SYSTEMATIC END TO IDEOLOGY

The 'ephemeralization',[11] dispersal and mobilization of architecture through easily transportable kits and capsules marked an important juncture in the non-plan story, promising to free architecture of fixed structure, making it more thoroughly transitory in time and space as if, in this age of the private motor car, physical mobility was commensurate with social mobility. The dream of setting structure as free as a touring caravan had attracted the young Cedric Price[12] and was intimated in Alison and Peter Smithson's romanticization of the Airstream caravan,[13] which the Archigram group's

---

7 Reyner Banham, The atavism of the short distance mini-cyclist, *Living Arts*, 1963, pp. 91–97, excerpted in David Robbins (editor), *The Independent Group: postwar Britain and the aesthetics of plenty*, Cambridge, MA: MIT Press, pp. 176–177.
8 See Kiyonori Kikutake, Kisho Kurokawa, Fumihiko Maki and Masato Otaka, Metabolism 1960 – a proposal for new urbanism (1958), a manifesto delivered to the 1960 World Design Conference. Quoted in Kisho Kurokawa, *Metabolism*, Boulder, CO: Westview Press, 1977, p. 27.
9 Peter Smithson writing on the Tokyo Bay project, *Architectural Design*, September 1964, p. 479, quoted in Jencks, *op. cit.*, note 5, p. 343.
10 Quoted in Kenneth Frampton, *Modern Architecture: a critical history*, London: Thames and Hudson, rev. edn. 1985, p. 277.
11 A term derived from Richard Buckminster Fuller.
12 Cedric Price designed a caravan as a youth.
13 See Alison and Peter Smithson, Caravan: embryo appliance house?, *Architectural Design*, September 1959, reprinted in Alison and Peter Smithson, *Ordinariness and Light*, London: Faber and Faber, 1970, pp. 114–122.

figure 12.2
RON HERRON, FREE TIME NODE, 1966

Ron Herron stacked into the neutral service frame of the multi-storey car park in his Free Time Node of 1966 (Figure 12.2). This was not entirely fanciful: by mid-decade, one in six single-family dwellings in the USA were classed as 'mobile',[14] many of them already plugged into service lines, and *Trailer Life* magazine projected the imminent arrival of city-centre high-rise trailer parks where capsules would be plugged into a service core.[15] The 1960s enthusiastically rediscovered attempts from the previous couple of decades to produce and distribute architecture in the same way as auto- and consumer goods. Richard Buckminster Fuller's archetypal 'kit-of-parts', the geodesic dome (under development since the 1940s), acquired quite simply iconic status, alongside Jean Prouvé's prefabricated buildings, Charles and Ray Eames's Santa Monica House (assembled from standard parts ordered through catalogues), the CLASP[16] school-building project (later emulated by SCSD), and the space-frame system of Konrad Wachsmann.

There was respectability in many of these ventures into the non-planned that would be inherited, in part at least, by the visions of the 1960s. They worked with a generally accepted precept of the modern movement – the alliance with engineering, and the aura of rationality that engineering brought with it.[17] But what exactly was 'the programme', floating amorphously amongst kits and capsules scrambled or set loose to create indeterminate outcomes?[18] Fixity itself, the predicate of the architect's capacity to 'resolve' the programme, had during the 1950s come to seem slightly irrational. Indeterminacy, meanwhile, became considered better-attuned to successful modern problem-solving. Once regarded as an inconvenience to the rational functioning of society and space, human variables offered a new challenge for progressive architec-

14 See Melvin Charney, Predictions for design, *Landscape*, Spring 1967, pp. 21–24, reprinted as Environmental conjecture: in the jungle of the grand prediction, in Stanford Anderson (editor), *Planning for Diversity and Choice: possible futures and their relations to the man-controlled environment*, Cambridge, MA: MIT Press, 1968, pp. 313–326. The statistic dates from 1965.
15 See David F. Lyon, High rise mobile home parks, *Trailer Life*, October 1964.
16 The Consortium of Local Authorities Special Programme was launched in 1957 to perfect a prefabricated system for school building.
17 See, for instance, Summerson, *op. cit.*, note 3.
18 Cf. Kenneth Frampton, Reflections on the opposition of architecture and building, in Gowan (editor), *op. cit.*, note 1, pp. 107–113.

ture – something, indeed, of a philosophical and political maxim in the wake of Karl Popper's seminal books, *The Open Society and Its Enemies* and *The Poverty of Historicism*,[19] just as Western intellectuals and artists were frantically disengaging with scientific, Leninist Marxism. The attempts by the masters of political philosophy – Plato, Hegel, Marx and, for that matter, Hitler – to impose a plan upon human history and action was, Popper argued, immoral, intellectually dishonest, and counter-productive. In its place Popper proposed a pragmatism of social openness, democracy, criticism and rationalism. Partly in a bid to provoke the prevalent closed-shop thinking that beset their own profession, progressive architects accepted the spirit of the Popperian challenge.

Yet the task of assessing and meeting the needs and desires of the citizens of the Open Society was fearsome. Gamely tackling apparently intractable design tasks, the foremost theorist of the problem, Christopher Alexander, would methodically identify all parameters – the competing demands of community and privacy, for example – and reconcile them, finally, as a plan. At first he charted design criteria in tree-like diagrams but, in his acknowledgement that spaces accommodate overlapping activities, announced in an essay of 1965 that 'A city is not a tree'.[20] So Alexander superimposed a 'semi-lattice' over his tree diagrams, conjoining criteria laterally as well as hierarchically. It was enormously influential, seen as lending credence to avant-garde attempts to erode rigid zoning, though some (Cedric Price, for one)[21] remained sceptical: Alexander's choice of design criteria might reduce the scope for error, but was ultimately arbitrary and provided only a snapshot of needs at a certain moment in time.

Cybernetics and computing suggested an alternative and more glamorous solution, which negated the necessity for an architectural methodology as such by handing the control levers of the environment over to its inhabitants. In the late 1960s, MIT's Nicholas Negroponte was the most intensive researcher into the management of the environment by humanely programmed computers, because he admired the machine's ability to handle the minutiae of 'the unique and exceptional'.[22] The architect, Negroponte noted (quoting another advocate of machine-management), 'is forced to proceed in this way ... because watching each sparrow is too troublesome for any but God'.[23] As if egging one another on in the realization of this cybernetic city – always feasible in theory, rather improbable in practice – Negroponte cited Archigram's Plug-In prefabs as the sort of architectural hardware that could be handled by his software.[24] Design decisions might be reached, Negroponte suggested, by the machines themselves 'sampling the environment for cheers and boos,'[25] or by some sort of central planning

19 Karl Popper, *The Open Society and Its Enemies*, vol. 1 1945, vol. 2 1966; and *The Poverty of Historicism*, London, 1957.
20 Christopher Alexander, A city is not a tree, *Architectural Forum*, May 1965 pp. 58–61 (part 1), April 1965 pp. 58–62 (part 2).
21 In conversation with Cedric Price, 9 April 1998. Price had met Alexander while both were studying at Cambridge University.
22 Nicholas Negroponte, *The Architecture Machine: toward a more human environment*, Cambridge, MA: MIT Press, 1970, p. 3.
23 B. Harris, The limits of science and humanism in planning, *American Institute of Planners Journal*, no. 5, pp. 324–335, September 1967, quoted in Negroponte, *op. cit.*, note 22, p. 3.
24 See Negroponte, *ibid.*, p. 63.
25 Negroponte, *ibid.*, p. 69.

agency monitoring feedback, a dream shared with the Yona Friedman 'Flatwriter' scheme and Charles Jencks' vision of consumer democracy (c. 1969)[26] (Figure 12.3).

figure 12.3
CHARLES JENCKS, CONSUMER DEMOCRACY, C. 1969

Thus far a sense of innocent value-neutrality clung to non-planning. Read alongside the anti-ideology of Popper, Daniel Bell's 1959 book *The End of Ideology* predicted that social decisions would increasingly be made on technical grounds.[27] In this promise of a rational redistribution of goods and abolition of politics, of a world of decision making supervised by technocrats, commentators at the time noted a return of Saint-Simonian and Comtean sensibilities.[28] But they noted almost as quickly the fallacies of anti-ideology. The commitment to economic growth unconstrained by the dynamics of political interaction and social conflict was itself a powerfully ideological stance. The displacement of the intellectual and the elected representative by the meritocrat – the 'noble savage engineer'[29] – elicited reactions ranging from contempt[30] to fear, culminating in Noam Chomsky's *American Power and the New Mandarins* (London: Penguin, 1969), which expressed alarm at the concentration of power in the hands of technicians avowedly indifferent to ideological constraint.

26 See Charles Jencks and Nathan Silver, *Adhocism: the case for improvisation*, London: Secker and Warburg, 1972, Chapter 4.
27 Daniel Bell, *The End of Ideology*, Glencoe, Il.: Free Press, 1959.
28 See, for instance, Bruce Mazlisch, Obsolescence and 'obsolescibles' in planning for the future, in Anderson (editor), *op. cit.*, note 14, p. 165, or Charles Jencks, *Modern Movements in Architecture*, *op. cit.*, note 5, p. 72.
29 Charles Jencks' phrase: see Jencks, *Modern Movements*, *op. cit.*, note 5, p. 73, which contains a useful discussion of these issues.
30 See Michael Young, *The Rise of the Meritocracy*, London: Thames and Hudson, 1958.

The cybernetic environment had, however, seemed so promising that there was a notable reluctance to let go of the idea, whatever its shortcomings, and opposition to it throughout the decade tended to create confusion rather than clarification. Within the ultra-left Situationist International, for example, the debate over technocracy very quickly provoked schism. At the landmark Archigram-convened Folkestone Conference of 1966, left-leaning students accused well-intentioned progressive architects of fascism, yet Buckminster Fuller, in many respects a technocrat *par excellence,* remained a hero throughout the decade, supplying the geodesic plans for drop-out communities (which soon discovered the domes performed indifferently in the absence of machine-precision construction). Charles Jencks understood as well as anyone that consumer society had always been supply- rather than demand-led, but saw the solution in the *expansion* of consumerism into a new 'consumer democracy': the provision of a greater choice of goods and of better information about them (through directories like *The Whole Earth Catalog,* launched 1968 (Figure 14.6), and new information technologies), backed, perhaps, by the political strength of the consumer lobby.[31]

three
PLURALISM AND SELF-DETERMINATION

Appropriating the latest developments in computer networking for his model of consumer democracy, Jencks had reached a compromise with centralized power, whereby the 'CIA FBI Pentagon etc. switch to handling relevant information'[32] while actually devolving decision-making to individuals. Riding on a belief in the capacity of the social body to develop its own environment, progressive architects steadily came to believe that their services would be best rendered in a merely advisory or even *laissez-faire* role, 'tuning' existing space rather than reconstructing it. At the same time it was possible to discern a cooling of the 'White Heat' of architectural management systems that had flourished in the earlier part of the decade.

To an extent this represented a return of the architect to her/his pre-modernist, local-level advisory role, though it remained nostalgic for the modernist ambition to cultivate social harmony. Harmony would be forged now not through architectural homogenization but through a new sensitivity to *pluralism,* reconciling competing social interests and identities.

'Pop', the daddy of Jencks' consumer democracy, still provided one of the most persuasive strategies. For Robert Venturi and Denise Scott Brown, the self-conscious deployment of pop was an aesthetic tactic in their search for greater 'complexity and contradiction' in modernist taste, and an ethical necessity if modernism was to be more 'inclusive' and recognize the cultural pluralism of the real world.[33] For members of the

31 See Jencks, *Modern Movements, op. cit.,* note 15, pp. 358–360, and Jencks and Silver, *Adhocism, op. cit.,* note 26, Chapter 4.
32 Jencks, Consumer democracy collage, c. 1969. In the late 1960s, computer networking was directed and funded by the Pentagon's ARPA-Net programme.
33 See Robert Venturi, *Complexity and Contradiction in Architecture,* New York: The Museum of Modern Art, 1966, and Robert Venturi, Denise Scott Brown and Steven Izenour, *Learning from Las Vegas,* Cambridge, MA: MIT Press, 1972.

Archigram group, pop came more naturally, as if speaking their own vernacular. Responding to the fickleness of popular grass-roots taste, Archigram realized, meant that the architect would have to eschew the making of monuments in favour of 'disposable' architecture. And in this pop was genuinely *provocative*.

'The notion of obsolescence', Bruce Mazlisch, Professor of History at MIT explained to architects and planners in 1966, 'goes against the time sense of both conservatives and liberals ... and it offends against our hopes of immortality'. In the case of the conservative this was obvious, but the liberal too 'wishes only the *old* order to be treated as obsolete. ... He does not wish his own "brave new world", his "new" order, to become obsolete'.[34] In the hands of Cedric Price or Archigram – a group which flaunted its own inconsistency of opinion as if ideas too were disposable – obsolescence began to seem so radical that the Smithsons, once champions of the concept with their House of the Future (1956), steadily distanced themselves from it in the 1960s, leaving its continued theorization in the hands of former Independent Group colleague Reyner Banham, one of the four authors of the remarkable *New Society* 'Non-Plan' feature of March 1969[35] (Figure 1.1).

The promotion of obsolescence and deregulation, since associated with the free-market policies of the New Right, appeared to its left-leaning advocates of the 1960s to be a truly radical anti-establishment stance. One way of reading the popular- and counter-cultural activities of the 1960s is to see them as acts of blatant enterprise, setting up boutiques, record labels, manufacturing and distributing drugs, zipping around in cars: the triumph of the sorts of consumer free-wheeling celebrated in Archigram's 'Living city survival kit' (1963)[36] (Figure 12.4). These, one could have argued, were such potent demonstrations of the desire to participate in culture that the traditional leftist maxims of orderly solidarity were made to seem distinctly backward. They broke more completely as well with the discredited, blatantly repressive central planning of the Soviet bloc, and here it is worth remembering the Popperian intellectual provenance of Non-Plan, from the tutelage of Friedrich von Hayek,[37] who, in works like *The Road to Serfdom* of 1944, had argued for a free-market libertarianism that approximated to the position taken by Banham, Price, Hall and Barker.[38]

To these four influential commentators, environmental planning was compromised by its dependency upon the grand, institutional, deadening paternalism of the Welfare State and its agencies, born of the major postwar British environmental legislation[39] and manifesting itself in the New Towns and public estates of dubious popularity and

34 Mazlisch, *op. cit.*, note 28, p. 155.
35 Reyner Banham, Paul Barker, Peter Hall and Cedric Price, Non-Plan: an experiment in freedom, *New Society,* no. 338, 20 March 1969, pp. 435–443.
36 Archigram, Living city survival kit, in Theo Crosby and John Bodley (editors), *Living Arts* no. 2, London: Institute of Contemporary Arts and Tillotsons, 1963, p. 103.
37 See Karl Popper, *The Poverty of Historicism, op. cit.*, note 19, p. iv.
38 For further discussion see Ben Franks' essay in Chapter 3.
39 The New Towns Act of 1946, the Town and Country Planning Act of 1947 and the National Parks and Access to the Countryside Act of 1949.

figure 12.4
ARCHIGRAM, LIVING CITY SURVIVAL KIT, 1963

quality, usually designed according to a rather conservative mainstream modernist repertoire of forms and solutions of the sort endorsed by the Royal Institute of British Architects. At the same time, *New Society*'s Non-Planners were fighting a rearguard action against the forces of traditionalism and conservation, gathered, for example, around The Council for the Protection of Rural England.[40] And so began a trend for selecting the sacred cows of the national imagination as targets of Non-Plan projects. Sprawling across greenbelt, and projecting American-style speculative development, the three experimental zones in which *New Society*'s Non-Planners proposed the complete suspension of environmental planning law were named after figures from the English pantheon of painters, writers and statesmen, and, in a sly bid to break down the one-nation myth underwriting the conservation movement, the issue was presented in embarrassingly frank class terms. The article claimed, for instance, that 'taking the lid off' planning procedures in the 'Constable country' of the Hertfordshire–Essex border 'would produce a situation traumatic enough ... to show how much is genuine concern for environmental and cultural values, how much merely class panic'.[41]

Rather than overthrow social convention in a revolutionary *coup d'état*, the avant-garde of the 1960s – with a few notable exceptions, like the Situationist International, often considered to be the last 'real' avant-garde in its incitement of absolute *resistance*, conceptual and physical, to State-directed urbanism – was attempting to transgress society

40 The CPRE was formed in 1926.
41 Banham, Barker, Hall and Price, *op. cit.*, note 35, p. 438.

146

from *within,* attacking the foot-dragging paternalism of the Welfare States by liberalizing local economies and empowering the ordinary citizen. The approach encountered many difficulties. A predilection for 'industrializing' culture and education threatened to reinstitutionalize socio-cultural patterns as fast as they were broken – through Price's plans for the Fun Palace and Potteries Thinkbelt (a 1961 project for a new university dispersed along an existing network of roads and railways across a forgotten part of England), Peter Cook's 'Info-Gonks' educational headset of 1968 (Figure 12.5), numerous student projects[42] and, eventually, Piano and Rogers' designs for the Pompidou Centre. Even the 'pop' deregulation of Non-Plan betrayed an increasingly passé optimism about affluence and equality still basically rooted in J.K. Galbraith's *The Affluent Society* (London: Hamish Hamilton, 1958). As urban planner Paul Davidoff, author of the seminal article 'Advocacy and pluralism in planning' (1965)[43] pointed out, euphoria over the vast increases in mobility the decade had witnessed was slightly illusory when, for example, only one-third of Americans had ever flown.[44]

figure 12.5
PETER COOK, INFO-GONKS, 1968

Highly suspect of technocratic elites ('a group of characters in search of a future'),[45] and of the logical positivism of planning that attempted to impose yes/no decisions upon complex urban societies riven by differences in culture and wealth, Davidoff had concluded that urban communities needed planners to represent them in much the same way that a plaintiff is defended by a lawyer. Inspired in part by the explosion of interest in participatory democracy and Black power, Davidoff's brass tacks approach began to dissolve the distinction between architectural planning and any other process of political culture, spelling the end of a normative social programme with a normative, socially closed solution.

42 See especially the work gathered together in James Gowan (editor), *Projects: Architectural Association 1946–1971*, London: Architectural Association, 1975.
43 Paul Davidoff, Advocacy and pluralism in planning, *Journal of the American Institute of Planners*, vol. 31, no. 4, pp. 331–338, November 1965. Davidoff was Professor of Urban Planning at Hunter College, City University of New York.
44 See Paul Davidoff, Normative planning, in Anderson (editor), *op. cit.*, note 14, pp. 173–187.
45 *Ibid.*, p. 175.

four
FROM CITIZEN TO WOODLAND IMP: ARCHITECTURE AND LIFESTYLE GAMES

The importance attached to the maintenance of social difference is significant, because it reversed the sense of bland socialist homogenization with which modernist planning had been saddled. Instead it initiated the search for, and cultivation of, ways of living that were more heterogeneous, 'authentic' and joyful.

A persistent sense of anthropological interest clung to non-planning's search for heterogeneity and 'authenticity'. At a time when the implications of structural anthropology were still being digested by a range of disciplines and professions, the need felt by planners to fraternize in some way with urban communities was compared with the anthropologists moving amongst Hottentots.[46] It was above all inspired by Jane Jacobs' *The Death and Life of Great American Cities*, her defiant 1961 celebration of the messy pluralism of the American city 'as found', unsullied by masterplans.[47] Davidoff, Jacobs and Archigram (in their Living City exhibition held at London's ICA in 1963) conceived of environmental determination as fought out by lifestyle-parties. These new approaches accommodated untidy consumerist appetites and subcultures, inspired by the seedy, stylish vibrancy of the London Soho of Archigram or the street-life of Jacobs' New York rather than the Team 10 ideal of the Italianate hilltown.

In the process earlier types of model citizens – modernism's subscriber to great humanist traditions, and sociology's 'Orgman'[48] – were jettisoned in favour of an entrepreneurial individualist confidently playing the currents of urban situations and fashion. In an Archigram audio-visual presentation, repressed, middle-aged suburbanite Norman Jones, married with children, expressed fulsome thanks to Mike Webb's Dreams Come True Inc. for selling him a new custom lifestyle which, as a side-effect, also released him from architecture's 'crushing impact upon human beings'.[49] Architecture now would do more than serve human desire: it would actively cultivate it.

At Living City, Archigram introduced the new ideal citizen as being akin to a comic-strip superhero negotiating the strange game that was city living.[50] 'Architecture', Nicholas Negroponte also decided, 'unlike a game of checkers with fixed rules and a fixed number of pieces, and much like a joke, determined by context, is the croquet game in *Alice in Wonderland*, where the Queen of Hearts (society, technology, economics) keeps changing the rules'.[51] Such playful delight in uncertainty was shared too by the Non-Planners of *New Society*, who illustrated their article with an indeterminate board game (Figure 1.8). So two rival economics of indeterminacy had become apparent, one rational, the other playful, both working in close proximity. Whereas

46 *Ibid.*, p. 32.
47 Jane Jacobs, *The Death and Life of Great American Cities*, New York: Vintage, 1961.
48 In Harold Rosenberg, *The Tradition of the New*, New York: McGraw-Hill, 1965.
49 Audio-visual presentation by Mike Webb and Dennis Crompton, c. 1970, based on Mike Webb, Dreams Come True project for Archigram, 1970.
50 Archigram, Man, in Crosby and Bodley (editors), *op. cit.*, note 36, p. 100.
51 Negroponte, *op. cit.*, note 22, p. 3.

non-planners like Buckminster Fuller trusted individuals to recognize the scarcity of resources for themselves, followers of Fuller, such as Archigram, urged individuals to playfully demand ever more from the community, testing freedom to its limits in a feeding frenzy of plenty. Yona Friedman urged members of his Mobile Architecture Study Group[52] to dump the expressive, art-historical baggage of architecture to concentrate on scientifically reasoned design methods, but one of those members, the Situationist architect Constant Nieuwenhuys, pressed on with his project for a city continuously re-created as a giant game. Constant's 'New Babylon' (Figure 7.2) may well have been the most magnificently odd project of the period, but its mission looked increasingly in tune with cultural trends (summarized by Richard Neville's book *Play Power* in 1970[53]) to turn the passive spectator into an active creator. Apparently a world away from Fuller's Dymaxion world, the bid to create communal psychodramas, to make art an open-ended lived process, had actually been nurtured by Fuller's sometime colleagues from Black Mountain College, John Cage and Robert Rauschenberg.

Communication, long a central concern of modernism, becomes an ecstatic condition in experimental work of the 1960s, the breakdown of the 'architectural interface' tantalizingly close in cybernetics, experiments with computer-aided design, and the welter of communications theory. If Marshall McLuhan could bring an insight into media, and Timothy Leary the hallucinogens, then the architectural avant-garde reckoned it might have the environmental techniques. Price's Fun Palace, conceived with theatre impresario Joan Littlewood for London's East End, was poised in 1964 to make Constant's utopian propositions into a built reality of festive interchange between people, performers and architecture. Soon after, the New Wave of Italian design emerged from work within the 'Piper' youth club scene. Andrea Branzi evokes its atmosphere:

> The spatial model of the Pipers consisted in a sort of immersion in a continuous flow of images, stroboscopic lights and very loud stereophonic music; the goal was total estrangement of the subject, who gradually lost control of his inhibitions in dance, moving towards a sort of psychomotor liberation. This did not mean for us a passive surrender to the consumption of aural and visual stimuli, but a liberation of the full creative potential of the individual.[54]

Non-plan methods could be culturally ruthless: by depriving people of the reassurance of habitual spaces, experiences, symbols and ways of life, they would be *forced* to reinvent culture from scratch.

Here was a new architectural ethos, a search for an architecture of intimacy that would pare away the barriers between one's mind, body, other bodies and the environment. New materials and techniques were critically important in literally, as well as metaphorically,

---

52 The Groupe d'Etude d'Architecture Mobile (GEAM), founded 1958.
53 Richard Neville, *Play Power*, London: Jonathan Cape, 1970.
54 Andrea Branzi, *The Hot House: Italian new wave design*, London: Thames and Hudson, 1984, p. 54. The original Piper hailed from the Coppedè quarter of Rome, 1965, and another opened in Florence the same year.

softening the architectural interface. Inspired by the wild bodily release of Viennese Actionism and an urge to continue reconstructing a social realm shattered by Nazism,[55] the architects of Coop Himmelblau and Haus-Rucker-Co let the public loose in spaces filled with giant inflatables and foam (Figure 12.6). The extreme transitoriness of tensile and pneumatic structures offered amazing possibilities for the refiguring of social space. In 1967–1968 the neo-Marxists of the Utopie group fell upon pneumatics as a cheap and quick way for the revolutionary class to collectively occupy space.[56] Meanwhile, Mike Webb's graphic depiction of joyous intercourse between two wearers of his Suitaloon (1967) showed how individuals were at liberty either to withdraw from mass society into a private cocoon or associate with others.[57]

This option to secede from the crowd was evident in non-planning's attraction towards de-urbanization. A taste for adventure that could no longer be satisfied plugged-in to the city would be supported instead by items like David Greene's Living Pod and Michael Webb's Cushicle (which shrank a fully equipped building into something like a hefty haversack), both 1966. Yet although this kit was clearly inspired by heroic efforts to inhabit the Arctic, space, the deserts, and the sea, it is noticeable too how often the vision of nature in experimental architecture is actually rather Arcadian. It is a wood-

---

55 For further discussion, see Eeva-Liisa Pelkonen, *Achtung Architektur! Image and Phantasm in Contemporary Austrian Architecture*, Cambridge, MA: MIT Press, 1996.
56 See Utopie, *Structures gonflables*, Paris: Musée d'Art Moderne, 1968.
57 For a full discussion of the role of bubble structures in experimental architecture, see Hadas Steiner, The limits of the bubble: Archigram and the ideal of the collapsible inflatable, unpublished paper delivered at the conference 'Reconceptualizing the Modern, 1943–68', Harvard University, April 1998.

opposite page figure 12.6
HAUS-RUCKER-CO, GIANT BILLIARD,
VIENNA, 1970

right figure 12.7
HAUS-RUCKER-CO, PULSATING
YELLOW HEART, 1968

land campsite where, like sociologist Herbert Gans in *The Levittowners* (1967), the pod occupant could rediscover something of the quiet pleasures of suburban living. Reyner Banham and François Dallegret imagined themselves brought together naked in the woods, ensconced in an 'Environment Bubble' of 1965, the camp-fire replaced by a home entertainment console and the weather tempered by a transparent pneumatic plastic membrane. David Greene gently aided people's return to the wild with his frighteningly discreet servicing of countryside powerpoints and wandering robotics (for, as Cedric Price announced in 1966, 'When the increasing invisible servicing now available in the advanced technical countries (and soon to be available elsewhere) becomes totally independent of position, then the importance attached to the actual location of any activity disappears').[58]

Modernism had once assumed that revelation would be achieved by contemplation of the fixed and ideal architectural object,[59] but non-planning promoted the notion of architecture as an event and situation which could only be realized by the active involvement of the subject. Philippe Boudon, surveying the Pessac housing, put the issue like this: 'the importance which he (Le Corbusier) attached to seeing things is understandable for, where the architect is concerned, looking at things, seeing things, is in itself an action. Ordinary people, on the other hand, do not spend their lives looking at their houses, they are more concerned with living in them'.[60]

five
SIMULATED ANARCHY

Yet the relationship between architecture and event became in turn reified. Non-planning's ambition to create 'event-spaces' and new types of living was sincere, but its legacy was very largely one of tremendous images, *representations* and *simulations* of architecture as a process.

58 Cedric Price, Initiation of the discussion, in Anderson (editor), *op. cit.*, note 14, p. 288.
59 See Pelkonen, *op. cit.*, note 15, pp. 13–14, for further discussion.
60 Boudon, *op. cit.*, note 4, p. 162.

With the intellectual authority of Banham's *Theory and Design in the First Machine Age* tucked under their arms, experimental architects of the 1960s had set out to recuperate the original futurist energies of modernism in a backlash against the 'lost years' of modernism's 'middle generation', willingly sacrificing ideal form in favour of an iconography of spontaneity. Services bristled, pneumatics generated wild forms, colour-coded components dazzled. Haus Rucker's Pulsating Yellow Heart (1968) (Figure 12.7), suckling the heads of its designers, confirmed all the fears voiced by Siegfried Giedion and the Smithsons that the likes of Archigram had opened the floodgates of aesthetic and social decadence.

From the start, the symbolism of the various non-plan techniques had been understood. Team 10's Shadrach Woods wrote that 'A point is static, fixed. A line is a measure of liberty. A non-centric web is a fuller measure',[61] and in the elevations of buildings too, by amplifying Louis Kahn's distinction between servant and served components, experimental architects symbolized process through a great preponderance of infrastructure. The enthusiastic attempt to facilitate spontaneity usually resulted in structures and systems so unrelenting that they represented anything but a withdrawal of architecture – 'the brutalization of local space', as critic Kenneth Frampton put it,[62] a fact mercilessly satirized in the literary/collage projects by Italian groups Superstudio and Archizoom, 'Continuous Monument' and 'No-Stop City' (1970). The Pompidou Centre was widely criticized for *monumentalizing* the 'neutral technological shed', *containing* the anarchic playfulness and participation so important to non-planners like the Situationists and Henri Lefebvre, and thrown into contrast by the piazza left empty for 'non-programmed activities'.

In the search for a genuinely anarchic strand of non-plan one turns finally to the 'guerrilla architectures'[63] of riot, squatting and nomadism. But if these environmental interventions successfully eschewed the employment of the architect, they could not escape architecture's imperious eyes and minds. Hence, perhaps, the strange appeal exerted over architects by the Peruvian squatting movement, or *barriadas*,[64] whose self-managed success was, sure enough, eventually rewarded by the intervention of professionals like Christopher Alexander and team (1969). Moving on from consumer democracy in his quest for the authentic look of pluralist society, Charles Jencks turned his attention to the grassroots, Do-It-Yourself, inconsistent making-do of 'adhocism', so that the very objects and actions that would otherwise have existed outside the designer realm could be brought back in. Jencks could even be found contemplating the ad hoc 'aesthetic' of the Parisian street barricades of 1968[65] (Figure 13.1).

61 Shadrach Woods, in John Donat (editor), *World Architecture II*, London: Studio Vista, 1965, p. 117, quoted in Jencks, *op. cit.*, note 5, p. 344.
62 Kenneth Frampton, Reflections on the opposition of architecture and building, in Gowan, *op. cit.*, note 1, pp. 107–113.
63 A term used by Robert Goodman in *After the Planners*, Harmondsworth: Penguin, 1972.
64 See, e.g. John Turner, The squatter settlement, *Architectural Design*, August 1968.
65 See Jencks, *op. cit.*, note 5, p. 93, and Jencks and Silver, *op. cit.*, note 26, pp. 22–23. Jencks provided similar 'appreciations' of women's lib, p. 14, and Yippie! publicity stunts, pp. 65–67, though in fairness it should be noted that Jencks was also attempting to theorize an adhocist politics. Jencks' pleasure in inconsistency was a phenomenon analogous to trends in literary theory, where pleasure was being taken in the disjuncture and incompleteness of texts. Indeed, the disrupted grids of 1960s non-planning would be inherited by the architectural Deconstructions of the 1970s and 1980s.

While the housing crisis continued to leave many involuntarily homeless both in the Third World and the West, the late 1960s also witnessed a conscious refusal of the paternalism of the State in the resolution of problems of environment and shelter in Europe and the USA. In the celebrations of nomadism and 'dropping-out' that began with the Beats in the 1950s and carried through to the 'alternative' culture of the American West Coast in the 1960s and 1970s, evidence of a conscious non-plan agenda abounds. Colorado's Drop City (1966) of geodesic domes fabricated from car tops epitomized aspirations for a static site (Figure 12.8). Ken Kesey's psychedelic bus 'Further' was the

figure 12.8
DROP CITY, TRINIDAD COLORADO. 1966

beacon of a joyous mobility, and the emergence of the rock festivals (above all Woodstock, 1969) suggested a workable, repeatable compromise. For Archigram, midway through its 'Instant City' project for a cavalcade of 'infotainment'-laden trucks and airships, the rock festival phenomenon must have appeared to be a case of life imitating art[66] (Figure 11.4).

66 Mark Fisher, an Archigram group-tutored student at the AA, went on to become the pre-eminent designer of mobile architecture for rock concerts.

Non-plan was certainly libertarian, but had it, in Archigram's phrase, led towards an 'anarchy city'?[67] 'Anarchy' is a word commonly corrupted in the English language into a byword for chaos, and in this sense it is certainly not applicable to non-plan, which was precisely a device to *manage* the forces of change. Anarchism is more properly understood as a doctrine advocating the abolition of the State; non-plan projects tended to *reform* the government of space rather than *abolish* it. Paradoxically, the free-market libertarianism of 'Non-Plan' came attendant in *New Society* and *Architectural Design* with several pages outlining the procedures necessary for the implementation of non-plan, and went on to project outcomes.[68] Modernism, it would be fair to say, was always a cult of the new, but lying at its heart was a conundrum, between the will to *manage* the new and the belief that *spontaneity* must be permitted in order to guarantee renewal, in an ongoing dialogue between 'closed' and 'open' systems.[69] Buoyed-up by a slightly fantastical imagining of contemporary society as one of exponential economic growth, liberalization and technical innovation, and by the decision to make architecture seem relevant by subjecting it to the vicissitudes of the moment rather than the solid ground of *Gestalt,* non-planning of the 1960s marked the most extreme phase of modernism's 'openness'.

THANKS to Ben Franks, Jonathan Hughes and Hadas Steiner for their comments and conversation during the preparation of this chapter.

---

67 Peter Cook, Control or choice, *Control,* 1967, reprinted in Peter Cook (editor), *Archigram,* London: Studio Vista, 1972.
68 Banham, Barker, Hall and Price, *op. cit.,* note 35, p. 438, and Cedric Price, Non-Plan, *Architectural Design,* May 1969, pp. 269–273.
69 For another exposition of this theory, see for instance Frank Werner, Constructive, not deconstructive work: on the city of the 21st century, remarks on the recent work of Coop Himmelblau, in Coop Himmelblau, *Die Faszination der Stadt/The Power of the City,* Darmstadt: Georg Büchner Buchhandlung, 1988, pp. 6–11.

#13
BEN HIGHMORE: THE DEATH OF THE PLANNER?
PARIS CIRCA 1968[1]

The struggle against alienation must concern itself with giving words their true meaning, at the same time as conveying their elemental force: So don't say: town planning. Say instead: preventative policing.[2]

Nothing happens exactly as planned (and is not that what historical dialectic is, the dialectic of the planned and the unplanned, the foreseen and the unforeseen?).[3]

one
THE CITY AS TEXT

In 1967 the French semiologist Roland Barthes gave a paper to the Institute of Architectural History at the University of Naples. His topic, 'Semiology and urbanism', was framed by the question of the possibility of a semiotics of the city: 'On what conditions or rather with what precautions and what preliminaries will an urban semiotics be possible?'.[4] This chapter is similarly concerned with such conditions of possibility and sets out to investigate the symptoms that emerge when the urban is *reduced* to semiotics, when the city as a space of *use* is reduced to a space that is *read*. For Barthes the necessary condition for a semiotics of the urban environment was provided by language and an understanding of the city as a text: 'the city is a discourse', 'a writing', 'a poem'. But if the city is a text, then for Barthes it is not a text with stable or fixed meanings that can be uncovered *behind* the text, rather, the city-as-text is seen as an endless play of possibilities, an 'infinite chain of metaphors'.[5] For Barthes, urbanists and planners may want 'all the elements of a city to be uniformly recuperated by planning',[6] but in actuality the urban text 'can never be imprisoned in a full signification, in a final signification'.[7]

The city in Barthes' essay is an open text, and while planners and architects may try to inscribe a meaning and an order on the city it will always exceed such meanings. But if meaning is not to be found in the intentions of the planners and designers then where

---
1 Thanks to Iain Hamilton Grant for walking through this text with me.
2 Vandalist Committee of Public Safety, untitled Tract published in Bordeaux in April, 1968. Republished in René Viénet, *Enragés and Situationists in the Occupation Movement, France, May '68*, New York: Automedia, 1992, pp. 127–128. Originally published in France in 1968 by Gallimard.
3 Henri Lefebvre, *Introduction to Modernity*, trans. John Moore, London: Verso, 1995, p. 249. Originally published in France in 1962.
4 Roland Barthes, Semiology and urbanism, in Roland Barthes, *The Semiotic Challenge*, trans. Richard Howard, New York: Hill and Wang, 1988, p. 191.
5 *Ibid.*, p. 199.
6 *Ibid.*, p. 194.
7 *Ibid.*, p. 198.

is it to be found? On this Barthes' position is precarious. On the one hand he calls for a more subtle form of analysis, one that can articulate the conflicts between the function of a space and its symbolic meanings, and one that can attend to both the microstructures and the macrostructures of the city. For Barthes this is a 'scientific' orientation that will need to divide the city into units and relationships. On the other hand, however, he suggests that the meanings of the city are to be found by attending to its *users*, those that live and read the city. So, for instance, the 'centre-city is instituted above all by the young, the adolescent', and 'is always experienced as the space in which certain subversive forces act and are encountered, forces of rupture, ludic forces'.[8] By emphasizing the users of the city, Barthes' urban semiotics stumbles up against a radical heterogeneity of urban meaning:

> And here we rediscover Victor Hugo's old intuition: the city is a writing; the man who moves about in the city, i.e. the city's user (which is what we all are, users of the city), is a sort of reader who, according to his obligations and his movements, samples fragments of the utterance in order to actualize them in secret. When we move about in the city, we are all in the situation of the reader of Queneau's *100,000 Million Poems*, where we can find a different poem by changing a single verse; unknown to us, we are something like the avant-garde reader when we are in a city.[9]

Here the (male) inhabitants of the city are a non-conscious avant-garde operating in the city undercover (they actualize meaning 'in secret'). It would be hard to imagine how this 'explosion' of meaning (100 000 million versions of the city?) could be accommodated by analysis, how an urban semiotics could contain the figure of the user. Here, however, use is already qualified: users *encounter* subversive forces rather than enact them; they *find* rather than make or produce the heterogeneity of the urban. If attention to use has the potential to disrupt and disqualify the scientific project of semiotics, suggesting that the production of meaning is not reducible to the city-as-text, not something that can be known in advance by attention to the semantic field of the urban, then in 'Semiology and urbanism' such a disruption is contained by reducing the user to a reader. By this reduction, interpretation of the city is shown as Barthes' exclusive concern and any activities that might occur *in spite* of the semantic properties of the city are obliterated in advance. In this move urban semiotics can be seen as an accumulation of readings *made possible* by the textuality of the city.

In places, 'Semiology and urbanism' reads like a spatial version of his more famous essay 'The death of the Author', an essay that ends with the words: 'the birth of the reader must be at the cost of the death of the Author'.[10] 'Semiology and urbanism' offers a version of this theme adapted for attending to an urban setting: the birth of the urban reader must be at the cost of the death of the Planner. Barthes' polemic is not aimed at

8 *Ibid.*, pp. 199–200.
9 *Ibid.*, p. 199.
10 Roland Barthes, The death of the Author, in Roland Barthes, *Image, Music, Text*, trans. Stephen Heath, London: Fontana, 1977, p. 148.

actual authors or planners (hence the capital letters), but at a mode of interpretation that would privilege their intentions (conscious or otherwise) over the business of reading. If the relationship between the reader and the city-as-text remains obscure, a closer look at 'The death of the Author' will make things clearer.

Barthes' 'The death of the Author' made its first public appearance in 1967, the same year as 'Semiology and urbanism'. Translated into English, it appeared in a special double issue of the American avant-garde magazine *Aspen*. Edited by Brian O'Doherty and dedicated to the work of Stéphane Mallarmé, the list of contributors to *Aspen* 5+6 reads like a directory of the contemporary avant-garde on both sides of the Atlantic and includes such luminaries as John Cage, Merce Cunningham, Robert Rauschenberg, Alain Robbe-Grillet, Michel Butor, Samuel Beckett, Susan Sontag, Sol Lewitt, Dan Graham and the arch avant-gardist Marcel Duchamp.[11] Barthes' essay is an attack on the limitations of an 'academic' approach to literature: 'to give a text an Author is to impose a limit on that text, to furnish it with a final signified, to close the writing'.[12] It is also a conceptualization of the nature of 'the text': 'a text is not a line of words releasing a single "theological" meaning (the message of the Author-God) but a multi-dimensional space in which a variety of writings, none of them original, blend and clash'.[13] By conceptualizing the text as space, Barthes argues that meaning cannot be *deciphered* by recourse to a specific 'place' (the topos of Author, Planner, Architect), instead the critic works to *disentangle* the play of meanings at work across the textual space. For Barthes the text requires a revolutionary refusal:

> Refusing to assign a 'secret', an ultimate meaning, to the text (and to the world as text), liberates what may be called an anti-theological activity, an activity that is truly revolutionary since to refuse to fix meaning is, in the end, to refuse God and his hypostases – reason, science, law.[14]

For an audience well versed in a tradition of avant-garde art centred on the refusal of the original and the negation of expression (Duchamp, Cage, *et al.*), or for anyone familiar with Susan Sontag's 'Against interpretation', and her demand that 'in place of hermeneutics we need an erotics of art',[15] Barthes' essay must have seemed unexceptional. For a Parisian audience involved in arguments about literary interpretation, the essay would have been seen as a synoptic version of arguments rehearsed in much more detail elsewhere.[16] Published the same year as Derrida's *Of Grammatology*,[17] both 'Semiology and urbanism' and 'The death of the Author' are symptomatic of the textualization of the world argued for by a chorus of 'avant-garde' French intellectuals.

11 For an account of the content of this magazine and its relation to Barthes' text see Molly Nesbitt, What was an author?, *Yale French Studies*, no. 73, 1987.
12 Roland Barthes, The death of the Author, *op. cit.*, note 10, p. 147.
13 *Ibid.*, p. 146.
14 *Ibid.*, p. 147.
15 Susan Sontag, Against interpretation, in Susan Sontag, *A Susan Sontag Reader*, Harmondsworth: Penguin, 1983, p. 104. This essay was first published in 1964 and went on to become the title essay of her first book of criticism: Susan Sontag, *Against Interpretation and Other Essays*, New York: Delta Books, 1966.
16 Roland Barthes, *Criticism and Truth*, trans. Katrine Pilcher Keuneman (editor), London: The Athlone Press, 1987. First published in France in 1966.
17 Jacques Derrida, *De la Grammatologie*, Paris: Les Editions de Minuit, 1967.

All this might seem familiar enough, but it is worth paying attention to the figuring of the 'reader' in this move from 'Work to Text'. Lest anyone should think that the 'birth of the reader' was indicating a move towards audience research (or pedestrian research) or that the envisaged reader might be *someone* who 'skims the page, ... dreams, ... skips sentences',[18] Barthes makes his position clear:

> The reader is the space on which all the quotations that make up a writing are inscribed without any of them being lost; a text's unity lies not in its origin but in its destination. Yet this destination cannot any longer be personal: the reader is without history, biography, psychology; he is simply that someone who holds together in a single field all the traces by which the written text is constituted.[19]

The 'birth of the reader' turns out to be just another name for the edifice of the text. The reader is a space not a body, a space of plenitude and unity, a space where the play of meaning in all its plurality can be seen and registered. The space of the reader is made coterminus with the space of the text. If 'The death of the Author' spatializes the reader as text, then 'Semiology and urbanism' textualizes space. While Barthes imagines a number of readings of the city (different navigations) he also imagines these being mapped (held together) by 'that *someone*', the semiologist of the urban. In the end the interpretative strategies of the semiologist subsumes the deviations and negotiations of actual walkers and users, of spaces and bodies as they intersect. What had seemed to be an unmanageable multiplicity of uses ends up being selected interpretations for the semiotician to disentangle, arrange and manage.

two

THE WRITING ON THE WALL

The following May Paris exploded.[20] Students and workers took to the streets, barricades were erected, cars overturned, and institutions occupied (Figure 13.1). While the initial spark of May 1968 came from demonstrations and expulsions at the new Nanterre University campus on the outskirts of Paris, the struggle soon moved to the symbolically central Latin quarter and the Sorbonne. On 10 May thousands of students and sympathizers ('who had come in from the outlying areas of Paris to help out the students'[21]), responding to the closure of the Sorbonne and to general feelings of dissatisfaction, barricaded an area of the Latin quarter and defended it against the police. The next day Pompidou had the Sorbonne reopened and it was immediately occupied by students and revolutionary groups. Although the events of May were initiated by students these sparks soon gave way to what was seen as a 'contagion':[22] teachers went on strike, workers at

18 Michel de Certeau, quoted in Brian Rigby, *Popular Culture in Modern France: a study of cultural discourse*, London: Routledge, 1991, p. 157. The quote is from Michel de Certeau, Pratiques quotidiennes, in G. Poujol and R. Labourie (editors), *Les Cultures Populaires: permanences et émergences de cultures minoritaires, locales, ethniques, sociales et réligieuses*, Toulouse: Privat, 1979.
19 Roland Barthes, The death of the Author, *op. cit.*, note 10, p. 148.
20 Henri Lefebvre's analysis of the May events is called, *L'irruption de Nanterre au sommet*, Paris: Editions Anthropos, 1968.
21 *L'Aurore*, quoted in René Viénet, *op cit.*, note 2, p. 29.
22 Bernard E. Brown, *Protest in Paris: anatomy of a revolt*, New Jersey: General Learning Press, 1974, p. 13. The word contagion was much used in the press at the time.

figure 13.1
BRUNO BARBEY, *PARIS, MAY 1968.*
© BRUNO BARBEY/MAGNUM PHOTOS

Sud-Aviation in Nantes locked up the management and occupied the factory, wild-cat strikes at Renault factories and elsewhere were followed by a general strike and the occupation of workplaces. If occupation was the means, self-management *(autogestion)* was the end that everyone had in mind – even the hundreds of professional football players who occupied the French Football Federation and demanded 'football to the footballers'[23] were taken up with the desire for self organization, for *autogestion*.

If the city was a text (an unauthored, unplanned text) for Barthes, then what kind of a text was it in May 1968? What kind of a text did those involved in the 'events' imagine it to be? Were the insurgents avant-garde readers of the city? Or were they writers, re-writers, and counter-writers? Does the analogy of writing break down at such moments, or does it require a rethinking of the textuality of the urban? And does the dream of *autogestion* suggest an urban environment that has to be re-authored, replanned? At the most literal level, Paris in May 1968 evidences a vivid textuality; graffiti. The writing on the walls of Paris resonated with a range of cultural and political references that mixed Surrealism with anarchist demands: 'I take my desires for reality because I believe in the reality of my desires'; 'Humanity will only be happy the day the last bureaucrat is hanged with the guts of the last capitalist'; 'We won't ask for anything. We won't demand anything. We'll just take and occupy'.[24] Throughout the improvised culture of May 1968, one particular historical reference should be noted: 'Vive La Commune'. The reference to the Paris Commune of 1871 conjures up a particularly telling moment of urban history. The radical reordering of Paris orchestrated by Georges Haussmann in the 1850s and 1860s transformed medieval Paris into 'the city of light'. Haussmann's urban planning, exemplified by a network of massive boulevards and expansive squares, was a response to a number of forces; commercial, sanitary and political. If Haussmannization opened up the city to facilitate the circulation of commodities, then the political pay-off was just as crucial:

> It meant the disembowelling of the old Paris, the quartier of uprisings and barricades, by a wide central street piercing through and through this almost impossible maze ...[25]

23 René Viénet, *op. cit.*, note 2, pp. 149–150.
24 *Ibid.*, pp. 52, 51, 54.
25 Haussmann, quoted in T.J. Clark, *The Painting of Modern Life: Paris in the art of Manet and his followers*, London: Thames and Hudson, 1985, p. 39.

The new boulevards were planned to dissuade insurrection, as Walter Benjamin put it: 'the breadth of the streets was to make the erection of barricades impossible, and new streets were to provide the shortest route between the barracks and the working-class areas'.[26] The fact that these same streets were then successfully barricaded and that Paris was 'won' by the popular uprising of the Commune in 1871 demonstrates the impossibility of planning to 'plan-out' oppositional practices. If the walls of Paris in 1968 declared that 'beneath the paving stones, the beach', then that beach and its associated festive pleasures, was not to be found in an act of interpretation but by following the example of the Communards – 'We'll just take and occupy'.

Amongst the myriad determinations at work in May, the aspects of space and urbanism stand out. The critical understanding of urban space that informed the oppositional culture of 1968 was a world away from Barthes' idea of the polysemic text. If Barthes offers an avant-garde book by Raymond Queneau as a fitting simile for the city, then the most adequate analogy for the city-as-text in the culture of 1968 would be the prescriptions of a user's manual like the *Highway Code*. Rather than figuring the city in terms of the play and plurality of meaning what is emphasized instead are limits and pressures performed by the built environment. The spatial language of this critical urbanism figures the city as functional; functioning to exclude, alienate, contain and control. So while Barthes argues for a structuralist account of meaning across the textual space of the city, here, urban space is conceptualized as structured and operational, acting on bodies.

For the insurgent students the initial rallying point was the issue of spatial exclusion and confinement in the university: in the months leading up to the May events a wave of demonstrations took place throughout the French university system over 'the right to entertain members of the opposite sex in dormitory rooms'.[27] While the issue of gender segregation might seem to evidence the non-fit between the traditional education system in France and a 1960s youth culture, it also evidences the importance of the perception of the lived environment as performing an ideological function. Similarly, the protests against US involvement in Vietnam, a galvanizing issue for the oppositional culture of 1968, recognizes a global spatiality animated by power and force. Such perceptions point to an understanding of space, not as something unplanned, but as something over-planned and over-policed.

Nowhere was the awareness of the over-planned environment more keenly pursued than in response to two aspects of post-war planning: the New Town and the *Grandes Ensembles*. These two elements coalesced in the production of urban space characterized by 'monotonous high-rise blocks of flats' with 'large areas of open space between the individual buildings' and where 'residential densities are often high'.[28] By 1969 'it was estimated that one person in six in the Paris region lived in a *grande ensemble*'.[29]

26 Walter Benjamin, *Charles Baudelaire: a lyric poet in the era of high capitalism*, trans. Harry Zohn, London: Verso, 1983, p. 174.
27 Bernard E. Brown, *op. cit.*, note 22, p. 7.
28 Ian Scargill, *Urban France*, London: Croom Helm, 1983, pp. 92–93.
29 Norma Evenson, *Paris: a century of change, 1878–1978*, New Haven: Yale University Press, 1979, p. 238.

Such developments generated a critical commentary that stresses function over and above the symbolic elements of the urban. If such an environment is seen as a textuality, then it is not the sign (always open to interpretation) that dominates the text but the instrumentality of the signal (always closing down on meaning and the movement and action of bodies). Writing in 1962 as the New Town of Mourenx is being built, Henri Lefebvre sees the production of an over-planned functional city:

> Mourenx has taught me many things. Here, objects wear their social credentials; their function. Every object has its use, and declares it. Every object has a distinct and specific function. [...] When an object is reduced to nothing but its own function, it is also reduced to signifying itself and nothing else; there is virtually no difference between it and a signal, and to all intents and purpose a group of these objects becomes a signalling system. As yet there are not many traffic lights in Mourenx. But in a sense the place is already nothing but traffic lights: do this, don't do that.[30]

Here it is not reading that is the necessary response to the city-as-text but movements and actions. In writings about the *grandes ensembles* and the New Towns, the alienating functionalism of the urban is not just understood as an intention of planners in their attempt to orchestrate the movements and activities of inhabitants, it is also seen as successfully achieved. In Christianne Rochfort's popular novel, *Les Petits Enfants du Siècle,* the protagonist Josyane, visits the most notorious *grande ensemble,* Sarcelles (Figure 13.2):

> A person could do no evil here; any kid who played hooky, they would spot him right off, the only one his age outside at the wrong time; a robber would show from miles away with the loot; anybody dirty, people would send him off to wash.[31]

Significantly it was women who were thought of as most at risk in these new conurbations. It was women who were perceived as most likely to suffer from 'Sarcelitte': 'total disenchantment, indifference to social life, insurmountable boredom, ending in nervous depression in benign cases, and suicide in acute cases'.[32]

Intellectual attention to the urban in France in the 1960s can be seen as divided by conflicting approaches: exemplified on the one hand by the idea of the city as 'non-plan', an open text whose meanings are not determined by the Planner; and on the other the idea of the urban as a planned and functional space that operates instrumentally. Across this conflict a number of meaningful oppositions are unevenly distributed: the city centre versus the suburbs, male versus female, active users versus passive receivers. Reading across the literature a picture begins to emerge of the city as a double space: an urban centre troped as masculine, rich in meaning and open to various interpretations; and an urban periphery troped as feminine, lacking in meaning and producing compliance and docil-

---

30 Henri Lefebvre, *Introduction to Modernity,* trans. John Moore, London: Verso, 1995, p. 119. Originally published in France in 1962.
31 Christianne Rochfort, *Children of Heaven,* New York: David Mckay Co., 1962, p. 92; quoted in Norma Evenson, *op. cit.,* note 29, p. 248.
32 Jean Duquesne, *Vivre à Sarcelles?,* quoted in Evenson, *op. cit.,* note 29, p. 247.

figure 13.2
SARCELLES FROM *INTERNATIONALE SITUATIONNISTE,* NO. 9, AUGUST 1964

ity. In the Parisian spring of 1968 the 'periphery' invaded the 'centre' and in so doing upset these divisions. The non-compliant insurgents of 1968 did not just encounter and experience 'certain subversive forces … forces of rupture, ludic forces' as they moved from the suburb to the centre-city, as Barthes would have it, they *generated* such forces in the clash of bodies and space, and they did so in response to a perception of the urban as a planned and ideological environment. The rupture of May 1968 problematizes both of the conflicting tendencies for writing the city. It vividly highlights the insufficiency of the city as polysemic 'open' text, by stressing the social power that regulates, patrols and encloses the spatial at both a micro (dormitory regulations) and a macro level (imperialism in Vietnam). But it also emphasizes the inadequacy of figuring the city as an *effectively* functioning space: May 1968 was, after all, a *refusal* to follow the script of the planned city.

three
WALKING IN THE CITY

In the wake of 1968 these polarized tendencies towards the city come together in the work of Michel de Certeau. Adopting and adapting the conflicting traditions of 1960s urban commentary, de Certeau can be seen as trying to navigate a path between and across the planned and the non-planned. Sharing similar concerns with a range of approaches to culture that materialized after 1968, de Certeau privileges a notion of popular culture,[33] but here 'popular culture' (or ordinary culture) does not designate particular cultural products (TV, comics or whatever) rather it designates a sphere of activity, a way of operating, of using, of making and of making do *(arts de faire)*. This attention to the use of culture and of urban space is central to de Certeau's work. His book, *The Practice of Everyday Life,* sets out his project of privileging 'use' as a tactical response to the extension of disciplinary power, both in academic approaches (Foucault, for instance) as well as in social life (urban planning, education, etc.):

> If it is true that the grid of 'discipline' is everywhere becoming clearer and more extensive, it is all the more urgent to discover how an entire society resists being reduced to it, what popular procedures […] manipulate the mechanisms of discipline and conform to them only in order to evade them, and finally, what 'ways of operating' form the counterpart, on the consumer's (or 'dominee's'?) side, of the mute processes that organize the establishment of socioeconomic order.[34]

33 See Rigby, *op. cit.,* note 18.
34 Michel de Certeau, *The Practice of Everyday Life,* trans. Steven Rendall, Berkeley: University of California Press, 1984, p. xiv.

Such an approach cannot be seen as part of a 'realist' project, rather it needs to be seen as an intervention into a field of study, an attempt to *use* texts and spaces to generate ruptures, a *practice* that offers a heuristic possibility, not for discrediting a view of the world as controlled by disciplinary techniques, but for opening up a space that allows for other ways of operating to be recognized. In 'Walking in the city', a much referenced and anthologized chapter of *The Practice of Everyday Life*, he turns his attention specifically to the urban environment. For de Certeau, the 'planned' city is 'a spatial order [that] organizes an ensemble of possibilities (e.g., by a place in which one can move) and interdictions (e.g., by a wall that prevents one from going further)'.[35] But this aspect of the city only exists as concept, never as use: 'the geometric space of urbanists and architects seems to have the status of the 'proper meaning'. ... In reality, this faceless 'proper' meaning cannot be found in current use'.[36]

This 'clean and proper' city is not the city of experience and use, and even though it sets in place certain limitations and pressures, the city user often 'multiplies the possibilities' of a space, going 'beyond the limits that the determinants of the object set on its utilization'.[37] An urban space may have been planned to order the movement of bodies by the strategic use of barriers, embankments and other obstacles, but for the skateboarder such a landscape only adds to the possibility of mobility. For de Certeau the figure of the walker stands in for this other side to the planned city, a side where tactical evasion and inventive use characterize space. In figuring the city as marked by use, de Certeau, like Barthes, textualizes it, but in doing so the terms are reversed: the user of the city is no longer a reader of the city, but a writer:

> The ordinary practitioners of the city live 'down below', below the thresholds at which visibility begins. They walk – an elementary form of this experience of the city; they are walkers, *Wandersmänner,* whose bodies follow the thick and thins of an urban 'text' they write without being able to read [...] The networks of these moving, intersecting writings compose a manifold story that has neither author nor spectator, shaped out of fragments of trajectories and alterations of spaces; in relation to representations, it remains daily and indefinitely other.[38]

If de Certeau maintains Barthes' insistence that such use is rarely fully conscious of itself, he departs from him on a substantial point. Here the urban is made up of a network of user's writings that have 'neither author nor spectator' and which remain 'other' to representation. De Certeau refuses the perspective of the urban semiotician who can weave all these networks together into a readable text. Such a perspective ends up looking surprisingly similar to the planner's view point: 'looking down on, totalizing the most immoderate of human texts'.[39] For de Certeau the use that the urban is put to necessarily has to 'elude legibility' if it is not to be 'reduced' to 'the grid of "discipline" '.

35 *Ibid.*, p. 98.
36 *Ibid.*, p. 100.
37 *Ibid.*, p. 98.
38 *Ibid.*, p. 93.
39 *Ibid.*, p. 92.

Here the 'discipline' of the urban exists not just in the form of the built environment, but also in the institutional forms of attention that it receives, including urban sociology and urban semiotics. De Certeau's position is, of course, impossible: he points to something that he cannot name, and can barely register. Ironically it is as a result of his overarching concept of power that he ends up producing an idea of 'resistance' that is both ubiquitous and invisible.

De Certeau's city is orchestrated by power but it is a power that is inconsistent: it is both total and inefficient; it saturates space but leaves gaps. For de Certeau the practices of everyday life are consequently marked by the precariousness of their position; 'these multiform, resistant, tricky and stubborn procedures ... elude discipline without being outside the field in which it is exercised'.[40] This is specifically a spatial paradox; 'they [the tactical practitioners of everyday life] escaped it [power, discipline, planning] without leaving it'.[41] In trying to negotiate an idea of the urban as both an 'open' and a 'planned' text, while at the same time privileging the tactical procedures that resist planning, de Certeau conjures up an urban space where the power of planning is never openly confronted or challenged as it was in May 1968. Planning, instead, is something that is sidestepped. The cost of doing this is that the practitioner of urban space is figured as irreducibly singular, both nomadic and monadic. It is monads (a multitude of singular beings) that 'escape without leaving'. What is sidestepped here are the forms of collectivity (however multiple, however minuscule) that emerge from these monadic threads and that are crucial to an understanding of social space. It is hard to imagine any form of territorialization, whether it is the momentary occupation of the Latin quarter, the possession of 'turf' by a group of kids, or the speculative practice of property developers, that is not a form of collective action. In attempting to overcome the conflicting approaches to the urban, de Certeau remains in their grip, 'playing them out' in an endgame that makes their limitations evident.

Writings about the urban, circa 1968, evidence a strange but seemingly inevitable omission. In that most social of texts what is missing is, precisely, the social. Caught between the plan and the non-plan the city-as-text vacillates between being overauthored and unauthored. The position of users, readers and pedestrians remains unchanged – the text cannot accommodate them. Or rather, to make the city-as-text inhabitable for them, 'readers' have to be figured in a number of ways: as text itself, or the point where it comes together; as the product of the functional text; or as an unrepresentable other, whose presence in the text can only be marked as an absence.

Meanwhile the homeless dream of *autogestion* continues to haunt the city streets.

40 *Ibid.*, p. 96.
41 *Ibid.*, p. xiii.

#14

JONATHAN HUGHES: AFTER NON-PLAN
RETRENCHMENT AND REASSERTION

Myth has it that modernism ended at 3.32 pm on 15 July 1972, at the point when a clutch of high-rise residential blocks in St Louis, Missouri, were dynamited – an act of destruction which has been taken to signal the bankruptcy of both the modernist project and State-sponsored mass-housing.[1] Such temporal and geographical precision inaccurately sensationalizes a single event; nonetheless it is clear that during the early years of the 1970s architectural culture in first world nations such as the USA and Britain underwent a fundamental reappraisal. Both the aesthetic and programmatic concerns of architects embraced alternative approaches, although a common aim prevailed: to re-engineer a sense of agency on the part of the public in the design process, to address the imbalance of power which appeared to operate in favour of developers and officials, as well as their servants the architects and planners. Yet whilst the responses were varied, they were often contradictory and occasionally ineffectual. Clearly, architectural design and the State planning machinery in Britain have evolved since the 1970s, although developers and the State have ultimately ceded little power to the public: the power brokers and professionals have listened, if not always talked, to the public.

one
TAKING A STAND

In 1972 Penguin published Robert Goodman's American book, *After the Planners*, in Britain. Its tone stridently denounced an ethically corrupt and socially divisive planning system which Goodman argued lay at the roots of urban development in the USA. For the benefit of British readers the book contained an introduction by John Palmer, alerting them to the domestic significance of Goodman's thesis. The explanation may not have been wholly necessary, for the cover illustration provided a well-known London parallel to Goodman's argument (Figure 14.1). From the rooftops of North Kensington terraced houses protestors had draped a banner proclaiming 'Get us out of this hell', whilst in the background Ernö Goldfinger's striking housing block, Trellick Tower (1966–1972), was rising floor-by-floor. The cause of the residents' anger itself skirted the curtilage of the houses: the new elevated urban motorway, the A40(M) Westway, which had rendered adjacent properties uninhabitable as it bulldozed its way through west London.

Goldfinger had himself long promoted the modernist vision of bold residential towers and aerial expressways set amongst verdant parkland,[2] a vision to which Trellick Tower

---
1 The buildings in question being the Pruitt-Igoe flats designed by Minoru Yamasaki, 1950–1954. For an account see Katherine G. Bristol, The Pruitt-Igoe myth, *Journal of Architectural Education*, 44, no. 3, May 1991, pp. 163–171.
2 Ernö Goldfinger, The elements of enclosed space, *Architectural Review*, vol. 91, January 1942, pp. 5–8.

figure 14.1
ROBERT GOODMAN,
AFTER THE PLANNERS, 1972

and Westway were both – consciously or unconsciously – indebted. Even if they lacked the greenery which should in theory have swathed them both, their construction was indicative of the pervasive authority of long-cherished tenets of modernism within the local government planning and architectural establishment of the late 1960s. And, although they were but two incidents in the uneven patchwork of post-war planning initiatives in inner London, the manifest sense of an alien new urbanism expunging the reassuring forms of the existing city in the name of 'progress' was becoming increasingly problematic outside the professions – not least for those in the path of the Westway, for whom progress meant either a life lived in the shadow of the new motorway or complete dislocation.

The protests against the construction and, subsequently, the operation of the Westway now stand as a *cause célèbre* of British urban activism in the early 1970s, for it was only after vociferous complaints from disgruntled residents that the Greater London Council (GLC) finally declared the housing closest to the flyover unfit for human habitation. Indeed, the widely publicized campaign only reinforced increasingly vocal public criticism of the planning authorities; and following the defeat of the Conservative GLC in 1973 the new Labour administration quickly scrapped the proposals it had itself previously supported for an extensive 'Ringways' motorway network within inner London.

Other triumphs for London's angry local communities were also achieved that year. In Covent Garden plans for the comprehensive redevelopment of the disused market were overturned in favour of piecemeal renewal and conservation,[3] whilst proposals to build the new British Library alongside Georgian Bloomsbury Square were also abandoned in the face of conservationist pressure.

The complaint was more accurately levelled at the developers and official bodies who wielded ultimate power; nonetheless it was the actual form-givers (the architects and planners) who bore the brunt of public criticism. Indeed, the public's confidence in modern architecture and urbanism had been thoroughly shaken by a series of widely reported misadventures. The well-publicized collapse of the system-built Ronan Point tower block in east London in 1968 (killing five people) was only one in a series of crises which undermined the professionally cherished image of the modern architect as a benign agent of positive social reform, harnessing technology to create a better environment for all. As Lionel Esher has reflected:

> In the first place, post-war buildings began to come to pieces: they blew up, collapsed, leaked, burnt out, had their roofs blown off. The spacious new houses and flats that people could not afford to heat suffered appallingly from condensation. In the high flats, the lifts failed and there was no one on hand to repair them: in the sealed office blocks, the air-conditioning failed or the external cladding fell off. Those who had the courage to employ expensive avant-garde designers found themselves at worst ruined or at best embarrassed by experimental technology that went wrong.[4]

Furthermore, the incarceration for corruption of architect John Poulson in 1974,[5] public concern over the failings of high alumina cement[6] and, not least of all, the stagflation of the British economy (along with the building recession and sharply declining workloads for architects which accompanied it) all challenged the assumptions of probity, professionalism and progress which had underwritten post-war architecture. Vocal critics and academics, like Pearl Jephcott and Alice Coleman, put the whole official bureaucracy (including architects and planners) on trial, and found them to be wanting – creating buildings and environments out of tune with public need or sentiment, imposing their designs without proper public consultation, and then failing to maintain them adequately.[7] The authors of 'Non-Plan' had, in 1969, sought to redress this imbalance of power, to make design more responsive to public desire by reasserting the relationship between the architect and the client – thereby simultaneously taming preconceptions of architectural arrogance and short-circuiting the planning authorities. What remained to be seen was whether they could rise to the challenge.

3 For a glowing account see Judy Hillman, *The Rebirth of Covent Garden: a place for people*, London: GLC, 1986.
4 Lionel Esher, *A Broken Wave: the rebuilding of England 1940–1980*, Harmondsworth: Penguin, 1981, p. 80.
5 See, for example, M. Tomkinson and M. Gillard, *Nothing to Declare: the political corruptions of John Poulson*, London: John Calder, 1980.
6 See, for example, President writes on high alumina cement, *RIBA Journal*, vol. 81, October 1974, p. 5.
7 Alice Coleman, *Utopia on Trial: vision and reality in planned housing*, London: Shipman, 1985; Pearl Jephcott, *Homes in High Flats: some of the human problems involved in multi-storey housing*, Edinburgh: Oliver and Boyd, 1971.

two
CAMOUFLAGE

The easiest way of countering accusations of rigid, authoritarian planning and the intrusive threat of redevelopment was simply to disguise the form of the building: undertake the work anyway, but couch it in aesthetic terms which would guarantee its public acceptance. By the 1980s, this could entail the wholesale revival of earlier languages of architecture, evinced most successfully at Quinlan Terry's Richmond Riverside office development (1984–1988, Figure 14.2). During the 1970s a more tempered, revisionist, course was charted between the old and the new, drawing on vernacular forms and materials which might communicate that sense of humanity, individuality and warmth which modernism was felt to have dispensed with. The skill was to marry tradition with some remnant of modernist novelty, invention or originality. Not that modernism had ever wholly dispensed with the vernacular at all, as Le Corbusier had demonstrated at his *Maisons Jaoul* (1951–1954), where the small scale of the buildings and the employment of simple forms and sympathetic materials produced dwellings far removed from popular preconceptions of machine-age modernism, whilst resolutely eschewing crude stylistic revivalism or patronising folkishness.

figure 14.2
QUINLAN TERRY,
RICHMOND RIVERSIDE,
1984-1988

Whilst the impact of such Corbusian work in Britain during the 1950s and 1960s was largely translated into the superficial effects of bold sculptural forms and roughly shuttered concrete surfaces (swept up under the label of 'brutalism') others married it with the usage of brick (via Alvar Aalto and his British apologists Leslie Martin and Colin St John Wilson) to create dense, medium-rise, brick buildings with reassuringly irregular and craggy silhouettes. Tellingly, the exemplar of this approach, Darbourne and Darke's Lillington Gardens mass-housing project in Pimlico, London (Figure 14.3) had been won in competition as early as 1961. Indeed, by 1964 the *Architectural Review* was able to warmly mock

figure 14.3
DARBOURNE AND DARKE, LILLINGTON GARDENS,
PIMLICO, LONDON, 1961-C.1975

what it labelled 'Neo-slum, kasbah, or troglodyte',[8] as the style was beginning to inform housing schemes across the country, as at Harlow (Bishopsfield by Neylan and Ungless, 1966) or Runcorn (The Brow, by Runcorn Development Corporation, c.1972).

For help, architects looked to vernacular building for exemplars of a more humane mode of design, one supposedly able to cater for an individual's unquantifiable, emotional needs. The appeal of the vernacular was underlined by the popularity of Bernard Rudofsky's 1964 exhibition and book, *Architecture Without Architects*,[9] a celebration of the world's 'non-pedigreed' building: those untutored, spontaneous architectures normally sidelined in historical accounts, forms apparently created innocent of the guidance of architects. What was at stake was the very programme of institutionalized modernist architecture and planning, a situation which recalled Nikolaus Pevsner's demands for a 'Twentieth-century picturesque' immediately after the Second World War, that is, a mode of modernism which Pevsner considered would 're-create a visual culture which will help re-create civilization'.[10] Pevsner's promotion of an irregular, informal, picturesque modernism during the 1940s and 1950s had been a means of countering the authoritarianism he considered implicit in the over-regimented, over-rationalized architecture of totalitarian States. A generation later, the picturesque was to be consulted once more as a means of visually countering the sense of modern architecture's subservience to exploitative big business or the bureaucratic Welfare State during the 1960s and 1970s.[11]

Such picturesque, neo-vernacular, schemes shared a rejection of rigid orthogonal planning in favour of a rambling, apparently disordered, arrangement of accommodation, often highly landscaped to suggest an informal pattern of accretion: an environment which had

8 Preview 1964, *Architectural Review*, vol. 135, January 1964, p. 9.
9 Bernard Rudofsky, *Architecture Without Architects: an introduction to non-pedigreed architecture*, New York: Museum of Modern Art, 1964. This was followed in a similar vein by, *The Prodigious Builders*, London: Secker and Warburg, 1977.
10 Nikolaus Pevsner, The second half century, *Architectural Review*, vol. 101, January 1947, pp. 21–26. See also, Nikolaus Pevsner, Twentieth-century picturesque, *Architectural Review*, vol. 115, April 1954, pp. 227–229.
11 For a discussion of the disingenuous nature of the picturesque, see Sidney K. Robinson, The picturesque: sinister dishevelment, *Threshold*, no. 4, Spring 1988, pp. 76–81.

apparently not been planned. Of course picturesque planning was just that: planning, albeit planning masquerading as natural growth, and its rules had been codified at least since the late-eighteenth century, only to reappear in 1973 in the highly influential *Essex Design Guide* published by Essex County Council.[12] Providing a set of aesthetic and design guidelines for private property developers within the county, the *Guide*'s aim was to engender a sensitivity for local historic architecture amongst such developers as Barratt and Wimpey. However, at worst, the result was a cosy-cosy mix-and-match appliqué of architectural forms designed to offer a suitably reassuring 'olde-worlde' effect, all deployed within a bastardized picturesque planning regimen, now stripped of any reference to modernism. With its half-timbered, tudorbethan-cum-cottage styling, forced inglenooks and preposterously mean gable ends, it was an architecture applied as unthinkingly to Ayreshire as it was to Essex. Its appeal to the vernacular was, more correctly, an appeal to *a* vernacular — one conceptually constructed in response to market-research of the house-buying public, and one physically constructed using standard, nationally available materials. Yet, regardless of its debatable faithfulness to any sense of an indigenous vernacular, local authority planning committees readily voted through such anti-modernist schemes, and major retailers soon realized that such neo-vernacular styling could ease the passage of their own increasingly massive out-of-town developments through the State planning machinery. Of course, whilst the style of the buildings might no longer have been modernist, the scale and pace of development showed little sign of abatement.

three
CONSERVATION

More radical attempts to redress the balance of planning power sought to prevent new building altogether, as critics of modernism and planning garnered support by focusing debate on the demolition of existing buildings which redevelopment inevitably involved. Although having failed to save the Euston Arch from demolition in 1962, increasingly well-informed advocates of building conservation, refurbishment and rehabilitation rallied supporters to their cause with growing success. The Civic Trust, founded in 1957 to improve the standard of town design, saw its ranks swell from thirty affiliated organizations in 1960 to ninety by 1974. Meanwhile the Victorian Society (founded in 1958 with Sir Nikolaus Pevsner at its head) joined the Georgian Group (founded 1935) and William Morris's Society for the Preservation of Ancient Buildings (1877) in the battle against the obliteration of historic architecture across Britain — their disputes catalogued in Colin Amery and Dan Cruickshank's 1975 polemic *The Rape of Britain*,[13] and the fortnightly 'Pilotti' column in the satirical magazine *Private Eye*.

The State had actually already provided a mechanism through which redevelopment might be tamed in the 1967 Civic Amenities Act, which permitted the designation by local planning authorities of Conservation Areas — 'areas of special architectural or his-

---

12 For a discussion see Sutherland Lyall, *The State of British Architecture*, London: Architectural Press, 1980, pp. 70 ff.
13 Colin Amery and Dan Cruickshank, *The Rape of Britain*, London: Paul Elek, 1975.

toric interest the character or appearance of which it is desirable to preserve or enhance'. By the mid-1980s Greater London had acquired over 300 such areas, including over 30 000 listed buildings.[14] Yet the system was far from unproblematic: listed buildings continued to be demolished (and any fine – if imposed – would rarely compensate for the lost building) whilst those subject to a conservation order could find the alteration of their property impossible if the local planning authority was unamenable to the proposed changes.

The desire to grant Conservation Area status to entire neighbourhoods equally exposed the social faultlines associated with the phenomenon of 'gentrification'.[15] In the north London working class district of Barnsbury the 1960s witnessed a dramatic rise in demand for its Georgian townhouses by the middle classes who had rediscovered Barnsbury's proximity to the City of London (Figure 3.2). This not only forced up property prices (and hence rentals for the indigenous working classes), traffic calming and conservation measures were also implemented to protect the character of the area. Local businesses reacted with anger to what they perceived as the threat to their livelihoods posed by official planning policies dictated by the incoming, conservation-minded, middle classes.[16] Conservation was still planning after all, albeit now concerned with the maintenance of the physical (though not necessarily the social) *status quo* and the preservation of the past rather than the processes of modernist comprehensive development. Clearly, it did not necessarily follow that the social impact of conservation would benefit all.

four
TECHNOLOGY

In opposition to the conservationist lobby, the modernist vanguard retaliated with a renewed statement of its belief in the fruits of technological progress. The authors of 'Non-Plan' had themselves declared their faith in the benefits of twentieth-century progress: the neon shop signs and the paean to the petrol station which peppered the article signalled *modernolatrià* writ large. Reyner Banham and Cedric Price had already nailed their colours to the mast of beneficent technological progress during the 1960s, even if in 'Non-Plan' the traces of Price's cybernetically responsive Fun Palace (Figure 2.2) and Banham's populist technophilia had been moderated for *New Society* readers. At their best, Price's projects, along with those of the Archigram group, had exploited the fallout from technological innovation with an imaginative radicalism and the occasional hint of irony: plug-in cities, living pods, and pop-up parliaments promised a future of spontaneity, choice and democratizing participation. Furthermore, Banham's

14 Quoted in Roy Porter, *London: a social history*, London: Hamish Hamilton, 1994, p. 368. By 1971 one-third of Westminster City Council's land had been granted Conservation Area status. In addition, the 1968 Town and Country Planning Act gave the GLC's Historic Buildings Board greater power to recommend the listing of buildings (Stephen Mullin, Change, conservation and the tourist trade, in Judy Hillman (editor), *Planning for London*, Harmondsworth: Penguin, 1971, pp. 112–123).
15 For a discussion see Sharon Zukin, Postmodern urban landscapes: mapping culture and power, in Scott Lash and Jonathan Friedman (editors), *Modernity and Identity*, Oxford: Blackwell, 1992, pp. 221–247. The term was coined by sociologist Ruth Glass in connection with the events in Barnsbury.
16 For a discussion see Donald Appleyard, *Livable Streets*, Berkeley: UCLA Press, 1981.

figure 14.4
GLC HOUSING (NABEEL HAMBDI AND NICHOLAS WILKINSON), ADELAIDE ROAD, CAMDEN, LONDON, C. 1977

championing of these architects during the 1960s helped sow the seeds for certain of the structural and stylistic innovations of 1970s' 'high-tech' architecture: most tellingly, Rogers' and Piano's 1970s Parisian Pompidou Centre displayed a clear resemblance to Price's 1960s Fun Palace project.

Archigram's Plug-In City (Peter Cook, 1964, Figure 11.3) had developed the notion of the individual as the consumer of disposable parcels of accommodation which could be plugged into an architectural framework and replaced, off-the-shelf, as necessary. This train of thought had already surfaced in Holland in Nicholas Habraken's 1961 work *Supports: an alternative to mass housing*,[17] in which he proposed serviced megastructures within which users could situate their individual tailor-made environments. Reminiscent of Yona Friedman's proposals for an *architecture mobile* (1958, Chapter 9) with its aerial space frame, and potentially a source for Archigram's Plug-In City, Habraken's text gained widespread currency in Britain, although it fostered few built examples. The recessionary climate of the 1970s soon curtailed the techno-optimism of the previous decade, and Habraken's utopian thesis had to be translated into more pragmatic solutions if it was to be implemented at all. Typical of the resulting compromise was the Primary Support Structure and Housing Assembly Kit (PSSHAK) developed in 1977 by Greater London Council architects Nabeel Hambdi and Nicholas Wilkinson, in which the future occupants of housing accommodation were given the opportunity to design the layout of their own dwellings.[18] Not that they were given complete freedom: the building envelope had already been determined, and the scope for the arrangement of partitions was constrained by the load-bearing brick cross-walls. The approach was employed on a group of outwardly neo-vernacular houses in Adelaide Road, Camden, London (Figure 14.4), although their design philosophy had already been superseded by RIBA president Alex Gordon's promotion of 'long life, loose fit, low energy' design strategies which dismissed as inefficient the notion of highly tailored buildings.[19]

The radical futures promised by Price and Archigram's experimental paper architecture remained largely unexplored. Those attempts at exploiting technology to design for flexibility which were realized were often either small-scale (Nicholas Grimshaw and Terry Farrell's Service Tower, Student Hostel, Paddington, 1967) or compromised by static 'high-tech' aesthetic effects (Richard Rogers' Lloyd's Building, London, 1978–1986).

17 Nicholas Habraken, *Supports: an alternative to mass housing*, London: Architectural Press, 1972. Originally published in Holland by Scheltama and Holkema NV, 1961.
18 See, for example, *Architect's Journal*, vol. 170, 27 February 1980, pp. 425–439; also Nabeel Hambdi, *Housing Without Houses: participation, flexibility, enablement*, New York: Van Nostrand Reinhold, 1991, chapter 4.
19 Alex Gordon, Architects and resource conservation, *RIBA Journal*, January 1974, pp. 9–12.

'High-tech' quickly joined the lexicon of architectural styles: at best it denoted a taut, inventive – even occasionally popular – architecture which vaunted its structural supports with aplomb; at worst, it degenerated into a rash of gaudy plastic-coated, crinkly tin sheds housing leisure centres and DIY superstores. The scope for employing technology to grant people a greater say in the creation of their environments had been reduced to providing shop-space for self-assembly kitchens. Not that such a retrenchment was wholly surprising: technological progress clearly troubled the British during the 1970s. Having promised a future of health, wealth and happiness, technology appeared only to have ushered in the menace of airborne international terrorism, the catastrophe of global nuclear war, and the threat of unemployment owing to automation, robots and computers. Little wonder, then, that the British house-buying public voted with their mortgages and sought reassurance in neo-vernacular spec-built cottages furnished with William Morris chintzes. The futuristic plug-in buildings and walking cities of the 1960s avant-garde were largely jettisoned for the less challenging – but not necessarily less sophisticated – *imagery* of shiny, static, high-tech architectural set-pieces.

five
TRAVEL

Even if it was viewed with considerable suspicion, technology was, however, far from *wholly* discredited: most notably the motor car, whose capacity for poisoning and maiming the public was widely criticized during the 1970s, nonetheless continued to exercise an irresistible allure over the British nation – the individual freedom it granted outweighing such concerns as safety or cost. Banham's interest in the liberating qualities of motor travel had underwritten his 1960 article, 'The city as scrambled egg', in which the car was judged to have fostered a contemporary urban realm in which human association could be facilitated by travel, and in which modernist functional zoning and the historic need for proximity had been superseded by the liberty of mobility (see also Figures 1.6–1.9).[20] The argument was also pursued by American planner Melvin Webber, whose 1964 article 'The urban place and the nonplace urban realm'[21] defended the sprawling, polycentric forms of American urbanism against the tight, focal urban forms of the first world (and possibly also provided a precedent for 'Non-Plan'). The stance was reinforced in 1972 by the publication of *Learning From Las Vegas: the forgotten symbolism of architectural form*,[22] by Robert Venturi, Denise Scott Brown and Steven Izenour, in which mobility was, once again, of primary importance since it granted the freedom to move about the expansive suburban realms of the USA, and helped determine the distinctive townscape of the Las Vegas Strip. In a similar fashion, and a year earlier, Banham had published his own hymn to the American West Coast, *Los Angeles: the architecture of the four ecologies*,[23] a work he dedicated to Cedric Price.

20 Banham aligned this transgressive freedom with Situationist Guy Debord's revolutionary urbanism (Reyner Banham, The city as scrambled egg, *Cambridge Opinion*, no. 17, 1960, pp. 18–23).
21 In Melvin Webber (editor), *Explorations into Urban Structure*, Philadelphia: University of Pennsylvania Press, 1964.
22 Robert Venturi, Denise Scott Brown and Steven Izenour, *Learning from Las Vegas: the forgotten symbolism of architectural form*, Cambridge, MA: MIT Press, 1972.
23 Reyner Banham, *Los Angeles: the architecture of the four ecologies*, London: Penguin Books, 1971.

Meanwhile the principles of their transport infrastructures were being incorporated into the planning of the British new town of Milton Keynes by Richard Llewelyn-Davies – Banham's colleague at University College London (Figure 8.10).

The prevalence of car ownership may well have sanctioned the sprawling, motor-dependent forms of Los Angeles and Las Vegas, and fostered populist architectures of advertisement, display and consumption, yet they remained fully inscribed within the logic of the capitalist free market. That is to say, it was an urbanism for those with mobility and the resources to consume. And whilst *Learning From Las Vegas* provided a neat semiological gloss on its dissection of the signs and symbols of the Strip, and Banham's tract offered an engaging architectural history of its subject, there was little consideration of those for whom the free market did not function perfectly. The reader would not know from Banham's text that in August 1965 Los Angeles had witnessed three days of rioting in the poverty-stricken and ghettoized Watts district, prompting world-wide press coverage.[24] By the late 1980s, Los Angeles' urbanism was once again creating its own body of criticism, albeit now focused on subverting the myth of the city as a sun-drenched Autopia, and promoting an alternative account of Los Angeles as a city of violently policed geographical exclusion and architecturally enforced physical segregation.[25] Clearly, if this urbanism had developed organically in response to the wishes of the market unfettered by the interference of the planning authorities – if it had indeed been non-planned – it had, all the same, developed within the bounds of a highly capitalized economy, subject to the constraints which the *laissez-faire* economy places on the scope for individual action – at least for those without the resources to travel and consume.

six
LAISSEZ-FAIRE

During the 1960s, commentators had already begun to question the assumptions of benevolent paternalism which had underwritten the role of the architect and the planner in the post-war period. In 1961 Jane Jacobs had, to great acclaim, dared to suggest that, somehow, cities were quite able to look after themselves without planners imposing their own values on existing communities. Unmotivated by any sentimentality for pre-modern urbanism, her work *The Death and Life of Great American Cities* (New York, 1961) sought simply to demonstrate that the flexibility, multiplicity of use, and self-policing mechanisms she witnessed in the traditional high-density urbanism of New York actually worked. Whilst, to the outsider, the apparent failings of these communities might have demanded redevelopment as the only viable corrective, Jacobs argued that external intervention would only serve to destroy what actually were vital

---

24 Including a discussion in Guy Debord's *Internationale Situationniste* (Le déclin et la chute de l'economie spectaculaire-marchande, *Internationale Situationniste*, no. 10, March 1966, reprinted in *Internationale Situationniste*, Paris: Librairie Arthème Fayard, 1997, pp. 415–423).
25 See for example, Michael Davis, Fortress Los Angeles: the militarisation of urban space, in Michael Sorkin (editor), *Variations on a Theme Park: the new American city and the end of public space*, New York: Hill and Wang, 1992, pp. 154–180. See also Edward Soja, *Postmodern Geographies: the reassertion of space in critical theory*, London: Verso, 1989.

figure 14.5
LONDON DOCKLANDS, WITH CANARY WHARF TOWER

and workable communities. In a different, but related, manner Aldo Rossi's work (most notably documented in his 1982 work, *Architecture of the City*[26]) evinced a respect for the historical development of urban form as the inscription of an ongoing series of social and ideological discourses. By implication, Rossi's approach suggested the need for a meaningful dialogue with previous architectural and urban forms, one which thereby challenged the established modernist cult of progress and originality.

Leaving cities to themselves had, of course, been central to 'Non-Plan', and it is not surprising that one of its authors, Peter Hall, developed the notion of *laissez-faire* 'enterprise zones' out of the original 1969 idea, subsequently to be adopted by the 1979 Conservative administration under Margaret Thatcher.[27] The most spectacular British enterprise zone was that created in London's Docklands in 1980 under the London Docklands Development Corporation (LDDC), and it has surely been the most controversial (Figure 14.5). The relaxation of planning controls and the medium-term exemption from business rates which enterprise zone status brought to the decaying Thames-side corridor in east London prompted the development of a highly striking – and equally problematic – form of late-twentieth century urbanism. The resulting diversity of architectural styles, the striking adjacencies of high-rise commercial offices and low-rise residential accommodation, and the long-criticized inadequacies of the Docklands Light Railway all testify to the 'free' market efficiently defining its own priorities regardless of the desirability of long-term strategic planning, the development of an adequate transportation infrastructure or the deprivations of those remaining enclaves of working class residents nearby. Not that Docklands evinced the operation of the free market anyway: the tax exemptions and other financial inducements offered to developers surely contradicted the Thatcher government's avowed antipathy to State subsidy. Nor has the experiment in freedom been one of unalloyed joy for the beneficiaries of the development incentives: most notably, Olympia and York, the developer of the striking centrepiece of the Docklands, Canary Wharf,[28] went bankrupt in 1993, just as an upturn in economic activity was about to generate a revival in the fortunes of the development.

26 Aldo Rossi, *The Architecture of the City*, Cambridge, MA: MIT Press, 1982.
27 Peter Hall's idea was originally canvassed in a 1977 speech to the Royal Town Planning Institute as the 'freeport solution'. It was subsequently adopted by Sir Keith Joseph and Geoffrey Howe in 1978 (see Stuart M. Butler, *Enterprise Zones*, London: Heinemann Educational Books, 1982).
28 Ironically, the Canary Wharf area of Docklands was itself subject to a master plan by architects SOM. See Brian Edwards, *London Docklands: urban design in an age of deregulation*, Oxford: Architectural Press, 1992.

seven
DOING IT YOURSELF

As a reaction to perceptions of the inertia, bureaucracy and remoteness of the State, the 1970s witnessed increasing support for the authority of grass-roots individual action. At its most mundane, the recessionary climate and the conservation movement conjoined to encourage the rehabilitation of property, and it became increasingly culturally acceptable and financially prudent to undertake one's own building, repairs and maintenance. 'Do it yourself' became a national pastime, and a lucrative retail market in materials and equipment was established. In a small but socially important way people were taking control of their own domestic environments. Of course, for more radical critics, the achievement of real architectural freedom implied a far more thorough-going project than domestic loft conversions and the installation of central heating. Various commentators sought to question more radically the limitations which the prevailing economic system imposed on the achievement of a liberating non-planned environment. For these critics, the desire for people to gain real freedom in the creation of their own environments demanded nothing less than the overthrow of the prevailing economic system and social institutions.

In the aftermath of the events of May 1968, radical proposals were offered for countering the injustices of modernist State planning: notably, Richard Sennett's 1970 work *The Uses of Disorder* (published London: Allen Lane, 1971) proposed an urbanism freed of State regulation and control, one constantly reforming itself through a process of tense anarchic challenge and negotiation, to be undertaken by those directly affected. If Jacobs' critique had evoked a cheery urbanism of expediently 'making do', Sennett's city was far more confrontational, ceaselessly participatory and actively challenging. Yet what both shared was a commitment to the individual and collective engagement of people and communities in the creation of their own environments, rather than the delegated and indirect actions of official planners and architects.

It was a spirit shared with academia: in 1974, in the catalogue to its 125th anniversary exhibition, the Architectural Association noted amongst students the 'universal rejection of 1960s myths ... large-scale planning exercises, massive urban renewal and public housing ventures'.[29] Instead of this out-dated modernism, viewers were presented with squatter housing in Turkey ('dweller control has become an essential theme of debate at the AA'), the miseries of impositional State planning ('Camden Council's intervention in the Prince of Wales Crescent area has aroused considerable community hostility') and the need for the restructuring of London's docklands.[30] The debate was furthered the following year by AA tutor Bernard Tschumi, whose article 'The environmental trigger' charted the potential for the enactment of radical politics within the urban environment. Tschumi proposed the urban realm as the arena within which political struggle could be enacted, and through which revolutionary change could be effected. Tschumi was clear about the role of architecture within this:

29 Architectural Association, *The A.A. 125 Exhibition*, London: Architectural Association, 1974, p. 20.
30 *Ibid.*, pp. 20–21.

Environmental knowledge (not building) can contribute to polarizing urban conflicts and inducing radical change. Architecture is the adaptation of space to the existing social structures. No spatial organization ever changes the socio-economic structure of a reactionary society. The only possible architectural action of a revolutionary nature is rhetorical.[31]

The construction of the *Maison du Peuple* in the Paris suburbs as part of the student insurgency of 1968 could only function as a rhetorical act indicating the scope for group behaviour and symbolizing meanings of revolutionary freedom; 'the space itself was neutral, but in order to prove that it had a political meaning, specific signs to this effect were necessary; to give it a name or, less crudely, to perform political acts involving building – in this case erecting a building for the people [without permission] on private or State property'.[32] The design of the building was largely irrelevant; it was the rhetorical act which was significant. Therefore Tschumi's prescription for architectural design was, in conventional terms, nihilistic. Whilst architecture could at best concern itself with questioning, critical, 'counter-design' (the work of the Italian group Superstudio being cited as an example) such work would, and typically had been, rapidly co-opted by the establishment. Far better that the struggle be undertaken directly within the urban realm, either through what Tschumi termed exemplary rhetorical actions or subversive analysis, through such practices as squatting or barricading. The 1970s did indeed witness the rise of squatting as an occasionally successful means of re-appropriating vacant property, and certainly the press attention typically granted to squatters fulfilled Tschumi's demands for rhetorical action.[33] Equally, at Greenham Common, the camp erected by women CND supporters protesting during the 1980s against the Cruise missiles stationed at the American air base provided a highly publicized example of a rhetorically articulate – and non-planned – settlement.

eight
SELF-BUILD

Examples of communitarian action were being widely publicized amongst architectural circles by the late 1960s. Suddenly architectural commentators were seeking out alternative settlements across the world, of which the most notable were the *barriadas* of Lima, Peru – makeshift self-build communities initially resisted but later tolerated by the authorities (Figure 4.3). *Architectural Design* had begun to publish articles on the *barriadas* in 1963,[34] and their author – John Turner – was to appear frequently in its pages by the end of the decade, his message of self-help and self-build for the poor in South America (and beyond) challenging entrenched policies towards settlements which had officially long been considered slums.[35] Others were making the pilgrimage

---

31 Bernard Tschumi, The environmental trigger, in James Gowan (editor), *A Continuing Experiment: learning and teaching at the Architectural Association*, London: Architectural Press, 1975, pp. 89–99.
32 *Ibid.*, p. 94. See also *Architectural Design*, Beaux-Arts issue, vol. 41, September 1971.
33 Ron Bailey, *Squatting*, Harmondsworth: Penguin, 1973.
34 John F.C. Turner, Pat Crooke, *et al.*, Dwelling resources in South America, *Architectural Design*, vol. 33, August 1963, pp. 360–393.
35 Turner's *Architectural Design* articles were published as *Housing By People: towards autonomy in building environments*, London: Marion Boyars, 1976.

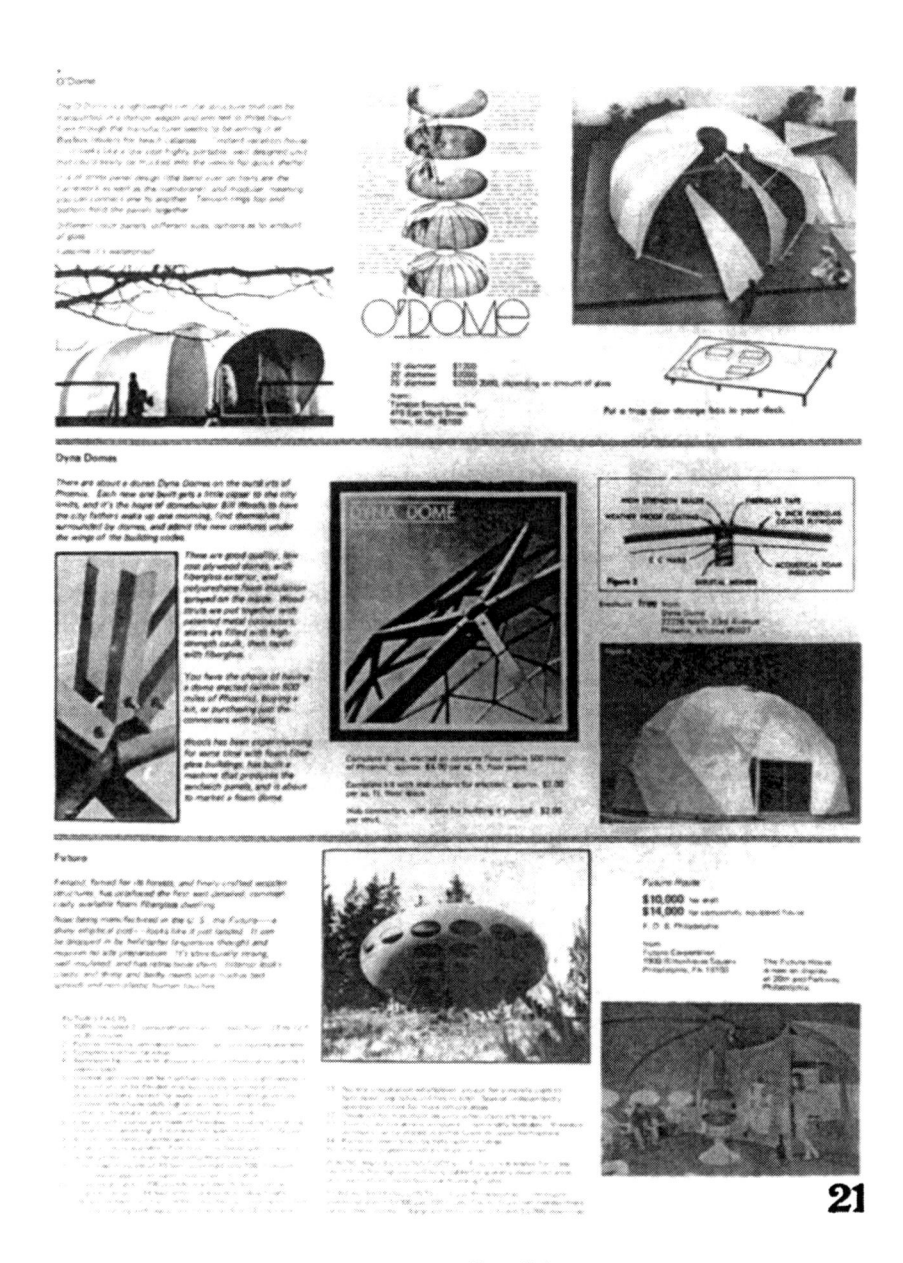

figure 14.6
HOUSING DOMES FOR SALE, FROM *WHOLE EARTH CATALOG*, SPRING 1970

to the Drop City, created in Colorado, 1966, by three former students of the University of Kansas (Figure 12.8). The community had chosen an alternative lifestyle, 'dropping out' from mainstream society, and creating its architecture out of the detritus of industrial society: car parts, waste building materials and the like. The model for the structures erected by the 'Droppers' was Buckminster Fuller's geodesic dome, a product which was popularized afresh to adherents of alternative lifestyles through Stuart Brand's *Whole Earth Catalog* (Figure 14.6).

179

Likewise, Martin Pawley's investigations into self-built 'garbage housing'[36] (see Chapter 18), created from such refuse as empty bottles, oil drums and cardboard tubing, offered a critique of both throw-away industrialized society and the disengagement of architecture and the user – all of which tallied with the critiques of developed western societies being offered by such commentators as Fritz Schumacher[37] and Ivan Illich.[38] The notion of self-build was most successfully expounded in Britain by the independent architect Walter Segal who, since the early 1960s, had employed standard building materials (especially timber) with a minimum of cutting and jointing to create housing which could be built by lay people at low cost. In 1978 Segal convinced Lewisham Council to fund a group of fourteen such houses, which were completed at significantly lower cost than traditional construction (Figure 14.7).[39] Segal himself assisted the self-builders on site, although residents subsequently undertook extensions and alterations to their houses with little or no help.

Notions of do-it-yourself and self-build were swept up by Charles Jencks and Nathan Silver in 1972 under the banner of 'adhocism', as a means of stressing the sense of spontaneity, invention and creativity evinced in such 'bricolaged' work.[40] The reference to Claude Lévi-Strauss' bricoleur (from his anthropological text *La Pensée Sauvage*, Paris, 1962) was symptomatic of the influence of structuralist thinking in academic circles by the end of the 1960s, and was employed by Jencks and Silver as an antidote to the rationalist, industrialized work of establishment architects and unimaginative engineers. The idea was treated with contempt by Banham, who viewed Jencks and Silver's opposition of the bricoleur and the designer as a false, reductive dualism. Designers, he argued, typically worked through a process of bricolage anyway:

> People who can believe that mass bricolage is a sovereign remedy for 'forces and ideas that hinder the fulfilment of human purposes ... large corporations ... philosophies of behaviourism ... modern architecture' because it is the opposite of the faceless 'technostructure' of engineering, should think again, carefully. Modern bricolage, on the evidence of the illustrations in *Adhocism* (and the pix, at least, do observe the real world) works only with the offcuts and discards of engineering ... The bricoleur's universe of instruments proves – in this version – to be just another colonial dependency of the dreaded technostructure.[41]

Banham's technophilia had, however, side-stepped the main argument of *Adhocism*: that lay people should have greater input into the design of their environments. Jencks and Silver's aim had, after all, been to promote pluralism and democracy in design, to counter the exclusionist professionalization of architecture and urbanism. All the same, it was clear that substantial differences of opinion could exist between proponents of non-planning, depending on whether or not one placed one's faith in design professionals.

36 Martin Pawley, *Garbage Housing*, London: Architectural Press, 1975.
37 E. Fritz Schumacher, *Small is Beautiful: a study of economics as if people mattered*, London: Abacus, 1973.
38 Ivan Illich, *Autocostruzione e tecnologie conviviali per un uso delle tecnologie alternativi nel costruire-abitare*, Bologna: Clueb, 1980.
39 See, for example, John McKean, *Learning From Segal: Walter Segal's life, work and influence*, Basel: Birkhaüser Verlag, 1989.
40 Charles Jencks and Nathan Silver, *Adhocism: the case for improvisation*, London: Secker and Warburg, 1972.
41 Reyner Banham, Bricologues à la lanterne, *New Society*, 1 July 1976, pp. 25–26.

figure 14.7
WALTER SEGAL, SELF-BUILD HOUSING,
LEWISHAM, C.1978

nine
ADVOCACY AND COMMUNITY

Rather than to promote unthinkingly or to dismiss out of hand the professions, a third approach to the issue of professional involvement in urban design was offered by those who proposed the redefinition of the role of the architect. Segal's direct, hands-on approach to self-building was rarely repeated, although the idea of emphasizing the architect's role as an 'advocate' for the community attracted growing support. The question was one of how to harness the talents of the professional to assist the 'uninformed' client – those for whom the legal and statutory mechanisms of architecture and planning were arcane and esoteric mysteries. Termed by the American planner Paul Davidoff in 1965, and informing the writings of critics like Robert Goodman, 'advocacy planning' sought to harness the professional skills of the architect in the service of the community, to act both as collaborator with and mouthpiece for clients. Confronting public perceptions of disinterested and even hostile planning and architectural professions, its tenor subsequently surfaced in Britain in the 1969 Skeffington Report on participation in planning, in which planners were exhorted to involve the public in their decisions.'[42]

Whether as a result of Skeffington or not, the notion of 'community architecture' soon caught the imagination of both the public and, after initial hostility, the profession during the 1970s.[43] In 1973, the new President of the RIBA, Frederick Pooley, declared prophetically: 'I see a new community architecture with a more human face, with form and detail suited to its own location, and in tune with the new social outlook on what life is all about'.[44] In Black Road, Macclesfield (1972–1976), architect Rod Hackney helped local residents protect their condemned terraced housing from demolition, and worked with them to refurbish their properties – to widespread media acclaim. Likewise at the Byker redevelopment in Newcastle-upon-Tyne (1969–1975), architect Ralph

---

42 Committee on Public Participation in Planning, *People and Planning* (Skeffington Report), London: HMSO, 1969.
43 For a history see Nick Wates and Charles Knevitt, *Community Architecture: how people are creating their own environment*, London: Penguin, 1987. As Theo Crosby put it, 'The words "community" and "participation" are the ping-pong balls of current fashionable discussion being batted around without a great deal of accuracy, usually hollow shells' (Theo Crosby, *How to Play the Environment Game*, Harmondsworth: Penguin, 1973, p. 256).
44 Fred Pooley, Toward a community architecture: a mirror to architecture today, *RIBA Journal*, vol. 80, December 1973, pp. 598–602.

Erskine opened an on-site office and permitted tenants an unprecedented degree of participation in the design of their new housing. It seemed that the involvement of the users of architecture in the design process was now a serious (and realizable) consideration. The need for such involvement was at its greatest in mass-housing projects where the official patron was the local housing authority, not the resident. Moreover, in these situations, the social differences between an overwhelmingly middle class architectural profession and the typically working class residents could be cited as an explanation for the failure of public housing.[45] Advocacy and community architecture sought to bridge this gap, not by changing the class of the architectural and planning professions, but by at least challenging their presuppositions through the direct participation of the ultimate users of the building.

Regardless of the well-meant attempts of socially minded architects to help people realize their own architectures, critics continued to attack the modernist establishment, a tirade which achieved new extremes of controversy with the populist interventions of the Prince of Wales, lambasting the arrogance of architects and the legacy of modernism and championing the wishes of the public. Clearly, his criticisms had been well-rehearsed from the late 1960s onwards, but it was at Charles's widely quoted RIBA speech of 1984 that the debate reached new heights of controversy in Britain.[46] His 'Vision of Britain' was subsequently broadcast by the BBC in 1988, exhibited at the Victoria and Albert Museum in 1989 and published as a book. By this point the debate was as much focused on stylistic issues as on attempts to involve the users of architecture. The simple employment of a classical idiom could now be deemed to vouchsafe public acceptability, even if participation had not been guaranteed. The exemplar of this approach, Quinlan Terry's Richmond Riverside (1984–1988), duly offered a series of erudite, revivalist façades to the Thames, and met with widespread popular acclaim (Figure 14.2). Otherwise the building was not exceptional: just another late-twentieth-century commercial development of open-plan offices and retail units, all policed with closed circuit television and pseudo-Roman signs declaring 'no public right of way'. Alongside the triumph of political conservatism signalled by the 1979 general election, then, architectural practice and history had, amongst certain quarters, also witnessed a retrenchment.[47]

ten
WHAT IS THIS POST–MODERNISM?

The Architectural Association's questioning of modernism reached an early crescendo in 1975, with the devotion of an issue of its journal to 'The menopause: beyond post-modern architecture'.[48] Yet what is now most revealing, in the light of the subsequent development of post-modernism, is the concentration in 1975 on the basic issues of

45 Alan Lipman, The architectural belief system and social behaviour, *British Journal of Sociology*, June 1969, pp. 190–204.
46 For a discussion see Charles Jencks, *The Prince, The Architects and New Wave Monarchy*, London: Academy Editions, 1988. Also, Maxwell Hutchinson, *The Prince of Wales: right or wrong?*, London: Faber and Faber, 1989.
47 One thinks of historian David Watkins' attack on modern architecture, *Morality and Architecture*, published in 1977, and the revival of classicism in the work of Quinlan Terry, John Simpson, etc.
48 *Architectural Association Quarterly*, 7, no. 4, October/December 1975.

self-determination, self-build and participation which were deemed to signal the bankruptcy of modernism. And whilst Tschumi's propositions of 1974 prefigured the philosophical nihilism of deconstruction, it is rather the issues of populism and participation which exercised contributors to this issue of the journal. Given the later emphasis on the stylistic novelties, theoretical complexities and knowing witticisms of the various strands of post-modern architecture, it is instructive to reconsider its origins in attempts to widen the scope for public involvement in design.

#15

CLARA GREED: CAN MAN PLAN? CAN WOMAN PLAN BETTER?

one
INTRODUCTION

This chapter seeks to provide an alternative perspective on the plan/non-plan debate, from a 'women and planning' viewpoint, with reference primarily to the situation in Britain. The presentation of the debate as a dualism in which there are only two options, to plan or not to plan, is limiting. Of course such a zoned, dualistic, mentality does not only affect town planning, it affects all aspects of western society and thought. Gillian Rose has discussed the dualisms and problematic binary oppositions identified by Hélène Cixous, and the implications for geographical thinking which, like planning, is obsessed with defining terms, amassing data and controlling perceived chaos.[1] Cixous's dualisms include man/woman, man/nature and activity/passivity – especially relevant to planning. One could presumably add plan/non-plan to this list. Some may imagine that women 'are not interested' in planning, or that they are likely to be on the side of non-plan or even anti-planning. However, this chapter proposes a third option to the plan/non-plan dualism: 'to plan differently', to transform patriarchal, bureaucratic planning. The discussion of this third way will be addressed through a wide range of ideas, policies and perspectives from 'women and planning' literature – for there is considerable enthusiasm among women for town planning.

I will discuss the problem that women have with the effects of planning on our towns and cities, with particular reference to the issue of zoning and its murky history. En route, I will offer alternative planning policies, and different ways of planning which might transcend the plan/non-plan dualism by transforming the nature and appeal of planning. I will look at three levels of spatial planning, namely the 'macro' city-wide level; the 'meso' district level; and the 'micro' local level of estate and building design. I will discuss for whom it is assumed that planning is done, and who is doing the planning, thereby exploring the planner/planned dualism. I will also consider how planning is undertaken, and the particular problems that its organization and operation present for women.

In the concluding section alternative approaches both within and without the statutory planning system are considered. I will argue that in order to change planning it is necessary to change patriarchal attitudes which are embedded not only within the sub-cultural values of the planning profession, but also in the private property sector and within wider society. Clearly, one cannot radically change the end product – the built environment – without changing how planners and other urban decision-makers

---

1 Gillian Rose, *Feminism and Geography: the limits of geographical knowledge*, Cambridge: Polity, 1993; Hélène Cixous, *Des Femmes*, Paris: Gallimard, 1980.

see the world or imagine it ought to be. After all, unplanned cities are not so great for women either but are problematic in different ways from planned developments. Replacing planning with nothing might lead to rampant property speculation, urban sprawl and chaos and joy for some – but not for most women. Planning functions might then be taken over by building inspectors, highways engineers, or perhaps a new department of 'style police' even keener than the planners on stamping out individuality, imagination and originality.

two
WHAT IS THE PROBLEM?

MACRO: CITY-WIDE LEVEL

Over the last twenty years the 'women and planning' movement has produced a vast amount of literature on the problems for women in the city of man.[2] Women planners and urban geographers have been concerned with the macro, city-wide, emphasis on land-use zoning which has sought to order the perceived chaos of the city by dividing 'work' (employment zones) from 'home' (residential areas). Yet, for women, home has always been a place of work, not a retreat from work, although nowadays most women also undertake paid work outside the home.

Within Anglo-American statutory systems planning has generally been equated with zoning at the macro level and, particularly in Britain, in the land-use-zoning-based 'Development Plans' which were introduced nationally under the 1947 Town and Country Planning Act – the foundation stone of post-war reconstruction planning. For many years, then, the choice for planners has been between zone or non-zone, order or chaos, with little space for alternative approaches based on a greater diversity of planning policy. Whilst in the nineteenth century this approach may have been justifiable in the name of public health and sanitary reform, such an argument is hardly valid in the twentieth century where the pollution created by commuters travelling by car between work and home far exceeds last century's industrial emissions. Many a city has been planned around the journey to work, which was conceived as an unbroken journey undertaken primarily by men from house to place of work. By contrast, for a working woman with a child under school age, and another at school, the journey to work and back is likely to comprise home, childminder, school, work, school, childminder and, finally, home.

Increasingly, however, the development plan system has applied specific planning policy initiatives across districts which overarch individual land uses, as manifest in the designation of, *inter alia,* urban conservation areas, urban regeneration areas, central

---

2 Gerda Wekerle, Rebecca Peterson and David Morley (editors), *New Space for Women,* Boulder: Westview Press, 1980; Dolores Hayden, *Redesigning the American Dream,* London: Norton, 1984; Clara Greed, *Women and Planning: creating gendered realities,* London: Routledge, 1994; Jo Little, *Gender, planning and the policy process,* Oxford: Pergamon, 1994; Christine Booth, Jane Darke and Susan Yeandle (editors), *Changing Places: women's lives in the city,* London: Paul Chapman Publishing, 1996; Linda McDowell and Joanne Sharp (editors), *Space, Gender, Knowledge: feminist readings,* London: Arnold, 1997.

business districts and local plan areas. Such an approach still evinces a spatial fetishism but is, arguably, more holistic and flexible than a purely zoning-based strategy. Nonetheless, in the national development control planning system (to which all development remains subject) one still witnesses traces of a zoning mentality and an enduring desire to plan by means of separation, categorization and by negative regulation. The planning system is structured around defining which land uses are forbidden in a particular setting, rather than pro-actively specifying what is to be positively encouraged, or what is simply to be left alone.

This desire for spatial separation is a manifestation of a deeper, centuries-old desire to separate public from private realms and to separate women from men. The etymology of 'zoning' is itself revealing.[3] From an historical perspective Marilyn French points out that the Hebrew for 'prostitute' is *zonah* and means 'she who goes out of doors' (outside the marital home), that is, she who is in the wrong place.[4] In Latin, *zonam solvere* means 'to lose the virgin zone', to get married or lose one's virginity. In many Mediterranean societies, both classical and recent, there has been a clear demarcation between outside/inside and public/private, with women being allocated to the latter realm.[5] Woman could have considerable power within the home, as in Ancient Greece, provided she 'accepted her role', as the good mother presiding over the private realm of hearth and home, looking after the fruit of the loins (significantly *zonē*), and did not seek to invade the public space or challenge the public/private dichotomies which underpinned society. Whether, and to what extent, these historical taboos continue to influence today's society is open to debate. Nonetheless, many women certainly feel from personal experience that even in societies which have ostensibly tried to make a conscious break with the past, traditional attitudes towards women and space linger on.[6]

For some of the founding fathers of modern town planning a mixture of Freudian, eugenic, occult, classical and evolutionary principles influenced conceptualizations of what planning ought to be about, not least the need to control women's sexuality.[7] Town-planner Patrick Geddes, for example, promoted the tripartate zoning of 'place, folk, work' as a basis of urban analysis and policy – paralleled by Le Play's 'man, place, work' and similar divisions made by many of the other forefathers of modern planning. This demarcation helped keep women out of 'work' and in the private realm of hearth and home. Such a mentality was echoed in Geddes' extreme opposition to women's suffrage and in his follower, Lewis Mumford's, obsession with women's body parts as 'sexual', 'maternal' and therefore 'other'.[8] The concept of 'zoning', then, contains within

---

3 For a discussion see Clara Greed, *Women and Planning: creating gendered realities*, op. cit., note 2, chapter 5.
4 Marilyn French, *The War Against Women*, London: Hamish Hamilton, 1992, p. 76.
5 Elise Boulding, *The Underside of History*, London: Sage, Volume I, 1992, p. 227; for the plaza/patio divide see Pilar Ballarin Domingo and Candida Martinez Lopez (editors), *Del Patio a la Plaza: las mujeres en las sociedades mediterraneas*, Granada: Universidad de Granada, 1995.
6 Domingo and Lopez, for example, address this issue from an anthropological historical perspective, reflecting upon post-Franco Spain, where women's place is now meant to be 'equal' and 'liberated'. Domingo and Lopez, *ibid.*
7 David Matless, Regional surveys and local knowledges: the geographical imagination of Britain, 1918–39, *Transactions*, 17, no. 4, 1992, pp. 464–480; Clara Greed, *Women and Planning*, op. cit., note 2, p. 80.
8 Clara Greed, *Women and Planning*, op. cit., note 2, pp. 75, 117.

it the idea of the separation of the sacred from the profane, the pure from the diseased, male from female, and the good from the bad, in order to achieve an ordered, 'uncontaminated' society (the words 'zoning' and 'sanitary' being etymologically linked).

Land-use zoning is essentially a religious exercise aimed at containing women and their powers, dating from times when the spiritual and the spatial were not separated – unlike today when little reference is made to spiritual forces within town planning, or within mainstream humanities and social sciences discourses.[9] Zoning's 'practical' value, so stressed by modern town planners is, arguably, quite secondary and incidental. For example, traditionally, in some Mediterranean countries, to ensure a new building was not contaminated a human sacrifice would be made – ideally by walling-up a virgin in its foundations. Manuela Antoniou recounts the derivation of the term 'milk of magnesia' as a reflection of a deep bau/frau (building/woman) enmity within western society.[10] In this complex story, of which there are many mainly Greek and Balkan versions and possible locations for Magnesia, the wife of the master builder (the architekton) was walled up in the foundations of the building as a sacrifice to ensure successful construction, since the building had constantly fallen down. Yet, when her baby cried, the walls of the building wept breast milk for the infant in sorrow, and the building (the work of man) acquired miraculous powers of healing as supplicants, especially the infertile, drank its milk. Other versions of the story allowed for a blood sacrifice, of some unlucky virgin or goat, in place of the builder's wife. This myth became conflated with, and echoed in, a range of Christian, masonic, and occult beliefs about the powers of blood sacrifice, propitiation and substitution, and about the powers of regeneration and salvation transmitted by building. Woman's power of procreation is thus transferred to the master mason, and life force is given to the building itself, whilst the place of women in construction resides murdered and unseen. No wonder planning remains a problem for women.

MESO: DISTRICT LEVEL

At the 'meso' or district level, women have long argued for a more balanced and mixed relationship of land uses. Eurofem members (the European 'women and planning' organization) have promoted the concept of 'the city of everyday life' as the solution.[11] This would be based upon the city of short distances, of mixed land uses, and a generous provision and abundant distribution of local facilities, shops, employment opportunities and services – so there would be no need to travel by car or commute. Such a vision would prove highly environmentally sustainable whilst also creating more jobs, particularly in local businesses, retail outlets and the service sector – especially for women – but would offend those who argue for the economies of (large)

---

9 Chris Arthur, Diversion around the God slot: how can the humanities ignore the human soul?, *The Higher*, 8 November 1991, London: Times Newpaper Group.
10 Manuella Antoniou, The walled up bride: an architecture of eternal return, in Debra Coleman, Elizabeth Danze and Carol Henderson (editors), *Architecture and Feminism*, Princeton: Princeton Architectural Press, 1996, p. 114.
11 R. Skjerve (editor), *Manual for Alternative Municipal Planning*, Oslo: Ministry of the Environment, 1993; OECD, *Women and the City: housing, services and the urban environment*, Paris: Organisation for Economic Co-operation and Development, 1996.

scale.¹² Ironically, this is what many European cities were like before town planning came into force, although nowadays this 'natural' state could only be achieved through artificial planning.

A major contributory factor to this state of affairs within British town planning has been the emphasis upon land uses rather than upon the users of the land, suggesting a use/uzer dualism (spelt as said, to emphasize difference). The ideal meso-level plan would, instead, put great emphasis upon social considerations and the needs of people. Of course, many of women's demands have been relegated to the non-planning side of the planning/non-planning dualism. Many of their practical demands for better childcare provision, baby buggy parking spaces outside shops, more public toilets and safer streets have been met over the years with such statements as, 'women? that's not a land use matter', 'that's *ultra vires*' or, simply, 'that's not part of town planning'. Indeed a vast list of topics which encompass just about every aspect of human life have been relegated to this no man's land of non-planning. In contrast, the provision of 'public' open space for sport, not least football, has always, paradoxically, been seen as a serious land-use matter, whereas adequate provision of childcare facilities (which would result in vast amounts of building and changes of land use¹³) has been marginalized as unworthy of consideration. Such a mentality demonstrates why women want to reconceptualize town planning and offer new definitions and approaches which are inclusive, not exclusive, of their needs.

MICRO LEVEL

The 'micro' level has often been assumed to be the focus of 'women and planning', although, as should be apparent from the previous discussion, women planners eventually intend to restructure the entire city of man. At the micro level, the issues typically of concern to feminist planners are those of safety and accessibility, the very basic but vital issues of adequate lighting, fewer steps, wider doorways and other such 'minor details' which have effectively kept women, especially those with babies and small children, out of the city of man. Whilst many progressive local authorities have now incorporated some of these issues into the plan-making process, there is still no Department of the Environment, Transport and the Regions (DETR) Planning Policy Guidance statement (PPG) on gender – nor for that matter disability or ethnicity. *The Building Regulations: Part M* document, does provide some control, but relates only to individual buildings, and mainly new ones at that.¹⁴

The new *PPG1* on *General Policy and Principles* does, however, state that 'the development of land and buildings provides the opportunity to secure a more accessible environment for everyone, including wheelchair users, and other people with disabil-

12 OECD, *Women and the City, ibid.*
13 J.B. Cullingworth and V. Nadin, *Town and Country Planning in Britain*, London: Routledge, 1994, p. 251.
14 The relative roles and jurisdiction of the building and planning regulations in respect of disability are discussed fully in Clara Greed and Marion Roberts (editors), *Introducing Urban Design: interventions and responses*, Harlow: Longmans, 1998, Appendix II.

ities, elderly people and people with toddlers or infants in pushchairs'.[15] It would seem that women are now likely to get some of their needs met under the category of disabled people. Or perhaps 'wheeled people', including people in wheelchairs and children in pushchairs, are now a recognized category in planners' shorthand, covering women and the disabled.

One problem for women – with urban design as much as with town planning – has been the tendency of the designer and planner to look down at the city street layout, seeing the city spread out on the drawing board from above, from a God's eye view. In contrast women, as the main carers, shoppers and users of public transport, have to battle through the streets at ground level, through wind and rain, often carrying heavy shopping and accompanied by small children. Virtual reality computer programs which seek to simulate walking through the proposed layout of an area often appear to be designed from the perspective of an energetic young man, carrying nothing more than a rolled-up newspaper, whistling as he weightlessly bounds through cyberspace.

The problems of negotiating the streets of man are even greater for small children: indeed, children may be seen as the last great minority which planning has yet to accommodate – the child/adult dualism cutting across our whole society and particularly affecting access to public space and facilities. The powerful but changing social construction of the child/adult dualism is reflected in the changing age limit put on the definition of childhood, which at present is defined by the United Nations as eighteen years. In 1998 The Children's Society publicized a series of projects to encourage children's participation in planning, which encouraged the re-examination of child/adult, and planned/planner dualisms within the context of the policy-making process, and the viewing of the city of man from a child's eye-level.[16]

Another problematic dualism within planning relates to the dichotomy between the inside and the outside of buildings. Legally, the planners' powers cease at the threshold to the building – the design and external appearance of the building – and the details of the inside and the building structure belong to the designers. But many of the issues, particularly in relation to accessibility, require a clear run between insides and outsides, involving decisions about entrance steps, door widths and ramps. Such factors are covered, at a basic level, by the Building Regulations, and policed by local authority Building Control officers, but the division of power and the difference in culture and attitudes between the building control and planning authorities on these matters is clearly unhelpful.

The reader will, no doubt, be able to think of many examples, especially in more progressive urban authorities, where negotiation, agreement or bluff, conservation controls and special planning controls have been used by planners to ensure careful design

---

15 DETR, *General Policy and Principles*, Planning Policy Guidance Note 1 (PPG 1), Department for the Environment, Transport and the Regions, London: HMSO, 1997, para. 55.
16 Eileen Adams and Sue Ingham, *Changing Places: children's participation in environmental planning*, London: Children's Society and Planning Aid for London, 1998.

control over the whole building, inside and out, and especially over the façade. County councils, in their role as highways authorities, also have considerable power on ensuring access, but critics may argue that the emphasis, even today, is likely to be upon meeting the needs of the motor car, rather than those of the pedestrian: for mobility rather than access.[17] And in each case women's interest typically coincides with the former, less powerful component, since women are less likely to be car drivers and also comprise the majority of pedestrians in shopping streets.[18]

The appearance of huge internal spaces for public use, such as covered shopping malls, airport structures and the Millennium Dome, is reconfiguring and challenging the traditional divisions between outsides and insides, and private property and public space. Nonetheless statutory control over the inside of buildings still only comes under the control of the Building Regulations, which are primarily concerned with structural rather than social or aesthetic considerations, and which are often a cause of frustration to both architects and planners.

three
SOLUTIONS: TRANSCENDING DUALISMS

IMPLEMENTING PLANNING

From a 'women and planning' viewpoint there is a central need to change planning policy, particularly to return to a more diverse, smaller scale, mixed form of development and to include social as well as physical considerations in planning policy. This gets us half way, but the continuing lack of statutory powers to implement 'women and planning' policies remains an immense problem for women.[19] However, even though the British planning system remains subservient to spatial fetishism, alternative possibilities and models exist elsewhere. In Italy, for example, women planners have pioneered – and progressive municipalities have implemented – 'time planning'.[20] Such temporal planning seeks to make more space for women in the city of man by co-ordinating the opening and closing hours of shops, schools, factories and public offices to enable women to fulfil all their tasks, whilst reducing rush hour traffic and enabling men to take on home-making tasks too. In Britain the cause of time planning has become confused with notions of the 'twenty-four-hour city',[21] and, whilst this may have honourable objectives with strong cultural advantages,[22] many women are suspicious of what they see as an over-emphasis simply upon pubs and clubs (the

17 Hugh Barton, Design for movement, in Clara Greed and Marion Roberts (editors), *Introducing Urban Design, op. cit.*, note 14.
18 Clara Greed, *Introducing Town Planning*, Harlow: Longmans, 1996.
19 Jo Little, *Gender, Planning and the Policy Process*, Oxford: Pergamon, 1994.
20 Carmen Belloni, A woman-friendly city: politics concerning the organisation of time in Italian cities, in OECD, *Women in the City: housing services and urban environment, op. cit.*, note 11; also, Clara Greed, Bad timing means no summer in the cities, *Planning*, no. 1209, 14 March 1997, pp 18–19.
21 J. Montgomery, The evening economy of cities, *Town and Country Planning*, 63, no. 11, pp. 302–307.
22 Franco Bianchini, The twenty-four hour city, *Demos*, no. 5, 1995, p. 47. Franco Bianchini and Clara Greed, Cultural and time planning, in Clara Greed (editor), *Social Town Planning*, London: Routledge, 1999.

'twenty-four-hour pub crawl'). Ideally, work and leisure – the functional and cultural dimensions of urbanism – should complement each other within gender-sensitive time planning. The incorporation of time planning into the statutory planning system is a likely future development, and women planners watch the situation with interest.

The sustainability movement – and environmentalist legislation – also offer means of incorporating social (including women's) issues into the planning system. Local Agenda 21 and Environmental Assessment requirements offer great possibilities for including women's issues into the mainstream agenda. This had been facilitated from the outset by the Rio Declaration, which stated that sustainability comprised three components: economic viability, *social equity* and environmental balance.[23] Women planners in other European countries have been effective in arguing that sustainability must contain a gender perspective which suffuses all aspects of policy.[24] Indeed, it is often more advantageous nowadays to promote 'women and planning' issues through the vehicle of 'sustainability' rather than to argue from the basis of practicality or discrimination.[25]

CHANGING PHILOSOPHICAL PERSPECTIVES

Women philosophers argue that the adoption of a holistic environmental perspective might break down traditional man/nature, science/instinct and planning/chaos dualisms by seeing both women and men as equal parts of an unfathomable natural world and ecosytem.[26] Indeed one must ask why man thought he was so different in the first place.

A whole crop of malestream[27] theories, purportedly without dualisms, are becoming popular[28] reflecting the current academic spirit of post-structuralism, relativism and diversity. But this does not mean that age-old dualisms have departed from the planning psyche, or that they no longer exist – although such problems are at least being discussed. Nor should one forget that as soon as women criticized and discredited as sexist and illogical much of mainstream traditional sociology (not least patriarchal class theory because it left women out of society) post-structuralism became popular and 'class' was suddenly declared irrelevant. Class was just another factor which, along with gender, race, disability and sexuality, provided a source of endless debate, publications and entire academic careers – whilst nothing really had changed.

---

23 Brundtland Report, *Our Common Future: World Commission on Environment and Development*, Oxford: Oxford University Press, 1987.
24 OECD, *Women and the City, op. cit.*, note 11; Christine Booth, Jane Darke and Susan Yeandle (editors), *Changing Places: women's lives in the city, op. cit.*, note 2; Dory Reeves, Women and the environment, Special Issue, *Built Environment*, 22, no. 1, 1996.
25 See Sule Nisancioglu and Clara Greed, Bringing down the barriers, in *Living in the Future: 24 sustainable development ideas from the UK*, London: UK National Council for Habitat II, pp 16–17, in which childcare and accessibilty are presented as primarily 'green issues'.
26 Karen Warren (editor), *Ecofeminism: women, culture, nature*, Bloomington: Indiana University Press, 1997.
27 Malestream = 'male mainstream', a popular, widely used contraction in feminist slang, source unknown (often confused, significantly, with maelstrom). Explained and used in J. Siltanen and M. Stanworth, *Women and the Public Sphere*, London: Hutchinson, 1984.
28 Deriving from M. Callon, J. Law and A. Rip, *Mapping the Dynamics of Science and Technology*, London: Macmillan, 1986; also Jonathan Murdock, Inhuman/nonhuman/human: actor network theory and the prospects of nondualistic and symmetrical perspective on nature and society, *Planning and Environment*, 15, no. 6, 1987, pp. 731–756.

Perhaps the same is happening in planning. As soon as planning is criticized, it is disowned. Some would still say that town planning is an irrelevance since the 'spatial' locality is of minimal significance in our modern mobile society, and that we should be concerned with wider economic issues. A strong sense of *déjà vu* overwhelms me, as this argument is so reminiscent of the arguments of the new left in the 1970s, in which I was regularly accused of 'just rearranging the deckchairs on the Titanic'. Many urban feminists and traditional planners (including myself) still maintain that space matters, since we do not float in a spaceless vacuum, in spite of attempts to 'unplace', 'unspace' and 'untown' planning.[29] In throwing away unhelpful dualisms we must not discard the vital components of town planning, most notably space itself. Yet although space matters, it does not follow that physical space is the same as social space, for women's experience of the city can be very different from that of men within the *same* locality.[30]

CHANGE AGENTS

One can never really change the nature of town planning, or break down unhelpful dualisms, unless the hearts – as well as the minds – of planners are changed. In my current research on the changing culture and composition of the construction professions,[31] I am fascinated by the question: 'How can change be generated and transmitted within professional sub-cultural groups?', and have been seeking to identify potential change agents and to map pathways of change. Increasing numbers of minority students are entering the built environment professions, especially town planning and housing, but easier access does not necessarily lead to greater representation and progress within the professions themselves. Far from altering the culture of the built environment professions, the entrance of a greater range of so-called minority professionals has led to a series of new sub-cultures with their own organizational structures. Significant groups include the Centre for Accessible Environments; Planning Aid for London; London Women and the Manual Trades; the Society of Black Architects;[32] Women's Design Service;[33] the London Regeneration Network;[34] and a host of other training, education, community groups and all-women practices (following the tradition of Matrix, the feminist architectural practice).

Those actively involved are few in number but they represent a force for change to the extent that they form part of a powerful network of alternative groups and are highly productive in publications, research and campaigning. In addition, their organizations offer models of alternative management structures, often based on a

---

29 Compare Linda McDowell and Joanne Sharp (editors), *op. cit.*, note 2; and Dolores Hayden, *op. cit.*, note 2.
30 A summary of the battle between the spatial and aspatial 'sides' of urban sociological theory, *vis à vis* the development of town planning is to be found in Clara Greed, *Introducing Town Planning, op. cit.*, note 18, chapter 11.
31 Material on the changing culture and composition of the construction professions derives from ESRC-funded research undertaken by the author during 1997 on 'Social integration and exclusion in professional subcultures in the construction professions'.
32 SOBA, Mentoring: to tame or to free?, Symposium notes, meeting of Society of Black Architects, 27 November 1997, Prince of Wales's Institute of Architecture, London.
33 WDS, Women's Design Service Broadsheet Design Series, London: Women's Design Service, 1997, includes *Policy planning and development control*, London: WDS.
34 LRN, *Still Knocking at the Door*, Report of the Women and Regeneration Seminar, held May 1997, London: London Regeneration Network in association with LVSC (London Voluntary Service Council), 1997.

more co-operative, inclusive attitude towards employees at all levels and greater communication with 'society' – particularly when their client is a community group, or a disadvantaged or under-represented minority group.

Indeed, many of those active in the 'women and planning' movement retain links with, and draw strength from, community and local minority groups, but they also network with other women professionals. I am fascinated by pan-professional women's groups within the construction industry, such as Constructive Women Professionals (subsequently degendered and renamed the Equal Opportunities Taskforce in Construction), which includes women representatives from all the chartered built environment bodies including the Royal Town Planning Institute and, of course, the RIBA. One of the ways ahead for 'women and planning' is surely through uniting forces with other such women's groups, for only 6 per cent of built environment professionals are planners, and only 6 per cent of all construction professionals are women.[35] The number of women planners has increased, but more does not necessarily mean better.[36] Only 5 per cent of women planners are in senior decision-making posts – that is in a position, potentially, to alter the nature of urban policy. Nor should it be assumed that just because women are women their policies will be different from equivalent men: much depends upon their level of awareness, education, class, life experience and personal perspective.

Studying the experience of women in other built environment professions who deal with the 'same' problems is extremely valuable.[37] I have become particularly interested in the wider construction professions and property development industry, because this is now where, I believe, the real power to create and plan the built environment resides. The powers of local government planners have changed during twenty years of political shift away from State intervention and control and towards an ostensibly freer, entrepreneurial national culture. 'Planning' as an ideology has become passé, with embarrassing socialist associations; and, although it continues to attract more women than most other built environment professions, female membership is now levelling off and there are signs it will drop in the future. It has been upstaged by environmentalism, and town planning courses are less popular, as it is unfashionable to be in favour of road building or development of any kind. Some would argue that an increase in the numbers of women and other minorities in a profession is a sure sign of declining status, not a sign of more progressive attitudes and increased social equality.[38] Indeed, I feel I have at times been arguing with the ghost of planning as it once was fabled to be: the plan/non-plan debate means little to my students, many of whom intend to go into the private sector.

35 See tables of membership figures in Clara Greed, The Changing Composition and Culture of the Construction Professions: quantitative report, Bristol: Faculty of the Built Environment, University of the West of England, Occasional Paper, 1998.
36 Clara Greed, Is more better? Mark II: with reference to the position of women town planners in Britain, *Women's Studies International Forum*, 16, no. 3, 1993, pp. 255–270.
37 Sandy Rhys Jones, Andrew Dainty, Richard Neale and Barbara Bagihole, *Building on Fair Footings: improving equal opportunities in the construction industry for women*, Glasgow: Proceedings of CIB (Construction Industry Board) Conference, 1996; CIB, *Tomorrow's Team: women and men in construction*, Working Group 8 Report of the Latham Committee, Construction Industry Board, 1996.
38 See also Sally Kirk-Walker, *Undergraduate Student Survey: a report of the survey of first year students in construction industry degree courses*, York: Institute of Advanced Architectural Studies (commissioned by CITB), 1997.

But the body of planning is still with us in the form of the statutory planning system and, without it, it does not follow that a non-planned situation would necessarily be better. Development, and thus the nature of towns and cities, would be planned by property and construction professions acting on their clients' orders, whose decisions would be more likely to be determined by considerations such as cost, profit, speed of construction, contractual arrangements and structural design considerations[39] – and not necessarily by social, environmental or aesthetic considerations (although these two sets of factors are not necessarily mutually exclusive). If we get rid of the planners we do not get rid of urban problems: the pressures created by the motor car, the market and environmental pollution would not go away. Whilst it can be argued that 'good design' enhances market values, and it is in everyone's interest to consider aesthetic factors, few developers appear to believe this. Much 'design' is, after all, based on considerations such as car-parking provision, floor space allocation and profit margins (although some seem to want not to acknowledge such constraints on good urban design[40]). I suspect that if there were no planners, other groups involved in the process of property development would soon take over the territory for their own ends, many of whom are quite anti-planning.[41]

In a non-plan situation, without any statutory town planning, we could go back to the situation where building control is the main regulator of the built environment. Pressure would then build up for building controllers to increase their powers beyond the scope of individual buildings, to control whole areas and to produce plans for towns, thereby re-starting the whole cycle of increasing State control over land and development we call 'planning'. The first chair of the Building Research Establishment (BRE) was the eminent planner Raymond Unwin, and there was a strong town planning section within the organization from the outset. Conversely, Desmond Heap has commented on the roots of the planning profession and noted that 'planners could only become planners after first either becoming architects or surveyors': he considered the early planning profession to be 'a little Cinderella' relative to the other construction professions.[42] If there was a situation of non-plan, these professions presumably would, by default, take on the role again, albeit possibly developing a different planning system based on alternative criteria, potentially reflecting less social awareness and less emphasis upon women's issues.

PUBLIC PARTICIPATION / PROFESSIONAL PARTICIPATION

It has been argued that to increase 'women and planning' policies (that is, policies for women) there needs to be an increase of 'women in planning' (that is, women who become planners).[43] In order to reshape planning policy there is a need for a wider and more representative range of people and ideas to enter the profession, be it from the

---

39 CISC (Construction Industry Standing Conference), *Occupational Standards, for Professional, Managerial, Technical Occupations, in Planning, Construction, Property and Related Engineering Services*, London: CISC, The Building Centre, 1994; Ivor H. Seeley, *Quantity Surveying Practice*, London: Macmillan, 1997 (second edition).
40 Prince of Wales, *A Vision of Britain*, London: Doubleday, 1989.
41 A fuller account of the actors involved in the process is to be found in Ivor H. Seeley, *op. cit.*, note 39; also Clara Greed, *Introducing Town Planning, op. cit.*, note 18, chapter 3.
42 *Planning*, 8 August 1997, pp, 16–17, 'A witness to the monumental Act' interviewed by Peter Baber.
43 Christine Booth *et al.*, *op. cit.*, note 2.

perspective of gender, ethnicity or disability. There is also a need to ensure greater representation of women on a range of key decision-making and regulatory committees which shape the nature of the built environment.

A criticism of the recent Single Regeneration Budget (SRB) programme which includes the State-funded City Challenge scheme (ostensibly set up to regenerate inner-city communities) has been that many of the managing boards and programme committees are almost entirely white and male. And whilst women have been numerous and prominent in community politics, this valuable resource is being ignored. Groups such as the London Regeneration Network have campaigned for inclusion of women and other minorities in decision-making processes, and for recognition of the fact that at least 50 per cent of inner-city residents are female.

Criticism has been levelled at so-called 'public participation' exercises, organized on 'hit and run' principles. Women have advocated and demonstrated that a gradual, long-term approach of building up local networks and programmes between the planners and the planned is more worthwhile. Needless to say, such exercises yield a demand for a range of policies concerned with social issues, which usually have been deemed not to be a planning issue by malestream departments. Not surprisingly, ordinary women feel let down if, after all their efforts, they find that their proposals have not been implemented.

One might ask 'what is the point of having professional planners, they always get everything wrong?'. It is argued that planners might still have a role – albeit more as brokers of ideas, as organizers or as advocates, rather than as 'master planners'. However, it must be acknowledged that ultimately, when planning *must* take place, someone has to take responsibility and make decisions. Those with a professional education are likely to see the whole picture more clearly, although the local knowledge of the 'uneducated' is also a valuable resource. 'Planners' are sure to be unpopular with someone, however hard community planners might seek to accommodate everyone's needs – such are the difficulties of attempting to adopt 'bottom up' (community) rather than 'top down' (bureaucratic) approaches to planning.

It would seem that, to be a really effective feminist planner, it is better to work for a community or pressure group within the voluntary sector than to work for local government. Become a member of the 'planned', and seek to implement policy by means over and above, or apart from, the mainstream planning system. There has been a tradition in North America of women creating their own settlements and schemes but then, as critics point out, 'they have the space and money to do it'.[44] There have also been some examples in Britain, in this century, of co-operative housekeeping schemes, model neighbourhoods and individual buildings designed and developed by women.

44 Dolores Hayden, *The Grand Domestic Revolution: feminist designs for homes, neighbourhoods and cities*, Cambridge, MA: Massachusetts Institute of Technology Press, 1981; Dolores Hayden, *Redesigning the American Dream*, London: Norton, 1984.

In London, these range from the work of Alice Melvin in Finchley in 1910, to that of the Jagonari Building, Asian Women's Centre in Whitechapel, built recently by the Matrix Group.[45]

In our highly urbanized situation, women planners are more likely to seek to change policies for existing areas than to build new schemes and there is a significant, but 'invisible', history of this in Britain. Women use any means available, including approaches not actually labelled 'town planning', although for all intents and purposes they are undertaking holistic urban area planning. For example the 'Peckham Experiment' in South London[46] in the inter-war period, prefigures much of what modern women planners have sought to achieve, integrating policies on housing, health, education, childcare and urban regeneration. Such schemes grew out of a deeper heritage of co-operative, organic, community-based, communitarian and self-help movements which predate modern 'planning'. But, like many inter-war social planning schemes, this project also embodied strongly 'classed' principles, which today would be seen as eugenic, paternalistic and even fascistic in character.

In a similar way, aspects of first wave urban feminism were, by today's standards, extremely politically incorrect due, in part, to the associations of some of its followers with eugenics, which was particularly strong in the early birth control movement.[47] Nowadays – to shatter the simplicity of the dualisms – some working class women are wary of what they see as middle class women planners who, along with social workers, housing managers and other 'interfering stuck-up cows', may be seen as the 'soft cops' of the capitalist system, there to keep working women 'under'.[48] Perhaps the fear of splitting feminist cohesion and hegemony has made much of urban feminist analysis surprisingly classless.

Women appear to have had little influence on the development of statutory town planning in the post-war reconstruction period, with some notable exceptions.[49] It was not until the 'women and planning' movement of the late 1970s onwards, which came in the wake of the 1960s 'second wave' of the feminist movement, that any impact began to be felt. The peak was reached when women's planning policies were incorporated into the Greater London Development Plan.[50] The GLC was abolished soon after, but the fall-out from the GLC spread far and wide. Nowadays most development plans have some mention, however small, of women's policies, although their implementation remains another matter altogether. Most men planners, by now, have learnt the 'script' and can say the right things about 'women and planning' but few seem to realize what it really means.

45 Lynn Pearson, *The Architectural and Social History of Co-operative Living*, London: Macmillan, 1988; Clara Greed, *Women and Planning, op. cit.*, note 2, pp. 62, 95.
46 Innes Pearse and Lucy Crocker, *The Peckham Experiment: a study of the living structure of society*, London: George Allen and Unwin, 1934.
47 The wider intellectual milieu of Edwardian women planners and individual liaisons is discussed in Clara Greed, *Women and Planning, op. cit.*, note 2, pp. 99 ff.
48 Derived from observations and comments made at various meetings over the years, as seldom is this written down.
49 Clara Greed, *Introducing Town Planning, op. cit.*, note 18, chapter 6.
50 GLC, *Greater London Development Plan*, London: London Residuary Body (unadopted plan), 1996; also see GLC, *Changing Places*, 1996 (key policy document on women and planning).

As a result, women have been looking at other governmental organizations which might enable change, including various central government agencies, such as funding bodies. These can insist upon higher levels of what the Americans call 'contract compliance' above current Building Regulation and employment legislation requirements as to, respectively, the design of what is built, and who builds it. For example, the Lottery, Millennium Commission, Sports Council and Arts Council all have higher equal opportunities requirements, access and disability design standards than are found under standard legislation.[51] Voluntary bodies representing minority groups are likely to be among the beneficiaries of grants, thus enabling them to produce exemplar schemes in terms of both design and employment practice. But some minority groups may still feel excluded even when other community groups gain recognition, particularly when it comes to competitions for new schemes (such as the controversy over the development of the Stonebridge site in Brent (London), in which black architects, especially black women architects, considered they were unfairly excluded.[52] Many are critical of the perceived racism of some housing associations who put black women built environment professionals on their management committee, 'because it looks good', but never actually use black professionals in construction projects.[53] Black built environment professionals have set up a range of network groups to raise the 'visibility' of all black practices and individual practitioners, and to counter further assimilation or exclusion.[54]

Many planners feel uneasy about the ad hoc nature of the 'lottery culture' and the lack of evidence of consideration of long-term strategic planning objectives in granting funding and setting priorities. Local authorities still have their uses; for example, planning departments can make it a requirement of any major planning permission that under a 'Section 106 Agreement'[55] certain equal opportunities measures, social policies and progressive design features should be integrated in the development, although, such 'planning gain' measures have frequently been subject to legal challenge, as *ultra vires*. Meanwhile, as stated, women continue to keep an eye on the continuing story of urban regeneration and the SRB.

Rather than having to adopt an opportunistic and ad hoc approach to getting 'women and planning' policies implemented, cobbling together precedents, enabling legislation and funding from a variety of sources, it would be so much better if there were clear central government guidelines and support to bottom-up groups, to enable implementation. But then planning would not be planning as we know it; it would be closer to non-planning, and might be all the more useful for it.

---

51 Arts Council, *Equal Opportunities: additional guide*, London: National Lottery, 1996.
52 Black firms get slice of Brent action, *Building Design*, 31 January 1997.
53 Bernie Grant, *Building E=Quality: minority ethnic construction professionals and urban regeneration*, London: House of Commons, 1996.
54 SOBA, *op. cit.*, note 32.
55 Section 106 of the Town and Country Planning Act.

#16
MALCOLM MILES: LIVING LIGHTLY ON THE EARTH

one
INTRODUCTION

This chapter considers a possibility for radical transformation in the construction of cities. The term 'construction' denotes the generation of the conceptual image to which a city corresponds as well as its built form. There is seldom a single image, and built form may correspond to that image, or resist it. Where a city has been built more or less in one piece, as in some colonial cities established to quickly announce the order of the colonizing power, form and concept are unusually close. Similarly, the planned cities of the Enlightenment order space as a metaphor for the rational state. But urban environments are complex, and informal acts of appropriation by dwellers construct a psychological space overlaying physical space. This is not chaotic; it is a different kind of order. The city of appropriation, being socially produced, may in the end be a more sustainable system. But why should this concern us now?

Half the human inhabitants of the Earth now live in cities, in luxury apartments or cardboard boxes, because they have chosen the excitements of an urban lifestyle or because they have no choice. Many recent immigrants to cities in the southern hemisphere live in informal settlements surrounding those cities. Elizabeth Wilson cites estimates that in the 1960s about one-quarter of the populations of Manila and Djakarta, one-third in Mexico City and one-half in Lima lived in such settlements, and that these proportions are increasing.[1] Within the cities of Europe and North America, enclaves of corporate development marginalize adjacent neighbourhoods. Gleaming office towers such as Canary Wharf or the World Financial Centre in Battery Park City are linked by information super-highways in a 'global city' of continuous dealing, an electronic realm with neither horizon nor nightfall.[2] But is there a disparity between the autonomy of a world accessed by computer terminals and modems and the everyday experiences of urban publics, between expectations of an ever-expanding economy and the destruction of natural resources? The free market on which the global city depends is expensive for people disaffected by gentrification, or subject to market rather than human values; its economy pillages the Earth, causing environmental damage in developing countries, but not only there. And, whilst the fastest rates of urban growth are in the southern hemisphere, the model of the western city is exported throughout the world in a kind of economic colonialism.

Contemporary views of the city, in the literature of urbanism, tend to negativity. Academics and architects are captivated by war-stories from the urban fron-

---

1 Elizabeth Wilson, *The Sphinx in the City*, Berkeley: University of California, 1991, p. 128.
2 Saskia Sassen, *The Global City*, Princeton, NJ: Princeton University Press, 1991.

tier.³ Their view is supported by scenes of violence and the breakdown of values in films such as *Clockwork Orange* and *Strange Days*. Yet for many of its inhabitants the city remains a viable place of informal mixing, unplanned encounters, cultural diversity and exhilaration – the positive image which draws people into metropolitan centres. Since Georg Simmel argued that the tumult of the metropolis brought about an 'increase in nervous life',⁴ urban publics have shown an ability to reconstruct webs of social support within the metropolitan environment, despite the effects of modern planning. In the UK, house renovation, or signs of ownership such as Georgian-style doors and stone cladding, mark a desire for identity. In Turkey, contrastingly and from economic necessity, people build whole houses from scrap materials, yet paint them bright colours.⁵ Despite their economic mismatch, could there be any relation between these cases?

two
DYSTOPIA AND ITS CAUSES

The perceived dysfunctionality of cities is, perhaps, a projection of a disintegrated subjectivity affirmed by a professional methodology. A naturalizing explanation – couched in the term planning blight with its sense of crop failure – paradoxically masks processes of regulation by professionals who establish a territory of expertise from which users are effectively excluded, and makes explicit the impact of such regulation. The term 'user' itself, according to Henri Lefebvre, is a linguistic marginalization which '... has something vague – and vaguely suspect – about it'.⁶

In a liberal society there is a supposition that urban planning serves the public good. And modernist architecture espouses notions of utopia. More often, today, both professions serve private-sector urban development.⁷ Geographer Aram Eisenschitz notes that the history of capitalism 'demonstrates its scant regard for human life' adding that to be poor means 'constraints in access to the basics of life and in the ability to participate in ordinary society'.⁸ David Widgery, a doctor in east London, reflects on Canary Wharf as an attempt to insert a USA-style financial district in Docklands, alluding to the way political economy and geographic imperative are presented as inevitable, and the development's portrayal as a 'great leap forward to freedom (redefined as the market) against all the unwanted nonsense of the Welfare State'.⁹ He notes the frequency with which people can be seen sleeping in skips, adding that Cesar Pelli, the

3 For instances see: Mike Davis, *City of Quartz*, London: Verso, 1990; J. Bird, B. Curtis, T. Putnam, G. Robertson and L. Tickner, *Mapping the Futures*, London: Routledge, 1993; R. Plunz, Beyond dystopia; beyond theory formation in P. Lang (editor), *Mortal City*, New York: Princeton Architectural Press, 1995, pp. 28–36; L. Woods, Everyday war, in P. Lang (editor), *Mortal City, op. cit.*, pp. 47–53; N. Smith, *The New Urban Frontier*, London: Routledge, 1996.
4 David Frisby, *Simmel and Since*, London: Routledge, 1992, p. 71.
5 M-A. Ray, Gecekondu, in S. Harris and D. Berke (editors), *Architecture of the Everyday*, New York: Princeton Architectural Press, 1997, pp. 153–165.
6 Henri Lefebvre, *The Production of Space*, Oxford: Blackwell, 1991, p. 362.
7 R. Deutsche, Uneven development – public art in New York City, in Diane Ghirardo (editor), *Out of Site*, Seattle: Bay Press, 1991, pp. 157–219; J. Bird, Dystopia on the Thames, in Bird *et al., op. cit.*, note 3, pp. 120–135; Sharon Zukin, Space and symbols in an age of decline, in Anthony King (editor), *Re-Presenting the City*, London: Macmillan, 1996, pp. 43–59.
8 Aram Eisenschitz, The view from the grass roots, in M. Paccione (editor), *Britain's Cities*, London: Routledge, 1997, pp. 150–176, p. 153.
9 Cited in P. Ambrose, *Urban Process and Power*, London: Routledge, 1994, p. 181.

architect of 'the fat Canary' has said that 'A skyscraper recognizes that by virtue of its height it has acquired civic responsibilities ... [a] unique and socially charged role'.[10]

Two factors characterize such developments: a polarization of corporate affluence and human poverty; and an erasure of the multi-layered past of the site. But the construction of a *tabula rasa* is the project of modernity as interpreted by Le Corbusier in *The City of Tomorrow and its Planning:* 'my settled opinion, which is a quite dispassionate one, is that the centres of our great cities must be pulled down and rebuilt ...'.[11] In modernity, the space of clearance is a site of inscription – a new city made in one go, a site for aesthetic autonomy in the design of signature buildings, or its parody in the grotesque vernacular-style of supermarkets. Yet whose is the city in which the gleaming towers rise? Sociologist Sharon Zukin writes that the question 'suggests more than a politics of occupation; it also asks who has a right to inhabit the dominant image of the city'.[12] She draws attention to the exclusion of women and marginalized publics from spaces which represent the city's dominant image.

The separation of a masculine public realm of affairs from feminine spaces of domesticity is ossified in urban planning and justified by an appeal to biological causes. Elizabeth Wilson writes of Patrick Geddes, whom she sees as an important influence on town planning, that, having been trained as a biologist, he emphasized sexual difference, 'since "what was decided among the prehistoric Protozoa cannot be annulled by Act of Parliament".'[13] A biological theory of urban growth characterizes, too, the concentric ring model of Chicago sociologist E.W. Burgess. Burgess saw urban expansion as analogous to anabolic and katabolic processes of metabolism, asserting that a segregation into discrete zones determined by class 'gives form and character to the city' because 'segregation offers the group, and thereby the individuals who compose the group, a place and a role in the total organization ...'.[14] Burgess's description has become a prescription as cities re-code their centres as central business districts.

Burgess's view of the city as biology masks its cultural production. Modern city form, whether following the ring or the grid plan, manifests the idea, for instance, of a purification beginning in the seventeenth century, giving rise to rigid spatial boundaries which widen divisions of gender, race and class. In 1656, deviant and non-productive elements of the urban population – the insane and the vagrant – were excluded from visibility and confined in the Hôpital Général.[15] The process of purification continues in the ending of burial in shallow graves around city churches for fear of contagious auras[16] and the introduction of sewers. Purification is accompanied by the appearance of vistas, turning the city from a space of occupation to one of representation.

10 *Ibid.,* p. 184.
11 Le Corbusier, *The City of Tomorrow and its Planning,* New York: Dover, 1987, p. 96. Originally published Paris, 1925.
12 Sharon Zukin, Space and symbols in an age of decline, in Anthony King, *op. cit.,* p. 43.
13 E. Wilson, *op. cit.,* note 1, p. 101.
14 Burgess in R. LeGates and F. Stout, *The City Reader,* London: Routledge, 1996, pp. 94–95.
15 Michel Foucault, *Madness and Civilisation,* London: Tavistock, 1967, pp. 38–64.
16 Ivan Illich, *H$_2$0 and the Waters of Forgetfulness,* London: Marion Boyars, 1986, p. 50.

In the subjectivity of modernity, the city is reduced to an object in the mental life of its designer, translated into actuality when planning and technology, in service of power and money, make this possible. When the city becomes unliveable, one solution is to re-construct the countryside as sub-urb. Edward Robbins sees such solutions as regressively anti-urban. He further argues that although modern planners and designers are well-intentioned, the disparity of the aim of social reform and the outcome of run-down estates of tower blocks follows prioritization of spatial form over social process: 'social reformers failed to look at the way their critique of space ... unwittingly destroyed the social and cultural energy' of working-class neighbourhoods.[17] The disparity between intention and outcome results from an abstraction of the city which allows professionals in a liberal society to plan development which is destructive in its impact. There are two locations for the origin of this abstraction: the subjectivity of Cartesian dualism; and money.

three
REPRESENTATIONS OF SPACE

Henri Lefebvre, relating what he terms representations of space, or the conceived spaces of plans and architectural designs, to the development of linear perspective, situates this in the new economic relations of Tuscany in the thirteenth century. He posits as a complementary form of spatial practice the representational spaces around the body, the spaces of feeling, appropriation and atmosphere which, he emphasizes, are not abolished by the dominance of representations of space. But it is in the inert medium of representation, characterized by a computer screen or a blank sheet of paper on which lines are drawn, that the conceptualization of the modern city, as Lefebvre sees it, takes place. He writes of the architect ensconced in a space bound to graphic elements such as plans and elevations,[18] the basis of which is Cartesian dualism.

Descartes, distrustful of sense impressions and writing in the secluded space of the study – described as 'an intellectual space beyond that of sexuality'[19] – articulated a realm in which the world is reduced to representation. In a passage from the *Discourse* (1637), he writes:

> ... buildings which a single architect has undertaken and completed are usually more beautiful and better ordered than those which several architects have attempted to rework ... Thus these ancient cities are normally so poorly proportioned, compared with the well-ordered towns and public squares that an engineer traces on a vacant plain according to his free imaginings.[20]

17 Edward Robbins, Thinking space/seeing space: Thamesmead revisited, *Urban Design International*, 1, no. 3, September 1996, pp. 283–291, p. 289.
18 Henri Lefebvre, *op. cit.*, note 6, p. 361.
19 Mark Wigley, Untitled: the housing of gender, in Beatriz Colomina (editor), *Sexuality and Space*, New York: Princeton Architectural Press, 1992, pp. 327–389, p. 347.
20 Descartes (1637) cited in C.B. Lacour, *Lines of Thought*, Durham, NC: Duke University Press, 1996, p. 33.

Representation takes the form of line, and is ordered in the self-contained systems of geometry and mathematics, in which problems can be reduced '... to such terms that a knowledge of the lengths of certain straight lines is sufficient ...'.[21] Claudia Brodsky Lacour comments:

> The act of architectural drawing that Descartes describes is the outlining of a form that was not one before. That form could combine reason ('qu'un ingénieur') with imaginative freedom ('tracé à sa fantasie'). It is not only new to the world, but intervenes in a space where nothing was, on a surface ('dans une plaine') where nothing else is.[22]

In solitude, Descartes conceives an image of an engineer drawing regular places on a blank ground.

four
MONEY

The abstraction of money parallels that of representations of space, distancing individuals from possessions. Simmel writes of the owner of shares, the creditor of a state and the owner of a leased estate as gaining independence through leaving their property to purely technical management by means of money,[23] from which follows the objectification of labour and deterioration of the position of the subordinate in the relation of capital to labour. The freedom of a money economy is contradictory. The way in which freedom presents itself is, Simmel argues, as irregularity and unpredictability; this leads to the anomalies of liberal political constitutions.[24] These anomalies include the liberty of free market economics to determine city form. The abstraction of money linked to that of representations of space produces a city in which urban publics are users of spaces regarded as value-free settings for a city which is not theirs.

five
URBAN TRANSFORMATIONS

Mapping the model of the modern city onto the urban fabric of older, inner-city neighbourhoods, or onto settlements in non-western countries, demonstrates its limitations. Ivan Illich notes that '... dwelling by people is transformed into housing for people. Housing is changed from an activity into a commodity'.[25] Abigail Goldberg, in a study of informal settlements in South Africa, contrasts an official view that such settlements pose a threat with an idea that they celebrate the do-it-yourself innovations of their inhabitants. State policy either acts like a farmer and scatters the birds; or allows settlements to exist but seeks to harness them by upgrading, developing as assets

21 *Ibid.*, p. 49.
22 *Ibid.*, p. 37.
23 Georg Simmel, *The Philosophy of Money*, London: Routledge, 1990, p. 333. Originally published 1907.
24 *Ibid.*, p. 338.
25 Ivan Illich, *op. cit.*, note 16, p. 54.

what a more authoritarian approach regards as liabilities; or ignores the problem until there is a crisis. The second option has pitfalls, but Goldberg sees it as the only humane and viable approach.[26]

The pitfalls are demonstrated in the case of Winterweld, taken by Goldberg as the basis for her article. This settlement arose from the forced removal of black people from Pretoria. An economy of shack farming produced a spontaneous and continuously modified development of single-storey shelters of mud block and corrugated iron, paths and enclosed open spaces used as meeting places. When the State attempted to introduce electricity without consulting dwellers the power boxes were stoned. Clearances took place in the late 1970s, and the spaces of informal meeting – people's parks – were destroyed. Since the 1980s, various consultants have proposed upgrading schemes or plans for new towns. One new housing scheme was constructed using modern technology and materials, termed Beirut by local people on account of its design.[27] The informal settlement remains and people's parks have begun to reappear. Goldberg concludes that schemes are more likely to succeed when the consultants adopt a non-business strategy of phasing themselves out. An extension of this would be to hand over to dwellers the power and resources to construct the settlement themselves. Some efforts to do this are beginning to happen in South Africa. An implication of such cases is that planning and design cease being practices of representation and become processes of participation in which the expertise of dwellers on urban living is equated in status with that of planners on planning and designers on designing. Professionals then become facilitators not controllers of the process. This dissolves the Cartesian split between concept and actuality, the subjectivity of the designer and the objectification of what is designed. But if this implication is to be more widely taken up, then models are needed which demonstrate its practicality.

Models of participatory practices exist in art, planning and architecture. Artist Suzanne Lacy uses the term new genre public art to describe art projects for social and ecological healing.[28] The use of urban design action teams has been proposed by the Urban Design Group in the UK, and advocacy planning in the USA was described by Paul Davidoff in the 1960s.[29] In some alternative, communitarian and ecologically responsible settlements, architecture becomes community building. Examples include Arcosanti, designed by Paolo Soleri in Arizona[30] and Findhorn in Scotland. Two cases of alternative settlement have been noted in critical writing: the Open City at Ritoque, Chile,[31] and New Gourna in Egypt.[32]

---

26 Abigail Goldberg, The birds have nested: design direction for informal settlements, *Urban Design International*, 1, no. 1, pp. 3–15, p. 6.
27 *Ibid.*, p. 9.
28 Suzanne Lacy, *Mapping the Terrain*, Seattle: Bay Press, 1995.
29 Paul Davidoff, Advocacy and pluralism in planning, 1965, in LeGates and Stout, *op. cit.*, pp. 422–432.
30 C. McLaughlin and G. Davidson, *Builders of the Dawn*, Summertown, TN: Book Publishing Company, 1985.
31 A. Pendleton-Jullian, *The Road that is Not a Road*, Cambridge, MA: MIT Press, 1996.
32 Hassan Fathy, *Architecture for the Poor*, Chicago: University of Chicago, 1973; originally published 1969.

NEW GOURNA

New Gourna, designed by Hassan Fathy and built by local masons, is a model of no-cost architecture for non-industrialized countries. Although intended to facilitate the resettlement of families from old Gourna (Figure 16.1) who, for generations, made a living from the proximity of their houses to archaic tombs, New Gourna can be seen as a model of the use of appropriate materials and technology serving a carefully researched pattern of village sociation. Although the Gournis refused to move, the village is now fully inhabited and supports a stable community. A second attempt was made by the Egyptian government, around 1995, to remove the population of old Gourna to a village of concrete houses built on an arid site near the Valley of the Kings. This, too, is occupied. When asked how people were persuaded to move there, a taxi driver replied: 'they shouted at them'.

figure 16.1
OLD GOURNA

In contrast to the technology of concrete, Fathy's work used mud brick. Cases of mud-brick vaulting survive in the nearby Ramesseum, dating from the nineteenth dynasty (Figure 16.2). Fathy began in 1945 by researching the social structures of village life. The spatial organization of New Gourna is determined by the social patterns generated by the extended family. Varying degrees of privacy and publicity are offered by house interiors; interior courtyards shared by related families; streets, some of which have detours to discourage strangers; open spaces outside public buildings – the mosque, the theatre, the khan – and the open market for produce and animals.[33] The courtyard is of particular importance:

33 *Ibid.*, pp. 54–62.

figure 16.2
MUD-BRICK VAULTING, RAMESSEUM,
NINETEENTH DYNASTY

In an enclosed space, a room or a courtyard, there is a certain quality that can be distinctly felt, and that carries a local signature as clearly as does a particular curve. This felt space is in fact a fundamental component of architecture, and if a space has not the true feeling, no subsequent decoration will be able to naturalize it into the desired tradition.[34]

Fathy sought to reproduce the social pattern of the village rather than to engineer changes to it, and replicates a traditional gendering of domestic space:

The inward-looking Arab house, made beautiful by the feminine element of water, self-contained and peaceful ... is the domain of woman ... Now it is of great importance that this enclosed space with the trembling liquid femininity it contains should not be broken. If there is a gap in the enclosing building, this special atmosphere flows out and runs to waste in desert sands.[35]

Fathy may have looked, in prioritizing the courtyard, to the houses of Cairo rather than to village models, and it could be argued that his traditionalism affirms structures of repression. On the other hand, if social structures are to change, the force for this needs to come from within those structures. Egyptian village life is conservative in its value structure, and Fathy has worked from the social processes which differentiate the village from the city. That the houses and public buildings are still in good condition, proudly shown to visitors by their inhabitants, testifies to the success of New Gourna (Figures 16.3–16.6).

Fathy sees New Gourna as an answer to the housing problem brought about by Egypt's rapid population growth:

What aspects of the problem does it solve? First, that of money. It is built entirely of mud and costs nothing. Second, that of space ... there is no limit to the size of the house; ten rooms are as cheap as one. Third, that of hygiene. Space means health, both physical and mental,

34 *Ibid.*, p. 55.
35 *Ibid.*, p. 57.

left figure 16.3
NEW GOURNA

right figure 16.4
NEW GOURNA

while the material, mud, does not harbour insects as thatch and wood do. Fourth, that of beauty. The demands of the structure alone are almost sufficient to ensure pleasing lines.[36]

Given that a substantial part of current urbanization takes place outside the western industrialized States, this model has obvious practical interest; it contrasts with schemes for expansion such as the new suburb of Esenkent, Istanbul.[37] But it goes further in redefining the role of the architect. At New Gourna, the practice of architecture is re-visioned to reclaim the representational spaces of dwelling. The process of building is not a replication of plans which are external to the site and superimposable on more or less any site, but a social process involving architect, dweller and builder – a continuation of traditions which have developed through adaptation.

This model of architecture in which form is determined by patterns of sociation can be mapped onto a society in which social structures are mediated by critical democratic processes. Then, it is likely that the production of space would be a process of continuous modification. The possibilities of self-build, or a situation in which dwellers are co-designers, offers more scope for this than the conventional methodologies of planning and design. New Gourna, then, constitutes a model of alternative design methodology for cities in the industrialized States; it entails an integration of the aesthetic and the social, the conceptual and the experiential; and a relation of architect and dweller in a process of negotiation of design possibilities.

36 *Ibid.*, p. 129.
37 A. Aksoy and K. Robins, Modernism and the millennium – trial by space in Istanbul, *City,* no. 8, December 1997, pp. 21–36.

left figure 16.5
NEW GOURNA

right figure 16.6
NEW GOURNA

RITOQUE

The Open City, sited on dunes by the sea at Ritoque, was founded in 1970 by the architecture school of the Catholic University of Valparaiso. Its buildings adapt to the constant movement of sand (Figure 16.7). Each is founded by a poetic act which establishes its site, and all are open to modification by common will; decisions on all issues affecting the community are made in open meetings. Machinery is not used in construction, which is carried out by the community. The city has no plan.

Ann Pendleton-Jullian writes that the group who founded the Open City, linking architecture with surrealist poetry through the persons of Alberto Cruz Covarubias and Godofredo Iommi, adopted a morality in which 'beauty is associated with the elemental, and wealth and power are rejected in favor of a "voluntary poverty".'[38] The city's founders see grandeur as too often linked to power and wealth, and instead look to inner potentialities. These do not denote a Cartesian subjectivity, but something closer to a Fourierist libidinization of work. Iommi proclaimed: 'the university must be erotic, if it is not erotic it stops to be a university'.[39]

The difficulty with Fourierism and the Open City is that they may entail a withdrawal from the mainstream of society; if such a withdrawal turns life into art, it may become a refuge for the unfree, whose captivation in it then prevents the realization of freedom. Yet alternative models are vital if urban societies are to avoid collapse. The Open City meets the needs of a city to be a grouping of buildings and a place for sociation, and constructs a communal means of acting. Its field of activity is set out in Iommi's poem

38 Pendleton-Jullian, *op. cit.*, note 31, p. 23.
39 *Ibid.*, p. 49.

'the amereida' (1965), which is its charter. Like New Gourna, it re-integrates the practice of architecture in the practice of everyday life. Pendleton-Jullian writes that the physical environment of the city evolves from this field of activity, in contrast to '... the hierarchical European Renaissance cities in which a built idealized architectural plan was expected to determine a higher state of living'.[40] In this it corresponds with the many communitarian settlements founded from the 1960s to the 1990s[41] which provide for the needs of their members through an ecologically responsible lifestyle.

six
URBAN DESIGN AS PRAXIS

Ernesto Laclau, in an essay on emancipation, arrives at a position of negotiated possibility between freedom and unfreedom. This is a way out of the logical contradictions of a concept which supposes a chasm between a past from which society emancipates itself and a future necessarily formed in that past.[42] His position suggests a praxis, revealing an understanding of preceding conditions which indicates possible future conditions, that is, imagining possible rather than ideal futures.

How, then, does a new social and ethical foundation for the production of city form arise? Does it mean the abolition of planning, or is there an equivalent to Laclau's negotiated possibility between freedom and unfreedom? Elizabeth Wilson writes:

> Planning is necessary if cities are to survive. What needs to change is the ultimate purpose of planning. Hitherto, town planning has too often been driven by the motor of capitalist profit and fuelled by the desire to police whole communities ... to create a city of order and surveillance rather than one of pleasure and opportunity.[43]

Wilson references Richard Sennett's *The Uses of Disorder*, and foresees a city which offers excitement and risk rather than conformity.

Perhaps it is the excitement, and acceptable levels of risk, which prevent a total collapse of metropolitan life. An alternative process of determining city form, then, requires that sociation produces form, rather than form, as a product of representation, coercing sociation. When the Cartesian split of subject and object is mended, it is possible to live lightly on the Earth, creating settlements which are both sustainable and convivial.

---

40 *Ibid.*, p. 125.
41 McLaughlin and Davidson, *op. cit.*, note 30.
42 Ernesto Laclau, *Emancipation(s)*, London: Verso, 1996, pp. 1–19.
43 Elizabeth Wilson, *op. cit.*, note 1, p. 156.

figure 16.7
RITOQUE

#17
CHINEDU UMENYILORA: EMPOWERING THE SELF-BUILDER

The word 'change' engages all our expectations at the threshold of the new millennium. For many people of the so-called developing world, in particular the continent of Africa, change will not be for the better, but a repetitive spiral of struggle and poverty. To others change is unwanted, lest it should somehow undermine the status quo that holds their world together. We in the richer nations must work together with our struggling partners in order to achieve change for the better, and the leaders of struggling nations must focus on the plight of their impoverished people.

'Empowering the self-builder' seeks to identify with the people caught up in this repetitive spiral. It examines the role of the architect in creating real tools of empowerment for the individual and the community through being more responsive and flexible in its approach to architectural and social needs. The intention is to complement indigenous patterns of life with a building process that results in a new urban vernacular, and to stimulate positive change. The building block for this strategy lies in assisting people to build for themselves, to become self-builders. This assistance will help produce low-cost houses and to access the architectural industry and the wider job market. This will be a new process which ultimately empowers the individual through the community, implementing enabling programmes that operate in partnership with local delivery agents.

one
PEOPLE CITIES

One can conjecture that the city does not only exist as an inhabited location whose boundaries are made up of a built fabric. Could boundaries – national or otherwise – reach their plateau of usefulness, converging towards a singularity that benefits all, making territorial posturing a thing of the past? As boundaries fragment and reconfigure, a new amalgamation of 'people as cities' results, defined through trans-migrational socio-economic networks.

'Trans-migrational cities' exist not only in the form of labour or social groupings as economic migrants, but also as economic and financial capitals establishing as communities; shifting like flocks with the flow of the markets. This recognition about boundaries shifting, dissolving and coming back together again indicates a move towards an 'openness', yet still within fixed parameters. This openness should be harnessed, through policy and through technologies like the Internet, to give access to those who have not traditionally benefited from the present system.

top figure 17.1
HOUSING FOR COMMUNITIES, SOUTH AFRICA

right figure 17.2
TOWNSHIP HOUSING, SOUTH AFRICA

Let us similarly consider architecture without boundaries, open and organic. This is architecture unconstrained by the rigidity of many rules whose regulations ultimately set up a means of State control. Rather it is a strategy to encourage and manifest freedom through the exploration of new avenues in architecture. Such an approach can ignite the spark of invention in marginalized sectors of our societies.

In establishing the process or mechanism, the collective of individuals – the 'people as city' – exchange skills to train and mobilize a 'pool of visions'. Self-build must not only embrace the idea of house building but, much more importantly, a vision of Self coupled with Community taking control of destiny. The emphasis must be to simultaneously help the grass roots to grow upwards, whilst also encouraging the downward devolution of power and access. This transformation of individual and collective lives must then be expressed in a language that may be market compatible, or in an indigenous social currency which in this case can best be realized through a locally manufactured batch production of architecture. An open-ended approach is crucial for empowerment to take place, implementing the programmes through an infrastructure which determines by the leap from micro-to-macro, people-to-city scale. Hence, gradually, the individual's capacity increases enough to be harnessed collectively to benefit the people city.

Demographic forecasters have predicted that up to 50 per cent of the population in the struggling nations of the Two-Thirds World will be living in cities by the year 2000. With population growth outstripping economic growth and food production, these suppressed nations lack the infrastructure to redress this balance beyond 2000, and the stage is being set for a major crisis. Reducing the impact of this urban explosion will require more than simple relief measures. It must involve land reform and community development in rural areas, together with new approaches to urban agriculture, architecture, sanitation systems and economic initiatives. Self-build harnesses a potential to deliver cities as fabric, and also building cities as people.

below figure 17.3
POVERTY AND SELF-BUILD, SOUTH AFRICA

left figure 17.4
INVENTIVENESS OF SELF-BUILD, SOUTH AFRICA

We have to implement climates of invention, ownership, autonomy and sustainability. This would involve not only complementing technology with environmental vision (particularly with regard to energy efficiency), but also reducing the burden of debt repayment costs potentially carried by the individual and the community as a whole. An infrastructure of support through workshops, resource centres, technical support networks and business outlets should also be established.

All this encourages the long-term sustainability required for community development, which in turn would create a local economic climate attractive to internal and external markets. The stimulus for attracting such markets lies in creating a vibrancy within the community that is accelerated by good communications networks. Once the spread of information is not restricted by national boundaries, then expressions of individuality and collectivity, and the demands for more freedom, will manifest themselves in more liberated forms of architecture.

Consensus politics has the intention to provide everyone with a decent quality of life, but lacks the capacity to reach those furthest from the centres of power. Activity and responsibility, knowledge and the power that comes with it must constantly be given to the margins, allowing access, involvement and opportunities to be gained from the whole process that leads to the delivery of architecture. We can ensure that the devolution of the architectural delivery mechanism ultimately manifests itself in the redistribution back into marginalized communities of some of the immense wealth generated by industry. Effort is being made to redress the divide between the rich and the

figure 17.5
STERILITY OF STATE HOUSING, SOUTH AFRICA

poor, a divide that is accelerating more and more rapidly in most countries of the world. By not addressing these issues, the building industry plays a part in adding to the worldwide housing problem that is challenging us today.

The cry that comes from isolated communities has been: 'give us the tools and the materials, and we will build our own houses the way that we want them'. The evidence indicates that when this happens, elegant, exquisite and radical forms of architecture spring up from within the communities. The constant hindrance to this happening has been access: access to materials of quality, access to high performance specialist tools and access to the training necessary for the delivery of quality architecture. Of course, these or any other infrastructural requirements typically cannot be delivered without substantial financial backing and support from government and big business. The problem is that the limited amount of money that is available has not so far found its way in adequate measure.

two
THE ROLE OF THE ARCHITECT

For newly emerging economies with their marginalized societies migrating towards the urban densities of the cities, housing inevitably takes on a charged expectancy. The emphasis should be more towards the individual and their empowerment, rather than solely on the architectural skin that envelops them. Devolving power can be looked at as 'establishing partnerships'. This forces a re-evaluation of traditional architectural practice. Should the architect continue to be the sole creator and deliverer of a designed product? Could the architect become a facilitator and an enabler to the client, ultimately empowering them? Should the architect focus on people as equally as material fabric, thus broadening the definition of the word 'building'? Can the architect strategically intervene using legislature and policy affecting the whole strata of society to bring about change? Or, can architects devolve our expertise to designers, engineers, project managers, developers and other aspiring deliverers? The process of self-build has the advantage of reducing the responsibility carried by the architect, redistributing the wealth generated through the housing industry, and incrementally delivering an architecture of quality through locally based workshops.

figure 17.6
VRYGRUND TOWNSHIP, SOUTH AFRICA. SITE PLAN SHOWING INFORMAL
SETTLEMENT SANDWICHED BETWEEN GOVERNMENT DEVELOPED AREA AND THE
PROPOSED PLANNING GRID OF FUTURE STATE DEVELOPMENT

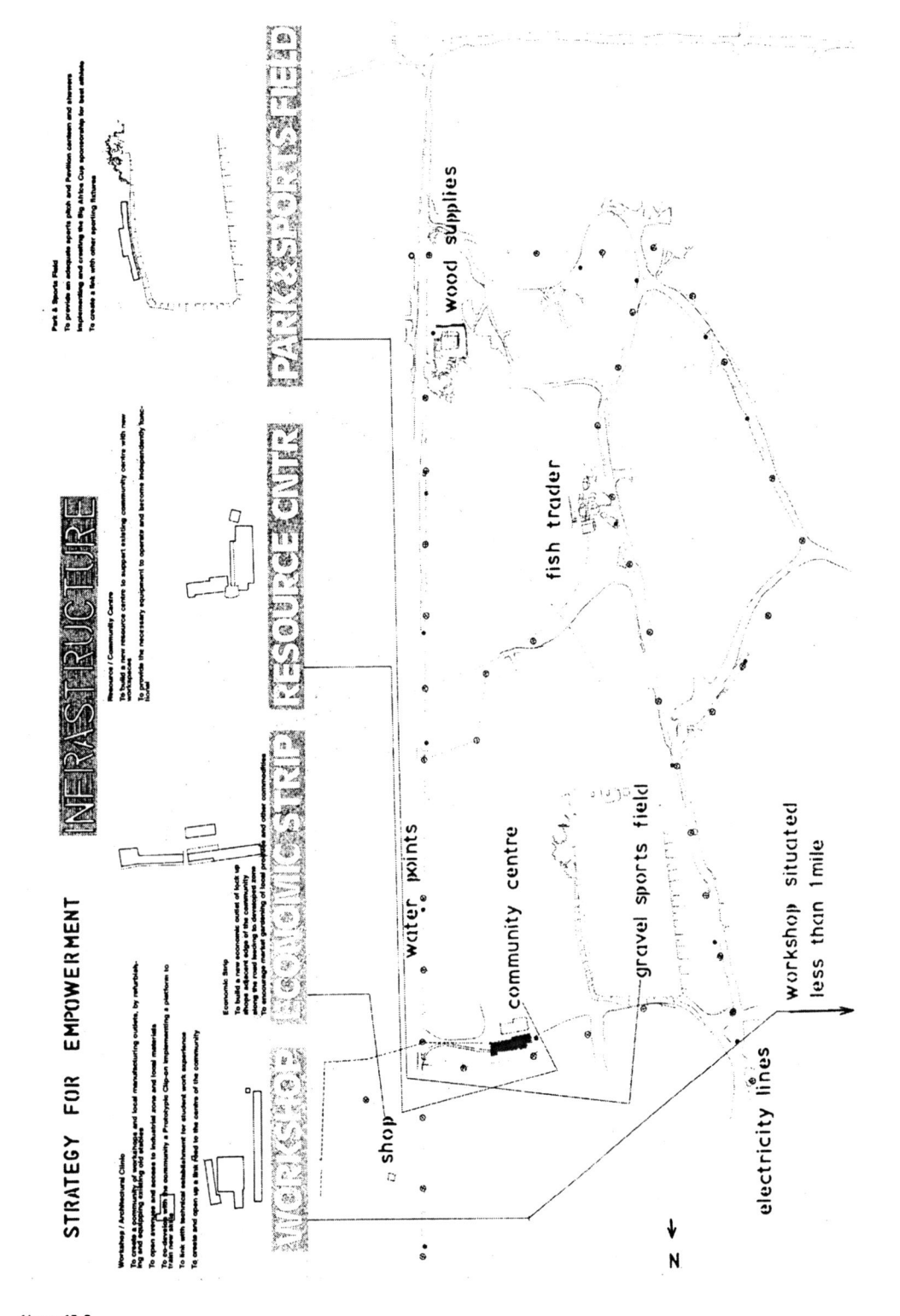

figure 17.7
STRATEGY FOR EMPOWERMENT IN THE INFORMAL SETTLEMENT.
RATHER THAN DESTROY THE VITALITY OF THE INFORMAL SETTLEMENT, HARNESS
THE RESOURCEFULNESS OF ITS PEOPLE THROUGH THE STRATEGY OF SELF-
BUILD TO HELP THEM IMPROVE THEIR HOUSING. A WORKSHOP/ARCHITECTURAL
CLINIC WOULD BE PROVIDED TO HELP LOCAL SELF-BUILDERS

kitchen — bedroom
storage shed

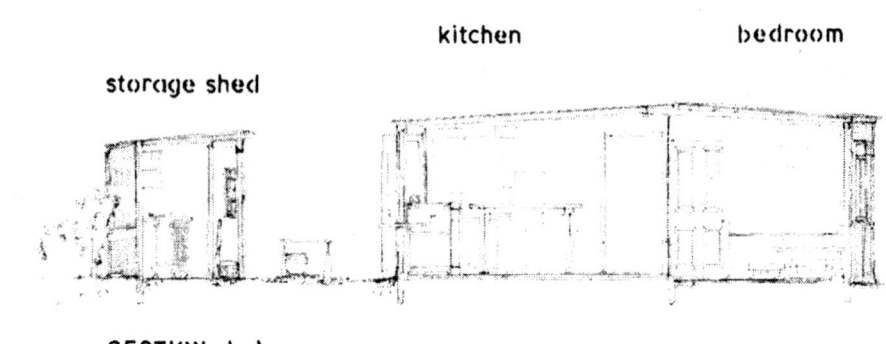

SECTION A-A

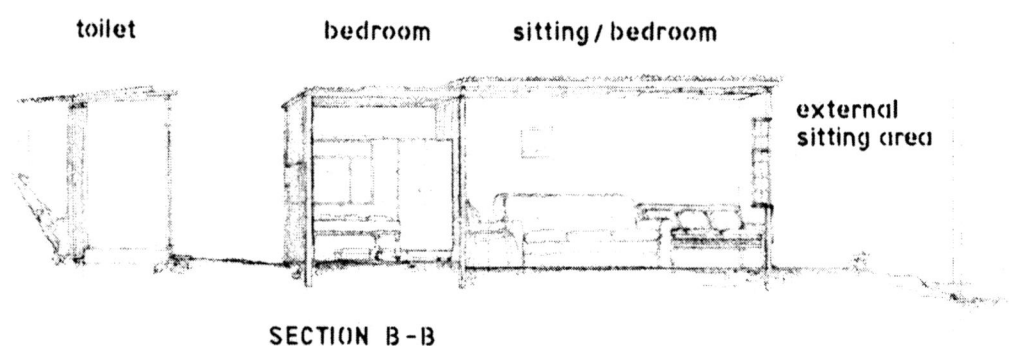

toilet — bedroom — sitting/bedroom — external sitting area

SECTION B-B

figure 17.8
REAL TOOLS: SECTIONS THROUGH THE EXISTING HOUSING WHICH
FORMS THE BASIS OF THE SELF-BUILDER'S SITE (THE HOUSING IS SHOWN
IN PLAN FORM IN FIGURE 17.11)

My own programme evolved by becoming a self-builder and as a result of a visit to South Africa. As my starting point for investigation, I took the notion of a 'kit-of-parts' to be an example of something that will be developed from its present preliminary version, responding to contextual issues of site, programme, space and vision. The 'kit-of-parts' therefore becomes a method of investigation and exploration into a free and liberating architecture. The idea is that the architect designs a 'seed' for self-built quality architecture, complete in its incompleteness, but fulfilling all the requirements for a modern standard of living through its programme. The product is completed in spite of its open-endedness, by establishing an architectural clinic/workshop that delivers the remaining architecture through a 'train and build' programme, complementing design quality with self-build choice. This can be seen as the 'flower', coming from the seed, which ultimately encourages a new vernacular.

three
ARCHITECTURE AS SEED

Conceptually the kit-of-parts acts as an architectural seed, packaged in modular componentized parts. It explores notions of architectural flexibility and adaptability for townships and informal settlements. The self-builder works with this to create the 'flower', accessing a support infrastructure and developed through community interaction. The architect designs the seed, and the self-builder creates the flower. Through this transformation, the basis for a partnership of sorts between the architect and the self-builder is provided. This can only come through an open design process. Self-build offers a real opportunity to the recipient builder in that it provides an income-generating platform and an educational platform at the same time, whilst facilitating the capacity of the individual to eventually create more work.

Self-build is now being adopted by many countries as a realistic alternative to large-scale labour-intensive and volume-build programmes. Such programmes are being implemented as part of the housing policy of poorer countries, particularly South America where it is a preferred alternative in housing, and Sri Lanka, whose homeless built a

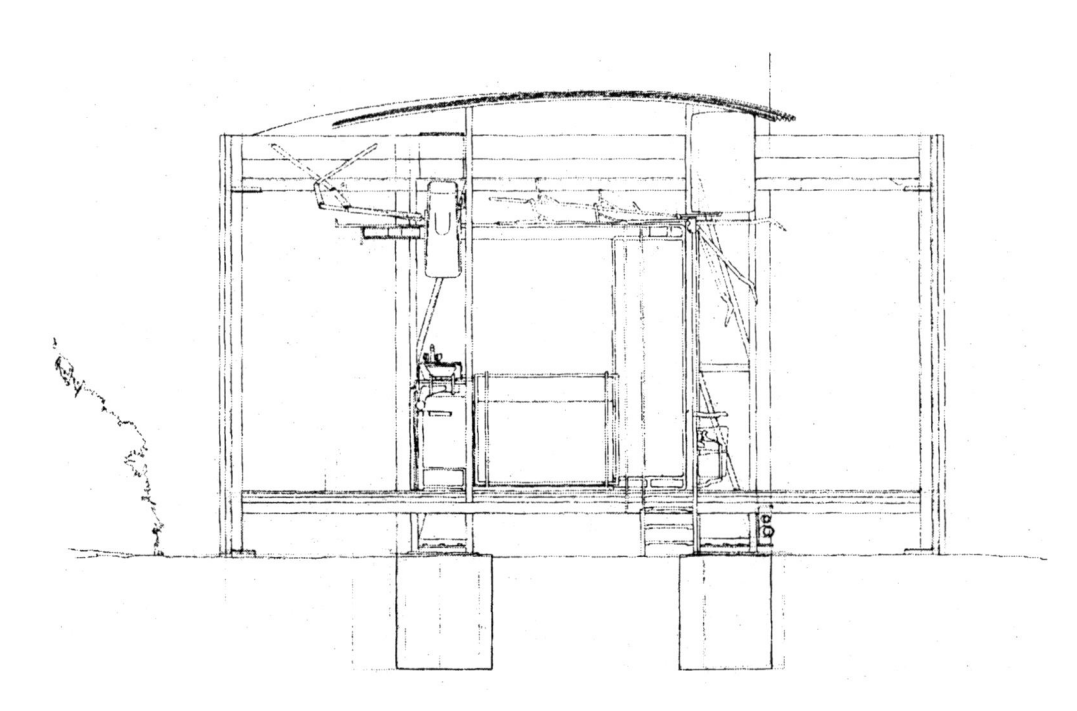

figure 17.9
THE KIT OF PARTS: A COMPONENTIZED ARCHITECTURAL 'SEED' WHICH
THE SELF-BUILDER MESHES INTO THE EXISTING ACCOMMODATION TO CREATE
A 'FLOWER', IN THIS CASE SANITARY AND OTHER FACILITIES

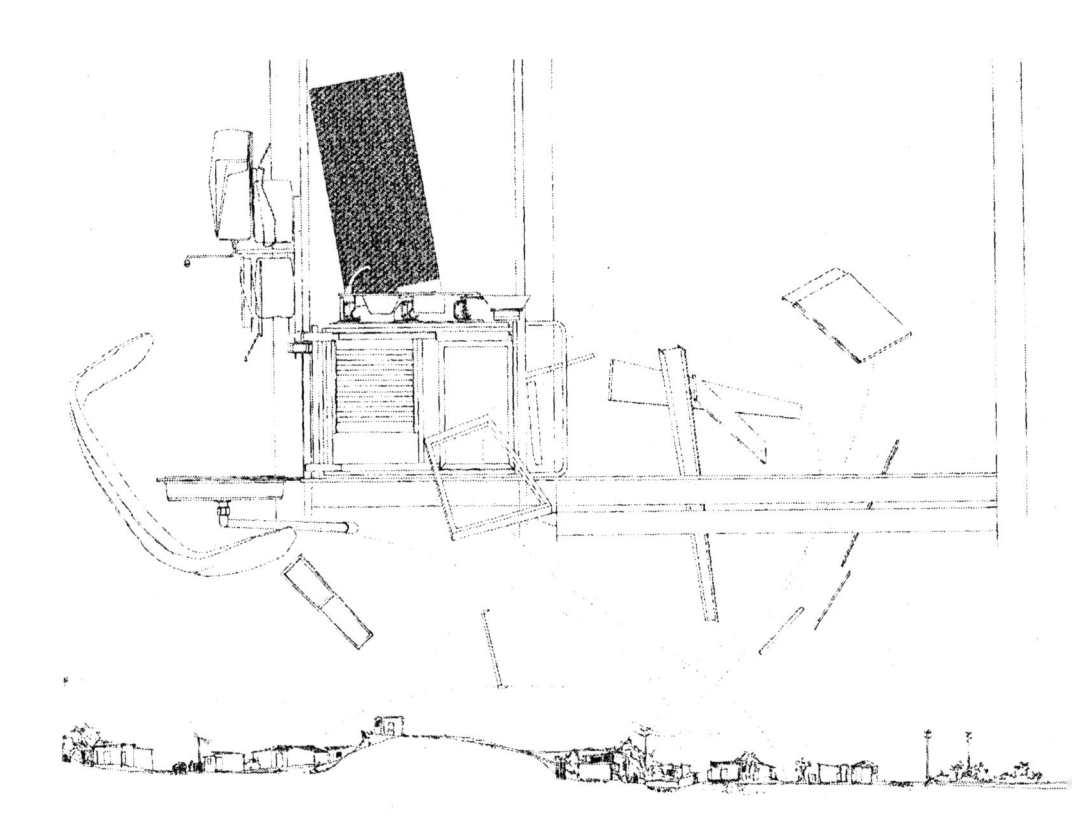

top figure 17.10
THROUGH PROGRAMMES OF RECYCLING, TRAINING AND EDUCATION, THE LOCAL
POPULATION CAN BE EMPOWERED TO BETTER THEIR OWN COMMUNITIES

opposite page figure 17.11
THE KIT OF PARTS SITED ALONGSIDE OR ON TOP OF THE EXISTING
ACCOMMODATION. ITS POTENTIAL FOR DEVELOPMENT WOULD BE HARNESSED BY
THE SELF-BUILDER IN CONJUNCTION WITH THE NEARBY ARCHITECTURAL CLINIC

AS SEED

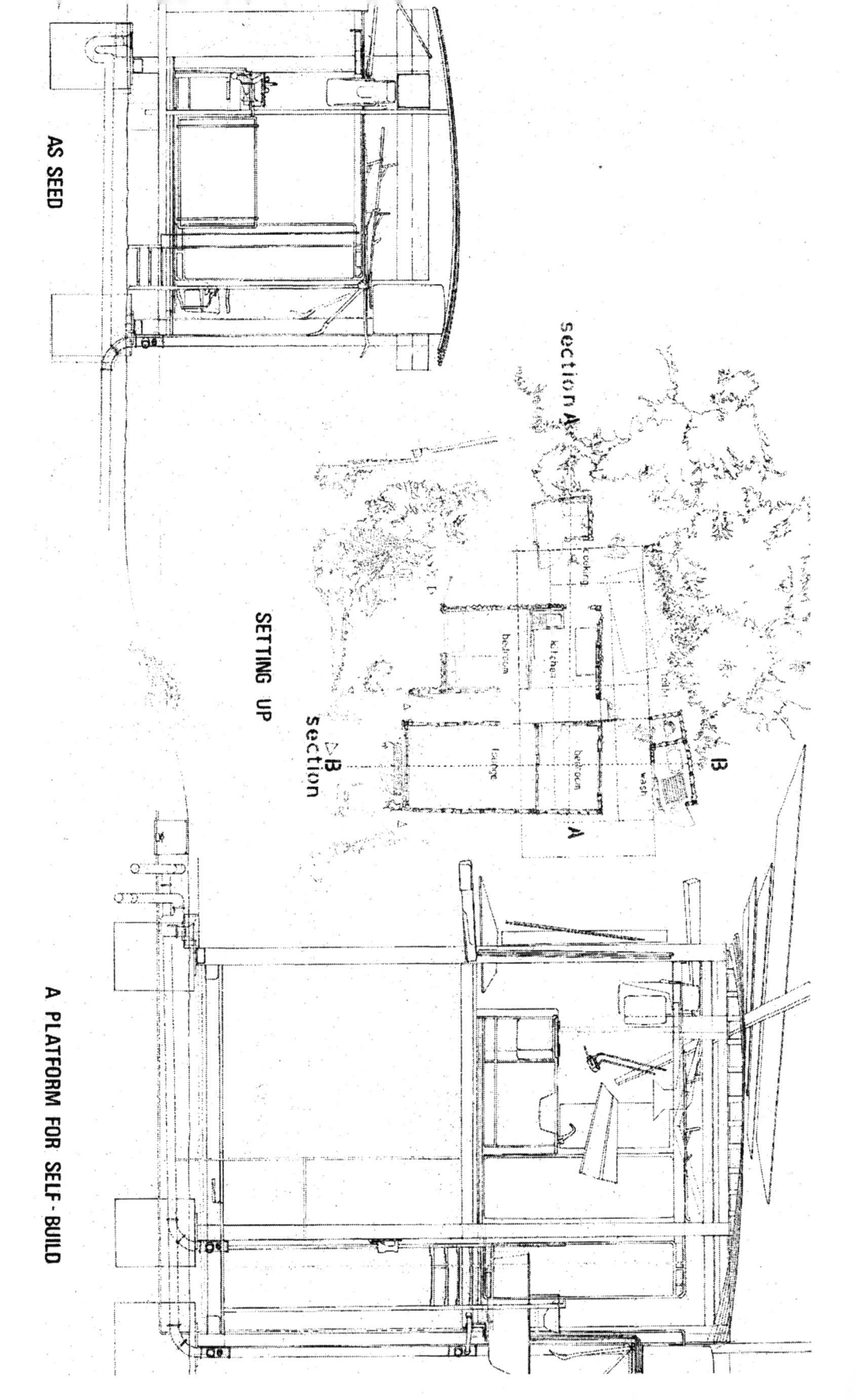

SETTING UP

A PLATFORM FOR SELF-BUILD

million houses between 1984 and 1989. Indonesia's poor run their own high-rise communities and, in Karachi, the poorest of the poor have laid out their own city, down to the last house and child care centre.

Most people in Africa already opt to build their own home. This option can be mobilized by governments as a means of introducing a bottom-up development strategy, by legitimizing the process and giving it credibility which, in turn, fosters self-worth. Rather than self-build being the single option, it complements extant housing programmes. This also entails strategies for reducing the cost of housing, by:

— redirecting housing subsidies into the hands of communities and individuals;
— changing planning and building legislation to make it accessible to non professionals;
— reducing the cost of designing, and allowing the client to become the designer;
— encouraging flexibility in the choice of materials, bringing in new technology, like reinforced earth blocks, restored materials, and technology transferred from other product manufacturers;
— encouraging the use and reuse of indigenous and appropriated materials;
— introducing workshops for mass or batch production;
— reducing cost by empowering people to do what they are good at, which is helping themselves.

A cellular management structure needs to be implemented in order to encourage autonomous work groups, in keeping with the move towards individual and personal empowerment. This is done by designing the kit-of-parts so that it is easily and quickly assembled, allowing a greater variety of possibilities in building type through its modular arrangement. Adaptability and flexibility are maintained through the accessibility of material resources in close proximity to the locality, stimulating interest in specialist fields of production by prefabricating parts, like walls, structures, floors, halls, landings, porches, entrances, etc.

To add to the system of flexibility, efficiency in production can be gained by making products to a batch-produced order, tailoring each kit-of-parts to particular needs. A light industrial manufacturing base can grow to deliver the kits-of-parts through local community enterprise. The system also allows various crafts people to work on one project, revisiting the Bauhaus notion of a building being a collective work of art, and thus being representative of an architectural language that is indigenous to its own environment.

The workshops need not only act as batch production lines, but also as restoration clinics for materials that have not outlived their usefulness. All this adds to the vital reduction of cost, which is necessary for sustainability. Glen Murcot, an Australian architect using and mixing reusable materials with newly ordered ones, was once asked, 'what was the procedure that allowed him to design a quality house with recycled materials?'. His answer: by working closely with the builder – a relationship which is kept entirely flexible all the way along, making the sourcing of materials revenue-efficient.

The builder keeps in constant touch with the sources of material, whilst also possibly encouraging the community to salvage and reclaim materials. Added to this is the suggestion that materials could be bought from the reclaimer before or after restoration, and then sold on to new customers as 'off the peg', allowing the reclaimer to share in the process.

There is uncertainty as to whether one can effectively design good communities, but we can assist and enable communities to design themselves. The main advantage of self-build is the potential to create work through an educational and an income-generating platform, implemented through architectural workshops/clinics where skills are taught and exchanged.

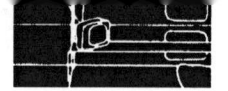

#18
MARTIN PAWLEY: TOWARDS AN UNORIGINAL ARCHITECTURE[1]

One day in 1935 there was a great scandal. The celebrated violinist Fritz Kreisler admitted to a journalist that for thirty years he had been inserting pieces of his own composition into recitals of the works of seventeenth- and eighteenth-century composers. Kreisler came under virulent attack, but he was unrepentant. If his listeners could not distinguish between the pieces he played and genuine baroque music, he argued, why should it matter whether they were forged or not?

The Kreisler episode has its analogues in architecture today. A modern building may be no more than a piece of industrial design, 'like an enormous typewriter', as Robert Venturi once put it, but its unique combination of industrial components is still considered to be intellectual property, like the compositions of Couperin, Stamitz and Albinoni that were actually Kreisler fakes. In this way architecture, like music, is inextricably bound up with an erroneous idea of individual creativity.

Why this should be is not clear. Architects know that getting a building built is not like writing a book or painting a picture. It is more like winning an election, after undergoing a process of immense and unfathomable complexity involving many personalities, products, consultancies, schedules, contractors, bureaucracies, statutes, regulations, budgets, policy committees, review boards, protest groups etc. Even a small building can involve a cast of thousands, amongst whom only one – the architect – is trying to create something original. In such circumstances creative architecture is a myth, as Kreisler proved.

Is there then a case for uncreative architecture? In *Theory and Design in the Second Machine Age*[2] I argued that the real, as opposed to the mythological, profession of architecture should shift its ground from meretricious claims of creativity based on art history and 'meaning' – a realm where, as the Prince of Wales has demonstrated, expertise is already completely consumerized – to the more challenging field of technology transfer.

Technology transfer is what happens when the methods or processes developed in one industry are applied to a completely different one. Its history is immense and uncharted, often bizarre. In the fifth century AD, the dome of the church of San Vitale in Ravenna was made from earthenware pots, still with their carrying handles, in a tour de force of technology transfer executed in pursuit of lightness. Fifteen hundred years later pots of

---

1 First published in *Architectural Record* (New York) under the title, The case for uncreative architecture, December 1992, pp. 20–21.
2 Martin Pawley, *Theory and Design in the Second Machine Age*, Oxford: Basil Blackwell, 1990.

a similar design were being fashioned out of worn-out car tyres. The middle ages saw a long series of largely undocumented transfers from wooden ship construction to timber roof construction. Later, pairs of scissors were adapted into the first spectacle frames and the machinery devised to make bone china was used to make the first European chocolate. In the nineteenth century hot-rolled iron beams, made to support the decks of ships, migrated ashore to become part of the structure of buildings and the model for railroad tracks. Forty years after a small reinforced concrete boat was exhibited in Paris, reinforced concrete building became common. In the same way all-steel ships preceded steel buildings, and the steel masts of steel ships led the way for radio transmission antennae and power transmission pylons. In modern times the cavity magnetron vacuum tube has made its equally unlikely way from airborne radar to the domestic microwave oven.

Technology transfer has all the unpredictable wonderment of genetic mutation and, in construction, its importance has been direct and seminal, although virtually unacknowledged. The auto industry, for example, has been a great source of technology transfers into building. Its cold-rolled steel chassis beams led to the birth of the family of round tubes, square tubes, angles, channels and space frame members that are widely used in construction today. At the behest of pioneer technology transfer architect Eero Saarinen, the auto industry adapted the neoprene gasket glazing developed for car windshields into a technique suitable for curtain walling systems. Aerospace too has proved a fruitful source. Complex alloy castings and large-panel raised floor systems for commercial buildings have been developed from those developed for use in large passenger aircraft. In the same way the vast array of composites and adhesives developed for aerospace applications by the chemical industry has filtered into innumerable applications in construction.

Stochastic and unplanned as it generally is, the adaptation of the technology of one field to advance another is a tremendously efficient process that offers unique synergetic advantages. In architecture its capacity to exploit the products of research and development in other fields without actually paying for it, adds up to a parasitic form of R&D well suited to the needs of an impoverished and fragmented profession with no profits to plough back into research of its own.

In short, technology transfer is a process far better attuned to the needs of a profession seeking to serve a globally organized construction industry than art historical aesthetics can ever be. All the more surprising then that even those architects who most dramatically exploit technology transfers in their work, still temporize over its importance. Sir Norman Foster is well known for his ingenious use of components and materials that have their origin in industries far removed from construction. His buildings have pioneered the use of solvent-welded PVC roofing derived from swimming pool liners; neoprene gaskets originally developed for cable-jacketing; structural glazing and enamel glass 'fritting' techniques borrowed from the auto industry; superplastic aluminium sandwich panels and metallized fabrics from aerospace; eaves-tensioning devices from articulated trailer sidescreens; raised floor systems from jetliners ... All of these, along with techniques of presentation culled from aviation magazines, are to be found in his buildings and projects: yet he does not believe that this interesting but uncreative process can ever supplant the art historical tradition upon which the architectural profession depends.

Like Sir Norman Foster, many other leading European architects including his former partner Sir Richard Rogers, Jean Nouvel, Terry Farrell, Benthem and Crouwel, Nicholas Grimshaw, Weber Brand and Richard Horden – who designed the 1984 Yacht House, a sophisticated technology transfer building with an alloy mast structural frame and many nautical components – acknowledge the presence of technology transfer in their designs and cite it as evidence of modernity in their buildings, but they too shrink from espousing it as a theory of architecture in itself.

The reason for their reluctance is connected with the self-image of the architectural profession. To conceive of the design of buildings as a technique founded on the pursuit of technology transfers, every one of them evolutionarily self-selected by Richard Buckminster Fuller's technological law of doing more with less, is to accept that architectural design is no longer a creative activity in the old art historical sense, but a mechanical process of multi-sourced element combination that can readily be undertaken by computers equipped with adapted search software. Properly established, an organization prepared to undertake the task of beginning the creation of a technology transfer data base could open up this process of combination to the whole genetic pool of scientific and industrial activity everywhere. It may be mechanical but it is an activity that is literally waiting for a profession to take it over.

figure 18.1
TECHNOLOGY TRANSFER CAN BE MORE OLD WISDOM THAN NEW TECHNOLOGY. THIS WATER CONTAINER IS MADE FROM WORN-OUT TRUCK TYRES TWISTED TO THE TRADITIONAL SHAPE. PHOTOGRAPHED IN USE IN TRIPOLI 1976

figure 18.2
A HOUSE WITH WALLS MADE OF BOTTLES SET
IN ADOBE MORTAR, NEVADA 1912

figure 18.3
A HOUSE WITH BOTTLE WALLS SET IN CEMENT
MORTAR, NETHERLANDS 1961. THIS STRUCTURE WAS
BUILT WITH SPECIALLY DESIGNED INTERLOCKING
BOTTLES AS PART OF A SECONDARY USE EXPERIMENT
BY HEINEKEN BREWERIES

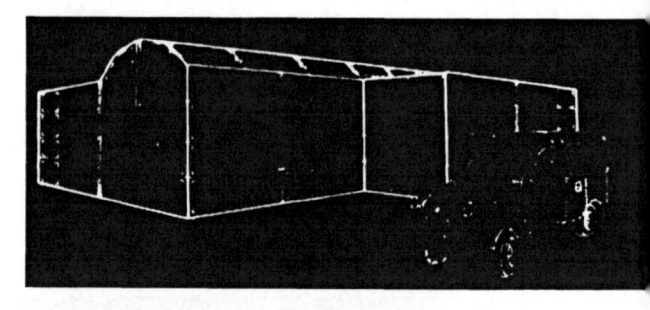

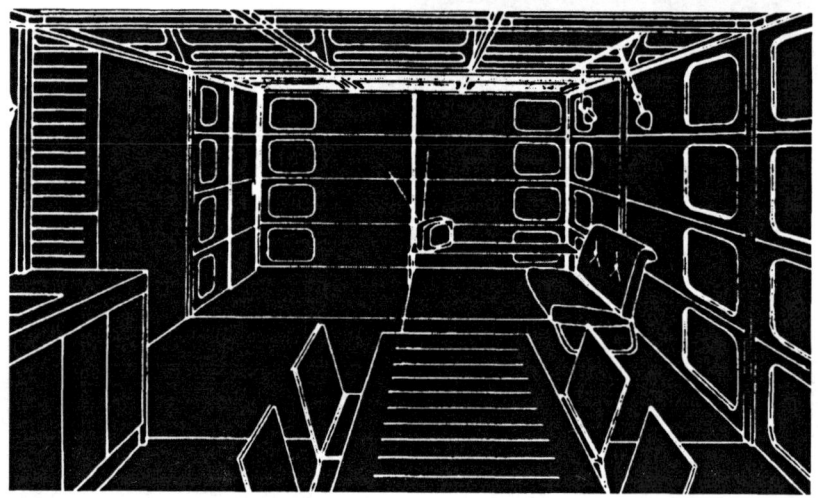

figure 18.4
THE AUTHOR'S 1973 PROJECT TO CONVERT PRESSED METAL CAR
BODY PARTS INTO AN EMERGENCY HOUSING SYSTEM FOR THE UNIDAD POPULAR
GOVERNMENT IN CHILE. CITROEN 2CV BODY PARTS FORM SIDING AND ROOF.
WINDSHIELD AND CAB PROVIDE CLERESTORY LIGHTING AND VENTILATION

figure 18.5
THE FIRST LONG-WAVE RADIO ('WIRELESS') AERIALS WERE RIGGED LIKE
THE MASTS AND SPARS OF SHIPS. THIS 1923 ADVERTISEMENT STRESSES THAT
THE ANTENNAE SHOWN ARE 'DESIGNED BY NAVAL EXPERTS'

figure 18.6
MODEL OF UNEXECUTED 1975 PROJECT BY
NETHERLANDS ARCHITECT RINUS VAN DEN BERG FOR
A HOUSE USING WELDED 55 GALLON OIL DRUM
COLUMNS; VOLKSWAGEN CAMPER ROOF PANELS AND
DOORS, AND TRANSLUCENT GLASS BOTTLE WALLS

figure 18.7
TWO TEST STRUCTURES BUILT BY THE AUTHOR
AND STUDENTS AT RENSSELAER POLYTECHNIC
INSTITUTE, TROY, NEW YORK, 1975. ONE USING
STEEL CANS BRAISED TOGETHER, THE OTHER
CARDBOARD TUBES, SCRAP STEEL STRAPPING
AND MILK CONTAINERS

figure 18.8
A 60M² HOUSE FRAMED IN CARDBOARD TUBES AND CLAD IN STEEL CANS, BUILT BY THE AUTHOR AND STUDENTS AT RENSSELAER POLYTECHNIC INSTITUTE, TROY, NEW YORK, 1976. THE ROOF TILES ARE NEOPRENE RUBBER OFF-CUTS. THE SKIN TREATMENT IS A COATING OF GLASSFIBRE AND SULPHUR. THE LIVING ROOM WALL IS OF COLOURED BOTTLES

figure 18.9
1978 SULPHUR-BLOCK-WALLED QUEBEC HOUSE UNDER CONSTRUCTION BY
THE MCGILL UNIVERSITY MINIMUM COST HOUSING UNIT

figure 18.10
TERRAPIN MATREX DEMOUNTABLE OFFICE BUILDING FOR NORSK HYDRO IN
ENGLAND, 1983, ARCHITECT NICK WHITEHOUSE. VERTICAL CLADDING PANELS
ARE INSULATED ROOFS FROM FREEZER TRUCK TRAILERS

figure 18.11
YACHT HOUSE, BY RICHARD HORDEN, 1985.
LOUVRED FRONT ELEVATION CONCEALS STRUCTURAL FRAME MADE FROM
ALUMINIUM YACHT SPARS. PANELLIZED ASSEMBLY ALSO FEATURES YACHT
DECK HATCHES AS ROOFLIGHTS

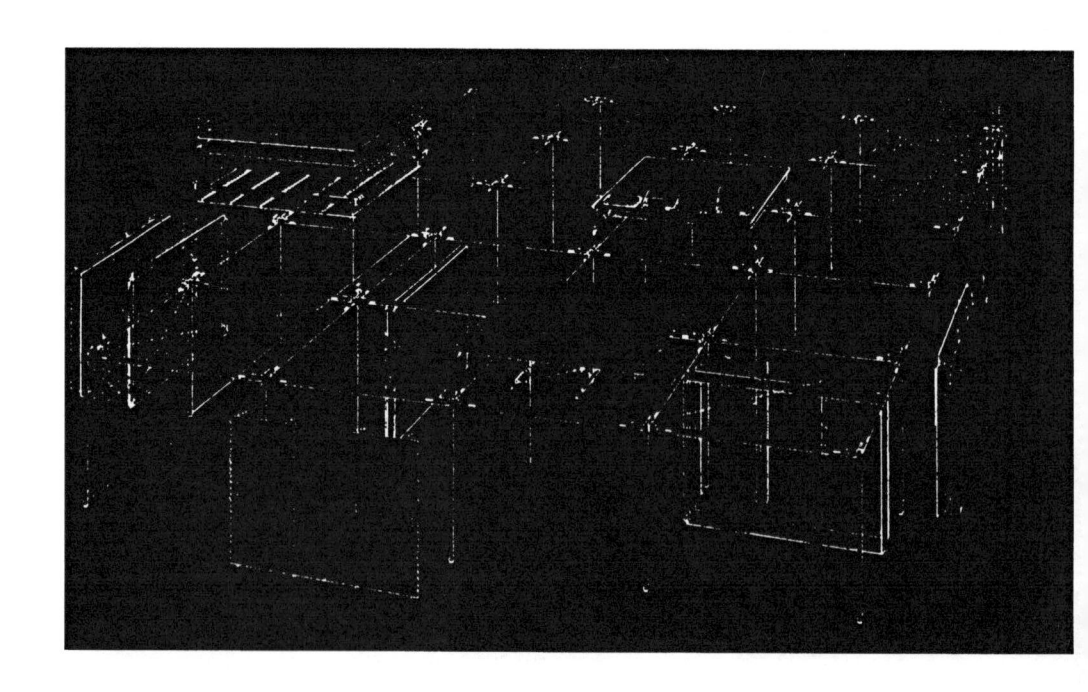

figure 18.12
FOSTER ASSOCIATES' 1986 HONGKONG AND SHANGHAI BANK CLADDING
SYSTEM ACHIEVED CAR-BODY PRECISION WITH UNIFORM SHUT-LINES BETWEEN
ITS PURPOSE-MADE PAINTED ALUMINIUM PANELS. PANEL SIZE AND SHAPE
CONFORMED TO PARAMETERS REQUIRED BY CAR MANUFACTURERS' MECHANIZED
PAINTING PROCESS

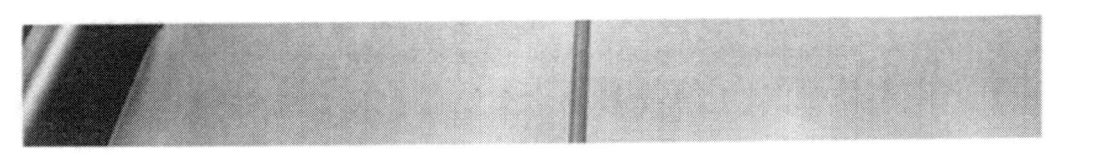

#19
MICHAEL RAKOWITZ: PARASITE

one
PARASITE

figure 19.1
*para*SITE

PARASITISM IS DESCRIBED AS A RELATIONSHIP IN WHICH A PARASITE TEMPORARILY OR PERMANENTLY EXPLOITS THE ENERGY OF A HOST.[1]

*para*SITE proposes the appropriation of the exterior ventilation systems on existing architecture as a means for providing temporary shelter for homeless people.

PARASITES LIVE ON THE OUTER SURFACE OF A HOST OR INSIDE ITS BODY IN RESPIRATORY ORGANS, DIGESTIVE ORGANS, VENOUS SYSTEMS, AS WELL AS OTHER ORGANS AND TISSUES.[2]

1 Kazimir Tarmon, *Osmove Ekologije*, text distributed by PARASITE Museum of Contemporary Art, Ljublana, 1990.
2 *Ibid.*

figure 19.2
paraSITE

The *para*SITE units in their idle state exist as small, collapsible packages with handles for transport by hand or on one's back. In employing this device, the user must locate the outtake ducts of a building's heating, ventilation and air conditioning (HVAC) system.

FREQUENTLY A HOST PROVIDES A PARASITE NOT ONLY WITH FOOD, BUT ALSO WITH ENZYMES AND OXYGEN, AND OFFERS FAVOURABLE TEMPERATURE CONDITIONS.[3]

The intake tube of the collapsed structure is then attached to the vent. The warm air leaving the building simultaneously inflates and heats the double membrane structure (Figures 19.1 and 19.2).

BUT A HOST IS CERTAINLY NOT INACTIVE AGAINST A PARASITE, AND IT HINDERS THE DEVELOPMENT AND POPULATION GROWTH OF PARASITES WITH DIFFERENT DEFENCE MECHANISMS, SUCH AS THE CLEANING OF SKIN, PERISTALTIC CONTRACTION OF THE DIGESTIVE APPARATUS, AND THE DEVELOPMENT OF ANTIBODIES.[4]

In April of 1997, I proposed my concept and first prototype to a homeless man named Bill Stone, who regarded the project as a tactical response. At the time, the city of Cambridge had made a series of vents in Harvard Square 'homeless-proof' by tilting the metal grates, making them virtually impossible to sleep on.

In his book, *City of Quartz,* Mike Davis describes a similar war on homelessness in Los Angeles. He lists a series of these hindrances throughout the city.

3 *Ibid.*
4 *Ibid.*

One of the most common, but mind-numbing, of these deterrents is the Rapid Transit District's new barrel-shaped bus bench that offers a minimal surface for uncomfortable sitting, while making sleeping utterly impossible. Such bum-proof benches are being widely introduced on the periphery of Skid Row. Another invention, worthy of the Grand Guignol, is the aggressive deployment of outdoor sprinklers. Several years ago the city opened a 'Skid Row Park' along lower Fifth Street, on a corner of Hell. To ensure that the park was not used for sleeping – that is to say, to guarantee that it was mainly utilized for drug dealing and prostitution – the city installed an elaborate overhead sprinkler system programmed to drench unsuspecting sleepers at random during the night. The system was immediately copied by some local businessmen in order to drive the homeless away from adjacent public sidewalks. Meanwhile restaurants and markets have responded to the homeless by building ornate enclosures to protect their refuse. Although no one in Los Angeles has yet proposed adding cyanide to the garbage, as happened in Phoenix a few years back, one popular seafood restaurant has spent $12 000 to build the ultimate bag-lady-proof trash cage: made of three-quarter inch steel rod with alloy locks and vicious out-turned spikes to safeguard priceless mouldering fish heads and stale french fries.[5]

PARASITES RESPOND TO THIS DEFENCE BY ANCHORING THEMSELVES WITH HOOKS AND SUCKERS ONTO SKIN, OR DIGESTIVE MUCOUS MEMBRANE, AND BY DEVELOPING PROTECTIVE DEVICES AND SUBSTANCES WHICH LESSEN DEFENSIVE CAPABILITIES OF THEIR HOST.[6]

The system by which the device attaches or is anchored to the building is designed to allow the structure to be adaptable. The intake tube can be expanded or tightened to fit the aperture of the vent through an adjustable lip made possible by elastic draw-strings. Hooks are attached to the metal louvres for reinforcement.

THERE IS 'TENSION' BETWEEN A HOST AND ITS PARASITE, SINCE THE HOST ENDEAVOURS TO GET RID OF THE FOREIGN BODY, WHILE THE PARASITE EMPLOYS NEW WAYS TO MAINTAIN THE CONNECTION WITH THE HOST.[7]

The connection of the inflatable structure to the building becomes the critical moment of this project.

From February 1998 until April 1998, I built seven prototypes of the *para*SITE shelter and distributed them to several homeless people in Cambridge, among them Bill Stone, George Livingston and Freddie Flynn, who worked closely with me on the design and production of these units. Most were built using temporary materials that were readily available on the streets (plastic bags, tape). While these shelters were being used, they functioned not only as a temporary place of retreat, but also as a station of dissent and empowerment; many of the homeless users regarded their shelters as a protest device

---
5 Mike Davis, *City of Quartz*, New York: Vintage Press, 1992, p. 233.
6 Kazimir Tarmon, *op. cit.*, note 1.
7 *Ibid.*

and would even shout slogans such as 'We beat you Uncle Sam!' The shelters communicated a refusal to surrender, and made more visible the unacceptable circumstances of homeless life within the city.

For the pedestrian, *para*SITE functioned as an agitational device. The visibly parasitic relationship of these devices to the buildings, appropriating a readily available situation with readily available materials, elicited immediate speculation as to the future of the city: would these things completely take over, given the enormous number of homeless in our society? Could we wake up one morning to find these encampments engulfing buildings like ivy?

This project does not present itself as a solution. It is not a proposal for affordable housing. Its point of departure is to present a symbolic strategy of survival for homeless existence within the city, amplifying the problematic relationship between those who have homes and those who do not have homes.

The issue of homelessness is of global proportions and it is foolish to think that any one proposition will address all the issues associated with this problem. There are many different types of homeless people. The mentally ill, the chemically dependent, those who are unable to afford housing, men, women, families, even those who prefer this way of life are included among the vast cross-section of homeless people in every urban instance. Each group of homeless has subjective needs based on circumstance and location. My project does not make reference to handbooks of statistics. Nor should this intervention be associated with the various municipal attempts at solving the homeless issue. This is a project that was shaped by my interaction as a citizen and artist with those who live on the streets.

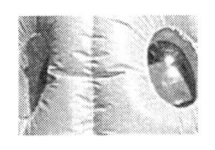

INDEX

Aalto, Alvar, 169
Abercrombie, Patrick, 69
Adhocism, 152, 180
Adshead, Stanley, 69
Advertising, 131
Advisory Service for Squatters, 43
Advocacy, and advocacy planning, IX, 181–182, 203
Aesthetics, 4, 66–79 *passim*
Africa, 62
Agora, 61
Aix-en-Provence, see Congrès Internationaux d'Architecture Moderne
Alexander, Christopher, 101, 142, 152
Alienation, 60, 156
Alloway, Lawrence, 56
America, see United States of America
Amery, Colin and Dan Cruickshank, *The Rape of Britain*, 171
Anarchism, and anarchy, 2, 5, 37, 44–51 *passim*, 151, 152, 154, 177
– 'ontological anarchism', 42
– anarchist-communism, 40
– *Anarchy* magazine, 38, 49
Anderson, Stanford, 25
– *Planning for Diversity and Choice*, 25
Angry Brigade, 40
Anthropology, Structural Anthropology, 148, 180
Antoniou, Manuela, 187
Apollo space craft, 127, 128
Archigram, V (frontispiece), 49, 77–78, 126, 129, 137, 126–137, 138–154, 138, 140, 145, 149, 152, 153, 172
– *Archigram*, magazine, 126, 127, 129, 132, 135, 137
– (Cook, Peter), Info-Gonks, 147
– (Cook, Peter), Plug-In City, 77, 131, 135, 139, 142, 173
– (Crompton, Dennis), Computer City, 135, 136
– (Greene, David), 130
– (Greene, David), Living Pod, 150
– (Herron, Ron),

Free Time Node, 141
– (Herron, Ron), Urban Action: Tune Up, 132
– (Herron, Ron), Walking City, 135, 137
– (Webb, Mike), 148
– (Webb, Mike), Cushicle, 150
– (Webb, Mike), Suitaloon, 150
– Folkestone Conference (1966), 144
– Instant City, 153
– Living City, 145, 146, 148
Architects' Co-Partnership (ACP), 45
Architectural Association School, London, 46, 177, 182
Architectural Design, 26–28, 33,
Architectural Review, 55, 75–77
– *Counter Attack Against Subtopia*, 77
– *Outrage*, 77
Archizoom, 152
Arcosanti, USA (Paolo Soleri), 203
Aristotle, and non-Aristotelianism, 94
Art schools, 130
Arts and Crafts, 73
Arts Council, 197
Ascoral group, 56
Aspen, 158
Attlee, Clement, 35
Auschwitz, 54
Australia, 10
Autogestion, 198–209
Avant-garde, 59
– in New York and Paris, 62
Axonometrics, 130

Bailey, Ron, 38, 48
Bakema, Jacob, 59
Banham, Peter Reyner, IX, 4, 5, 7, 28, 32, 34, 126, 130, 136, 140, 145, 151, 172, 174, 180
– *Los Angeles*, 174
– 'Revenge of the Picturesque', 77
– *Theory and Design in the First Machine Age*, 152
Banjo stencils, 130
Barker, Paul, IX, 2–12, 28, 32, 34–35, 145

Barr, John, 24
Barriadas, 152, 178–179
Barthes, Roland, 60–61, 156
– 'Semiology and urbanism', 156–165
– 'The death of the Author', 157, 158
Bartlett School of Architecture, 3
Baudelaire, Charles, 83
Bauhaus, America, 130
Beckett, Samuel, 158
Bell, Daniel, *The End of Ideology*, 143
Benjamin, Walter, 161
Bergamo, see Congrès Internationaux d'Architecture Moderne
Berger, John, 4
Berkman, Alexander, 40
Bernstein, Michelle, 82
Bethnal Green, London, 133
Betjeman, John, 75
Beverley Hills, 34
Bey, Hakim, 42
Biba, 40
Biotechnics, 92–93
Birkbeck College, 9
Birmingham, 39
Birth control, 196
Black Power, 147
Bloch, Ernst, 62
Body, 57
Bofill, Ricardo, 80
Bottom-up planning, 195, 220
Booker, Christopher, *The Neophiliacs*, 2, 5
Boudon, Philippe, *Lived-in Architecture*, 151
Bournemouth, V (frontispiece), 34
Boys, Jos, 63
Brand, Stuart, 179
Brand, Weber, 224
Branzi, Andrea, 149
Bricolage, 49, 180
Bridgwater, see Congrès Internationaux d'Architecture Moderne
Bridgwater, Shepheard and Epstein, 45
British Petroleum, 35

Brixton squatting centre, 41
Broad, Chris, 38
Brunel, Isambard Kingdom,
  Renkioi Hospital, 97
Brutalism, 54, 61, 95, 100, 169
Budapest, 36
Building Regulations, 188–190, 197
Building Research Establishment
  (BRE), 194
Bureaucracy, and planning,
  44–51 *passim*, 184–197 *passim*
Burgess, Anthony, *Clockwork
  Orange*, 199
Burgess, E. W., 200
Butor, Michel, 158

Cage, John, 98, 149, 158
Calder, Alexander, 59
Campaign for Nuclear
  Disarmament (CND), 178
Canada, 10
Cape Canaveral, 127, 137
Capitalism, and urbanism, IX, 34,
  39, 42, 61, 62, 84, 86ff,
  102–103, 120, 124, 175–176,
  198ff, 208
Caravans, 24, 140, 141
Carlo, Giancarlo de, 63
Cars, and traffic, 2, 56, 72, 113
– and freedom, mobility and
  access, 24, 101, 120, 140,
  174–175, 190
Carter, Angela, 4
Cartesianism, see Descartes, René
Cathy Come Home (BBC), 38
Caulfield, S.B., 44
Central Advisory Committee on
  National Planning, 68
Central Committee for the
  Architectural Advisory Panels, 69
Central Land Board, 68
Centre for Accessible
  Environments, 192
Centre for Political Studies, 6
Centrepoint building, 40–41
Chalk, Warren, see also Archigram
  (Chalk, Warren), 127
Chamberlin, Powell and Bon, 45
Children, childcare, and planning,
  184–197, 188–189
Children's Society, 189
Chomsky, Noam, *American Power
  and the New Mandarins*, 143
Chtcheglov, Ivan, 84
Cinema, 57–58, 64
– Film noir, 60
City Challenge Scheme, 195
Civic Amenities Act (1967), 171
Civic Trust, 171
Cixous, Hélène, 184

Claremont Road protest, 42
Class, 7, 10, 26, 34, 39, 42, 62
Class War, 40
Classicism, 61
Clip-Kit, 126, 132
Clip-On, design strategy, 139
Cobra movement, 85, 88
Coca-Cola, 34
Code du Plan, 84
Cold War, 52, 62, 123, 124
Coleman, Alice, 168
Collage, 100, 130
Colombia, 56
Comics, 131, 148, 163
Communalism, 123
Communications Theory, 149
Communism, 5, 6, 145
– anarchist-communism, 40
– Communist Party, 36, 37
Community, 26, 42
Community Architecture, and
  Community participation, 181,
  192–197, 203, 206, 210–221
Computers, see also Internet, 98,
  136, 137, 142, 149, 173, 198
Congres Internationaux
  d'Architecture Moderne
  (CIAM), 52–64, 133
– CIAM 4 Conference, 56
– CIAM 6 Bridgwater
  Conference, 54
– CIAM 7 Bergamo
  Conference, 55
– CIAM 8 Hoddesdon
  Conference, 52, 64, 133
– CIAM 9 Aix-en-Provence
  Conference, 53, 64, 133
– CIAM 10 Dubrovnik
  Conference, 54
– CIAM Grille, 133, 134–135
– 'Four Functions', 54
– *Heart of the City*, 52–64 *passim*
– Otterlo, 64
– see also Team 10
Conservation, 8, 34, 68,
  146, 171–172
– Conservation Areas,
  171–172, 185
– see also Council for the
  Preservation of Rural England
  (CPRE), 69
Conservatism, 2, 5
– Set Britain Free Tories, 11
– Conservative Party, 36, 38, 53
Constructionism, 90–103
Constructive
  Women Professionals, 193
Constructivism, 85
Consumerism, and consumers,
  IX, 34, 40–41, 52

Control of Elevations Joint
  Committee, 69
Control of Land Use, 67
Cook, Peter, see
  Archigram (Cook, Peter)
Coop Himmelblau, 150
Council for the Preservation of
  Rural England (CPRE), 69, 146
Counter-culture, 123, 124,
  145, 152
Cousteau, Jacques, 127
Covarubias, Alberto-Cruz, 207
Criminal Justice Act, 42
Crompton, Dennis, see
  Archigram (Crompton, Dennis)
Crooke, Pat, 47
Crowds, 57
Cubism, 131
Cumbernauld, 10–11
Cunningham, Merce, 98, 158
Cybernanthropes, 80–89 *passim*
Cybernetics, 84, 85, 96, 126, 128,
  142, 144, 149
– Cybernetic Serendipity (1968),
  98
Czechoslovakia, 5, 36

Dada, 41, 131
Daily Express, 11, 34, 37
Daily Telegraph, 6, 11, 34, 37
Dallegret, François, 151
Darbourne, John and Geoffrey
  Darke, Lillington Gardens, 169
Darwinian thinking,
  90–103 *passim*
Davidoff, Paul, 147, 148,
  181, 203
Davis, Mike, *City of Quartz*,
  199, 233
De Carlo, Giancarlo, 46–47
De Certeau, Michel, 156–165
De Gaulle, Charles, 5
De Syllas, Phoebe, 99
Debord, Guy, 8ff
Deconstruction, 183
Democracy, 36, 52, 55, 56,
  63, 88, 142, 206
Denmark, 40
Department of the Environment,
  Transport and the Regions
  (DETR), 188
Derby, 34
Deregulation, 33
– see also Regulation
Dérive, 63, 82ff
– see also Situationism
Derrida, Jacques, *Of
  Grammatology*, 158
Descartes, René, 201, 198–209
  passim

237

Determinism, 142
Development Plans, 184–197
Dictatorship, see Totalitarianism
Difference, 62, 76, 89
DiMaggio, Joe, 132, 133
Disability, and planning, 188–189, 192ff
Discrimination, and planning, 184–197
Do It Yourself, 50, 152, 177, 180, 202
Doncaster, 34
Dorset, 8
Drop City, Colorado, USA, 152, 179
Dualisms, and planning, 184–197
Dubrovnik (CIAM 10), 54
Dubuffet, Jean, 99
Duchamp, Marcel, 158
– and ready-mades, 131
Dymaxion House, see Fuller, Richard Buckminster

Eames, Charles and Ray, Santa Monica House (Eames House), 141
East Anglia, 33
Education, 25, 26
Eesteren, Cor Van, 133
Ehrenkrantz, Ezra, SCSD Schools, 139
Eisenschitz, Aram, 199
Elstree, 73
Empowerment, 210–221
Endlessness, 97
Engineering and engineers, 66–67
– and modern architecture, 141
Enlightenment, the, 198
Enterprise Zones, 6, 176
Entrepreneurialism, 148
Environmentalism, 5, 42, 191
Equal Opportunities Taskforce in Construction, 193
Equal opportunities, and planning, 184–197
Eroticism, and planning, 86, 207
Erskine, Ralph, Byker, Newcastle, 181
Esher, Lionel (Lord), 168
Essex Design Guide, 171
Ethnicity, and planning, 188–189, 192ff, 197
Euclid, and non-Euclidean theory, 94
Eugenics, 196
Eurofem, 187
Everyday life, 58–59, 61, 64, 89
Evolutionary models, and architecture, 90–93
Existentialism, 59–61

Expendability, 90–103 *passim*
Extended families, 204
Eyck, Aldo van, 55, 82, 140
Eysenck, Hans, 11

Fabianism, 5
Facilitation, and planning and architecture, 203
Fairlie, Simon, 50
'Family of Man', 60
Farrell, Terry, 173, 224
Fascism, 63
– see also Dictatorship; Totalitarianism
Fathy, Hassan, New Gourna, Egypt, 204–206
Felt pens, 130
Feminism, 62
– and planning, 184–197
– see also Gender; Sexism; Women
Festival of Britain, 54, 61–62
Fibonacci Series, 93
Film, see Cinema
Findhorn, Scotland, 203
Firmitas, 128
Fluxus, 41
Folkestone Conference, see Archigram, Folkestone Conference
Ford, Henry, and car production, 119, 120, 124
Form, 106–107, 111–112
– Formalism, 116–125
Foster Associates, Hong Kong and Shanghai Bank, 231
Foster, Sir Norman, 223–224
Foucault, Michel, 163
Fourierism, 207
Fragmentation, 28, 52, 77, 89
Frampton, Kenneth, 152
Francé, Raoul, 92
Free market, 33–34, 37, 90–103 *passim*, 102–103, 122, 145, 175–176, 198, 199
Freedom Press, London, 45ff
Freedom, 34, 37, 78
– and American values, 120
– and planning and architecture, 44–51 *passim*, 138, 208
Freedom, 44–51 *passim*
French, Marilyn, 186
Friedman, Yona, 128, 139, 143, 149, 173, 104–115
– *Vers une Architecture Scientifique*, 139 (note 5)
– *Ville Spatiale* (Spatial City), 139
Fry, Maxwell, 54
Fuller, Peter, 4
Fuller, Richard Buckminster, 116–125, 144, 149, 224

– 4D, 117, 118
– Dymaxion Deployment Unit, 122
– Dymaxion Dwelling Machine (Wichita House), 122, 123
– Dymaxion House, 118, 119, 120, 128, 149
– Geodesic Dome, 123, 141, 153, 179
– Institute, 117
– *Nine Chains to the Moon*, 117
– Undersea Island, 127
– *Utopia or Oblivion*, 117
– world map, 120
Function, 104, 109, 111–112
– functionalism, 55, 60, 104, 111
– anti-functionalism, 80ff
Futurism, 89, 131

Galbraith, J.K., *The Affluent Society*, 147
Games, 33
Gans, Herbert, 4
– *The Levittowners*, 151
Garbage, 180
Garden Cities, 9, 129, 133
Gasset, Ortega y, 61
Gaviria, Mario, 80
Geddes, Patrick, 9, 46–47, 186, 200
Gender, 60, 162, 184–197
– see also Feminism; Sexism; Women
General Development Order, 69
Gentrification, 40, 172, 198
Geodesic dome, see Fuller, Richard Buckminster
Georgian Group, 171
Georgian style, 9, 55
Germany, 40
Giedion, Siegfried, 53, 55, 56, 58–61, 63, 152
– *Space, Time and Architecture*, 53
Gill, Eric, 44
Glasgow, 39
Global economy, 198, 210–221
Gold, John, *The Experience of Modernism*, 48
Goldberg, Abigail, 202–203
Golden Section, 93
Goldfinger, Ernö, Trellick Tower, 166–167
Goodman, Robert, 39
– *After the Planners*, 166–167, 181
Gordon, Alex, 173
Gowan, James, 77, 95
Graffiti, 160
Graham, Dan, 158

238

Granta, 24
Greater London Council (GLC), 6, 167, 196
Greater London Plan, 69
Greene, David, see Archigram (Greene, David)
Greenham Common, 178
Grid, 56, 60, 71
Grimshaw, Nicholas, 173, 224
Gropius, Walter, 120
Groupe d'Etude d'Architecture Mobile, 149
Guardian, The, 11
Guerrilla architecture, 39, 43
Gummer, John, 6

Habraken, Nicholas, *Supports*, 173
Hackney, Rod, Black Road, Macclesfield, 181
Hall, Peter, IX, 4, 5–7, 28, 32, 34, 37, 145, 176
– *Cities of Tomorrow*, 32
Hambdi, Nabeel & Nicholas Wilkinson, PSSHAK, 173
Hamilton, Richard, 94–96, 99
Hampstead Garden Surburb, 9, 33
Hardy, Dennis, 50
Harlow
– New Town, 12, 34
– Bishopsfield (Neylan and Ungless), 170
Harraway, Donna, 62
Hastings, H. de Cronin, 75–76
Haus-Rucker-Co, 150, 151
– Pulsating Yellow Heart, 152
Haussmann, Baron Georges, 10, 160
Hawkes, Jacquetta, *The Land*, 61
Hawthorne, Nathaniel, *The House of the Seven Gables*, 116, 125
Hayek, Friedrich, 32–37, 39–41
– *The Road to Serfdom*, 145
– *Constitution of Liberty*, 34
Heap, Desmond, 194
Heath, Adrian, 93, 99
Heath, Edward, 6
Hegel, 142
Heisenberg, Werner, 95, 96–7
Henderson, Nigel, 94, 133
Herron, Ron, see Archigram (Herron, Ron)
Hewison, Robert, *Too Much*, 2
Highlands, 10
High-rise blocks, 9, 56, 73–74
High-Tech, 173–174
Highway Code, 161
Hill, Anthony, 93
Hippies, 116
Hitler, Adolf, 142

Hoddesdon, see Congrès Internationaux d'Architecture Moderne
Hollies, The (Essex), 38
Homelessness, 153, 232–235
Hook New Town, 26
– Hook Plan, 26
Horden, Richard,
Yacht House, 224, 230
Housing Act, 68
Housing Manual, 70–74, 72–76
Housing, 10, 37–40, 69–72, 74
Howard, Ebenezer, 9, 129
HRH Prince of Wales, 222
– *Vision of Britain*, 182
Hugo, Victor, 157
Humanism, 52–55, 60–64
Hunt, Albert, 4

Illich, Ivan, 180, 202
Imaginary Bauhaus Movement, 85
Imperial Chemical Industries (ICI), 35
Imperialism, 116
Independent Group, 54, 64, 90–103, 131, 145
– *Growth and Form*, 94–95
– *Parallel of Life and Art*, 94–95
– *This is Tomorrow*, 99
Indeterminacy, 90–103, 141, 148
India, 56
Indians, North American, 121
Indochina, 36
Industrialized building, 67, 74, 76
– see also Prefabrication
Inflatables, see also Pneumatics, 150, 232–235
Institute for Contemporary Arts, London (ICA), 64, 94
Institute of Building, 69
Institute of Economic Affairs, 36
Internet, 210
Iommi, Godofredo, 207
Isle of Wight, 34
Istanbul, Esenkent, 206
Italy, 56
Ivain, Gilles, 84
Izenour, Steven, 174

Jacobs, Jane, 64
– *Death and Life of Great American Cities*, 148, 175, 177
Jeffersonianism, 116, 120
Jencks, Charles
– and Nathan Silver, *Adhocism*, 152, 180
– *Consumer Democracy*, 143, 144, 152
– *Modern Movements in Architecture*, 130, 138

Jephcott, Pearl, 168
Johnson, Edward, 44
Jorn, Asger, 83, 85
Joseph, Keith, 6, 36
Judge, Tony, 44

Kahn, Louis, 152
Karachi, Indonesia, 220
Kesey, Ken, Psychedelic Bus, 153
Kit of parts, 22, 90–103 *passim*, 216ff
Knight, Richard Payne, 71, 76
Kofman, Eleonore and Elizabeth Lebas, *Henri Lefebvre: writings on cities*, 81
Korn, Arthur, 138
Kosmos, 33, 37
Kosuth, Joseph,
'Art after philosophy', 137
Kreisler, Fritz, 222
Kropotkin, Peter, 40, 46
Kurokawa, Kisho
– Nakagin Capsule Tower, Tokyo, 22
– see Metabolism (Kurokawa, Kisho)

Labour Party, 53
– see also Socialism
Laclau, Ernesto, 208
Lacour, Claudia Brodsky, 202
Lafargue, Paul,
Droit à la Paresse, 85
Lahr, John, 4
Laissez-faire, 63, 144, 175–176
– see also Free market
Lake District, 12, 34
Landau, Royston, 28
Land-use Planning, 184–197, 187–188
Larry, 22
Las Vegas, 34, 63, 174–175
Le Corbusier, 53–54, 58, 60, 76, 133, 138, 140
– Algiers Project, 140
– Maisons Jaoul, 169
– Marseilles, Unité d'Habitation, 100
– Pessac, see also Boudon, Philippe, 138, 151
– *The City of Tomorrow*, 200
Leary, Timothy, 149
Leavis, F.R., 63
Lebas, Elizabeth, see Kofman, Eleonore and Elizabeth Lebas
Lefebvre, Henri, 59, 61, 80–89 *passim*, 129, 152, 162, 199, 201
– *Critique de la vie quotidienne*, 84ff
– *Du rural à l'urbain*, 86

- *Introduction à la modernité*, 86
- *La production de l'espace*, 86
- *Le droit à la ville*, 82, 86
- *Le romanticisme révolutionnaire*, 81
- *Le temps des méprises*, 80
Léger, Fernand, 55
Legislation, 12, 27, 66–79 *passim*
Leisure, and urbanism, 59, 80–89 *passim*
Léja, Michael, 60
Leninism, 142
Les parapluies de Cherbourg, 12
Lethaby, W.R., 44
Lévi-Strauss, Claude, 61
- *La pensée sauvage*, 180
Lewisham, 38
Lewitt, Sol, 158
Littlewood, Joan, 23, 32, 149
Llewelyn-Davies, Richard (Lord), 77, 101, 175
Llewelyn-Davies Weeks,
- Milton Keynes New Town, 45, 101-2, 175
- Northwick Park Hospital, London, 90–103
- see also Llewelyn-Davies, Richard, and Weeks, John
Local Agenda 21, 191
Local Area Plans, 186
Local authorities, 68–71
London Docklands Development Corporation (LDDC), 176
London Regeneration Network, 192, 195
London Women and the Manual Trades, 192
London, 11, 37, 39, 54
- Adelaide Road (Nabeel Hambdi and Nicholas Wilkinson), 173
- Barnsbury, and gentrification, 172
- Bethnal Green, 9
- Biba building, 40
- Bomb damage, 59 (Fig. 5.6)
- British Library Redevelopment, 168
- Brixton squatting centre, 41
- Camden, 8, 10, 40
- Canary Wharf Tower (Cesar Pelli), 176, 198, 199–200
- Centrepoint building, 40–41
- Chelsea, 10
- Claremont Road, 42
- Covent Garden Redevelopment, 168
- Crystal Palace (Joseph Paxton), 22, 92
- Docklands, 6, 176, 177, 198, 199–200

- East End (Fun Palace project), 23
- Elephant and Castle, 10
- Euston Arch, 171
- *Greater London Plan*, 69
- Greenwich, Millenium Dome, 190
- Hoxton, 40
- Hyde Park, 56
- Inter-Action Centre (Cedric Price), 30
- Islington, 40
- Jagonari Building, Whitechapel (Matrix Group), 196
- Lillington Gardens (John Darbourne and Geoffrey Darke), 169–170
- Lloyd's Building (Sir Richard Rogers), 173
- London School of Economics (LSE), 4
- London Squatters Campaign, 37–38
- Northwick Park Hospital (Llewelyn-Davies Weeks), 90–103
- Notting Hill, 40
- Oxford Street, 24
- Paddington Station, 12
- Paddington, Service Tower (Nicholas Grimshaw and Terry Farrell), 173
- Peckham, Pioneer Health Centre (Owen Williams), 196
- Polytechnic of Central London (Greater London Council), 101
- Redbridge, protests, 48ff
- Regent's Park, 9
- Richmond Riverside (Quinlan Terry), 169, 182
- Roehampton, Alton Estate, 76
- Ronan Point Collapse, 168
- Southwark, 10
- St John's Church, Red Lion Square, 44
- St Pancras Hotel, 9
- Stepney, 40
- Stonebridge Development, 197
- Trellick Tower (Ernö Goldfinger), 166–167
- Westminster, 26
- Westway (A40M), 166–167
Long life, loose fit, 173
Los Angeles, 101, 174–175
Watts Riots, 175
Low impact development, 51

Macclesfield, Black Road (Rod Hackney), 181
Magnesia, Milk of, 187
Malestream, 191

Mallarmé, Stéphane, 158
Malpass, Peter, 46
Malraux, André, 84
'Man the Hunter', 62
'Man', 52, 59–63
Market, 52
- see also Free market
Marshall Plan, 35
Martin, Kenneth and Mary, 93–94
Martin, Leslie, 169
Marxism, Marxists, 2, 87, 142, 150
- Marxist-Leninism, 36
Massachusetts Institute of Technology, 25
Matrix Group, 192
- Jagonari Building, London, 196
Mazlisch, Bruno, 145
McCallum, Ian, 58
McHale, John, 100
McLuhan, Marshall,
 Understanding Media, 131, 149
Mechanization, 85
Megascope, 126–127
Megastructures, 138, 173
Mellor, David, 57
Melville, Herman,
 The Confidence Man, 117
Melvin, Alice, 196
Meritocrat, 143
Metabolism, 139, 140
- (Kurokawa, Kisho), Helicoids Project, 139
Millenium Commission, 197
Milton Keynes, New Town (Llewelyn-Davies Weeks, planners), 10, 45, 50, 101–102, 175
- Greentown Proposals, 50
Ministry of Education, Architects and Buildings Branch, 45
Ministry of Town and Country Planning, 67
Mises, Ludwig von, 36
Mixed-use Planning, 184–197
Mobile architecture, 111
Mobile Study Architecture Group, see Groupe d'Etude d'Architecture Mobile
Mobile town planning, 113
Mobility, physical and social, 7, 24–25, 59, 192
'Modern Man', 52
- see also 'Man'
Modernism, VIII, 32, 52–55, 58, 60, 63, 75–78
- Modern Movement in architecture, 119, 126, 133, 138, 152, 166, 177
Moholy-Nagy, Laszlo, 130

Mondrian, Piet, 97
Money, and planning, 202
Monomorph, 106
Monroe, Marilyn, 132, 133
Morocco, 56
Morris, William, 46, 171, 174
Moscow, 12
Motels, 34
Mourenx, France, 81–82, 162, 163
Mumford, Lewis, 46, 186
Murcot, Glen, 220

Nagakin Capsule Tower, 22
Nanterre,
University of Nanterre, 159
Napoleon III, 10
Nash, John, 9
Nationalization, 7
Navarrenx, France, 81
Negroponte, Nicholas, 142, 148
Neira, Eduardo, 47
Neo-Georgian, 73
Netherlands, 40
Neville, Richard, *Play Power,* 149
New Gourna, Egypt (Hassan Fathy), 198–209, 204–206
New Left, 32, 34–37,145, 192
New Right, 32, 35–37, 145
New Society, IX, 2, 4, 24, 26, 28, 32, 38
New Towns, 10–11, 26
- (Britain), and New Towns Act, 22–3 *passim*, 133, 145, 175
- (France), 81, 89, 161, 162
- (Holland), 81
- (South Africa), 203, 210–222 *passim*
- Cumbernauld, 10–11
- Harlow, 12, 34
- Mark I, 26
- Milton Keynes, 10
New Wave, 149
New York, 58
- World Financial Centre, 198
Newbury, 42
Newcastle, Byker (Ralph Erskine), 181
Nieuwenhuys, Constant, 80–89 *passim,* 149
- New Babylon project, 80–89 *passim,* 149
Nomadism, 63–64, 87, 120, 121, 152, 153
'Non-Plan' (*New Society,* 1969), IX, 2, 8–21, 27–30, 32–43 *passim,* 49, 102–103, 145, 146, 148, 154, 168, 172
- 'Constable Country', 12, 34–35, 37
- 'Lawrence Country', 12, 34–35

- 'Montagu Country', 12, 28, 34–35
- see also Price, Cedric, 'Non-Plan'
Nottingham, 34–35, 39
Novel, Jean, 224
'Null-Plan', 28
Nuthampstead, 12

Obsolescence, 90–103 *passim,* 145
O'Doherty, Brian, 158
Olympia and York, 176
Open systems, 99, 138–154
Organicism, and architecture and planning, 52–53, 61–64, 76, 90–103, 117, 200, 232–235
Originality, and architecture, 222-231
Orwell, George, 2
Otterlo (CIAM), 63
Outrage, 77
Oxbridge colleges, 10

Pang, Alex Soojung-Kim, 123, 124
Paolozzi, Eduardo, 94, 99
Parallel of Life and Art, 64
Parasitism, 232–235
Paris, 5, 10
- 1968, Paris Riots, May 1968, 152, 156–165, 177
- Paris Commune (1871), 160
- Champs Elysées, 59
- Haussmannization, 10
- Maison du Peuple, 178
- Pompidou Centre, 5, see also Rogers, Sir Richard and Renzo Piano, Pompidou Centre
- Sorbonne, 159
Parti Communiste Français (PCF), 80–89 *passim*
Participation, 10, 181–183, 192–197, 210–221
Pasmore, Victor, 93
Paternalism, 34–37
- patriarchy, 184–197, 184, 191
Pawley, Martin, ix, 180
- *Theory and Design in the Second Machine Age,* 222
Paxton, Joseph, Crystal Palace, 22, 92, 97
Pearson, John Loughborough, Truro Cathedral, 44
Peckham Experiment, 196
Pendleton-Jullian, Ann, 207–208
People cities, 210ff
Percy, Graham, 35
Permanence, 118
Peru, 56
- barriadas, 47ff, 178–179, 198
Pessac, see Le Corbusier, Pessac
Pevsner, Nikolaus, 44, 75–76, 170

- *Englishness of English Art,* 76
Phenomenology, 57
Photography, 60
Photomontage, 131
Piano, Renzo, 5
- see also Rogers, Sir Richard and Renzo Piano, Pompidou Centre
Picturesque, 55, 58, 66–79 *passim,* 170–171
Pidgeon, Monica, 49
Pipers, 149
Planners and planning, 4, 8–12, 26, 28, 32–34, 37, 41–42, 52–53, 56–57, 60, 63–64, 77, 184–197 *passim*
- Planning blight, 199
- Planning gain, 51, 197
Planning Aid for London, 192
Plato, 142
Play, 43, 111
- and urbanism, 80–89 *passim*
Plotlands settlements, Essex, 49–50
Plug-In City, see Archigram (Cook, Peter)
Pluralism, 63, 144
Pneumatics, see also Inflatables, 127, 150, 152, 232–235
Poetry and planning, 80ff, 207–208
Pollock, Scotland, 41, 42
Pollock, Jackson, 95, 99
Polymorph, 106
Pompidou Centre, 5, see also Rogers, Sir Richard
Pooley, Frederick, 45, 181
Pop culture, 90–103 *passim,* 144, 145, 146, 147, 163
Popper, Karl, 135 (note 36), 143, 145
- *The Open Society and its Enemies,* 95, 142
- *The Poverty of Historicism,* 142
Portoghesi, Paolo, 64
Portsmouth, 34
Post-modernism, VIII, 54, 62, 182–183
Post-structuralism, 64, 191
Potlatch, 82–83
Poulson, John, 168
Power, Anne,
Property Before People, 44
Pragmatism, 142
Prebble & Co., 40, 40 (Fig. 3.2)
Pre-fabrication, and system building, 46, 74, 100, 222–231 *passim*
- see also Industrialized building
Preservation, see Conservation
Price, Cedric, IX, 4, 5, 7, 22–31, 32, 34, 37, 22–31, 129, 134, 136, 139, 140, 142, 145, 151, 172, 174

241

– Fun Palace, 23, 32, 139, 147, 149, 172–173
– Inter-Action Centre, London, 30
– Magnet, 31
– Mechanical Mobility, 24
– 'Non-Plan', 27, 33–34
– Pop-Up Parliament, 26–27
– Potteries Think Belt, 25, 26, 147
– 'Principles', 29
Price, Uvedale, 70–72, 76–77
Primary Support Structure and Housing Assembly Kit (PSSHAK), 173
Primitivism, 59–60
Private Eye, 171
Propaganda, 124
Proportion, 93–95
Prouvé, Jean, 141
Pruitt-Igoe Flats, St Louis, Missouri, Minoru Yamasaki, 166
Psychogeography, 59, 83, 85

Queneau, Raymond, 157, 161

Race, 62
Radford, Jim, 48
Radio Times, 24
Ramessum, Egypt, 204–205
Rand, Ayn, 36
Rasmussen, Steen, *London: The Unique City*, 8
Rationalism, and architecture and planning, 61, 63, 86, 110, 141–142, 198
Rauschenberg, Robert, 149, 158
Read, Herbert, 64
Reconstruction, 54, 60–61, 67
– Reconstruction Committee, 68
Recycling materials, 210–221 *passim*, 222–231
Redbridge, 37–38, 42
Regulation, 33–34, 53, 70
– see also Deregulation; Planners and planning; Zoning
Reichardt, Jasia, 98
Reid, Alex, 30
Religion, and planning, 86, 184–197 *passim*
Renkioi Hospital (Isambard Kingdom Brunel), 97
Revolution, 38, 42
– events of 1968, 5, 36
– revolutionary action, see also 1968 Paris Riots, 80–89 *passim*, 120, 177–178
Rhone Valley, 12
Richards, J.M., 8, 56, 76
– *Castles on the Ground*, 76
Ringways, 167
Rio Declaration, 191

Rioting, 22, 23, 152, 175
Ritoque, The Open City, Chile, 198–209
Ritson, Don, 50
Roads and streets, 8, 9, 24, 58, 61, 64, 71–73, 77
– 'Main Street', 62, 64
– roads protests, 42
Robbe-Grillet, Alain, 158
Robbins, Edward, 201
Robinson, Sidney, 71, 77–78
Robots, 173
Rochfort, Christianne, *Les Petits Enfants du Siècle*, 162
Rock festivals, 153
Roehampton, Alton Estate, 76
Rogers, Ernesto, 59
Rogers, Sir Richard and Renzo Piano, Pompidou Centre, 147, 152, 173
Rogers, Sir Richard, 5, 224
– Lloyd's Building, 173
Rohe, Mies van der, 97
Romanticism, 70, 76
Ronan Point, 9, 12
Rose, Gillian, 184
Ross, Kristin, 62
Rossi, Aldo, *The Architecture of the City*, 176
Rowe, Colin, 55
Royal Institute of British Architects (RIBA), 66–79 *passim*, 181, 193
Royal Town Planning Institute, 6, 69, 193
Rudofsky, Bernard, *Architecture Without Architects*, 170
Rue corridor, 58
Runcorn, The Brow (Runcorn Development Corporation), 170
Russia, 22

Saarinen, Eero, 223
Safeway, 35
Saffron Walden, 34
Sanitation, and planning, 184–197, 198–209
Sarcelles, France, 162
Sartre, Jean-Paul, 59
Schumacher, Fritz, *Small is Beautiful*, 180
Schuster Report, 69
Science fiction, 85, 126–137 *passim*, 138–154 *passim*, 132
Scott, George Gilbert, St Pancras Hotel, 9
Scott Brown, Denise, 144, 174
– on little magazines, 126 (note 4)
Scruton, Roger, *The Aesthetics of Architecture*, 119

Section 106 Agreements, 197
Segal, Walter, 180–181
Self-build, 41, 47, 49, 178–180, 183, 199, 202, 198–209, 210–221
Self-help, 47, 196
Self-planning, 111
Semiology, and urbanism, 156–165
Sennett, Richard, 64
– *The Uses of Disorder*, 177, 208
Serial repetition, 131
Sert, Josep Lluis, 55, 56, 58, 62
Service stations, 11–12
Sexism, 42
– see also Feminism; Gender; Women
Sharawaggi, 75
Sharp, Thomas, 60
Sheffield, 34–35
Shelter, 38
Sherman, Alfred, 6, 37
Simak, Clifford, *City*, 85
Simmel, Georg, 63, 199, 202
Single Regeneration Budget (SRB), 195, 197
Situationism, 41, 80–89 *passim*, 131, 144, 146, 149, 152
– *dérive*, 63
– psychogeography, 59
Skeffington committee, 10, 181
Slums, 61, 68
Smith, Adam, 93, 96, 103
Smithson, Alison and Peter, 77, 93, 95, 131, 133, 134–135, 140, 145, 152
– Cluster City, 99
– Golden Lane Project, 132, 133, 134–135, 139
– House of the Future, 145
– Sheffield University Project, 99–100
Smithson, Peter, 140
Socialism, 5, 32–33
– libertarian socialism, 37
Society for the Preservation of Ancient Buildings, 171
Society of Black Architects (SOBA), 192
Sociology, 6, 52, 56
Software, 135
Solent, 12
Soleri, Paolo, Arcosanti, 203
Sontag, Susan,
'Against interpretation', 158
Southampton, 34
Soviet Union, 36
Space race, 126, 127, 150
– space travel and exploration, 63
Spontaneity, 7, 12, 33–34, 42, 58, 64

242

INDEX

Sports Council, 197
Squatting, 37–42, 44–51 *passim*, 152, 177, 178
St John Wilson, Colin, 46, 169
Staffordshire, UK, 22, 26
State, 34, 37, 43, 63, 66
Stirling, James, 77, 95
Streets, see Roads, also Cars
Structural Anthropology, see Anthopology
Structuralism, 54, 61, 64, 156–165, 180
Structure, 107, 109
Subcultures, see also Counter-culture, 64
Suburbs, 162
Superheroes, 132, 148
Superstudio, 152, 177
Surrealism, 41, 83, 131
Sustainability, 191, 184–197 *passim*, 198–209, 210–221
Sweden, 40
Symmetry, 70
Systems, 78

Taxis, 33, 37
Taylor, Basil, 56
Team 10, 61, 63, 138, 140, 148, 152
Technocracy, 62
Technology, IX, 9, 59, 66, 77, 80–89 *passim*, 117, 126, 127, 136–137, 143, 144, 147, 172–174, 180, 222–231
– Technology transfer, 222–231
Tecton, Finsbury Housing, 140
Telford, Lightmoor Project, 50
Temporary Autonomous Zone, 42–43
Terry, Quinlan, Richmond Riverside, 169, 182
Thatcher, Margaret, 6, 36, 37, 176
Thompson, D'Arcy Wentworth, *On Growth and Form*, 92–95
Thompson, E.P., 2
Time planning, 190–191
Times, The, 8, 11
Tokyo, Nakagin Capsule Tower (Kisho Kurokawa), 22
Topology, 95, 105
Totalitarianism, 52–53, 57
Town and Country Planning Acts, 10, 67–70
Town and Country Planning and Housing Committee, 68
Town planning, 11, 67, 113
– mobile town planning, 113
– see also Planners and planning;
– see also Royal Town Planning Institute

Townscape, 76–77
Tradition, and architecture, 52, 75–77, 169, 176, 182, 205
Traffic, see Cars
Training, and self-build, 216ff
Transcendentalism, 116
Trees, 68, 70–71, 73
Trocchi, Alexander, 32
Truman, Harry S., 35
Tschumi, Bernard, 177, 183
Turner, John, 46ff, 178
Tyrwhitt, Jane, (ed.), *The Heart of the City*, 52–64 *passim*
Tyrwhitt, Jane, 60

Un Homme et Une Femme, 12
Uncertainty Principle, see Heisenberg, Werner
UNESCO, 62
Unitary Urbanism, 84ff
United States of America, 4, 5, 10, 34–35, 56
– Navy, 22, 116, 122, 124, 127
– Beverley Hills, 34
– Las Vegas, 34, 63
– literature, 60
– New York, 58
'Universal Man', 62
Universities, 26
University College London, 4
– Bartlett School of Architecture, 32
Unwin, Raymond, 9, 194
Urban Design Group, 203
Urban Regeneration Areas, 185
Uthwatt Report, 67
– see also Royal Town Planning Institute
Utopia
– and modernism, 199
– and social harmony, 80–89 *passim*, 144
– and technology, 80–89 *passim*, 117–118, 127, 129
– utopianism, 54
Utopie, 150

Venice, 55 (Fig. 5.2), 56
– Architectural Biennale, 64
Venturi, Robert, 5, 144, 174, 222
– see also Scott Brown, Denise
Vernacular, 60, 171, 210–221, 210, 217
Victorian Society, 171
Vietnam War, 5, 22, 36, 161, 163
Virilio, Paul, *Speed and Politics*, 122
Virtual Reality, and planning and design, 189, 191–2, 198
Voelcker, John, 138

Volontà, 46
Vrygrund, South Africa, 210–221

Wakefield, Peter, 8
Ward, Colin, IX, 5, 42, 44–51
Warhol, Andy, 98
Wates, Neil, 28
Webb, Mike, see Archigram (Mike Webb)
Webber, Melvin, 8, 101, 139, 174
Webern, Anton, 98
Weeks, John, 30, 77, 90–103
Weiner, Norbert, *The Human Use of Human Beings*, 85, 98
Welfare State, 35–36, 45, 72, 103, 145, 168, 199
Weller, Ken, 46
Welwyn Garden City, 9, 33, 70
Westway (A40M), London, 166–167
Whole Earth Catalog, 144, 179
Widgery, David, 199
Wiener, Paul, 59
Wilkinson, Nicholas, see Hambdi, Nabeel and Nicholas Wilkinson
Willmott, Peter, 6
Wilson, Elizabeth, 198, 200, 208
Winterweld, South Africa, 203
Wittkower, Rudolph, 55
– *Architectural Principles*, 93
Wolfe, Tom, 4
Women and Planning Movement, 184–197
Women, 60
– see also Feminism; Gender; Sexism
Women's Design Service, 192
Wood, Michael, 5
Woods, Shadrach, 152
Woodstock Festival, 153
World War Two, 134
Wright, Frank Lloyd, 11, 76

Yamasaki, Minoru, Pruitt-Igoe Flats, St Louis, Missouri, 166
York Minster, 32
Young, Michael, 6
Youth culture, 161
'Yuppies', 40

Zevi, Bruno, 63
Zip-a-Tone, 130
Zoning, 33–34, 41, 56, 62, 68, 71–72, 77, 99, 184–197, 184–186, 200
– Control of Land Use, 67
– see also Temporary Autonomous Zone (TAZ)
Zukin, Sharon, 200

DESIGN TINA BORKOWSKI